Demographic Anxieties

REPRODUCTIVE JUSTICE: A NEW VISION FOR THE TWENTY-FIRST CENTURY

Edited by Rickie Solinger (senior editor), Khiara M. Bridges, Laura Briggs, Krystale E. Littlejohn, Ruby Tapia, and Carly Thomsen

1. *Reproductive Justice: An Introduction*, by Loretta J. Ross and Rickie Solinger
2. *How All Politics Became Reproductive Politics: From Welfare Reform to Foreclosure to Trump*, by Laura Briggs
3. *Distributing Condoms and Hope: The Racialized Politics of Youth Sexual Health*, by Chris A. Barcelos
4. *Just Get on the Pill: The Uneven Burden of Reproductive Politics*, by Krystale E. Littlejohn
5. *Reproduction Reconceived: Family Making and the Limits of Choice after Roe v. Wade*, by Sara Matthiesen
6. *Laboratory of Deficiency: Sterilization and Confinement in California, 1900–1950s*, by Natalie Lira
7. *Abortion Pills Go Global: Reproductive Freedom across Borders*, by Sydney Calkin
8. *Fighting Mad: Resisting the End of Roe v. Wade*, edited by Krystale E. Littlejohn and Rickie Solinger
9. *Fatal Denial: Racism and the Political Life of Black Infant Mortality*, by Annie Menzel
10. *The Pregnancy Police: Conceiving Crime, Arresting Personhood*, by Grace E. Howard
11. *Youth Organizing for Reproductive Justice: A Guide for Liberation*, by Chris A. Barcelos
12. *Queering Families: Reproductive Justice in Precarious Times*, by Tamara Lea Spira
13. *We Are Pregnant with Freedom: Black Feminist Storytelling for Reproductive Justice*, by Stacie Selmon McCormick
14. *From the Clinics to the Capitol: How Opposing Abortion Became Insurrectionary*, by Carol Mason
15. *Abortion and Reproductive Justice: An Essential Guide for Resistance*, by Marlene Gerber Fried and Loretta J. Ross
16. *Reproductive Justice, Queerly*, by Carley Thomsen
17. *Demographic Anxieties: Bodies, Borders, and Reproductive Injustice in Palestine/Israel*, by Gala Rexer

Demographic Anxieties

BODIES, BORDERS, AND REPRODUCTIVE INJUSTICE IN PALESTINE/ISRAEL

Gala Rexer

UNIVERSITY OF CALIFORNIA PRESS

University of California Press
Oakland, California

Library of Congress Cataloging-in-Publication Data

Names: Rexer, Gala, author.
Title: Demographic anxieties : bodies, borders, and reproductive injustice in Palestine-Israel / Gala Rexer.
Other titles: Reproductive justice ; 17.
Description: Oakland, California : University of California Press, [2026] | Series: Reproductive justice : a new vision for the 21st century ; 17 | Includes bibliographical references and index.
Identifiers: LCCN 2026003485 (print) | LCCN 2026003486 (ebook) | ISBN 9780520412521 (cloth) | ISBN 9780520412538 (paperback) | ISBN 9780520412545 (ebook)
Subjects: LCSH: Women, Palestinian Arab—Health and hygiene. | Reproductive rights—Palestine. | Reproductive health—Government policy—Israel.
Classification: LCC HQ1728.5.R485 2026 (print) | LCC HQ1728.5 (ebook)
LC record available at https://lccn.loc.gov/2026003485
LC ebook record available at https://lccn.loc.gov/2026003486

GPSR Authorized Representative: Easy Access System Europe, Mustamäe tee 50, 10621 Tallinn, Estonia, gpsr.requests@easproject.com

35 34 33 32 31 30 29 28 27 26
10 9 8 7 6 5 4 3 2 1

CONTENTS

ACKNOWLEDGMENTS

This book wouldn't exist were it not for my research participants' time and willingness to share their experiences with me. I thank the Palestinian women who generously taught me what it means to live, resist, and care under Israeli settler colonialism. I am deeply grateful to Najla Fawwaz, my longtime collaborator, interpreter, and friend, without whose support and labor this project wouldn't have been possible. I am also grateful to Rafa Musmar and Mary Khadija for working with me and letting me see Palestine through their eyes. Thank you, Najla Fawwaz, Sally Abazeed, Danielle Rahal, and Raed Mansour, for translating audio interviews and other texts. Your translation work did much more than just carry text from Arabic to English. Through working with you and discussing the politics and ethics of this work, I learned what translation actually means. I am indebted to all the Palestinian healthcare workers, activists, scholars, comrades, and friends who met with me and explained things to me that Palestinians knew all along. I am also grateful to the Jewish Israeli activists, scholars, comrades, and friends committed to fighting against occupation, apartheid, and genocide.

This book also wouldn't exist without the support, mentorship, and encouragement I received from many. Thank you, Gökçe Yurdakul, for opening this path for me. When you asked me if I wanted to become a scholar, I didn't know that this was something I could do. You not only made me believe in myself but also equipped me with the necessary resilience, perseverance, grace, and humor to embark on this journey. Your guidance has been everything. Thank you, Tariq Jazeel, for being such a brilliant, kind, and caring mentor. You have modeled for me how to *be* in academia. Thank you, Beate Binder, Jasbir Puar, Naika Foroutan, and Talja Blokland, for accompanying me on my academic journey early on, for teaching me, and for believing in me and this project. Ghada Majadli, Osama Tanous, Sophia Goodfriend, Himmat Zoubi (Zu'bi), Siggie Vertommen, Guy Shalev, Shvat Eilat, Khaled Furani, Nihaya Daoud, Ann Laura Stoler, Dána-Ain Davis, and Nadera Shalhoub-Kevorkian, thank you for supporting what would become this book in its various iterations. Our conversations and your critical feedback have significantly shaped this project, and I am grateful for the work you do.

At Humboldt-Universität zu Berlin, I owe gratitude to our small but excellent PhD cohort: Özgür Özvatan, Seyran Bostancı, and Tunay Altay. At UCL's Sarah Parker Remond Centre, I thank Paul Gilroy, Tariq Jazeel, Paige Patchin, Luke de Noronha, and Kaissa Karhu for establishing an intellectual space like no other. The center's core belief in antiracism as a nonidentitarian project and its commitment to thinking multidisciplinarily have significantly shaped this book. Pragya Dhital, Pavan Mano, and Elizabeth Cooper, thank you for our conversations and for the breaks from work. Thanks to the 2023/24 cohort of the MA in Race, Ethnicity, and Postcolonial Studies for your critical thought, curiosity, and for holding space for everyone during an insane year. Thanks to Gabriel Rahman for our collaboration and for thinking together. Also at UCL, I am grateful to Xine Yao, Lara Choksey, Nicola Miller, Megan Vaughan, Tom Western, Gargi Bhattacharyya, Seth Anziska, Anne Irfan, Simon Lock, Stephen Hughes, Alex Hyde, Noémi Tousignant, keisha bruce, Sarai Kirshner, and the UCL SPRC PhD cohort and research community for their generous support, conversations, feedback, check-ins, and organizing. At the University of Warwick, for support, comradeship, and collegiality, I thank Goldie Osuri, Claire Blencowe, Jamie Shenk, Hannah Jones, and Nerea Calvillo. Thank you, Ali Meghji, John Solomos, Gurminder Bhambra, Sophie Marie Niang, Billy Holzberg, Niharika Pandit, Howie Rechavia-Taylor, R. Sánchez Rivera, Aideen O'Shaughnessy, Rémy-Paulin Twahirwa, Rishita Nandagiri, Anna Horn, Caroline Bazambanza, Patricia Hamilton, Anna Shadrina, Hannah Boast, Sarah Arens, Lilly Markaki, Simon Fleury, Yener Bayramoğlu, Fran Tonkiss, and Alice Mah, for welcoming me into UK academia and for your generous support. Thanks to Sociologists in Solidarity with Palestinians for a sense of purpose and community. Toward the end of this project, I received profound encouragement and invaluable guidance from the sociology and gender studies community at Yale University—thank you to Kalindi Vora, Rene Almeling, Alka Menon, and Marcia Inhorn for welcoming me to Yale and for our conversations. I am also deeply grateful to colleagues and friends at NYU's Department of Social and Cultural Analysis for hosting me and for the intellectual support they offered throughout my time there. Thank you, Nikhil Pal Singh, Julie Livingston, Kessie Alexandre, and Linda Luu. Marisa Kriangwiwat, Andréa Becker, Didi Tal, Maya Perry, Heba Gowayed, and Weeam Hammoudeh, thank you for our ongoing conversations, for dinners, going to events, and for making NYC feel like an intellectual home.

Noémi Tousignant, Osama Tanous, and Ghada Majadli—thank you for your close reading and deep and critical engagement with my manuscript. It is so much clearer thanks to your insights. Maya Mikdashi and Laleh Khalili, your encouragement and feedback in the early stages of this project meant a lot—thank you for asking me the right questions at the right time. Rickie Solinger, my series editor, thank you for believing in this book from when I first reached out to you. Your support, encouragement, and generosity throughout this process meant everything to me. There were many things I didn't know as a first-time author navigating three different academic systems and norms, and I am grateful to Naomi Schneider and Aline Dolinh at UC Press for seeing this project through and giving me support along the way. I am also deeply grateful to Leah Caldwell for her thoughtful suggestions and guidance through the copyediting process, as well as the whole production team at UC Press. For carefully reading chapters, sections, and proposal materials, I am indebted to Sophia Goodfriend, Chen Liang, Ulrike Bialas, Bettine Josties, Michelle Pfeifer, Edna Bonhomme, R. Sánchez Rivera, Niharika Pandit, Elizabeth Berman, Hania Tayara, Paige Patchin, Nicola Miller, Paul Gilroy, Tariq Jazeel, Anne Irfan, and Ashjan Ajour. For answering all my questions about publishing and offering valuable and generous support, I owe gratitude to Xine Yao, Kelly Underman, Heba Gowayed, and Ulrike Bialas. I am immensely grateful to the two reviewers of my manuscript for their care and support in seeing this text through an ongoing genocide, for pushing me theoretically and methodologically, and for reading this book from their own perspectives of working on and in Palestine. Thank you, Ghada Majadli and Yasmine Kherfi, for discussing my book's cover art with me. The beautiful cover image comes from Tanya Habjouqa. Thank you for your work and for letting me use it.

After our interviews, one of my research participants, Reem, who also holds a PhD, told me, "Doing a PhD is a very lonely endeavor; don't make your life about it." To my friends Enya, Laura, Morgana, and Milena—thank you for making a life together. I wouldn't be here without you. Lilly, thank you for what already feels like a lifelong friendship and for making London home. Johnny, Humza, Awut, Sarai, Yuli, and Gabi, thank you for making London sweet. In Berlin, my forever home, I thank everyone at *diffrakt | centre for theoretical periphery*, which made me the thinker I am today. Lux, Lukas, the cats, and my whole Berlin crew, thank you for reminding me of my *other* life. To my parents, thank you for making me anticapitalist and feminist, to my grandparents, and to my whole family, thank you for your love and support. Thank you, Dorothee, for fully seeing me. And thanks to Yoav. Once, as I was struggling to grasp where this project was going, you told me, "Theory is like a poem, it's neither real life nor representation, but it helps people understand things." Thank you for thinking with me every day.

And finally, this book is dedicated to all academic outsiders and underdogs, the nondisciplinary and undisciplined, punks and weirdos, the shy and quiet grad students no one knows or is interested in, scholars from academic institutions no one has heard of before, and people who came to an academic "career" on a different path. I see you.

. . .

Parts of this book have appeared in written form before. Chapter 3 draws in part on arguments I have developed in "Borderlands of Reproduction: Bodies, Borders, and Assisted Reproductive Technologies in Israel/ Palestine," published in the special issue "The Sexual Politics of Border Control," *Ethnic and Racial Studies* 44, no. 9 (2021): 1549–68. Chapter 5 is based on my article "The Materiality of Power and Bodily Matter(ing): Embodied Resistance in Palestine," *Body & Society* 29, no. 4 (2023): 3–28, but expands both its scope and argument.

Introduction

REEM LIVES IN OCCUPIED EAST Jerusalem; Celine is from Bethlehem in the occupied West Bank; and Christeen, a Palestinian citizen of Israel, lives in a remote village in the north of the country. They all have one thing in common: For different medical and personal reasons, they are trying to get pregnant in Israeli fertility clinics. Reem is forty years old, born and raised in East Jerusalem, where she lives with her husband. She has been trying to get pregnant via in vitro fertilization (IVF) for over two years, and her legal and political status characterizes her experience in Israeli hospitals. Israel occupied East Jerusalem in 1967 during the Six-Day War and subsequently annexed it by applying Israeli law and implementing demographic markers to control its population. East Jerusalem Palestinians like Reem are granted permanent residency, a fragile status whose renewal depends on residents' ability to prove their constant center of life in East Jerusalem. Permanent residents are allowed to work in Israel, receive social benefits, and are included in the Israeli healthcare system. This means Reem accesses Israeli hospitals like Jewish Israeli citizens and gets the state's unmatched financial subsidies for fertility treatment. And yet, her status as a Palestinian living under occupation intersects with her comparatively easy access to Israel's thriving fertility economy. Reem received her PhD in history from a prestigious university in the UK, and she speaks English with a British accent. But for practical and political reasons, and like many other East Jerusalemites, she is not fluent in Hebrew, and language barriers shape her experience of trying to get pregnant. In addition, the cumulative effects of everyday hostilities, military control in Jerusalem, and what anthropologist Dána-Ain Davis has termed "obstetric racism" affect her general health and well-being.[1] For Reem, these circumstances are political. Reproduction is a "demographic struggle," and the historical and present-day context of Israeli governance determines Reem's understanding of reproduction as a mode of Palestinian resistance.

Celine is a medical professional in her mid-thirties and lives with her husband and three children in Bethlehem in the occupied West Bank. Celine's husband suffers from a severe genetic illness that causes infertility and cannot be treated in West Bank hospitals due to their lack of specialization as a result of being a healthcare system under occupation. He has been treated in Israeli hospitals since he was three years old, and nowadays, the couple uses his health-related permit to cross the border into Israel to enable Celine to undergo fertility treatment in an Israeli fertility clinic in Jerusalem. Since the beginning of the Second Intifada in 2000, Israel has imposed unprecedented restrictions on the movement of Palestinians in the occupied territories. Palestinians in the West Bank and Gaza must apply to the military authorities to cross the border into Israel. Dating back to British practices of colonial control, this form of population management has transformed the West Bank into a closed military zone, perceiving the Palestinians who live there as a security threat and "surplus population."[2] Despite having to engage with the deliberately opaque permit regime, Celine conceived their three children in Israeli hospitals. For each cycle of IVF (some of which were unsuccessful), the couple traverses the border and Israeli checkpoints up to ten times a month. Whether they can cross easily is unpredictable and depends on the political situation. For Celine, these circumstances have become routine. She hopes that one day her children will be able to get permits to work in Israel because Celine cannot imagine that they will have a "good life" in the West Bank.

Christeen is thirty years old and lives in a small village in the north of Israel with her husband and their newborn daughter. Most of Israel's Palestinian citizens, who comprise 21 percent of the population, live in the Northern Galilee, the Triangle area, or the Naqab (Negev in Hebrew) desert in the south. Palestinian citizens of Israel are those Palestinians who stayed inside the newly established borders of the Israeli state after they were expelled, dispossessed, or transferred from their homes by Zionist militia forces leading up to 1948. These roughly 150,000 Palestinians were granted Israeli citizenship and included in the liberal settler state.[3] However, Israel defines itself as the nation-state of the Jewish people and effectively bifurcates "nationality" and "citizenship" based on racialized categories and demographic concerns.[4] Palestinian citizens are subjected to more than sixty Israeli laws that discriminate against them, ranging from political participation, housing, and education to culture and language.[5] In her five-year journey to get pregnant, Christeen encountered many of these inequalities. After experiencing racism and medical neglect in the small public healthcare center close to her village, she moved to a private fertility clinic in Tel Aviv. The clinic was a two-hour car drive away, and Christeen had to pay for the IVF treatment privately, but she got pregnant within months. She attributed her successful pregnancy to a "private clinic that would convey a different feeling." Christeen understands her class position and reflects on how her network and financial resources enabled her to navigate Israel's stratified health infrastructures to avoid medical racism.

What unites Reem, Celine, and Christeen[6] is not only their desire to have children and the different medical or medicalized reasons why they are pursuing a pregnancy via fertility treatment, but also how their experiences are shaped by the Israeli state's demographic concerns and politics. Various borders, infrastructures, laws, and documents restrict Palestinian women's efforts to become pregnant. The Israeli state presents the separation and monitoring of Palestinians and their fragmentation into different jurisdictions as an absolute necessity to protect itself and its citizens. This necessity, what feminist legal scholar Nadera Shalhoub-Kevorkian calls Israel's "security theology," results from the settler state's demographic and territorial interests.[7] Since the establishment of the Israeli state in 1948, Israeli policymakers recognized that control of the land alone would be impossible without producing and maintaining a Jewish majority. Demographic considerations were thus a key feature of Zionist settlement in Palestine and continue to be central to Israeli politics.[8] Given the Palestinians' historical and ongoing resistance against their dispossession and expulsion, managing the Palestinian population—within the 1948 borders or in the occupied territories—lies at the heart of the Israeli state's security concerns.

Today, about seven million Jewish Israelis and seven million Palestinians live across the territory between the Jordan River and the Mediterranean Sea. The Israeli state holds governing power over this area and controls the Palestinian population's movement in and out of it. In the short descriptions of the circumstances under which Reem, Celine, and Christeen are trying to get pregnant, the broader contours of Israeli spatial, political, and demographic control appear clearly. However, Israeli demographic anxieties affect these three women in a particular way *because* they are trying to get pregnant. Reem, Celine, and Christeen embody in the most apparent way what the Israeli state and its politicians regularly call a "demographic threat." *Demographic Anxieties* explores the articulation of this condition and how it turns

Palestinian women's reproduction into a site for settler colonial surveillance and control but also into a vessel for Palestinian resistance and freedom.

This book takes inspiration from sociologist Ruha Benjamin's reformulation of W. E. B. Du Bois's famous opening question from *The Souls of Black Folk*: "How does it feel to be a problem?"[9] Benjamin suggests rephrasing the question in the context of reproductive justice: "How does it feel to be a . . . *population*?" For, "to be a racialized population, after all, is to be a stubborn *problem* and an insistent *people*."[10] While Benjamin writes in the context of US racial relations, her reformulation also offers a crucial analytic for racialized reproductive injustice in other settler colonial contexts.[11] In this book, the question "How does it feel to be a . . . *population*?" allows me to show how Palestinian women like Reem, Christeen, and Celine indeed constitute, in the eyes of the Israeli state and its institutions, a "stubborn problem." This lens opens a window into the affective dimension of demographic concerns and politics. A "politics of fear" structures the demographic project of Israel, from the early Zionist settlement in Palestine and the 1948 creation of the state of Israel (the Nakba, which is Arabic for catastrophe) to today's right-wing, Jewish supremacist Israeli government.[12]

Asking this question also allows me to center Palestinian women's experience of reproductive injustice as well as their resilient insistence on being *a people*. Thinking with Du Bois via Benjamin points to an important methodological dimension of this book. Du Bois writes: "To the real question, How does it feel to be a problem? I answer seldom a word."[13] Throughout *Demographic Anxieties*, I trace how Palestinian women resist their interpellation as a population, a problem, a number, an object of knowledge—by the Israeli state, their fertility doctor, and sometimes the researcher asking them all these questions. "How does it feel to be a . . . *population*?" is an invitation to ask what we can learn about reproductive freedom and autonomy when we listen to Palestinian women. It approaches Palestine as a generative site to theorize reproductive justice as a transnational feminist framework. However, it also alerts us to ethnographic refusals and probes the epistemological dimensions and ethnographic limits of transnational feminist approaches to Palestine.[14]

• • •

I met Reem, Christeen, and Celine in 2018 and 2019. At the time—or, to be precise, before October 7, 2023—their experiences could have been complemented by those of a woman in Gaza, getting pregnant in a fertility clinic there, or trying to get a health-related permit to travel to the West Bank or Israel. They could have also been discussed in contrast to the reality of the more than 5.9 million Palestinian refugees who are largely banned from entering Israel and cannot, like any other medical tourist from Europe or the United States, enjoy one of the world's most advanced fertility economies. However, what has happened since October 2023 changes the meaning of such comparisons. The reproductive injustices that Palestinian women like Reem, Christeen, and Celine experienced set the scene, or chronicle the threshold, to a more violent reality. Since 2023, Israel's demographic control and management of Palestinian women's reproduction has shifted from the various forms of reproductive injustice I discuss in this book to what anthropologist Sarah Ihmoud terms Israel's "reproductive genocide" in Gaza. Israel has since not only sought to "uproot and dismember the individual and collective Palestinian body," deploying various forms of military, spatial, psychological, environmental, and gendered and sexual violence against Palestinians in Gaza, but has also centrally targeted Palestinian forms of kinship, care, and other social relations.[15]

As I finalize this manuscript in January 2026, Israel has killed more than seventy thousand Palestinians in Gaza, a number that is vastly underestimated, as it doesn't account for the many indirect deaths from causes such as reproductive, communicable, and noncommunicable diseases.[16] This number amounts to 10 percent of Gaza's pre-2023 population. About 90 percent of the population of the Gaza Strip has been displaced, many repeatedly. At the same time, 81 percent of the Strip has been transformed into Israeli-militarized zones or is under displacement orders.[17] Since October 2023, Israel has also killed 1,046 Palestinians in the occupied West Bank, including East Jerusalem.[18] Reports from Gaza chronicle the forced starvation that people have suffered from after Israel's blockage of basic humanitarian supplies such as food, medicine, or fuel from entering Gaza. As of October 2025, 455 malnutrition-related deaths have been reported in Gaza, including 151 children.[19] On October 7, 2023, fighters from the Qassam Brigades, the armed wing of Hamas, and other Palestinian groups broke Israel's siege on Gaza and attacked Israeli military structures as well as civilians. During the attack and through Israeli crossfire, 1,200 Jewish Israelis, Palestinians, and other nationals were killed, and 250 Israelis, Thais, and one Filipino person were taken into captivity in Gaza. Despite Israel and its Western allies' framing of the ensuing genocide as a justified war, Israeli politicians were clear about their annihilatory goals in Gaza from October 8 onward. The aim to seize the whole territory and ethnically cleanse all of its Palestinian inhabitants has been openly stated since, supported by a majority of Israeli society.[20]

The destruction of Gaza and the killing of thousands of Palestinian women, men, and children alone are enough to understand how this is a reproductive justice issue. Israel's genocide in Gaza is an assault on present and future generations of Palestinians, an assault on Palestinian children and childhoods, an assault tearing apart families.[21] "The women of Gaza are not just statistics; they are mothers who mourn the loss of children they will never know," write medical scholars Bilal Irfan, Abdallah Abu Shammala, and Khaled Saleh, pointing to imminent intergenerational trauma.[22] The destruction of health infrastructure in Gaza has forced Palestinian women to give birth under unsafe conditions, in overcrowded shelters, often without medical assistance or necessary medical supplies. Women also lack access to pre- and postnatal care, which poses a high risk of maternal, neonatal, and stillbirth deaths.[23] Surviving physical injuries, reproductive health challenges, as well as the emotional toll of caring for their children when there is no food, shelter, medicine, healthcare, and the ongoing threat of displacement and destruction, additionally affects Palestinian women's mental health. Testimonies of women from Gaza expose a severe and disproportionately gendered mental health crisis, which is exacerbated by two years of genocidal violence and intensified gender-based violence.[24] In addition to that, the destruction and degradation of built and natural environments in Gaza expose Palestinians to waste, chemical weapons, and other hazardous materials, with severe long- and short-term (reproductive) health consequences.[25]

As various critical health scholars and international organizations have argued, the repeated bombing of hospitals, the targeting and killing of doctors, aid workers, and medical staff, and the ongoing blockage that restricts the entry of medical supplies are not side effects of a brutal war, but a strategy of Israeli warfare.[26] This deliberate destruction of reproductive and sexual healthcare, blocking women's access and availability to maternal healthcare, the reproductive harms of starvation, and Israel's systematic use of sexual and gender-based violence are central to understanding Israeli violence in Gaza.[27] Under such circumstances, and writing two years into the genocide, "there can be no reproductive justice that does not consider Gazan suffering," as sociologist Sharmila Rudrappa puts it.[28]

I drafted the previous paragraphs numerous times in the last two years, and if I were to write them again next week, these numbers, news items, and political statements would be different ones. Finalizing these few paragraphs feels wrong, as the suffering continues. How do I contextualize my reach to prove, evidence, collect, and illustrate what we have known for two years? Such is the challenge of writing about a genocide that is ongoing.[29] I could go on with the listing of atrocities, with a critique of the institutions and scholarly discipline I write from,[30] and with a reflection of my own complicity and role as a witness, as per my passport, and my current place of residency.[31] But having written this book, I believe my task is not only to chronicle that which is unfolding but to connect it to what I have studied in the past ten years.

In this book, then, I contextualize and connect stories like those Reem, Celine, and Christeen shared with me within the new reality since 2023.[32] I argue that their stories show how reproductive injustice has remained central to the Israeli settler colonial state, beginning with the 1948 Nakba and continuing in Gaza today.[33] The forms of reproductive injustice and violence that Reem, Celine, Christeen, and many other Palestinians experienced in Israeli hospitals, and on their way there, set the scene for such extreme forms of violence, destruction, and annihilation to be allowed to happen. While getting pregnant in an Israeli fertility clinic may reflect less overt and less visible forms of violence, the fact that such practices persist—and, as I demonstrate in this book, are implemented and supported by the majority of Jewish Israeli doctors—underscores the central argument of this book: Israeli demographic politics make the Palestinian population into a "problem" to be managed, a process that fundamentally relies on their racialization and dehumanization.[34] By focusing on Israel's management and control of Palestinian women's reproduction pre–October 7, *Demographic Anxieties* sets the scene for understanding how the escalation that Israel's genocide in Gaza presents is not a rupture or a single event but part of an ongoing structure of settler colonial statecraft.[35]

At the same time, I consider Reem, Celine, Christeen, and other Palestinian women's experiences of trying to get pregnant as reflective of their own time, place, and political reality. The same applies to the interviews I conducted with Jewish Israeli and Palestinian medical staff in Israeli fertility clinics, as well as with Palestinian activists, scholars, and healthcare providers. In the empirical chapters that follow, I thus contextualize the politics, documents, sentiments, experiences, and narratives I have collected as the ongoing history of the present. I connect empirical examples and ethnographic data to the unfolding reality of new developments in 2023, 2024, and 2025, including bringing in new data to draw out the continuum of reproductive injustice and violence in the Israeli healthcare system and beyond. This is, however, an open-ended endeavor, and many things will have changed once you get to read this book; new statistics will have been released, and perhaps a new political reality will have arrived. In that sense, *Demographic Anxieties* also chronicles how I grappled with my role as a witness. Like writer Sarah Aziza reflected in early 2024, to be a witness to this genocide "is to make contact, to be touched, and to bear the marks of this touch," witnessing the ongoing violence, and our own implication in it.[36] In seeing this book through, I tried to strike a balance between past and present, offering an analysis of how they are interwoven, and reflecting on my own role in writing about Palestine/Israel at this time.

THE SLOW VIOLENCE OF DEMOGRAPHY

Since the early days of Zionist settlement in Palestine, and increasingly so with the Israeli state's inception in 1948, concerns about the demographic composition across Palestine/Israel were considered central to Israeli governance and shaped public opinion.[37] Demographic concerns are inscribed into some of the most foundational laws of the country. In 1950, one of the first legislative acts of the newly formed Israeli parliament (Knesset) was to pass the Law of Return. This law entitles all Jews to receive Israeli citizenship if they wish to settle in Palestine/Israel. The Law of Return does not apply to Palestinians. This includes Israel's refusal to grant 5.9 million registered Palestinian refugees the right to return to their families' birthplace or to reunite with their remaining family members.[38] East Jerusalem permanent residents cannot automatically pass their residency status to their children. They must ensure that their children are born in a recognized Israeli hospital and only then are they eligible to begin the process of child registration to receive a permanent residency status with an Israeli number, which is later required again if the person wants to continue to obtain residency in Jerusalem.[39] Children born to Jewish Israeli citizens are entitled to citizenship, whether born in Israeli hospitals or elsewhere. Given the current demographic balance and a possible watershed, Israel has recently restricted Palestinians' rights to build and have a family.[40] For instance, in March 2022, the Israeli parliament passed the so-called citizenship law, denying naturalization to Palestinians from the occupied West Bank or Gaza who are married to Israeli citizens. The regulation replaces a decree renewed annually since 2003, forcing thousands of Palestinian families to live apart.

While these are just a few of the most obvious ways in which Israeli law governs Palestinians' intimate lives, family-building, and kin-work, more direct references to Palestinian women's birth rates abound and are effectively connected to "security issues." Comparing Palestinian and Jewish Israeli birthrates has been commonplace in Israeli public discourse since the establishment of the state. In 1949, the Israeli state established the so-called heroine mothers award to honor women who gave birth to more than nine children. Ten years later, the award was discontinued when it became clear that most award recipients were Palestinian women.[41] At the same time, Israel's first prime minister, David Ben-Gurion, stated that Israeli population policies aim to increase "the number of Jews and not the population of the state."[42] In the early 1970s, then-prime minister Golda Meir confessed that she would "have to wake up every morning wondering how many Arab babies have been born during the night."[43] In June 2020, right-wing Israeli politician Bezalel Smotrich, now the minister of finance, stated that the Palestinian Bedouin population's birthrate was a "bomb that must be handled."[44] In October 2022, a video of an Israeli physician addressing Israel's far-right minister of interior, Ayelet Shaked, circulated on social media. In it, the head of the cardiothoracic surgery at Soroka Medical Center in Beersheba talks about the "matter of population growth and the more problematic population," referring to Palestinian citizens of Israel. He finds that their birthrate, dehumanized as "the Arab womb," is a factor to be considered and questions why the state "encourage[s] it with all the child allowances."[45] As per the International Court of Justice's provisional order from January 2024, Israel's intent to destroy, in whole or in part, the Palestinian population in Gaza points to the demographic dimensions of the genocide.[46] Indeed, in December 2023, Smotrich went on record to state his vision of a depopulated Gaza Strip. He said: "If there are 100,000 or 200,000 Arabs in Gaza and not 2 million, the whole discourse about the day after will be different."[47] Itamar Ben-Gvir, Israel's right-wing minister of national security, similarly called the war an opportunity to encourage "the migration of the residents of Gaza."[48] Taken together, these statements and their underlying sentiments seamlessly fuse security and demographic concerns. They manifest in laws and state policy, and in militarized everyday language and practices. This book traces the formation of such demographic anxieties and explores how they shape Palestinian women's reproductive rights, health, and decision-making.

In their quest to become pregnant, Reem, Celine, and Christeen enter a significant contemporary site of innovation that the Israeli state invests in to keep up the Jewish Israeli birthrate: the country's thriving fertility economy. With twenty-five fertility clinics, mainly situated in majority Jewish Israeli areas, Israel has one of the highest rates of fertility clinics per capita.[49] The sector is animated by Israel's comparatively liberal stance regarding the regulation of a range of assisted reproductive technologies (ART) for heterosexual couples, such as IVF, surrogacy, or preimplantation genetic diagnosis (PGD), as well as by the state's unique subsidization of ART. Citizens or residents like Reem and Christeen are entitled to up to two fully subsidized IVF cycles leading to a live birth, while Celine, like other "medical tourists" (except she isn't a tourist to Israel), can access the Israeli fertility sector if they pay for treatment privately.

Including Palestinian citizens or residents in the settler state and its medical institutions is often presented as proof of Israel's democratic and liberal character. Compared to Palestinians in the West Bank and in Gaza, Palestinian citizens and residents have relatively easy access to the Israeli health sector and are comparatively visible within it as patients and staff.[50] Unsurprisingly, Israeli media, politicians, and doctors often use Palestinian physicians' presence in the Israeli medical sector to present it as a neutral sphere of coexistence and humanitarianism.[51] This has changed since the genocide in Gaza, and Palestinian physicians have expressed experiences of silencing and repression if they offer empathy for the Palestinian victims in Gaza in the Israeli medical sphere.[52] Based on the experiences of Palestinian women trying to get pregnant in Israeli fertility clinics, this book further challenges an understanding of Israeli medical institutions as neutral, apolitical, and humanitarian.

Israel's rule over the Palestinian population is often presented through spectacular and disastrous forms of violence. The genocide in Gaza, the military occupation of the West Bank, forceful evacuations of Palestinian neighborhoods in occupied East Jerusalem, and the racialized depiction of Palestinians as dangerous dominate the news and public opinion. These circumstances affect Palestinian women's lives, their reproductive decision-making, and family planning in multiple and intersecting ways. But the modalities of Israeli power can also be traced in the less spectacular, often overlooked sites of settler colonialism. How are demographic sentiments and politics implemented and contested in everyday encounters between Israeli medical staff and Palestinian women who want to become pregnant? Israeli hospitals, fertility departments, delivery rooms, and maternity wards offer a unique window into the formation of Israeli demographic anxieties.

Demographic Anxieties explores how these sites of "tender violence" and care infrastructures are foundational for the Israeli settler state to implement its sexual and demographic politics. It argues that these quotidian forms of surveillance, control, and "slow violence" unfold alongside Israel's broader and more clearly defined population politics and shape Palestinian women's reproductive choices and pregnancy outcomes.

The conceptual notions of "tender violence" and "slow violence" are central to the argument I make in this book. American studies and gender scholar Laura Wexler deploys the notion of tender violence in her book of the same title.[53] She introduces the term as an analytic to explore how white women photographers in the late nineteenth century framed American domesticity through a sentimental lens, coding racial hierarchy and subordination of domestic relationships as benign or even benevolent. Tender violence captures how this framing of racialized subjects, mostly formerly enslaved Black women, produces them as objects of white sympathy and care while maintaining power over them. It thus refers to a type of violence that claims to be caring and protective but upholds broader structures of dominance, such as colonialism, imperialism, and slavery. Anthropologist Ann Laura Stoler takes up a similar argument in her edited volume *Haunted by Empire*.[54] Interested in foregrounding intimacy as a central site to consolidate colonial power, she explores the "tense and tender" relationships between colonizer and colonized in intimate encounters in the domestic sphere, education, or public health. Stoler's focus on intimacies foregrounds the "human dimension" of the colonial encounter and illustrates how intimate encounters of various qualities are a crucial part of imperial and racial statecraft.[55] Humanities and environmental scholar Rob Nixon offers a different yet related formulation of violence. Concerned with ongoing environmental catastrophes and toxic pollution, he is interested in capturing the discounted casualties and agents of climate change and toxicity. To rethink the politically neglected and often invisible violence of environmental harm, he suggests "slow violence" as a notion of violence "that occurs gradually and out of sight, a violence of delayed destruction that is dispersed across time and space, an attritional violence that is typically not viewed as violence at all."[56]

These multidisciplinary conceptualizations of violence are central to my endeavor in this book. I am interested in the encounter between Palestinian fertility patients and Israeli healthcare providers, and how the structural violence of settler colonialism shapes these encounters and a system that is usually described as beneficial and caring for Palestinians. Furthermore, this book shows how the discrimination Palestinians experience in the Israeli fertility economy might not be spectacularly violent or obvious to everyone. Instead, it is precisely in the colonial encounter that violence is concealed and shapes Palestinian lives gradually, injuring them slowly and affectively. I thus use tender and slow violence as an analytic to explore how such violence requires different representational, methodological, and narrative strategies.

RESEARCHING DEMOGRAPHIC ANXIETIES: METHODS AND TRANSLATION

To this end, I conducted fieldwork in Israel, occupied East Jerusalem, and the occupied West Bank over the span of six years (thirty months in total) between 2015 and 2021. This book's main body of documentation draws on in-depth interviews with eighty interview participants, many of whom I met several times and stayed in touch with via messenger services; ethnographic research in Israeli fertility clinics; and legal documents and media reporting on reproductive technologies in Palestine/Israel. Thirty-five interviews with Palestinian women were conducted with three Palestinian interpreters and collaborators, Rafa Musmar, Mary Khadija, and Najla Fawwaz. It is important to note that their translations and transcriptions from Arabic to English conveyed much more than just language. Each collaboration, and especially my work with Najla, enabled me to understand the multilayered nature of Palestinian women's lives under Israeli governance and control, and transcriptions and translations of Palestinian women's narratives in this book bear Rafa, Mary, and Najla's contextualization. Interviews with thirty Jewish Israeli and Palestinian medical staff in Israeli fertility clinics and with fifteen Palestinian legal service providers, activists, religious leaders, and social workers were recorded in English and sometimes partly in Hebrew.

This research includes multiple accounts of Palestinian women's access to the symbolic and material resources needed to get pregnant in Israeli fertility clinics. I combine narratives, explanations, and practices from a variety of actors. These include the experiences of Palestinian women with Israeli citizenship; women from occupied East Jerusalem; West Bank residents who were trying to or got pregnant in Israeli fertility clinics; and women who got pregnant in fertility clinics in the West Bank as part of the practice of sperm smuggling. I also analyze interviews with Jewish Israeli and Palestinian medical staff and medical staff involved in providing and regulating reproductive technologies in Palestine/Israel, as well as Palestinian activists, scholars, and legal service providers. My analysis is also informed by meetings with various actors in sexual and reproductive health and rights (SRHR) in Palestine/Israel, and my volunteering with the Israeli nongovernmental organization Physicians for Human Rights Israel in cooperation with the Gaza Community Mental Health Programme.

My firsthand interactions with Israeli medical staff and Palestinian fertility patients open a window into highly personal and contesting narratives. On the one hand, interviews and observations of those providing or regulating reproductive technologies in Israeli hospitals reveal the formation of demographic anxieties and the implementation and legitimization of such policies in the Israeli fertility economy, as well as how Palestinian women, their bodies, and their children are perceived in a political system that is based on their dispossession. On the other hand, how Palestinian women experience this environment demonstrates how these processes, interactions, and sentiments affect their reproductive health, decision-making, and pregnancy outcomes. Combining the voices of these different actors conveys how settler colonial demographic and territorial claims are produced and contested in everyday encounters between Jewish Israelis and Palestinians. This juxtaposition reveals the complexity and ambivalence of how the demographic and sexual politics of a settler colonial state are translated—sometimes patchily, sometimes straightforwardly—in and through the provision of fertility treatment.

Collecting these materials, I was keenly aware of how my presence in Palestine/Israel and the history of what Sa'ed Atshan and Katharina Galor have termed the German-Israeli-Palestinian moral triangle would affect the empirical evidence I discuss in *Demographic Anxieties*.[57] While this book examines the formation of Israeli demographic anxieties and Palestinian women's experiences in Israeli hospitals, this is not its only purpose. Alongside this work, I also trace how the "geographies of intimacies" between a German sociologist, Israeli medical staff, and Palestinian fertility patients shape my narration of *Demographic Anxieties*.[58] I treat these methodological questions of intersecting modes of oppression and multidimensional memory[59] not as separate from the topic of reproductive injustice but as generative to exploring what reproductive justice means—in Palestine and as a transnational sociological lens.

SETTLER COLONIALISM

At the heart of *Demographic Anxieties* is an understanding of the intimate relationship between settler colonialism and demographic concerns, and how the latter further encourages and legitimizes the legal, economic, and biopolitical management of Palestinians' lives. Led by Palestinian scholars,[60] the past two decades have seen a resurgence of scholarship that describes Zionism as a settler colonial movement and Israel as a settler colonial state.[61] While colonialism relies on the establishment of labor economies, exploitation, and resource extraction as a primary mode of capital accumulation in the metropole, settler colonialism is characterized by the need to control native land and populations to enable a community of settlers to form a new society, guarantee their security, and support the continued growth of settler economies. The settler colonial "dual structure of destroy to replace" describes various strategies of appropriating land and resources to dispossess and replace, ranging from cultural, political, economic, military, and psychological forms of power.[62] Key to the settler colonial project is the political desire to limit the Indigenous community's ability to reproduce socially over time.[63] To be a settler is not necessarily about individual intention but describes a structural position in which settlers benefit from Indigenous dispossession and the accumulation of land and resources.[64] In this book, I explore how Israeli political subjectivity and its collective structure of feeling are founded on the control and restriction of the Palestinian population's reproduction.[65] In other words, I argue that reproductive injustice is a feature, not a bug, of the settler colonial project.

The Zionist movement and the Israeli state today rely on a powerful narrative to justify the historical and ongoing settlement of Palestinian land. Palestine was imagined to be sparsely populated, and Zionist settlement was premised on the conviction held by Jewish and Christian Zionists that God and the Bible had given the promised land to the Jewish people. As a nineteenth-century response to nationalism and growing antisemitism in Europe, this secular movement mobilized biblical language to make the argument for their religiously sanctioned and morally legitimized right to "return" to the land of Palestine.[66] Famously captured by the slogan "a land without a people for a people without a land," the Zionist movement called for and justified settlement based on the imagination of Palestine as terra nullius. This doctrine originates in the idea of Australia as an ostensibly empty wasteland and thus available for European discovery and settlement.[67] It has since been deployed to describe other settler colonies, such as North America, to foreground the foundational link between imagining land as belonging to no one and thereby constructing Indigenous people as outside the category of the human and without any rights to land ownership.

Writings by early Zionists illustrate the relationship between spatial imagination and ontological erasure. While settlement was driven by the idea of Palestine as an empty land, Zionist accounts clearly show that they were well aware of the existence of Palestinians who were already living there.[68] The notion of terra nullius thus served as a powerful fiction to legitimize claims to the land. It implied that Palestinians were not a people who existed.[69] The conflation of settler colonialism and theological ideology crystallized in 1917 with the Balfour Declaration, when Britain declared its support for establishing a "national home for the Jewish people," disregarding the presence and political aspirations of the majority of Palestine's residents.[70]

Racial hierarchy constituted the legitimizing epistemological framework for European indifference toward Palestinian existence. While the particularity of Zionist settlement in the context of European antisemitism and the Holocaust is evident, it was a development of its time, based on hundreds of years of colonial and imperial expansion legitimized by the racialization of the colonized.[71] As Edward Said explains in his foundational essay "Zionism from the Standpoint of Its Victims": "From the earliest phases of its modern evolution until it culminated in the creation of Israel, Zionism appealed to a European audience for whom the classification of overseas territories and natives into various uneven classes was canonical and 'natural.'"[72] Zionist pioneers, in their attempt to escape Nazi Germany and European persecution, established a nation-state for the Jews by reproducing the parameters of European colonial and racial hierarchies and property relationships.[73] In a bid for "colonization-cum-modernization," Zionist settlers imagined themselves as transmitters of Western values, rationality, science, technology, and medicine.[74] The racial subjugation of the Palestinian population was central to establishing the material conditions that Zionist settlement required. Today, the Israeli state continues to enact the same racial technologies of segregation, categorization, and discrimination that the Zionist movement relied on.[75] Ashkenazi Israelis (the Jewish diaspora population from Europe) occupy the structural position of whiteness, while Arabs—and Palestinians in particular—constitute their racialized Other.[76] The biblical claim of the "chosen people" was thus entwined with the racial grammar of

European colonialism, which, in turn, served as a legitimization for the settlement in Palestine and continues to shape the Israeli state's raison d'état.

Settler colonialism is an ongoing process. As per Patrick Wolfe, it is a structure of invasion, not a single event.[77] In the Israeli context, this allows for a critical historicization of the colonization of Palestine that extends beyond the 1948 foundation of the State of Israel.[78] Indeed, attempts to challenge the settler colonial analytic by exceptionalizing Israeli state-building as a single outcome of European antisemitism and the Holocaust falter with a brief look into the Zionist archives. Political Zionists proudly characterized their undertaking as "colonization" and described their presence in the "colonies."[79] A settler colonial perspective also challenges an epistemological division between events such as the 1948 Nakba and the 1967 occupation of the West Bank. It connects these instances to a continuous structure of invasion that began in the late nineteenth century.[80] Furthermore, adding to the temporal dimension, understanding Israel through a settler colonial lens explores the implications of the fragmentation of Palestinians into different jurisdictions under Israeli control, first in 1948, then in 1967, and in 2007, following the Israeli state's disengagement but ongoing control of Gaza. Palestinians in the occupied territories and Palestinians in Israel are routinely described as separate entities. Jewish Israelis usually refer to the latter group as "Israeli Arabs," which falsely but conveniently subsumes Palestinians with Israeli citizenship as a minority group just like other immigrants in Israel and disconnects them from the broader Palestinian struggle.[81] This fragmentation, often mirrored in scholarship on Palestinians and Palestine, reproduces the ontological difference the "Green Line" seeks to imply.[82] Situating Israel alongside other nineteenth-century colonial and nationalist endeavors thus challenges Israel's exceptionalism beyond comparison. The settler colonial framework enables a more nuanced understanding of how the territorial and demographic interests of the Israeli state are structurally implemented across time, space, and bodies.

RELATIONAL HISTORIES: REPRODUCTION, SEXUALITY, AND PARENTHOOD IN (SETTLER) COLONIAL STATES

The management of reproduction is central for nation-states to implement their racial politics, territorial interests, and the organization of labor and capital accumulation. While Michel Foucault has foundationally articulated the connections between sexuality, race, and what he terms biopower, feminist theorists further emphasize how sexuality and reproduction have become a central target for nation-states or national, capitalist, or colonial projects to institute their politics along racial fault lines.[83] Control of the reproductive body, surveillance of people's sexualities and relationships, and questions of who is regarded as a legitimate parent were central to the transatlantic slave trade and plantation slavery, colonialism, and imperialism, and continue to shape today's border and immigration regimes. A historical and comparative lens to the contemporary politics of reproduction is central to the arguments I develop in this book. This means that an understanding of the connected sociologies of reproduction across what American studies scholar Lisa Lowe calls the "intimacies of four continents" is as important to my analysis as tracing the history of racializing reproduction in Palestine/Israel.[84] This section provides a brief (and necessarily cursory) overview of both.

Scholars concerned with the history of slavery and reproduction have shown how Black women's bodies were systematically exploited to sustain both capitalism and the transatlantic slave trade.[85] Sociologist and legal scholar Dorothy Roberts emphasizes how reproductive control has been a key tool of racial oppression, tracing it from slavery to modern practices like forced sterilization.[86] Slavery placed Black women outside the bounds of gender, motherhood, and white femininity, thereby reducing their bodies to mere property and denying them the right to motherhood and protection from sexual violence.[87] What Black studies scholar Hortense Spillers terms the "ungendering" of Black women's bodies also allowed slaveholders and medical doctors to exploit their bodies in medical experiments to advance American gynecology and innovate in the field of women's health more broadly.[88]

During and after the abolition of slavery, racial reproductive politics continued and found a new outlet in eugenic thinking and pseudoscience. Imperialist policies reinforced gendered and racial hierarchies, with European colonial powers extending their control over the reproductive and sexual practices of colonized people and shaping ideologies of white motherhood and womanhood both within the metropole and colony.[89] In the early twentieth century, notions of motherhood were constructed as central to nation-building, justifying invasive intervention in poor and racialized women's lives and instituting who was deemed fit or unfit to become a mother.[90] Eugenics, imperialism, and the idealization of motherhood created a landscape in which reproductive control became a central tool of both social and political domination.

In the mid-twentieth century, women's rights to control their sexuality were central to debates about birth control, sterilization, and abortion, and access to the resources to implement individual reproductive decisions was refracted along the registers of race, dis/ability, sexuality, and class. In North America, Puerto Rico, India, Bangladesh, Brazil, Mexico, France, and other (post)colonial nation-states, sterilization campaigns targeted Black, nonwhite, disabled, and poor women.[91] Meanwhile, publicity surrounding coerced sterilization and other reproductive abuses, as well as the export and global circulation of North American and European eugenic thought and technologies, raised awareness among feminist activists and reformers.[92] In the wake of decolonization and Cold War anxieties, racialized fears of overpopulation and high fertility rates took center stage, and nonwhite and poor women's reproduction was perceived and targeted as an obstacle to modernity and progress, furthering the globalization of reproductive control.[93]

In contemporary settler contexts, sexual politics and the regulation of the reproductive behavior of settlers, natives, and their children continue to be central to establishing cultural, demographic, and territorial control and hegemony.[94] For the US context, historian Brianna Theobald shows how the forced sterilization of native women, medical abuse in federal birth clinics, and the removal of native children from their families to transfer them to foster homes or white families actualized civilizational discourse in the mid- to late twentieth century.[95] The so-called Sixties Scoop in Canada, where thousands of Indigenous children were forcibly removed from their homes and placed within white families, further exemplifies such racialized reproductive violence. In a large-scale project between the 1950s and 1980s, Canadian social workers removed Indigenous children from their families and communities, often without the consent of their families or proper investigation.[96] Alongside practices of coerced sterilization and abortions, such practices of child theft and transracial adoption represent the continuity and range of postcolonial or settler colonial reproductive control. The notion that Indigenous or colonized women are unable to provide for their children and that their reproduction and birthing practices need to be observed and managed further echoes similar experiences by Black women from the time of slavery until today.[97]

Feminist writer and antiracist activist Françoise Vergès calls attention to the relational histories of reproductive oppression. The archive of eugenic thought and praxis, racialized notions of overpopulation, and coercive reproductive and sexual politics provide ample evidence of continuous similarities across different places.[98] As a response to Israel's genocide in Gaza, gender studies scholar Nadine Naber considers US and Israeli state reproductive injustices as not merely similar but interlinked settler colonial practices, waged against Indigenous, Black, and poor mothers and caretakers in both contexts and across history.[99] In the opening vignettes, we have seen how various Israeli policies restrict Palestinian women's reproductive freedom. With the current right-wing, ultranationalist, and Jewish supremacist Israeli government that wages a genocidal war against Gaza, the conditions that limit Palestinian women's fertility have only been exacerbated. But such conditions of state reproductive injustice are neither new nor do they only affect Palestinians. Israeli demographic anxieties are deeply rooted in the political structure of the Israeli settler state and its structural anti-Arab and anti-Black racism.

The history of the Israeli state is rife with examples illustrating how the regulation of reproduction, sexuality, and parenthood works across different registers of racialization. While Palestinians continue to represent Zionism's ultimate Other,[100] the question of who (re)produces the Jewish nation—biologically and culturally—sits squarely at the core of Israeli nation-building.[101] Reproductive injustice in Palestine/Israel is not only an issue along the settler/native divide. It is helpful to recall two historical examples here to illustrate the vast range of strategies the settler colonial state and its medical personnel have applied to build a settler nation modeled after the European nation-state and its reliance on racism and racial categories to denote belonging and non-belonging.[102]

From 1948 to 1954, more than fifty thousand Yemenite Jews immigrated to the newly founded state. Due to housing shortages, most were accommodated in crowded transit camps and administered by Israeli medical and welfare organizations. The conditions in these tent cities were dire, and testimonies of Yemenite families who had lived there reveal a pattern of shared experiences. Women who gave birth in the overcrowded hospitals didn't get to see their newborns and were later told that their babies had died. Many of these women never received a death certificate or saw their child's grave. Other families were instructed to leave their children at one of the state-run nurseries, but their children were gone when they returned to pick them up.[103] Research shows that, during those years, one out of every eight Yemenite babies had been taken away from their parents without them knowing what was happening or giving consent.[104] In many cases, these missing babies and children were given up for adoption by Ashkenazi families or transferred to state institutions. Doctors, nurses, and social workers played a crucial role in managing these transfers. Still, Israeli health officials long denied that systematic abductions of Yemenite children happened altogether, and an official acknowledgment by then-prime minister Benjamin Netanyahu was issued only in 2021.[105]

Archival materials such as newsletters and testimonies show that implementing these child transfers was ideologically driven by Zionist organizations' racist perception of Yemenite women as unfit mothers. Medical staff, social workers, and state officials viewed Yemenite families as "primitive," "dirty," and unable to raise children properly to serve the newly established settler state.[106] It is important to stress that these families were Jewish. Different Zionist strategies sought to actively dislodge Asian and African Jewish communities to enlarge the Jewish population of the newly founded state. The work of cultural theorist Ella Shohat demonstrates how the integration of non-European Jews (Mizrahim or Sephardim) points to a rupture in the hegemonic Zionist narrative of state-building. Not unlike Palestinian Arabs, Mizrahi and Sephardi Jews were governed through the lens of modernization. Israeli authorities and individuals classified them as "underdeveloped," "backward," and thus in need of civilizing state intervention.[107] The act of kidnapping Yemenite children based on racialized notions of child-rearing, motherhood, and culture thus resulted from the foundational Zionist beliefs in the inferiority of Jews from Arab or Muslim countries. While situated differently vis-à-vis the Jewish nation-state, the racialization of Mizrahi Jews relied on anti-Arab racism, fueled by notions of hygiene and Western civilizational discourse, which were part of the conceptual toolkit of nation-building following the European colonial example.[108] These practices of abduction, disappearance, and assimilation of racialized children mirror similar histories in other settler colonial contexts, such as Canada, the United States, and Australia.[109] While the abduction of Yemenite children speaks to the historical specificity of raising, assimilating, and integrating *Jewish* children to become settler citizens of the newly established Israeli state, what unites these cases is how racialized mothers are deemed as unfit to properly raise their children based on racial hierarchy and civilizational discourse.

In the 1990s and 2000s, a similar scandal unfolded along the racial fault lines of Israeli body politics. The so-called Depo-Provera affair symbolized how anti-Blackness is inscribed into the fabric of Israeli institutions and society. In 2008, investigative journalists first documented how Israeli health organizations helped to administer Depo-Provera shots to female Jewish Ethiopian immigrants in transit camps in Addis Ababa, Ethiopia, and in camps upon their arrival in Israel. Depo-Provera is a long-acting contraceptive administered through injection.[110] The contraceptive was given to the new Jewish immigrants without their knowledge and without ensuring informed consent. Medical reports reveal how the Ethiopian community's birthrate declined rapidly in the following years. For instance, there was only one birth in three years among fifty-seven families living in Bnei Brak, a neighborhood just outside of Tel Aviv.[111] The Depo-Provera scandal sheds light on the complex racialization of reproduction in Israel. As gender scholar Bayan Abusneineh argues, the forced sterilization of Black Jews further complicates the understanding of Israeli settler colonialism as solely configured around a settler/native binary. This case indexes the internal racialization of the figure of the settler and the Israeli state's goal to become a white (European) nation.[112] This preoccupation with engineering a "chosen body"[113] according to European racial parameters and colonial logics of whiteness manifests in the policing of other nonwhite bodies *within* the settler state.[114] Taken together, the Depo-Provera affair and the abduction of Yemenite children illustrate how Israeli reproductive and sexual politics are contested along a Jewish-Palestinian divide and complicated by intra-Jewish racial hierarchy. As settlers, nonwhite Jews are included in the political structure of the Israeli state. Still, the anxieties around Black and Arab Jews' reproductive behavior demonstrate how notions of racial purity are central to the Israeli settler colonial project.

My intention here is not to compare the testimonies of Yemenite families and those of Ethiopian women to the experience of Palestinian women trying to get pregnant in Israeli fertility clinics, nor to equate the structural positionalities of Black women and Indigenous women in settler colonies. Instead, I propose to consider these cases as a lens through which to examine the relationality between different modalities of oppression targeting the reproductive body.[115] In this book, the relational structure of settler colonial reproductive injustice allows me to draw out how similar historical narratives and Israeli strategies of selective pronatalism and eugenic thinking shape Palestinian women's reproductive freedom and fertility.

FEMINIST DEBT: REPRODUCTIVE JUSTICE AND ANTICOLONIAL FEMINISM

In today's Israel, fertility clinics and hospitals are crucial and obvious sites to analyze how Israeli demographic sentiments and politics are formed and implemented. Feminist historian Sigrid Vertommen demonstrates how the Zionist movement's goal of establishing and maintaining a majority population translated into Israel's thriving "reproductive-industrial complex," in which military and demographic interests of the settler state and a growing bioeconomy merge.[116] Israel maintains a leading role in the global fertility economy. This is animated by the country's comparatively liberal stance regarding regulating, implementing, and subsidizing assisted reproductive technologies.[117] The Israeli state publicly funds IVF for up to two live births for Israeli citizens and residents between the ages of eighteen and forty-five, and health insurance companies' rates for more treatment cycles are comparatively affordable. However, Israel's pronatalism and techno-optimism are geared toward Jewish Israeli consumers.[118] Indeed, as sociologist Michal Nahman writes, "Israeli IVF cannot be examined outside the history and contemporary discursive practices of state Zionism."[119] Legal definitions of practices such as surrogacy or egg donation illustrate the state's ideological stance. Israeli law does not allow surrogacy for gay couples, and cross-religious egg donation and surrogacy are prohibited if either the intended mother, the egg donor, or the surrogate is Jewish, to ensure a matrilineal genealogy.[120] These regulations show how Israeli reproductive policies work to reproduce heteronormativity as well as narrowly defined Jewish cultural, religious, and political notions of kinship, motherhood, and body politics.[121]

Moreover, Palestinian women's experiences and needs in undergoing fertility treatment in the Israeli fertility economy are largely missing from the scholarship on reproductive technologies in Palestine/Israel, mirroring the target consumers of the fertility and health sector and their implication in the settler colonial project.[122] Israel's liberal stance and subsidization of fertility treatment and other biomedical interventions are often explained from a cultural and historical perspective. A large body of work focuses on the importance of childbearing and the role of motherhood in Israeli society and Judaism. It stresses the "Jewish quest for survival" in light of the centuries-long experience of antisemitism and the Holocaust.[123] While most of the scholarship on the Israeli fertility economy mentions the state's "intense demographic anxiety" about Palestinians' high birth rates, it fails to connect demographic concerns to settler colonial expansion and the question of territorial sovereignty.[124] Himmat Zu'bi succinctly notes that despite the accelerating pace at which new research on Israeli reproductive technologies is produced, what "these technologies mean for Palestinian women, who are excluded from the state's self-definition while having a contingent access to its health system, remain unstudied."[125] If, however, as reproductive sociologist Sarah Franklin puts it, IVF "has become a looking glass through which we see ourselves," it is imperative to address the omission of Palestinian women's experiences in the Israeli fertility economy and to explore what that tells us about the Israeli settler colonial state at large.[126] In analyzing Palestinian women's narratives and the formation of demographic anxieties among Israeli medical staff, I stage a theoretical conversation between a settler colonial reading of the Israeli fertility economy and the Black feminist framework of reproductive justice.

In response to the choice-centered, majority white and middle-class reproductive rights movement of the 1970s, Black and women of color feminists coined "reproductive justice" at a 1994 pro-choice conference in the United States. This paradigm challenges liberal feminism's focus on the legal right to abortion and foregrounds the entanglement of reproduction with questions of race, ethnicity, sexuality, gender, dis/ability, and class.[127] Centered around three interconnected human rights values, reproductive justice includes the right not to have children using safe birth control and access to abortion, the right to have children under the conditions the parents choose, and the right to parent those children in safe and healthy environments.[128] As an analytical tool, a theoretical concept, and a framework for activism, reproductive justice thus demands reproductive freedom, sexual autonomy, and gender expression for everyone.[129]

Demographic Anxieties takes the Palestinian case to spell out the conditions of a justice-based approach to reproduction and a right to have a family. Reproductive justice serves as an overarching theoretical framework for this book that enables me to analyze how reproductive *injustice* is a foundational function of Israeli settler colonialism as a political system. It also serves as a political and methodological commitment to contribute to the struggle for Palestinian women's liberation and to develop a transnational perspective on reproductive justice in which the Palestinian case is central. In the last decade, feminist scholarship has begun to analyze Palestine through a reproductive justice lens. Several works are important to mention here: Layaly Hamayel, Doaa Hammoudeh, and Lynn Welchman's study on reproductive health and rights in East Jerusalem; Ayesha AlRifai's work on abortion in occupied Palestine; Bayan Abusneineh's research on Zionism and anti-Black racism through the lens of the reproductive body; Nada Elia's book on internationalism, feminism, and Palestinian liberation; Sarah Ihmoud's work on Israel's racialized politics of the womb; Frances Hasso's historical account of life, death, reproduction in Palestine; and Nadera Shalhoub-Kevorkian's long-standing work on Palestinian women's sexual and reproductive rights.[130] Israel's genocidal war in Gaza has renewed this focus on reproductive justice as central to Palestinian liberation.[131] This book is in conversation with these scholars and activists who have begun developing this perspective.

To approach Palestine through the lens of reproductive justice contributes to an anticolonial analysis of Palestinian women's reproductive rights and health that centers on the complex gendered dynamics of Israeli statecraft. Gender and sexual violence are central to Israeli settler colonial power and establish a racialized hierarchy in which Palestinian women are either depicted as visible or invisible, as hypersexual or hyper-oppressed beings with attendant logics of governance or rescue.[132] Complementing this construction of female Palestinian sexuality, the male Palestinian body is portrayed and treated as dangerous and aggressive, not only toward the occupying power but also as a potential perpetrator that Palestinian women need to be protected from.[133] Such representations serve to dehumanize Palestinians and legitimize further oppressive measures against them. They also form the Orientalist backdrop against which Jewish Israeli subjectivities and my positionality as a white German researching Palestine/Israel are established as civilized and innocent.[134] An anticolonial or decolonial feminist framework recognizes how European colonialism and its legacies shape the everyday lives of marginalized communities and takes the experiences and struggles of oppressed women, nonbinary people, and queers as a central analytic for the broader feminist project.[135] This perspective not only allows for a comprehensive understanding of the gendered and racialized operations of Israeli settler colonialism but also centers Palestinian women as main actors in challenging how liberal and Western feminists approach the question of Palestine and its broader relevance in thinking about (reproductive) justice.

I am following anthropologist Sarah Ihmoud's proposal "to think with decolonial Palestinian feminism" as an "invitation to consider what this place has to offer us" as part of a feminist struggle toward anticolonial futures.[136] Given the history of liberal feminism, which is necessarily also the history of my feminist coming-of-age, this is an important yet complicated endeavor.[137] While *Demographic Anxieties* is a book about reproductive justice for Palestinian women, it also explores how the entangled histories of oppression and multidirectional memory between a German sociologist, Jewish Israeli or Palestinian medical staff, and Palestinian women and their families unfold in researching Palestinian women's access to fertility treatment in Israeli hospitals.[138] It asks what Palestine as a site of knowledge production enables, complicates, or demands from a transnational feminist perspective on reproductive justice.

I approach doing feminist research on Palestine from a position of "feminist debt." This proposition, formulated by political theorist Sumi Madhok, highlights the generative epistemological and methodological interventions that a critical and reflexive politics of location enables. Feminist debt is a "debt that cannot be repaid."[139] Instead, it calls for acknowledging responsibility and ethics in producing feminist scholarship. Madhok understands ethics as the responsibility to open up new ways of thinking and contribute to reshaping the conditions of "thinkability" outside Western frames of reference.[140] From a Palestinian perspective, sociologist Sarab Abu-Rabia-Queder similarly foregrounds the ethical dimensions of research with Palestinian women. She calls "upon all those who conduct research on the Palestinians in general, and Palestinian women in particular, to produce 'ethical knowledge' that brings research justice to the women, who, until now, have been researched from an 'Israeli' perspective."[141] This appeal to responsibility means taking Palestine seriously as a place to study the gendered and embodied effects of empire, European colonialism, and global white supremacy.

Writing through the lens of "feminist debt" has methodological implications. Two points are essential to highlight here. First, as described above, this book centers on Palestinian women's experiences. I take their narratives as a vantage point to theorize reproductive justice. But this book is not about "giving voice" to Palestinian women, as the interviews and data I have gathered here are as incomplete as such attempts at representation can be, both epistemologically and empirically.[142] Instead, it centers on Palestinian women's perspectives as key to discussing the broader implications of reproductive justice under settler colonialism *as* a transnational feminist praxis.[143]

This book thus asks what we can learn about reproductive freedom and autonomy when we listen to Palestinian women. It explores which new insights into the workings of settler colonialism and reproduction are enabled when their stories are the springboard for theorizing.[144] It also highlights the epistemological, political, and practical conditions that facilitate or foreclose listening to Palestinian women in the first place. This is related to a second concern. I also explore the limitations and possibilities of researching Palestine/Israel in this book. Being a German-passport holder, white, and culturally Christian allowed me to spend time in Israel and to freely cross its borders in and out of the West Bank. Moreover, it also granted me a sense of political freedom and curiosity that crucially shaped my access to Israeli institutions, such as hospitals, and to talk to Israeli medical staff and health service providers. I pay attention to how the histories of European colonialism, the Holocaust, and whiteness produce my positionality in and toward Israeli institutions. It is from the complicated standpoint of access, nonbelonging, and complicity, and a position of refusal and the commitment to producing feminist counter-knowledge about the nation-state, that I carefully unfold the complexity of Ihmoud's invitation to center Palestine as a space for enacting a transnational feminist praxis.[145]

An anticolonial feminist perspective on Palestinian women's reproductive freedom and autonomy challenges the Israeli state's presentation as humanitarian and benevolent toward Palestinian women. *Demographic Anxieties* intervenes in scholarship that frames Palestinian women's (reproductive) rights through the settler state's notions of inclusion, access, and recognition. Palestinian scholars and scholars in Palestine studies emphasize how the narrative of Palestinians' "inclusion" in the Israeli state and their resulting transformation into a "minority population" obfuscates the oppressive dimensions of this inclusion and the liminal status it assigns to Palestinian citizens of Israel. Granting citizenship to internally displaced Palestinians was based on various legal and bureaucratic mechanisms to maintain their status as "outsiders" or "settler colonial citizens" while gaining international legitimacy.[146] Palestinians in Israel fall on a spectrum of inclusion and exclusion, while Palestinians living under occupation are included via their exclusion as occupied subjects under the control of the very same state.[147] These mechanisms continue to dispossess Palestinians across Palestine/Israel, and Palestinian women bear the brunt of their legal status's gendered and racialized dimensions.[148]

In centering the experiences and realities of Palestinian women with different legal statuses vis-à-vis the Israeli state, this book offers an anticolonial feminist critique of Israeli attempts to feminist- or pinkwash Palestinian women's access to and varying degrees of inclusion into the Israeli state and its institutions.[149] Palestinian women's access to the resources needed to get pregnant is not solely a question about their de jure inclusion or exclusion from Israel's medical system and fertility economy but questions the system of Israeli settler colonialism itself, which relegates Palestinian women to the margins and considers their existence in the healthcare sector through the lenses of deservingness, security, and respectability. *Demographic Anxieties* shows how liberal paradigms like citizenship or recognition are an insufficient lens to understand the obstacles Palestinian women face if they want to undergo fertility treatment and give birth in an Israeli hospital. By approaching the question of reproductive justice from the perspective of Palestinian women it calls into question the Israeli state and its political system as a reference point for reproductive justice.

"GEOGRAPHIES OF INTIMACY": METHODOLOGY AND QUESTIONS OF SOLIDARITY

The experiences of Palestinian women getting pregnant in Israeli fertility clinics, as well as their encounters with Jewish Israeli medical staff, reveal the interlocking processes of the making of racial hierarchy and the long history of state-sanctioned reproductive injustices. This case affirms the historical and transnational connectedness of the systems of oppression that shape Black, Brown, Indigenous, and poor people's reproductive rights and health. In his book *Geographies of Liberation*, cultural historian Alex Lubin argues that throughout history, but especially in the twentieth-century, Jews in the diaspora, Black Americans, and Palestinians share a central insight. These subaltern groups have been understood and positioned as "the Other" vis-à-vis modernity and its central institution, the nation-state.[150] Based on this condition and united through a shared concern with global power, the twentieth century sees various movements of solidarity that engage with the other Other's oppression. These relationships, which legal scholar Noura Erakat, drawing from Lubin, terms "geographies of intimacy," function as an infrastructure for transnational alliances and forms of solidarity.[151] While never symmetrical, these geographies of oppression, liberation, and intimacy form the analytical and historical background for this book and its relational methodology. I take the Black feminist framework of reproductive justice to Palestine to offer an anticolonial feminist critique of settler colonialism and the nation-state form, in Israel and beyond.

Understanding Palestine as a site to trace the global conditions of European colonialism, racial hierarchy, and Indigenous dispossession is an ongoing intellectual project.[152] A careful analysis of these shared conditions and histories of violence, as well as the forms of resistance and solidarity they engender, exposes critical insights about colonial modernity. Cultural historian Maha Nassar shows, for instance, how as early as the 1930s, Palestinian anticolonial intellectuals linked their struggle against Zionism with anti-Black racism in the United States. This interconnectedness became more prominent in the 1950s and '60s, when '48 Palestinians began to compare their inclusive exclusion into (or from) the liberal settler state to the experiences of Black Americans in the United States.[153] The 1967 conjuncture marks a crucial point in time, not only in Palestine but also globally. Struggles over hegemony in the United States become increasingly entwined with Israeli relations of rule and its occupation of the West Bank, the Syrian Golan Heights, Gaza, East Jerusalem, and the Egyptian Sinai Peninsula. It is in this context that Black Americans and other racialized groups in the United States connect their fight for civil rights with the Palestinian liberation movement.[154] Placing Black solidarity with Palestine in the legacy of the Black radical tradition, Noura Erakat and Marc Lamont Hill argue that a shared understanding of imperialism, colonialism, and white supremacy *as* global phenomena crystallized in response to anticolonial revolts in the 1960s and the 1967 war.[155] Or, as Nadine Naber puts it, "the US and Israel Make the Connections for Us" (also the title of her essay).[156] Importantly, this shared political vocabulary of global power structures does not disregard the different histories and realities of oppression in the United States and Israel, but focuses on similar but distinct local structures of domination.[157]

Antiracist and anticolonial forms of Palestine solidarity were curtailed in the 1970s when Israel's occupation became progressively more permanent, and both Israel and the United States experienced a rightward turn in their respective political cultures. An investment in counterterrorism, embodied by the racialized figure of the Muslim/Arab terrorists, as well as strategic, material, and military circuits, further united the nascent Reagan administration in the United States and the Likud government in Israel.[158] The World Conference Against Racism, held in Durban, South Africa, in 2001, was an important moment in the history of Black–Palestinian and transnational solidarity for Palestine. On the agenda were reparations for the transatlantic slave trade, and Israel as a racist apartheid state. Protesting this, both the United States and Israel withdrew their delegations from the official forum. This refusal, as well as ongoing civil society discussions about the topics at hand, provided an infrastructure of connection between the struggle for Palestinian liberation and the fight against racism in the United States, South Africa, and Palestine.[159] In 2014, Israel's war on Gaza and the protests around the police killing of Michael Brown in Ferguson, Missouri, engendered a renewal of such ongoing Black–Palestinian forms of solidarity. Central to this movement is an exploration of the conditions of solidarity itself. Black–Palestinian forms of transnational solidarity emerge as an "engaged practice," questioning the usefulness of certain forms of solidarity, such as witnessing, reciprocity, a shared critique of state violence, and recognition of historical and contemporary differences.[160] Since Israel's genocide in Gaza began in 2023, a recognition of the transnational ties between various forms of oppression and resistance has only been strengthened. Then and now, women of color and queer of color activists have been at the forefront of such forms of conjoined struggle.[161]

Feminist and queer writers and scholars discuss Palestinian women's experiences of oppression and their fight for liberation through the lens of interconnected struggle against settler colonialism and racism in the United States.[162] As historian Rana Barakat draws out in her essay "Reading Audre Lorde in Palestine," an intimate connection links Black feminism and anticolonial refusal in Palestine.[163] The Black American essayist and poet June Jordan is a paradigmatic figure for these connections. In her famous poem "Moving towards Home," written in 1982 in the aftermath of the Phalangist-Israeli Sabra and Shatila massacre in Lebanon, Jordan writes, "I was born a Black woman | and now | I am become a Palestinian," expressing her identification with the Palestinian struggle through the lens of Black womanhood and shared experiences of oppression.[164] Jordan deepens this relational analysis in a column titled "Finding Our Way Home," written in 1989 for the magazine *The Progressive*, where she draws out how imperial and domestic violence penetrate the home, both in the United States and in Palestine:

> I believe that the issue of a home for Lisa Steinberg [a six-year-old girl killed by her abusive father] and the issue of a home for the Palestinian people is one and the same: The question is whether non-Europeans, and whether children, everywhere, possess a human right to sanctuary on this planet.[165]

The relational analytic crystallizing in Jordan's pivot between Black and Palestinian positions points not only to the transnational dimensions of gendered racialization but also, implicitly, touches on the subject of reproductive justice. As ethnic studies scholar Keith Feldman writes, Jordan's relational focus on "the home" points to a commitment to "the merely human practice of making home, a space to dwell and laugh and thrive and resist."[166] In that sense, Jordan addresses reproductive justice in its widest articulation. She points to the right to raise children in a safe and healthy environment—a home in which they can thrive—while opening up a transnational horizon to reveal such conditions. In *Demographic Anxieties*, I build on these existing links between Black feminist thought and anticolonial Palestinian feminism, as articulated by Rana Barakat in Palestine in 2023 or June Jordan in the United States in 1985.[167] These comparisons and connections provide the historical, analytical, and relational background for me to explore a transnational perspective on reproductive justice in Palestine.

However, I am not part of that "we" Barakat evokes, and I am also not part of the "we" of Black feminists and women of color who developed the reproductive justice framework. I am part of a different "we," or set of relationships between Germans, Israelis, and Palestinians. What Sa'ed Atshan and Katharina Galor term a "moral triangle" connects us through the historical events of the Holocaust and the Nakba, and the complex ways in which they live on through trauma, guilt, memory/memorialization, and conflict, both in my home country of Germany and in Israel.[168] The notion of this triangle challenges the invisibilization of Palestinians as victims of the historical circumstances of antisemitism in Europe and the Nazi German genocide of six million Jews during World War II, which led to Germany's and the Allied forces' unwavering support of the Israeli state.

The notion of intimacy in its various iterations is relevant here. Erakat theorizes "geographies of intimacy" as forms of Black–Palestinian transnational solidarities that are not based on identity politics but are not a given. Solidarity must always be negotiated across social, political, and affective registers. The conditions that enable political commitment and recognition of a shared struggle "are produced through a politics of location and engagement, which unsettles identity as an ontological point of departure and emphasizes the contingency of solidarity."[169] Here, Erakat references Adrienne Rich's notion of the politics of location,[170] emphasizing the specificity of site—place, time, culture, movement—of feminist knowledge production to explore the preconditions of the forging and political affect of intimacies.[171] However, intimacies do not always yield transnational solidarity, political kinship, or friendship and comradeship. Intimacies can also be violent and constitute another site for nation-states to exert (colonial) control and domination.[172] Lisa Lowe uses intimacies as a heuristic to observe how, analogous to the colonial divisions of humanity, colonial intimacies afford stratified access to liberal personhood, with its attendant categories of interiority (feeling) and property (possession).[173]

In researching and writing this book, I encountered and embodied both forms of intimacy. As a German, I share a violent relationship of intimacy with Jewish Israelis and Jews in the diaspora, in which my liberal personhood historically relied on their racialization and genocide, and continues to determine property relations in Germany. A structurally similar but reversed intimacy crystallized when I began fieldwork in Israel. In the increasingly Jewish-supremacist state in which the ideal Jewish body is constructed along European whiteness, masculinity, and dominance, my gendered whiteness and Europeanness constituted a shared horizon of white innocence and, at times, supremacy.[174] Being white and German in Israel positioned me near the Ashkenazi elite. It animated many of my Jewish Israeli interlocutors to rely on a shared racial framework based on Palestinians' dehumanization. I would get called into this narrative by way of comparing Palestinians in Israel to Germany's "struggle" with Muslim migrants or by comments on how my own appearance (white, blue eyes, blonde hair) was the desired appearance of an egg donor.

At the same time, I developed relationships similar to those described by Erakat based on a mutual understanding of the importance of an anticolonial perspective on Palestine, both with Palestinians and with some Jewish Israelis. Many of my Palestinian interlocutors mentioned the importance of foregrounding their experiences of pregnancy and childbirth. They asked for their stories to be shared in a European context, which they (rightly so) perceived as anti-Palestinian. Both in personal conversations as well as in the literature, Palestinian healthcare providers, activists, scholars, and policymakers emphasize a need for research on Israel's fertility economy and the healthcare system more broadly that approaches Palestinians' health not from a minority perspective of "inclusion," but that views settler colonialism and structural racism as essential health determinants.[175] However, to establish relationships with Palestinian interlocutors and research collaborators to do the critical scholarship Palestinians call for, one must also be allowed in. By implementing specific regulations on obtaining visas or restricting travel from several Muslim-majority countries, Israel's border and visa regime controls who can conduct research in Israel or the occupied Palestinian territories. Palestinians, Arab citizens of other countries, and scholars critical of the Israeli state face significant limitations on what kind of ethnographic or qualitative field research they can envision and conduct.[176] This has crucial methodological and epistemological consequences regarding what type of knowledge is being produced about Palestine/Israel.

Thus, my location allowed different geographies of intimacies to unfold across the local and global conditions of European colonialism, racism, and accumulation by dispossession. In this book, I write with and against them. However, I am not doing this by myself. Adrienne Rich also reminds us that "there is no liberation that only knows how to say 'I'; there is no collective movement that speaks for each of us all the way through."[177] I am writing in conversation with those Black and Palestinian feminist scholars and thinkers who offer us the crucial tools to critically address the realities of Palestinian women trying to get pregnant under settler colonialism. And I am writing in solidarity with those Palestinian women, scholars, activists, friends, and comrades who shared their experiences, homes, snacks, and politics with me. The geographies of intimacies across the German-Israeli-Palestinian triangle are necessarily fragile, and political and personal commitments need to be forged and nourished, but they constitute the affective and political foundation for my development of a transnational perspective on reproductive justice that takes Palestine as its point of departure.

ARGUMENT AND ORGANIZATION OF THE BOOK

Israeli demographic policies, settler colonial politics, and attendant racialized feelings of fear of the Palestinians and their reproduction are the objects of my analysis in this book. I argue that Israeli demographic concerns and politics limit reproductive justice for Palestinian women and analyze how they shape the everyday encounters between Palestinian women and their Jewish Israeli doctors or the Israeli healthcare system writ large. Central to this is an insistence on looking at and for the more invisible and often concealed forms of "slow" or "tender" violence.[178] Such forms of violence develop alongside and in tandem with more spectacular and obvious forms of violence, such as Israel's genocide in Gaza. Focusing on slowly and gradually unfolding violence allows me to explore how a collective political subjectivity and affective economy of Israeli fears and security concerns are linked to questions of reproduction, demography, and territory.

Slow or tender forms of violence, which are often not named or recognized as violence, require different representational, methodological, and narrative strategies.[179] In *Demographic Anxieties*, I trace these forms of violence in the encounter between Palestinian bodies and the borders set up to protect the Israeli state. In so doing, I pay attention not only to the colonial imposition of borders and geographies but also explore how, in the encounter between Palestinian women seeking to get pregnant and the Israeli healthcare system and fertility economy, borders are constantly made, unmade, and remade.[180] My analysis of these encounters between bodies and borders unfolds across different conceptual or material sites and is in conversation with various disciplinary approaches to Palestine/Israel, reproduction, gender, sexuality, and health. The former is reflected in the organization of this book. Structurally, I move from the population as an object of study and a mode of subjectification to infrastructure and settler colonialism, zooming closer into the affective economy of Israeli hospitals, to finally explore intimacies and the body as sites where Israeli demographic anxieties are articulated and reproductive injustices are manifested. The latter is apparent in this book as a multidisciplinary project. I am taking inspiration from Black studies scholar Katherine McKittrick's generative suggestion that "[d]oing anticolonial work in the academy and talking about race in relation to discipline and interdiscipline can be enriched by thinking across texts and places."[181] I draw from the fields of settler colonial and Palestine studies, medical sociology, and anticolonial or decolonial feminist theory to explore the formation of demographic anxieties and their effect on Palestinian women's everyday lives and health, their reproductive decision-making, pregnancy outcomes, and kin-work. As this introduction makes clear, this is necessarily a relational endeavor, thinking with and through different geographies and histories of race and gender, the politics of reproduction, and how they shape our present. While my analysis at times takes me back into history or sideways into theoretical discussions, it is grounded in the experience of Palestinian women who are trying to get pregnant in Palestine/Israel in the twenty-first century.

In chapter 1, I draw from interviews with Jewish Israeli medical staff and Palestinian patients in Israeli fertility clinics to illustrate how the relationship between demography and reproduction crystallizes in the various ways in which "population" appears as an object of knowledge and a mode of subjectification. I show how Jewish Israeli fertility doctors present a "demographic race" as a normalized condition of life in Israel, and how early Zionist population politics fold into notions of overpopulation and Orientalist tropes of reproduction shared by medical staff today. The second part of this chapter explores how Palestinian women perceive their interpellation in numbers and how Israeli demographic anxieties shape their everyday lives. Attending to Palestinian women's experiences of obstetric racism, fears of being mistreated, and reflections on what it means to become an object of demographic knowledge, the chapter closes with some reflections on population as a "felt condition."

Chapter 2 is based on the narratives of female Palestinian and Bedouin doctors, nurses, policymakers, activists, and social workers from Israel and occupied East Jerusalem who describe how health infrastructures limit Palestinian women's reproductive freedom. The chapter illustrates how Israeli demographic anxieties find their concrete shape and form in the built environment and affective economies. These include actual military infrastructures and the occupation, urban segregation, a lack of pre- and postnatal services in predominantly Palestinian areas in Israel, racial segregation in Israeli maternity wards, language barriers in East Jerusalem, and a lack of culturally appropriate health services in hospitals in Israel. These examples reveal how Palestinian women's reproductive decision-making, pregnancy outcomes, parenting practices, and reproductive and sexual health are altered by a lack of appropriate infrastructures or choppy infrastructures of care. In this chapter, I argue that Israeli health infrastructures are crucially embedded in the settler colonial project of nation-building and, as such, impede reproductive justice for Palestinian women.

Chapter 3 introduces Israeli hospitals as a crucial site of encounter between Jewish Israeli medical staff and Palestinian patients. Fertility treatment requires close and intimate contact between those providing it and their patients, as care, attention, familiarity, and tenderness affect the chances of getting pregnant. As an entry point of inquiry, the fertility clinic provides a way to focus on what haunts those social relations that emerge precisely through intimate encounters of care. Based on interviews with Palestinian and Jewish Israeli medical staff in fertility clinics, this chapter challenges the hegemonic Israeli imaginary of the hospital as a medically and politically neutral site. It discusses how this spatial imagination of harmonious coexistence and humanitarianism sits strategically within the broader context of Israeli settler colonialism. The chapter argues that notions of security, belonging, respectability, and deservingness affect Palestinian women's reproductive health and rights, in that they determine their access to goods, information, emotive state, and support needed to engage self-confidently and actively in doctor-patient encounters, and to have a successful pregnancy.

Chapter 4 builds on my theorization of intimate encounters. It is based on the narratives of Palestinian women trying to conceive in Israeli fertility clinics and fertility clinics in East Jerusalem and in the occupied West Bank. In a close ethnographic account, the reader will meet Reem from East Jerusalem, Celine from Bethlehem, and Christeen from the Galilee, and follow their journeys of becoming mothers. Their different positionalities vis-à-vis the Israeli state and in Palestinian society illustrate the complex lived realities, intimate decision-making, and practices of everyday-life resistance of Palestinian women. I discuss Palestinian women's reflections on whether to have children under conditions of extreme violence, their understanding of reproduction as a politics of resistance, or their experiences of obstetric racism. This chapter thus further advances the argument that intimacies, proximities, and care are sites of consolidation and contestation of settler colonial power and illustrates the granularity of Israeli sexual and demographic politics.

The last empirical chapter, chapter 5, discusses how Israel's demographic anxieties translate into a carceral horizon. Based on interviews with the wives of Palestinian prisoners who managed to smuggle a sperm sample out of Israeli prisons and into West Bank fertility clinics for their wives to get pregnant, this chapter introduces the reader to sperm smuggling as a form of embodied resistance Palestinians have deployed to challenge the Israeli occupation. The chapter shows how Israeli military authorities assign evidentiary status to Palestinian bodies and examines how Palestinian families challenge the Israeli carceral system through new modes of embodied resistance and kin-work. It finds that bodies, embryos, or sperm figure as central actors in sperm smuggling stories and argues that bodies and bodily matter are constitutive of the relationship between oppression and resistance. This chapter closes with a discussion of how settler colonial militarism, politics of resistance, and heteropatriarchy shape and are being shaped by bodies and their materiality.

I conclude *Demographic Anxieties* with three scenes from 2023 and 2024. I reflect on how the genocide in Gaza alerts us to the manifold ways in which this ongoing assault is also a question of reproductive justice. I share the experiences of silencing, dehumanization, and repression of Palestinian healthcare professionals in Israeli hospitals since October 7 and discuss how the long history of Palestinian racialization as Europe's Other legitimizes the genocide. Demonstrating the continuation of Israeli structures of domination and oppression from the time when I conducted research for this book to the current moment, these spotlights capture how *Demographic Anxieties* sets the scene for understanding how the escalation that Israel's genocidal war on Gaza presents is not a rupture but part of an ongoing structure of settler colonialism. Here, I reiterate my argument about why a focus on everyday forms of violence is central to understanding the various forms of reproductive injustice that Palestinian women experience. I end the conclusion with a meditation on reproductive justice as an analytical lens and an organizing framework, tracing how it travels between the local case of Palestine and the global conditions of connected sociologies of reproduction.

The afterword is an interview I conducted with the Palestinian health scholar Yara in the fall of 2024. Yara, whose voice also appears across the empirical chapters, shares her thoughts on questions of Palestinian health, Israeli healthcare, reproduction, and Zionism, one year into Israel's genocide. The interview is unedited and remains without interpretation to offer direct insight into what it has meant to be a Palestinian scholar of healthcare during the Israeli genocide, and to end with a Palestinian perspective on Gaza.

NOTES ON LANGUAGE

As anthropologist Julie Peteet remarks, "In Israel-Palestine, language is a minefield, literally part of an arsenal that one must tread through cautiously."[182] This begins with her calling the territory of historic Palestine "Israel-Palestine," while, as per the title of this book, I chose "Palestine/Israel." Indeed, some have critically inquired why the book is not titled "reproductive injustice in Palestine," to counteract the normalization of the Israeli state on Palestinian land. This question of naming is an unresolved issue for me and, I am sure, for many scholars of the region. I chose the articulation of Palestine/Israel for various reasons. First, the formulation of Israel *and* Palestine seems to be misleading, not least because the borders of what is "Israel" are constantly and deliberately shifted, and Israel has, de facto and de jure, control over all of the borders surrounding and fragmenting historic Palestine.[183] For many Palestinians who reside inside Israel's 1948 borders, the land they live on is the same Palestine as the Palestine of the occupied West Bank, East Jerusalem, and Gaza. It is thus unclear where Israel ends and where Palestine begins. Second, this book is about the violent effects of the *Israeli* state, its institutions, and the forms of subjectivation it created and cultivates. The reproductive injustices that I trace in this book wouldn't exist were it not for the existence of this state. It would therefore be misleading not to name the existing state and its policies, politics, and mechanisms of injustice. However, Israel is a settler colonial state on the land of historic Palestine. And Israeli politicians, policies, and laws have made abundantly clear that a two-state solution is not an actual political horizon in Israel, at least since 1967, and most definitely since 2023.[184] To capture this reality—the ongoing expansionist existence of the state of Israel, which relied on Palestinian dispossession, ethnic cleansing, and expulsion to come into being, as well as the actual existence of a state called Israel that controls the lives of all Palestinians across the territory of historic Palestine—I refer to the territory in question as Palestine/Israel.

In colonial contexts, the naming and discourse to describe the conquered and settled land, as well as the Indigenous population, is a central mechanism of control and hegemony.[185] I thus refer to Palestinian self-identifications such as '48 Palestinians (unless they self-identify differently), as well as to how they call the place or land they live in. This means that in addition to framing the book as a whole through the lens of Palestine/Israel, I also often refer to Palestine in the singular as a political project, horizon, and the name of the homeland of many of my interlocutors. Similarly, I also refer to Israel, mainly when I talk about the territory of Israel's 1948 borders, and my engagement with the institutions that make up this state. What can be read as an inconsistency, then, is simply a reflection of the fact that Palestine "is as much a when as it is a where."[186]

Another point of contention between various readers of this manuscript was how to render Palestinians referring to Jewish Israelis. The majority of Palestinians I interviewed, either in English or in the Arabic translation, referred to Jewish Israelis as Jews. I discussed the question of whether to translate or change "Jews" to "Jewish Israelis" with many different people, Jews and Palestinians alike, including some of the translators I worked with. In the end, I chose not to change what my interlocutors said. This is for ethical reasons (I also don't correct Jewish Israelis when they refer to Palestinians as "Israeli Arabs"), but also for political ones. As writer Mohammed El-Kurd puts it, it sometimes seems to matter more how Palestinians speak about their oppressors than the condition of oppression itself.[187] I trust my reader to develop their own understanding of how my interlocutors' references to Jews reflect the nature of the state that represents itself, as the *Jewish* state, including its investment in linking Jews in the diaspora to this national project. However, I also hold firm to the distinction between Zionism and Judaism, and I understand how this distinction can at times seem blurred in this text.[188]

ONE

Population

The calculation of the ratio between Jews to "Arabs" and the often violent separation, rigidification, and essentialization of these identities is a cornerstone of the imagined community of Israel.

RHODA ANN KANAANEH,
Birthing the Nation

Who and what is counted, who does the counting, and how do these numbers carry an affective charge?

M. MURPHY,
The Economization of Life

I SAT IN A CAFÉ on top of Mount Carmel, overlooking the port city of Haifa, with Leen and Mary. Mary is the Palestinian interpreter I was working with, and Leen is a twenty-eight-year-old Palestinian from a small town in the Galilee region who works as a medical technician. Leen has been married to her husband, a lawyer, for three years, and the couple has been trying to get pregnant for a while now. After they found out that there was a problem with his sperm count, the couple opted for fertility treatment. At the time of our interview, Leen was preparing for her next round of IVF. After an unsuccessful previous cycle, she still had some fertilized eggs left to be used once she was ready for the tiring hormone injections again. As a citizen of Israel, Leen receives fully state-subsidized fertility treatment in Israeli hospitals. On paper, she is benefiting from Israel's world-renowned fertility economy, and as a well-educated middle-class woman, Leen knows how to navigate Israel's medical system. However, her experience of trying to get pregnant is shaped by what it means to be a '48 Palestinian, which is how many Palestinian citizens of Israel self-identify, referring to Israel's 1948 borders and their successive inclusion in the liberal settler state.[1]

In the hegemonic Israeli imagination, Palestinians in Israel, whom Israelis often refer to as "Israeli Arabs," are a separate group from Palestinians under

Israeli occupation and siege in the West Bank, East Jerusalem, and Gaza.[2] The legal classification of Palestinians into different categories is central to Israel's governance of all Palestinians on the territory between the Jordan River and the Mediterranean Sea. Demographic considerations inform this mode of governance. While Israel has occupied the West Bank and East Jerusalem since 1967, has held Gaza under siege since 2006, and has invested in its destruction since 2023, it does not want to absorb these populations so as not to disrupt the demographic balance within Israel's 1948 borders.[3] Israel's spatial fragmentation of the Palestinians also serves to hamper Palestinian political unity and impede Palestinians' freedom of movement. But for Leen and many Palestinians in Israel, holding Israeli citizenship doesn't sever their relations with other Palestinian localities. Kinship ties, professional or political exchange, and other relationships unmake the borders and boundaries that seventy-five years of Israeli settler colonialism have imposed on them.[4]

Leen's pregnancy journey illustrates this. When we met Leen, she was being treated by a Palestinian physician in a local Israeli health-insurance-run fertility clinic in Haifa. But before that, she had tried to get pregnant in the occupied West Bank. While Palestinian women with Israeli citizenship have access to the Israeli healthcare system and fertility economy that women in the occupied territories are not afforded, many '48 Palestinians are also seeking fertility treatment in the West Bank. When I talked about this with Jewish Israeli medical staff, they would often be confused or ignorant about this decision, especially as Palestinian women would have to pay for their treatment in clinics in Nablus or Ramallah privately.[5] However, the Palestinian women I encountered who had also been treated in the West Bank cited greater cultural and linguistic understanding, more personalized or religiously sensitive care, avoiding discrimination, as well as distrust in Israeli medical institutions, as reasons for choosing to undergo treatment there.[6] Additionally, in comparison to Israeli hospitals, West Bank clinics are subject to more lenient regulatory mechanisms from the Palestinian Health Ministry and may offer alternative treatments or protocols, for example, regarding nonmedical sex selection or the number of embryos transferred in a single IVF cycle.

Personal connections and word-of-mouth are also among the reasons Palestinians in Israel cross the border into the West Bank to become pregnant. Leen's mother-in-law is a family doctor in Israel, and many of her Palestinian patients have undergone fertility treatment in West Bank clinics.

Leen had asked her for a recommendation and went to a clinic in Nablus. However, there she experienced what I often heard from '48 Palestinians who had access to both Israel's fertility economy and the Palestinian healthcare system, crumbling under the occupation: "I just didn't feel comfortable, it was not organized."[7] She explained that in Israel, specialized departments and sometimes even hospitals cater to the different stages of undergoing fertility treatment, from gynecological tests and hormonal treatment, to fertilizing and inserting the extracted egg cells, and giving birth. In the West Bank, she said, "the doctor has just one room, so she could be talking with you and then taking the oocytes from another person and then doing the insertion for another person. So, I felt she was lost; there was no order." In addition to that, Leen felt that because of the situation in the West Bank, the clinic there was more focused on making money than on providing a good service. After her experience in the West Bank, Leen was thus happy to go to the Israeli healthcare system. And while she remarked that she would not have cared if her doctor had been Jewish Israeli, she also mentioned that speaking Arabic with her current physician and having a shared cultural understanding made her experience more comfortable.

Leen's story is not unusual for middle-class Palestinian women with Israeli citizenship who struggle with infertility. While she has access to Israel's fertility economy and state-subsidized fertility treatment for up to two live births, as a Palestinian in Israel, her first impulse was to try to get pregnant in the West Bank, even if she had to pay for it privately. In Israel, she experienced the marked differences between a healthcare system under occupation and a state-subsidized fertility economy. Leen's story points to the central contradiction at the heart of this book. Israel is renowned for its thriving and advanced fertility economy and large biomedical sector.[8] As a liberal state and as the self-proclaimed "only democracy in the Middle East," Israel must grant all of its citizens access to its institutions. However, as a state built on Palestinians' dispossession, ethnic cleansing, and expulsion, the history and proclaimed goal of the state is to maintain a Jewish population majority. Palestinian women's access to state-subsidized fertility treatment as citizens thus sits squarely between Israel's population politics and being a liberal democracy. Palestinian women like Leen can access Israeli institutions and receive fertility treatment, but they are also considered a "demographic threat" to the Jewish character of the state.[9]

Leen's everyday experience and family planning as a Palestinian woman in Israel point to this contradiction. When we talked about the baby that would hopefully soon be on the way, she reflected on her future child's identity as a Palestinian in Israel. Mary, the interpreter, asked her: "Do you think it will have the same opportunities that the Israeli Jewish child is going to have? Will it have equal opportunities?" Leen replied: "No, not really. We live in a state that doesn't consider itself ours, so we will always be second degree. We live together, we are able to have education, we share a life with them, but the Israeli child will always be the priority." Leen describes the biopolitics of the Israeli state, whose life is fostered and encouraged, and whose will always be "second degree."[10] She makes clear that the optics of coexistence and inclusion in Israeli institutions like the educational system, the labor market, the healthcare sector, or so-called mixed cities like Haifa cannot hide whose child will be the Israeli state's priority. At the same time, Leen also talked about the pressure Palestinian women experience from Palestinian society to become pregnant and follow certain traditions, explaining that "the way they see it is different than the way I see it. For me, family means to be safe, not the traditional idea of getting married and having to have children so that society won't call me 'sterile.'" Various forms of gendered expectations and settler colonial governance thus shape Leen's pregnancy journey.[11] In addition to that, it is not only since Israel's genocide in Gaza that Israeli military violence against Palestinians in the occupied territories also reveals the necropolitical dimensions of Israeli population politics.[12] It becomes increasingly clear that Israel's mass killing of Palestinians also serves the state's self-proclaimed demographic goals. What connects these forms of power over Palestinians' lives and deaths is the management of women's reproduction and their interpellation as mothers.[13]

Palestinian women's reproduction, birth rates, and bodies have been subjected to Israeli surveillance and control since the early days of statehood. In her book *Birthing the Nation*, anthropologist Rhoda Ann Kanaaneh shows how Israeli demographic and reproductive policies are centered around what Michel Foucault termed political arithmetic, an investment in counting, classifying, and studying the Palestinian population and, in so doing, making it into an object of knowledge.[14] Today, this calculative form of governance still finds expression across various scales. These include citizenship and immigration law, land distribution and settlements, residential planning, municipal budget allocations, education and knowledge production, family planning, policies targeting the body, relationships, or reproduction, as well as, since 2023, Israel's genocidal war in Gaza.[15] Whether large-scale or intimate, most of Israel's demographic or territorial policies are concerned with maintaining a Jewish population majority while containing Palestinians and their reproduction. Or, as historian Laura Briggs has formulated it, all politics are, in some way or another, reproductive politics.[16]

Central to Israel's demographic politics and the circulation of attendant feelings—demographic *anxieties*—is the making of the Palestinian population into a problem that needs to be managed. In this chapter, I take the condition that Leen described—"the Israeli child will always be the priority"—as a starting point for investigating the relationship between population, demography, and reproduction. I draw from interviews I conducted with Jewish Israeli medical staff in fertility clinics and their Palestinian patients to illustrate how the relationship between demography and reproduction crystallizes in the various ways in which "population" appears as an object of knowledge and a mode of subjectification. I show how Jewish Israeli fertility doctors present a "demographic race" as a normalized condition of life in Israel, and how early Zionist population politics fold into notions of overpopulation and Orientalist tropes of reproduction shared by medical staff today. The second part of this chapter explores how Palestinian women perceive their interpellation in numbers and how Israeli demographic anxieties shape their everyday lives. Attending to Palestinian women's experiences of obstetric racism, fears of being mistreated, and reflections on what it means to become an object of demographic knowledge, the chapter closes with some reflections on population as a "felt condition."[17] Focusing on the links between population and racialization reveals the continuum between the dehumanization of Palestinians and their reproductive decision-making before October 2023, and the making of the Palestinian population—in Gaza and beyond—into a "problem" that can be solved by annihilatory means.

THE "DEMOGRAPHIC RACE" AND ISRAELI POPULATION POLITICS

Demographic concerns are often framed as an economic problem, presenting states' (or, more recently, planetary) interests through the lens of the detrimental economic effects of presumed or projected population growth.[18] Such demographic anxieties are also deeply racialized and gendered and shape law and state policy.[19] However, in settler colonial contexts, economic, racial, and gendered factors are as important as the creation, maintenance, and increase of the group of settlers in relation to the native population. In Israeli society and policy, the notion of a demographic race or battle and the idea of encouraging population growth as a political tool are commonplace.[20] Historically, the creation of a homeland for the Jews in Palestine was tightly linked with concerns about demography and the number of Jews versus non-Jews.[21] Sociologist Nira Yuval-Davis thus finds that "a 'demographic race' between Jews and Arabs in Israel is seen as crucial to the survival of Israel, not only as the state apparatus of the population living in it but as the state for Jews everywhere."[22] Moreover, as Palestine scholars argue, if a state is conceived of in ethnonationalist terms and subordinates other population groups to its interest in maintaining a population majority, protecting this majority becomes essential. This legitimizes an easy slippage into perceiving other groups' birth rates and reproduction as dangerous or a "security threat."[23]

The notion of a demographic race or problem was formulated in many of my interviews with Jewish Israelis. It was presented as something obvious, a backdrop to life in Israel. Irit, a Jewish Israeli gynecologist in her late forties, put it like this: "Yes, of course, there is a demographic race between Palestinian people and Israelis, we know that." However, Irit presents this as a structural condition that has little to do with people's lives and everyday decision-making. Instead, she explained reproduction and pronatalism through an individual lens: "But when it comes to the very sensitive point of the individual couple that strives for a son, an offspring, politics doesn't count. You know, people want kids everywhere. It doesn't matter on what cultural grounds it stays. It's just that it's very natural." This framing of a "demographic race" foregrounds the importance of childbearing through a universalist lens but detaches individual choice from enabling or restrictive state structures.[24]

Others, such as Galit, a gynecologist who works in the fertility department of a hospital in the center of Israel, also disagreed that the notion of a "demographic race" had implications for people's everyday lives. However, she contextualized the importance of having children historically and culturally. Galit explained: "We are raised like this, we need kids, children are our future. For Jews, it comes from the Holocaust, and they have to rebuild the country, and for the Arabs, they also always used to produce many kids, so I don't see any difference." In this explanation, a small but significant racialized difference between Israeli and Palestinian reproductive behavior appears and gives texture to the seemingly universal and natural desire to have children. Jewish Israelis have to reproduce to rebuild the country, whereas the Arabs have always reproduced at a high rate. Galit's reference to the Holocaust and the need of the Jewish state to make up for the six million Jews killed by Nazi Germany has been discussed extensively as a driver for Israeli pronatalism.[25] Her explanation further points to Israeli family ideology and the importance of childbearing in Judaism.[26] Both Irit and Galit also foreground reproduction as a shared feature of Jewish and Palestinian or Arab culture, pointing to the fact that this is a possible ground for shared alliances and vulnerabilities.[27] However, while these explanations can coexist in nuanced and contingent ways, both doctors fail to recognize that, on a structural level, chances to get pregnant and access the resources to implement this individual decision are not distributed equally. Irit's "we need kids, children are our future" must be contextualized by Leen's "the Israeli child will always be the priority." Settler colonial population politics connect and contextualize these two statements.

Central to the question of whose child counts, and whose child is always already presumed as part of an unidentified mass of "too many," is the concept of population. Feminist historian M. Murphy shows compellingly how what they call the economization of life ushered in a new era of calculative practices beginning in the mid-twentieth century. Producing knowledge about populations and their quantification—counting, assigning categories and territories, and translating these into an aggregate figure—produces differential worth of human lives to exploit those for economic purposes. Importantly, Murphy demonstrates how these calculative practices put the question of reproduction center stage.[28] Cast through the lens of overpopulation, racial difference is reshaped through the register of "economic futures" and designates those lives better not born.[29] This relationship is articulated with a particular intensity in settler colonial states.[30] If the central premise of settler colonialism is a logic of elimination, Indigenous lives are classified not only as surplus population but also as a target to manage, minimize, and eliminate—culturally, linguistically, economically, or genocidally.[31]

In Israel, the relationship between demographic concerns, population, and reproduction is as old as the Israeli state itself. Population politics was central to establishing a Jewish state in historic Palestine. Despite the opposite retelling of this history, the fact that a majority of Arabs already populated Palestine was well known among Zionist settlers.[32] They methodically devised strategies for the surveillance and political control of the Palestinian population at least since the 1920s, implemented with the outspoken goal of destabilization, disorganization, and eventual expulsion of the Palestinians.[33] With the Nakba and the inception of the Israeli state in 1948, the Palestinian population—both within and beyond its nascent borders—solidified as a "problem," specifically in regard to internally displaced Palestinians and those who stayed in their homes after the 1948 war. The archives of the early years of statehood show how Zionist settlers and later Israeli politicians, planners, trade unionists, and others discussed how to deal with what they conceived of as an "Arab minority," referring to the remaining 156,000 of 900,000 Palestinians in Israel. For instance, discussions between Israeli politicians and planners in the early 1950s reveal that while there was some debate on strategy, the Palestinians' existence in Israel was seen as impermanent; their eventual expulsion was supposed to be the main goal.[34] However, when it became clear that this could not be achieved as easily without losing international support for the young state, discourse moved gradually from exclusion to control, proposing strategies such as counting, classification, and spatial distribution of the Palestinians.[35]

In its formative years and the period of the Military Administration from 1948 to 1966, the Israeli state thus implemented a variety of laws targeting the Palestinian population as a "dangerous population."[36] The two most important legislative acts were the institution of the Law of Return in 1950, granting Jewish people worldwide the right to immigrate to Israel and acquire citizenship while excluding Palestinians born in Palestine from that right, and the 1952 Nationality Law, which determined the status of Palestinian citizens in Israel and classified them as distinct legal subjects, separate from Palestinian refugees outside of the country. While Palestinians were granted Israeli citizenship, which was debated controversially, it was also clear that they would never acquire the same rights as Jewish Israelis, for the state's foundational character as a *Jewish* state should not be changed. A strict bifurcation between Jewish and Palestinian citizens, which materialized in the legal distinction between "nationality" and "citizenship," was the result of Palestinians' legal inclusion.[37] To institute this distinction, Israeli law, policy, and policing sought to control and render the Palestinian population manageable and transparent for governance.[38] Counting, registering, labeling, and monitoring Palestinians and their movement became crucial tools of Israeli statecraft, both internally as well as in its occupied territories.[39] With the 1967 occupation of the West Bank and increasing attempts to Judaize the Galilee and the Naqab desert, the sentiment of a demographic race and a hyperfocus on Jewish and Palestinian birthrates only intensified.[40]

The early years of Zionist population politics are thus key to understanding the state of Israel today. Social scientist Ahmad Sa'di shows how it was precisely in the period of the late 1940s and early '50s that Israeli politicians and other officials articulated what would become "common understandings" regarding the official policy toward Palestinians in Israel. Not long after, this discourse would be translated into concrete action and representation. Sociological analyses of Palestinian class structure, percentage markers of how much the group of Palestinians in Israel was allowed to grow, or Israel's focus on Palestinians through the lens of security, were produced and communicated at that time.[41] These calculative practices were mediated through the presumed inferiority of the racialized Other, be it "uncivilized" Palestinians in need of modernization and progress or (future) "terrorists" who need to be surveilled in the name of national settler security.[42] Notions such as the "demographic race" became normalized and common knowledge during the early days of statehood, and we can see how they live on in Jewish Israelis' understanding of reproductive politics today.

"GOLDEN SPERM": BIRTH RATES, RACE, AND MODERNITY

While the "making" of the Palestinian population as a problem that needs to be managed was translated through legal classification and policy, these articulations have also sedimented into how Jewish Israelis encounter Palestinians in their everyday lives. This affective register of population politics is crucial to understanding the multilayeredness of demographic anxieties. The racialized trope of overpopulation and Palestinians' high birth rates plays a key role in implementing such markers of difference between Jewish Israelis and Palestinians, especially given the shared cultural narrative of larger families and the importance of children. This became apparent in how Jewish Israeli fertility doctors and nurses would describe their Palestinian patients and their reproduction. Like in Galit and Irit's accounts, high fertility rates and big families were usually explained through the lens of tradition and culture. However, to distinguish themselves from Palestinians and their similar reproductive behavior, Jewish Israelis would compare the Palestinian population to "third world" countries and societies and place their high birth rates in a broader, racialized discourse of overpopulation.

During our interview, Eran, the Jewish Israeli head of an IVF center in a hospital in Tel Aviv, produced a small illustration on a piece of scrap paper to illustrate demographic trends in "traditional" and "modern" societies. He drew two graphs, one triangle-like shape for what he called Muslim or "third world" countries, indicating age on the y-axis and birth rates on the x-axis, and a similar graph with a smaller basis, a thick middle part, and a sharp top for European countries like Germany or Sweden, which he then compared to Israel:

> In the Palestinian society, in all Arab societies, or traditional Muslim societies, basically third world [societies], even in places where they are very affluent, like in the Gulf states, it's always "make as many children as you can." . . . So if you look in these countries [draws]—this is the graph of the population, this is the age, they have a triangle-like graph. If you look at Germany, it should look like something like this [draws], if you take out the immigrants, or in Sweden, and they bring in a few immigrants to make it like this, so there will be people to pay the high pension. And in Israel, it should be something like this as well, because we have many children as well, not as sharp as this, because our elders also live very long, it goes something like this as well [corrects the tip of the "European" graph by broadening it].

Referencing the well-known racialized narrative of overpopulation in the Global South and aging populations in the Global North, his visualization of populations as an aggregate, graph-like form can be situated in the long history of illustrating population *as* a problem.[43] These figures of "massified life" offer an epistemological framing of the population that allows for a differential designation of the economic worth of human lives.[44] The notion of overpopulation as such carries with it the burden of a devalued future, whereas those countries with lower birth rates are the ones threatened by these masses of racialized others. In this narrative and Eran's visualization, Israel is like a European country, but with a less sharp tip at the top of the graph. Interestingly, the way he drew these two graphs, Palestinians don't figure in the Israeli graph. Like in the case of Germany, he drew these illustrations by already extracting the threatening racialized other, pointing to an imagined future of population growth. The graph of traditional or Muslim society, on the other hand, represents the threat of "make as many children as you can," emanating from an imagined elsewhere (migrants, Gulf states, Palestinians).

Michael, a middle-aged Jewish Israeli senior physician who works in the fertility department of a hospital in the south of the country, presented a similar narrative and connected fertility rates to notions of progress and civilization, inflected by his own gendered racism. The hospital Michael works at has a large Bedouin clientele, as most of the Palestinian Bedouin population lives in the south of Israel, in the Naqab desert. The Indigenous Bedouin population is a group within the population of Palestinians in Israel, suffering from ongoing Israeli dispossession, forced urbanization, and the Judaization of the Naqab (see chapter 2).[45] About two-thirds of the population live in towns the Israeli state built from the 1960s to the 1980s, while the other third rejected this move and stayed in unrecognized villages. Bedouins in the unrecognized villages are constantly threatened by demolition and criminalization of their housing and infrastructure, with many of them living in temporary dwellings as a result. The situation of the Bedouin population has been described as a form of organized abandonment and as one of the most evident cases of how structural racism is inscribed in Israeli law and policy.[46]

Michael told me that around 40 percent of the patients at his hospital are Bedouins, and the other 60 percent are Jewish Israelis. However, he noted that "in terms of the need for fertility services, the Muslim population is much more active. We serve them more like 60 percent." He continued to explain why:

> Many of them have several wives. So, a Muslim male can, let's say, legally, by his religion, be a husband to three wives here in Israel. We do not just let them have three wives, we even help them to have kids from three wives. And most of that is free of charge. Even in vitro fertilization, which is a very expensive treatment, is free of charge, because the government will sponsor that kind of treatment.

His explanation for the higher need for fertility treatment in the Bedouin population is interesting in several different ways. What stands out is Michael's juxtaposition of Israel not just "letting them have three wives" but also "helping them to have kids" from all of them, free of charge. It points to the central contradiction of the Israeli fertility economy, a settler colonial institution that is embedded in the historical and ongoing quest to achieve and maintain a Jewish majority in Israel. However, due to Bedouin Palestinians' inclusion into the state, generous state subsidies for assisted reproduction must also be granted to them, as well as to other non-Jewish citizens of Israel.

In addition to that, his explanation points to the legal acrobatics the Israeli state performs to subjugate and control its Bedouin population. Polygamy is indeed a contentious topic among feminist Bedouin Palestinian scholars. According to Israeli law, polygamy is prohibited. However, in the case of the Bedouins in the Naqab, as part of its pluralist legal system, the Israeli state grants Shari'a regulations oversight of personal status law. This policy of nonenforcement of antipolygamy laws means that the Israeli law incorporates, and thereby sanctions, Shari'a in its legal system.[47] Legal scholar Rawia Aburabia argues that this long-standing and unofficial policy fulfills a crucial function for Israel's governance over the Bedouin population in keeping them a subjected and isolated minority, supporting tribalism, and enshrining the most conservative versions of religious law among Bedouin communities.[48] Aburabia calls this an "unofficial political bargain with the Bedouin community," which ultimately serves the state, keeping the Bedouin population satisfied and pacified and strengthening internal patriarchal rule.[49]

At first glance, it might seem counterintuitive for Israel to allow the practice of polygamy to proliferate—a sentiment that shines through in Michael's statement: Why should Bedouins be allowed to have so many children, from different wives, free of charge? However, Aburabia furthermore shows that the practice of nonenforcement is only applied to Bedouins who already hold Israeli citizenship. Antipolygamy law is strictly enforced in the case of marriage between a Bedouin with Israeli citizenship and a Palestinian from the West Bank or Gaza. Israel's Ministry of Interior categorically denies family unification requests if one of the spouses is already married to a third party. In other words, the state's de facto acceptance of polygamy in the case of Bedouin citizens is only acceptable to enshrine further indirect control of Bedouins who are already Israeli citizens.[50] Such demographic considerations also concern the broader Palestinian population. In March 2022, the Israeli parliament passed the so-called citizenship law, denying naturalization to Palestinians from the occupied West Bank or Gaza who are married to Israeli citizens.[51] Israeli politicians and demographers carefully consider how to classify different parts of the Palestinian population under Israeli rule or occupation and restrict their freedom of movement and intimate decision-making in various ways.

Such demographic politics are often undergirded by racist and Orientalist assumptions. The case of polygamy in the Bedouin community offers another insight here. Aburabia suggests that Israel's policy of nonenforcement also has an ideological purpose. Enshrining Shari'a in Israel and thereby perpetuating patriarchal norms and conservative legal interpretations serves to uphold Israel's own perception as a modern, civilized state. While the Bedouin population can be characterized through an Orientalist lens as "backward" and "uncivilized," treating their women badly, Israel can assume the role of the civilized savior of Muslim women.[52] Michael's description of the Bedouin population is a case in point. When I asked him why he thinks having many children is more common among his Bedouin patients, he gave a long and slightly contradictory response:

> I can just tell you that the Bedouin population increased immensely since the State of Israel came up. There were about eight thousand Bedouins in the Negev in the south and versus now, maybe five hundred thousand. This is an immense increase, not just because fertility [treatment], of course, but especially because of the medical treatments for kids, because in the old world, from ten kids, maybe two or three survived because there was no water, no medications, no kitchen, you know.... So, they now survive almost as the Jewish population. They increase immensely because they have ten kids, twelve kids, and two or three women. Imagine a mature person having thirty kids and forty kids. Wow! From three or four women, of course. Can you imagine? I am calling them golden sperm, you know, if one has thirty kids, his sperm is very, very good. So, this will explain the immense increase in the Bedouin population since the State of Israel came up. And these small tribes of Bedouins became huge cities.

In this explanation for the Bedouin's high fertility rates, population, territory, and gendered racialization collapse into each other.[53] Michael explains that the increase in the Bedouin population has not only to do with their access to state-funded fertility treatment but also with Israel's civilizational transformation of the Naqab desert. Michael subsumes what many Bedouins and scholars describe as historical and ongoing forms of dispossession, forced urbanization, structural racism, and ongoing displacement under the umbrella of Israel's civilizing effect on "these small tribes."[54] Bringing Western medicine, hygiene, and technology to a backward and uncivilized population is a well-worn narrative of the colonization of historic Palestine.[55] However, in Michael's narrative, it is not only that Israel brought civilization to the Bedouin tribes, resulting in population growth. He also describes polygamy and what he perceives as the Bedouin men's exceptional virility as reasons for their presumably higher birth rates. His amazement and exaggeration are palpable in the second half of his response. Calling me into the narrative several times—"Imagine a mature person having thirty kids and forty kids.... Can you imagine?"—Michael conjures the Bedouin man, with his several wives and thirty to forty children, as a hyper-fertile man, the embodiment of potency and masculinity.[56] He has "golden sperm."

Michael's affective response to his patients is both racialized and gendered. His narrative brings together the civilizational discourse of health and medicine with an Orientalist frame of sexuality and virility.[57] In his view, the practice of polygamy, sanctioned by Israeli law, only reinforces the Bedouin men's potency and contributes to the "immense increase" in the Bedouin population. Here, the work of quantification and the "making" of a population are articulated on the affective and perhaps even subconscious level.[58] Imaginaries, feelings, and phantasmata are part and parcel of the discursive and affective production of the Palestinian population as an exotic, sexual, but also potentially dangerous population. These notions coproduce the calculative practices of quantification, classification, and territorialization that culminate in a broader discourse about why the Palestinian population across historic Palestine needs to be surveilled, controlled, and managed.

Like in other interviews with medical staff, my presence in the interview with Michael is used to establish a shared framework of Palestinians' racialization. The way that Michael addresses me several times—as a German, and a white woman—points to the fact that he wants me to agree with his Orientalist characterization of the Bedouin population as both "backward" and hyper-fertile. The racialized trope of the Brown man with his several wives is articulated in response to Michael establishing *our* oppositional identities; supposedly, German and Israeli men are not like the Bedouin man. This also echoes Eran's interpellation of my identity in his comparison of "Arab" birth rates to those of Germany and other European countries. It is in the relationality of our encounter—a young, childless German woman talking to an older male Jewish Israeli fertility doctor about their Palestinian patients—that such Israeli demographic anxieties are textured.

PALESTINIAN SURVIVABILITY AND REPRODUCTIVE JUSTICE

Palestinian women trying to get pregnant in Israeli fertility clinics are well aware of their interpellation as a population, and how sentiments such as those expressed by Michael or Eran are a reflection of state policy and settler colonial law. Mariam is a thirty-seven-year-old citizen of Israel from a village in the Triangle area and a teacher of alternative medicine. She gave birth to her son one month before our interview after six failed attempts to conceive via IVF. Despite these difficulties, Mariam described her pregnancy journey as relatively easy, mainly because she trusted her doctor, the same Palestinian gynecologist Leen eventually went to see. However, once our conversation moved on to the structural circumstances of trying to get pregnant, Mariam shared how she understands Israeli state policy regarding Palestinian reproduction: "Politically and speaking about the state, yes, of course, demography plays a role. This is all politics; they try as hard as they can to reduce the number of Arabs, to make it tighter for them. So, yes, this is the state's policy for sure." Inquiring further, we asked her how the state was trying to reduce the number of Arabs and make life more difficult for them. Mariam thought about it for a moment and then said:

> By killing them. With reproduction, they don't have control, but the state can make things more difficult. Making it more difficult and killing [people], those are all the state's strategies, meaning they kill Palestinians because they don't want their state to grow; this is what they can do, but they cannot control reproduction.

Mariam brings together a few important arguments. First, she talks about the limited reach of population politics. Even if it is Israeli state ideology to reduce the number of Palestinians and make it difficult for them to access the resources to implement their reproductive choices, there is a limit to the actual impact politics and policies have on individual people's lives, choices, and resilience.[59] However, as Mariam notes, while there is a limit to population politics in the biopolitical sense—surveilling, controlling, and managing reproduction, making it more difficult to have children for *some* people—Israeli rule over the Palestinian population is also necropolitical in its scope, exerting control over "human existence and the material destruction of human bodies and populations."[60] Mariam describes a scale of interference with the Palestinian population. The (limited) control the state has over Palestinian reproduction is accompanied by the actual control the military has over Palestinians' lives. Her remark that Israel is killing Palestinians to curb the growth of a Palestinian state is the underbelly of how Jewish Israeli medical staff like Galit or Irit described the "demographic race" through the lens of (Jewish) children as the state's future.

This tension between access to the means of reproduction—in Mariam's case, one of the world's most advanced fertility economies—and the Israeli military's direct monopoly over people's lives, points to a crucial and transnational question of reproductive justice. In the wake of the Black Lives Matter movement in the United States, sociologist Zakiya Luna writes about the racialized relationship between assisted reproductive technology and survivability:

> Of course, no matter the advances in ART, particular bodies remain under surveillance for their appropriateness for producing children. Further, as the Movement for Black Lives has helped the public understand, people of colour, particularly Black people, have to think about the reality that authorities can kill their children without any recourse for justice. It is no small issue that there are Black people and other racial minorities throughout the world who worry about the survivability of their children. White parents and potential parents have the privilege to worry only about the health of the baby and finances. Minority families often worry about discrimination that their child will face from an early age, or even death.[61]

The simultaneity of having access to advanced fertility treatment while knowing that Palestinians are routinely getting killed by the Israeli army characterizes the various registers of a "demographic race" in Palestine/Israel. Like Black women in the United States, Palestinian women like Leen or Mariam worry about the discrimination their (future) children might face. To the question of whether Mariam's one-month-old son will have equal opportunities as a citizen of Israel, she replied: "No, of course not, there is no equality here, it is not the same, this is obvious. But we are living here, aren't we? One tries his best to give his child some equality." The lack of equality that Palestinian citizens of Israel face, per the definition of the Israeli state as a Jewish state, is a matter of reproductive justice. Mariam made that point even clearer. She explained in detail how a lack of access to the resources needed to raise a child characterizes having children as a Palestinian in Israel:

> First of all, to have what it takes to raise a child, to have equality, to be in a peaceful place, *atmosphere* [Hebrew], especially at home. Parents need to have enough time to raise their children. Nowadays, work takes up most of our time, which means we are mostly not in our homes.... The parents should have time for their children, to raise them, to teach them. This is what is important, this is if you want to give society humans who get life right, there is a difference between giving birth to two children and giving birth to twelve children.

Her description of what it takes to raise children highlights the importance of reproductive justice, not just reproductive rights.[62] Through the lens of a liberal, rights-based approach, Mariam's access to state-subsidized assisted reproduction would be sufficient to point to the recognition of her status and rights as a citizen in a liberal democracy. However, understood through the lens of reproductive justice, Mariam's inclusion as a "settler colonial citizen" is more complicated.[63] While Israel, as a liberal state, must grant Mariam rights, like access to its medical institutions and economy, it is simultaneously invested in impeding Palestinian women's reproduction across various other scales. Mariam points to this contradiction. While she has access to advanced medical treatment, Israel kills Palestinians on the street (and, since 2023, on a mass scale, in Gaza). And while many parents struggle with raising their children under the time constraints of late-stage capitalism, Palestinian women carry the intersectional burden of racialization, gender, and class via their inclusion into the Israeli labor market and settler colonial society more broadly.[64] This also ties in with Mariam's concern about how many children to have and how to raise them. For her, there is a difference in giving birth to "two or twelve children," and she finds that you can only prepare them well for a good life if you have enough time and resources to raise them. This is a well-known consideration in Palestinian society, characterized by questions of modernization, resistance, and access to capital. Rhoda Kanaaneh shows how the question of whether to have large or small families lies at the core of Palestinian individual and nationalist responses to their interpellation in numbers by the Israeli state.[65]

Mariam's reproductive rights and intimate decision-making remain legally, politically, and economically circumscribed by the limits of the Israeli state, its institutions, and its economy, which are centered around the reproduction, well-being, and safety of its Jewish citizens. In Israel, Palestinians have, by definition, not the same rights as their Jewish citizen counterparts, and the state relentlessly demonstrates that their existence is tolerated, at best, or a threat that needs containment or elimination. The experience of women like Mariam thus calls into question the Israeli state and its political system as a guarantor for their reproductive rights. A state built on and maintained on the dispossession, expulsion, occupation, and the potential state-mandated killing of half of the people on the territory it controls can never grant women (and men) full (reproductive) freedom and autonomy.

I discussed similar questions about the limits of inclusion and Palestinian family planning with Douha and her husband, Hassan, along with Najla, my interpreter and research assistant, during an afternoon at the family's house in a village in the north of Israel. Douha is a thirty-eight-year-old stay-at-home mom and Bedouin Palestinian citizen who conceived three of her four children via IVF, both in private and public hospitals in Israel. Her husband, Hassan, a mechanic, was actively engaged in our interview. Najla knew the family, and the three of them discussed the topic of family size controversially. When Najla asked the couple what they thought about the state encouraging Jewish Israelis to reproduce, Douha at first didn't really have an opinion, but Hassan said, humorously: "Like, it's not about the quantity, it should be about the *quality* [Hebrew]. Look at the people in the Knesset, in the elections, they're all *stupid* [Hebrew]." Thinking about Najla's question further, he mused on whether to have larger or smaller families, arguing that if one considered population growth in the Arab population, nothing good would come out of that mindset for the Jews either, opening up a debate about the "quality" or "quantity" of smaller versus larger families:

HASSAN: It would affect the Jews, not us. Like, look at the Arabs now, from seventy years till now, we're a quantity, or do you think we're a quality?

NAJLA: You can't measure it like this. Of course, we also have difficulties. We're living under occupation at the end of the day. We don't have the same opportunities and rights. Just think of the national law that they issued recently.

HASSAN: But also, there are successful Arabs, like if you work hard, you'll do better.

NAJLA: If you have enough support from your family, society.

DOUHA: Look, we're in a better situation than the ultra-Orthodox Jews. Our only weapon is education in this country.

NAJLA: But it's different, we work hard and get educated to earn money, they don't go to school, they don't work, and still the government gives them money.

HASSAN: So, is life only about money now?

NAJLA: No, I meant the comparison isn't fair.

HASSAN: Of course, Jews have better opportunities. We live, at the end of the day, in [name of their village]. We don't have the same opportunities. We're a *minority* within a *minority* [Hebrew].

Hassan and Douha's argument points to what Kanaaneh terms Palestinian modes of self and categorizations of reproduction, characterized as "reproductively modern" versus "reproductively primitive."[66] The former alludes to a "modern way of life," established via consumption, education, and family size, while the latter ostensibly points to being backward and stuck in time.[67] While Douha puts forward the argument that education, and thus "quality" (i.e., smaller families), is Palestinians' only weapon in Israel, Najla's interjection challenges this view from a structuralist perspective, pointing out that having or not having many children is also a question of resources, resources that are not afforded to Palestinians in Israel. Najla questions Hassan's neoliberal point of "if you work hard, you'll do better" by pointing out that it doesn't matter how hard Palestinians work, as they are not equipped with the same resources as Jewish Israelis, exemplifying this by referring to the ultra-Orthodox communities' receipt of welfare. In the end, Hassan agrees, conceding that as a Bedouin minority within the minority of Palestinians, the "quality" of the Palestinian population writ large cannot simply be compared to the Jewish Israeli population.

After this exchange, Najla linked the conversation back to the couple's experience with IVF. They all agreed that politically, the Israeli state is invested in establishing and maintaining a population majority, specifically the more religious sectors of society, as Douha pointed out, "the ultra-Orthodox [want to be the majority], to control the country more." I asked her whether she thinks that a similar politicized understanding of reproduction exists in Palestinian society and culture, to which she replied, reiterating her earlier point: "No, we only need education, that's how we become better." Hassan added, "It's not easy financially, like, if I have two kids and I pay for their education, it's enough." In this conversation, a smaller Palestinian family size appears as both a tool to fight against Israeli domination to become "better," but also an outcome of the very conditions of Israeli governance.[68]

Rima, a twenty-eight-year-old physician who works in an Israeli hospital in Jerusalem, has a similar view on Israeli and Palestinian demographic politics and reproductive choices. Rima has been married for 1.5 years, and when we met, she was in the middle of her second round of IUI treatment (intrauterine insemination), a less invasive form of fertility treatment usually deployed before patients are advised to go for IVF. Rima and I sat in her office at the hospital where she worked and had an engaging conversation during a break in between seeing her patients. We talked about the role of Palestinian mothers, and Rima echoed the sentiment expressed by Douha and Hassan, explaining that being a Palestinian mother is not just about having children for the sake of Palestinian society, but that it also comes with concerns about how to best raise them:

> I think it's the most important role because if we stop having children as a society, we'll end soon. But another role, which is also important, is, OK, you have a baby, that's good, all the women—have babies, but how to raise the baby, that's the important thing. Not to have babies babies babies, but how to raise them, how to become a person who's good, kind, respectful, that's the kind of people we need.

Rima's understanding of Palestinian motherhood, having children for the sake of Palestinian society, but also how to best raise them, needs to be contextualized by her lived reality as a Palestinian under Israeli occupation in East Jerusalem. Israel illegally annexed East Jerusalem in 1967, and East Jerusalemites like Rima were included in the Israeli state but not granted Israeli citizenship. Instead, they hold a temporary residency status, which grants them more rights than Palestinians in the West Bank and Gaza, but less than Palestinian citizens of Israel.[69] Giving birth and raising children as a Palestinian resident of East Jerusalem comes with particular hardship and difficulties (chapters 3 and 4). Everyday encounters with the Israeli military, having to prove that one's center of life is indeed East Jerusalem to keep securing one's residency status, as well as inclusion in Israeli institutions such as the medical sphere and labor market, often while not speaking Hebrew, are some of the particularly gendered experiences of being a woman and mother in East Jerusalem.[70]

I thus asked Rima how the context of Israeli occupation shapes how she imagines her future children's lives. Rima exhaled exhaustedly and said: "It's the same as we live . . . let me be direct to you, every Israeli is superior over Palestinians, like we are under occupation, also in here, also in work, every day, every day you feel that, but you have to live with this feeling, it becomes normal for you." The heaviness of projecting her life into her future children's lives was palpable at this moment, and I still thought about Rima many years after meeting her. Her description of the condition of Israeli settler colonialism, the fact that, by law, every Israeli is superior to every Palestinian, is central to living across Palestine/Israel as a Palestinian. But similar to Mariam, who said that "one tries their best to give their child some equality," Rima shared how living under occupation becomes normal, and you "have to live with that feeling." For her, the hardship of raising children in East Jerusalem is also a reason why people in Jerusalem wouldn't have as many children as Jewish Israelis. Rima said: "It's a political thing for religious Israelis, they sometimes have ten, eleven, or twelve children. But for Palestinians in Jerusalem, no. I tell you why: Because it is hard, and it also costs money, if you want schools, universities, it really costs money, so . . ." Connecting the conditions of living under occupation in East Jerusalem to Palestinian women's reproductive choices puts the question of reproductive justice center stage. Access to the resources needed to raise children is scarce and part and parcel of their subjugated status as occupied residents.

Palestinian women are keenly aware of their interpellation in numbers, and that the Israeli state encourages high Jewish birth rates while complicating their own reproduction. From the standpoint of Palestinian women, Israeli population politics and demographic anxieties limit their reproductive freedom and autonomy. For Rima, Douha, or Mariam, having children is not simply a choice, it is also determined by their access to the resources needed to implement reproductive decisions and shaped by questions of what is best for the Palestinian body politic from a nationalist, liberationist, or individual point of view.

Their experiences also reveal various dimensions of Israeli demographic politics and how they shape Palestinian women's reproductive lives. As Bedouin citizens, Palestinian citizens, and East Jerusalemite residents, these women's experiences of being classified by the Israeli state differ and implicate various legal, social, and political limitations to their reproductive choices and decision-making. Mariam's pregnancy journey has been relatively easy, and she is rather "assimilated" in Israeli society, recounting that she has many Jewish Israeli friends and coworkers. However, for her, the broader structural implications of Israeli settler colonialism and biopolitics and necropolitics are clear. While the Israeli state might want to curb Palestinian women's reproduction, there is a limit to its reach into people's personal lives. There is, however, no limit to its necropolitical power, which the genocide in Gaza has revealed. As a Bedouin minority of the Palestinian "minority," Douha and her husband reflect on reproduction through the lens of modernization and "internal" betterment. For them, having fewer children is a reaction to Israeli settler colonial rule over the Palestinians. The couple's reflection on family size shows how the conditions of living under Israeli rule force Palestinian families to consider both economic as well as national or liberatory considerations in their reproductive decision-making. Similar to Mariam's reflections, the couple's experience highlights internal class differences between Palestinians and how these shape family planning and reproductive decision-making. Rima's lived experience similarly reveals the contours of reproductive injustice for Palestinians living under Israeli rule. She also stresses the national importance of having well-educated children as a

Palestinian woman, but she points to the particular limits that living in East Jerusalem places on her and other East Jerusalemite mothers. For her, having fewer children is a result of the lack of access to the resources needed to have children, as well as a decision made to invest in a "better" Palestinian society. These experiences demonstrate the various ways in which the Israeli state classifies and fragments Palestinians and their reproduction, and how Palestinian women, in turn, challenge such Israeli politics through their reproductive decision-making.

While Rima, Douha, or Mariam's narratives represent various jurisdictions, identities, and corresponding geographies of Israeli control, their experiences also reveal the continuum of Israeli rule over time—from 2018 to 2019, when I met them, until the time of writing this, while having witnessed the genocide for two years. Gender studies scholar Nadine Naber draws out how various Israeli tools of oppression are part of the same settler colonial power structure, manifesting differently at various political conjunctures. She writes in late 2023:

> Israel's killing of more than four thousand children in one month continues its same settler-colonial legacies that pressure Jewish Israelis to reproduce while obstructing Palestinian birthing—whether by blocking pregnant Palestinian women in labor at checkpoints from reaching medical facilities, or Israeli state practices that deny Palestinians the right to bury their children.[71]

While Rima, Douha, and Mariam's experiences are less obviously violent, all three women are keenly aware that the Israeli state encourages Jewish Israeli birth rates and wants to limit their own. Their experiences can thus be understood through a longer historical and ongoing settler colonial logic of (cultural, political, and actual) elimination, from East Jerusalem to the north, to Gaza today.

THE UNDERBELLY OF ISRAELI DEMOGRAPHIC ANXIETIES: HAUNTED BY DEMOGRAPHY

Israeli demographic anxieties, policy, and settler colonial politics also engender anxieties in Palestinian women when it comes to their experience of Israeli medical space. In my interview with Rima, I shared with her that while Jewish Israeli medical staff would usually describe their working environment of the fertility clinic as a rare site of coexistence and humanitarianism, some medical staff would also admit that "behind closed doors," they are wondering if what they are doing helps Palestinians to "have future terrorists" (see Ziva, chapter 3). These sentiments are not lost on Palestinian patients and physicians who work in Israeli hospitals, like Rima herself. Israeli biopolitics, what physician and health scholar Osama Tanous calls "racism by numbers," also shapes how Palestinians enter medical encounters with Jewish Israeli doctors.[72] When I told Rima about these instances in some of my interviews with Jewish Israeli medical staff, she recalled: "I've sometimes heard that a lot of Palestinian women said that if it's a baby boy, they [medical staff] told them that there is a problem with the baby, that you have to miscarry. Not here, but I've heard. From my experience, I don't know, this is just like talking, talking, talking." Other women I interviewed similarly expressed a suspicion that Palestinians might be treated differently from Jewish Israeli patients. They would share stories they had heard from other women who were told that there was an issue with their pregnancy or their baby, and that the doctors would recommend an abortion. Similar stories about doctors who would transfer Palestinian women's retrieved eggs to Jewish Israeli patients' wombs also circulated throughout the interviews. While some of these rumors are probably indeed just "talking, talking, talking," and point to an emotional response to being aware of Palestinian women's interpellation as "wombs" and incubators of "future terrorists," other experiences corroborate similar fears.[73]

Riham is a thirty-five-year-old stay-at-home mom who lives with her four-year-old son and her husband in a neighborhood in occupied East Jerusalem, near the Old City. When Najla and I arrived at Riham's house in the evening, it was already late, but Riham wanted to meet after iftar, the breaking of the fast during Ramadan. Riham's sister-in-law Israa, a twenty-eight-year-old stay-at-home mom, was present as well. She had also undergone IVF treatment and wanted to participate in the interview. They were both extremely welcoming, offering us sweets, coffee, and tea. Our conversation was lively and long as we smoked cigarettes, and we talked until it was almost midnight. Riham's pregnancy story began almost fifteen years ago when she realized she wouldn't get pregnant normally. Her health insurance company referred her to a small hospital in West Jerusalem, known for its maternity ward and its high percentage of ultra-Orthodox patients. Riham was treated there unsuccessfully for six years, first trying IUI and later IVF. Her attending physician told her that the issue was with her husband's infertility, which turned out to be a false diagnosis. In addition to that, the waiting times at the hospital were unusually long, and Riham felt extremely uncomfortable. After a while, a friend suggested she try another clinic, and Riham went to a larger Israeli hospital in East Jerusalem. She took her medical file with her and showed it to her new doctor. The previous physician had handwritten the number of injections she had given her on the file but never explained what they were for. Riham recounted: "I don't understand these things. When I went to a different doctor in [the other hospital], and he saw the file, he asked me, 'Why would you take these amounts of injections?' He saw all the files. He told me that if I kept taking all these medications, I would never be able to get pregnant." After this stressful experience and seeing her new doctor, Riham took a break from fertility treatment. After a while, she started again and got pregnant immediately with her now four-year-old son. In the following exchange, Riham and Israa reflect on the quality of the treatment they receive in the large East Jerusalem hospital, comparing it to the medically neglectful experience Riham had had in West Jerusalem:

RIHAM: When we went to [the new hospital], they also checked, and my husband didn't have problems, like she [the previous doctor] had shamed him. When I went to [the new hospital], he didn't even have to take any medications, and the doctor there said I should've been pregnant a long time ago; I didn't have any issues. She would give me so many injections, and I didn't know. And also, many Arab women went to see her, and she gave all of us the same amount of injections. When we talked about this issue, they found that she did give them high dosages of injections. This would mess up the hormonal levels, and that's why I didn't get pregnant. Really, that's what she did. I didn't understand her motives, but I suffered. She would let me wait for one paper and go back all the way and get the paper, and then she won't see me. When I was there, I would ask the Arab women there, and they would say the same. She was so mean to us. I tell you, the difference between [the new hospital] and [the previous one] is from the land to the sky. And there's no racism. They're respectful. There's a huge difference between the treatments, the medical staff, and the secretaries.

ISRAA: They're really nice and helpful. They even spoil us.

RIHAM: They know me there; they call me by my name. And they say I have a good smile [laughs]. There, they were ugly and terrible. They wouldn't explain how to take the medications. If I did something wrong, they didn't explain. She would yell and shout at us. And she would fight with my husband, and then we would leave her office. Six years of my life went for nothing, in vain, honestly. Once I left her, in [the new hospital], it worked the first time I did IVF, thank God.

Riham suggests that her physician at the West Jerusalem hospital not only misdiagnosed her but also mistreated her and other Arab women at the hospital. Comparing her experiences between the two hospitals, the blatant racism of the West Jerusalem one comes into stark relief. Riham's experience points to various levels of mistreatment at the hands of racist medical staff, from administering the wrong dosage of hormones and misdiagnoses, to making patients wait and failing to communicate medical procedures properly.[74] These experiences amount to what anthropologist Dána-Ain Davis terms "obstetric racism."[75] Following up on that, Najla asked Riham how she would explain this behavior, and Riham said: "She's racist, it's personal to her," but specified that this was not the case for all Israeli hospitals, only in the West Jerusalem hospital, "they treated Arabs in a bad way and were racist." There, racist behavior was clearly targeted at her and other Palestinian women simply because they were Palestinian. While this treatment could be the case of one specifically racist physician and an enabling medical context, the question of reproductive politics looms large over Riham's experience. Najla brought up the context of Israeli demographic anxieties and asked the sisters-in-law if they thought the racist physician's behavior was politically motivated. They disagreed:

RIHAM: I don't know.

ISRAA: Yes, so they can outnumber us and control the country and take it all.

RIHAM: But we also have a lot of kids. They also have infertility problems, and we go to the same hospitals.

While explicit demographic politics immediately comes to Israa's mind, Riham has a more nuanced view. However, implicitly, her reference to the fact that Palestinian women also have a lot of kids echoes the shared political arithmetic that shapes how both Palestinians and Israelis view reproduction, even if asymmetrical in power, as her own experience exemplifies. Whether articulated in straightforward political terms like Israa, or through an individual lens of shared vulnerability to infertility, medical encounters like Riham's are embedded in the larger context of Israeli population politics.

Israeli demographic anxieties don't have to amount to actual policy, medical misconduct, or racist behavior to be felt by Palestinian women. Lina, a forty-one-year-old secretary who lives in a refugee camp outside of Jerusalem and holds residency status, expressed suspicion concerning IVF treatment in

Israeli hospitals. When Mary and I met her, Lina already had two children and was in the process of undergoing fertility treatment again after having successive experiences of miscarriages in the IVF process. As usual, at the end of each interview, Mary and I asked the interviewee if she wanted to add something. Given her several miscarriages, Lina had spent a considerable amount of time in fertility clinics. She wanted to share with us that during that time, she had met many Palestinian women who were told by their Jewish Israeli doctors that there was a problem with their children and that an abortion was advisable. However, Lina recounted that these were religious women, and "they had persistence within them, saying, 'No, it's whatever God gives us with the baby, we will be satisfied,' and the shock was that the baby came out healthy, without any problems." Lina insisted that she had met more than one woman like that and that with all of them, the ostensible problems only arose after their fourth or fifth pregnancy. Lina took these rather anecdotal examples as a starting point for a broader argument about racialization and mistrust in the medical encounter. Coming back to some of the earlier questions we had discussed in the interview, she said:

> But seriously, if we want to speak again about trust, or differences in religion, the racism plays inside you, so that you . . . you keep on saying, "Is what she is saying true?" which means I don't know whom to listen to. I could go undertake an exam with the Arab doctors to make sure. It becomes your reaction, you see?

The history and presence of Israeli racism against Palestinians and their birthing bodies haunt clinical encounters in the Israeli fertility clinic. Whether based on experience, rumors, or broader political ideology, Israeli demographic anxieties also determine Palestinian women's ability to trust their fertility doctors. This relationship between racialization and mistrust in the Israeli medical system not only characterizes Palestinian experiences but has also been documented for other marginalized communities in Israel, such as Ethiopian, Yemenite, or Mizrahi Jews.[76] It is also reminiscent of the experiences of Indigenous women in North America who have pointed out that their exposure to sterilization abuses at the hands of American doctors and nurses amounts to genocide.[77]

Maysam is thirty-four years old and lives with her husband in the Old City of Jerusalem. She first started fertility treatment in 2006, with her then-husband, but she never got pregnant. After getting married to her second husband in 2009, she again started IVF treatment. At the time of our interview, in 2019, she was still not pregnant and was undergoing IVF at the same Israeli hospital as Riham and Israa. Similar to Leen, Maysam had also tried to get pregnant in a West Bank fertility clinic but didn't feel like they treated her well. She also had to cross the border and go through checkpoints to get there and had to pay for treatment privately. Her decision to try a clinic in the West Bank instead of undergoing state-funded fertility treatment in an Israeli hospital had initially been informed by friends and family telling her to go to an "Arab hospital." Maysam recounted, specifically addressing Najla, who was conducting this interview with me:

> Because you know how we think that they treat Jews better than they treat Arabs. Also, they say they do experiments on us. Even Arab doctors would say that. They also say that sometimes they might take your fertilized eggs and give them to Jews. But I also heard of Arabs who went there and got treated with IVF, and they got kids. My mother-in-law didn't want me to go to [the hospital in East Jerusalem]. But I insisted on going there.

Like in the stories Lina recounted, fear of mistreatment or even experimentation shapes some Palestinians' perception of the Israeli medical sphere.[78] Israeli demographic anxieties find their mirror image in these stories.

Similar to Riham's case, it is also remarkable that Maysam has been in unsuccessful treatment for such a long time, over ten years, with her second husband. Maysam shared that language barriers were a main factor exacerbating her pregnancy journey.[79] Maysam doesn't speak Hebrew and relies on her husband to translate for her, but if he's unavailable, she will ask another Palestinian person at the hospital to help her. In her experience, the doctors and nurses at the hospital would not speak Arabic and didn't make an effort to help her understand how to take the medications or when to schedule another appointment. During our interview, the extent to which Maysam lacks access to culturally and linguistically appropriate resources and an understanding of how fertility treatment works became painfully clear. I told Maysam about the availability of translation services at the hospital where she was treated, and Najla tried to explain to her the difference between male and female factors in infertility. We both left the interview feeling sad and defeated. While Maysam didn't directly experience racism or misconduct at the Israeli hospital, it was also clear that her long pregnancy journey was at an extreme structural disadvantage and that none of her attending physicians seemed to care that she didn't fully understand the treatment.

While such stories mainly appear in the already tense atmosphere of East Jerusalem, the Israeli political arithmetic and the state's demographic politics writ large are also recognized within '48 territory. I talked to Haya, a thirty-one-year-old mathematics teacher with Israeli citizenship who lives in a small Palestinian town in Israel close to the "Green Line." At the time of our interview, Haya was eighteen weeks pregnant after undergoing fertility treatment with a Palestinian physician in a women's health clinic in their town and later in a large hospital in central Israel. As a Palestinian teacher in an Israeli school, Haya is keenly aware of the political context her child will enter as a Palestinian with Israeli citizenship. Similar to Leen and Mariam, she talked about Palestinian children being at a disadvantage when it comes to education and the job market. Drawing from her own experience, Haya shared that Palestinians must work extra hard to be accepted: "We think about this all the time, that it's hard to accept us in the school or workplace like Jewish people, you have to be excellent, an excellent one." Haya's experience illustrates Palestinian citizens of Israel's inclusion in an educational system and labor market centered around Zionist values and Palestinian dispossession. In this context, Palestinians' respectability and deservingness are measured according to their assimilation into or acceptance of the Israeli state narrative.[80] Anthropologist Maya Wind shows the various ways in which Palestinians in Israeli educational institutions—institutions central to Israeli demographic and territorial expansion—need to perform like a "good Arab" to be accepted.[81]

Given her profession and interest in research, Haya also talked about the Israeli state's investment in Jewish Israeli versus Palestinian birth rates. She remembered reading a study about demography and drew her own conclusions: "I saw that they do research about the average number of children in the family, in Hebrew. I think they are happy that the Arab people have a lower average, and here in [her hometown], the average is 2 or 1.4 for every family. I think they prefer small Arab families." Haya is keenly aware of Israel's political arithmetic and that the preferred outcome is low Palestinian birth rates. As discussed earlier, the Israeli state's investment in producing demography data on Jewish Israeli and Palestinian birth rates, and its monitoring of changing proportions between Jews and Palestinians, both within and beyond its borders, has been well documented. Analyses of newspapers and academic texts further show how anxieties about Israel's demographic character are bound to questions of security and Israel's existence as a Jewish state.[82] It is not surprising that this "common knowledge" about demographic anxieties is referenced by Palestinians and shapes how they perceive the Israeli fertility economy and their reproductive lives and freedom under Israeli settler colonialism.

Israeli population politics, as well as individual or institutionalized demographic anxieties, haunt Palestinian women's reproduction.[83] When Palestinian women share rumors, stories, or experiences of reproductive injustice or violence, they alert us to how Israeli settler colonialism and its demographic logic shape their everyday lives, reproductive decision-making, and bodies—sometimes directly and sometimes more obliquely. Indeed, as feminist legal scholar Nadera Shalhoub-Kevorkian shows, gendered settler colonial violence not only has devastating material implications for Palestinian women but also enters their psyche, reappearing in nightly dreams and shaping dreams of the future.[84] Shared rumors or stories of mistreatment draw our attention to seventy-five years of unresolved gendered Israeli violence against Palestinian women.

In talking about fears of medical neglect or loss of bodily autonomy, Palestinian women direct us to the affective and embodied impact of ongoing oppression and psychosocial governance.[85] Rima, who is a physician in an Israeli hospital, has heard such rumors about medical neglect. But she believes them to be just stories (stories she nonetheless shared with me). Riham's experience in the West Jerusalem hospital, on the other hand, points to experiences of obstetric racism and medical neglect. Lina and Maysam both shared how the circulation of rumors and fears made them suspicious of their medical staff. Haya recounted how Israeli demographic anxieties engender concerns about her children's future and that they will always have to work harder to be successful, and she connected this to Israeli institutions collecting data on Palestinian birth rates. These experiences provide insight into how Israeli demographic anxieties work on a more affective and psychological level. These stories also foreshadow how experiences and fears of dehumanization, surveillance, and control within Israeli medical institutions would appear much more obviously after October 7. As health scholar Ghada Majadli's writing on the militarization of Israeli medical spaces post–October 2023 documents, Israeli hospitals have become increasingly militarized, with the line between Jewish Israelis who are both active reserve soldiers in Gaza and also doctors being blurred. She shows how this context leads to the dehumanization and surveillance of Palestinian doctors, who might express empathy with the people of Gaza or protest the Israeli war effort. Palestinian doctors in the Israeli healthcare system talk about how some of their Jewish Israeli colleagues shared personal photos from their military service in team meetings or staff group chats, while other Jewish Israeli doctors talk openly about their participation in the elimination of Palestinians in Gaza.[86] While Majadli's work doesn't discuss how this context affects Palestinian patients, it makes clear that the fears voiced by Rima, Riham, Lina, Maysam, and Haya reflect an acute awareness of how settler colonial militarization and racialized governance shape Palestinians' experiences of Israeli medical space.

DEMOGRAPHIC ANXIETIES: POPULATION AS A FELT CONDITION

This chapter opened with two quotations. Rhoda Ann Kanaaneh refers to the ongoing Israeli practices of calculating the ratio between Jewish Israelis and Palestinians, and the categorization and essentialization that come with these calculative practices. Palestinian women like Leen, Mariam, Douha, or Rima describe how they experience Israel's population politics. Their reflections illustrate how the structural conditions of Israeli settler colonialism result in conditions of systemic reproductive injustice for Palestinian women. While these women have access to Israel's fertility economy and derive benefits from state-subsidized IVF treatment, they also share how their individual reproductive choices are limited due to living in the settler state. Questions such as how many children to have and worries about accessing the means to raise them are accompanied by a broader knowledge that while they are trying to get pregnant, other Palestinians and their children are being shot, violated, or incarcerated. The ways in which the Palestinian women in this chapter address questions of reproductive injustice, demographic considerations, or the politics of reproduction are reflective of the fact that the ratio between Jewish Israelis and Palestinians is central to the Israeli state and its institutions.

The second quotation by M. Murphy asks about the specifics of the counting inherently at work in assessing birth rates or population growth. It asks who does the counting and what counting entails. For Jewish Israeli physicians Galit and Irit, a "demographic race" is a normalized and obvious part of living in Israel, but its calculative impetus happens in the background and doesn't affect ordinary people who just want children. At the same time, they talk about the importance of (Jewish) children for the (Jewish) state, at least implicitly recognizing that the "demographic race" is centered around the maintenance of a Jewish population majority. While Irit and Galit's counting is both abstract and conjures shared Israeli and Palestinian pronatalist values and culture, Eran and Michael's counting produces difference. Palestinian society is compared to other "third world" countries and their problems of overpopulation. The Bedouin population of the Naqab is referenced as a case in point, an uncivilized population that is not only "allowed" to over-reproduce because the Israeli state offers them access to assisted reproductive technology but is also fueled by their men's extraordinary virility. In these narratives, space, gender, and race collapse into each other to differentiate between civilized and uncivilized high birth rates.

This counting is an expression of Israel's ongoing expansionist demographic and territorial politics, established during the early years of Israeli statehood. Palestinian women's experiences testify to how these structures, institutions, and sentiments shape their reproduction today. However, as Murphy indicates, this counting also does something else. Counting carries "an affective charge." Implementing population politics, separating and fragmenting the Palestinian population, surveilling their movement and intimate relationships, and studying their birth rates also intervene on an epistemological-affective level. Murphy shows how affect not only animates numerical sums (such as the "immense increase" of the Bedouin population, or that Palestinians "make as many children as they can") but how it is also "purposively propagated by the infrastructures that do the counting."[87] Affect is central to the institutions, policies, and tools employed in the service of calculative practices, and it is amplified by their outcomes: statistics, numbers, reports, and "common knowledge" that establish that high Palestinian birth rates are at best concerning and at worst dangerous for the Israeli state. The production and circulation of demographic knowledge about the Palestinians is central to the transformation of Israeli demographic concerns into demographic *anxieties*.

Demographic anxieties are tightly knit together with Israel's articulation of security concerns. As shown in the historical excursion of this chapter, if a state is centered around the production and maintenance of a population majority, the birth rates of *other* citizens, residents, or neighboring countries are often classified as threatening and dangerous. One of the emotional drivers of Israel's securitization of demography is fear. Conjuring affective atmospheres of a demographic threat is thus central to the need to count, surveil, and manage the Palestinian population. As Nadera Shalhoub-Kevorkian demonstrates, Israel's security regime and rhetoric rely on the production of a dangerous Palestinian Other; primitive, barbaric, and uncivilized.[88] In this context, Palestinians' reproduction is produced both as proof of and legitimization for their subjugation. Affect, materializing as racialized fears of overpopulation or Orientalist tropes of masculinity, exceeds the calculative rationalities of population-making and becomes the driver *and* outcome of numbers, statistics, birth rates, and ratios. It is in that sense that the "making" of the Palestinian population does not only rely on calculative practices that categorize and group people, but the idea of a population itself also becomes "a felt condition."[89]

From a hegemonic perspective of Israeli statecraft, Palestinians feel like a dangerous threat, always already too many, possibly terrorists. As a result of these politics of fear, the Israeli state employs a variety of strategies to maintain low Palestinian numbers. It "surveils, counts and manages Palestinians to ensure that they do not resist, express their political views, raise the issue of their identity as Palestinians or produce too many children who might change the demographics of the ruling majority."[90] From a Palestinian perspective, such demographic anxieties and politics engender reproductive anxieties of their own. Women like Lina and Maysam ask themselves whether they can trust their Israeli physicians, while the experiences of Riham and Israa, as well as shared rumors and stories, corroborate such fears. Women like Haya further reflect on their awareness of how they have become subjects of Israeli calculations and how this condition shapes their own and their (future) children's lives.

In attending to the close relationship between counting and affect, or between demography and security in the Israeli vernacular, I propose to understand demographic anxieties not just as politics and policies, but as an affective economy of knowledge production under settler colonialism. This framing of demographic anxieties provides important insight into the production and circulation of Israeli hegemonic feelings and sentiments about the Palestinian population and their social and biological reproduction that may add to our understanding of how Israel's genocide in Gaza has been legitimized for over two years. Israeli demographic anxieties work to collapse territory, population, and racialization into each other. Like in the graph that Eran drew, the Palestinian population is presented through a dehumanizing lens of an aggregate state, massified lives that need to be controlled, surveilled, and contained. Whether this concerns Palestinians in Israel, the occupied West Bank, or Gaza, a "demographic race" is presented as a normal and naturalized feature of Israeli society, in which some children are the future and some are better not born. Central to this understanding of population as a "felt" condition is the racialization of Palestinians as Zionism's ultimate Other, which oscillates between racialized notions of overpopulation in a civilizational frame and their nonexistence as a people and political entity that is as deserving of self-determination, freedom, and peace. However, the Palestinian women I interviewed, and Palestinians in Gaza, the West Bank, or Jerusalem today, challenge and resist their interpellation as mere numbers and offer us important insights into the gendered and affective forms of settler colonialism.

TWO

Infrastructures

> For many years, Palestinians' health was neglected, not just because their health was not affecting the Israelis' health, but also because they lacked power and were automatically related to the enemy. The Palestinians are on the other side, so why take care of them? And I'm talking about general policy in the Israeli healthcare system.
>
> NAJWA, *Palestinian health scholar*

> To broaden the scope of this question to all Palestinians: how do a people reject this pessimistic narrative and imagine a life that is livable and worth living when all metrics, policies, donors, infrastructures, and health advocates have rendered them disposable and prescribed for them premature death?
>
> DANYA M. QATO[1]

PALESTINIANS' HEALTH OUTCOMES ARE shaped by Israeli settler colonialism and institutional racism. In the occupied West Bank, numerous Palestinian health issues and deaths result from movement restrictions instituted by the Israeli occupation. In occupied East Jerusalem, Palestinian residents are included in the Israeli healthcare system while struggling to prove their right to exist and remain in the city. Within Israel's 1948 borders, Palestinian citizens of Israel have significantly worse health outcomes compared to the Jewish Israeli population, despite, in theory, having access to the same healthcare system. In the Naqab desert, the Bedouin Palestinian population's health is impacted by ongoing Israeli land grabs and the destruction of their villages. Since 2023, Israel has been deliberately destroying health infrastructure in Gaza, with bombings of hospitals having become a normalized part of Israel's strategic warfare. Across Israel and the occupied territories, Palestinian women trying to get pregnant in Israeli hospitals or receiving reproductive and sexual healthcare services more broadly are particularly affected by Israeli governance and control over their bodies.

The opening quote by Najwa, a Palestinian scholar of health, calls attention to the complex topography of Palestinian health. I spoke to Najwa toward the end of doing research for my PhD, and we met on Zoom on a cold November day in 2020, at the height of the Covid-19 pandemic. The global pandemic is a crucial backdrop to how Najwa talks about Palestinian health, as it puts into stark relief the interconnectedness of Palestinians and Israelis from a critical global health perspective. In the Israeli public health imaginary pre-Covid, Palestinians in the occupied Palestinian territories were separated—politically, materially—from the Israeli state. At the same time, Palestinians within Israel's borders were equally invisible, with many of them living segregated from Israeli society.[2] Palestinian health was thus not a matter of concern or investment for the Israeli healthcare system, as Palestinians' health was not perceived to be threatening to the Israeli body politic. This changed during the Covid-19 pandemic. But instead of taking our planetary connectedness as a starting point to rethink Palestinians' access to health, Israel's response was to reinforce separation. Checkpoints from the West Bank and Gaza were closed off, and the state initially blocked the administering of vaccines to the West Bank.[3] While Palestinian health became a matter of concern, the pandemic reinscribed the spatial logic of occupation. Located on "the other side" of the separation wall, locked in the besieged Gaza Strip, or within Israel's borders, Palestinians are perceived through the lens of "the enemy," trapped not only in a settler colonial state but also within its security theology.[4] The spatial parameters of the occupation and the legal bifurcation between Jewish and non-Jewish citizens and residents translate into Israeli health policy and shape Israel's medical sphere at large.

The Israeli healthcare sector and its thriving fertility economy exemplify in a biopolitical sense how the Israeli state invests in the health and future of its Jewish Israeli citizens. While Palestinians are variedly included or have limited access to Israeli health services, their access to medical technology, knowledge, and specific treatment they might need is slowed down, choppy, limited, or outright denied. Who can access advanced fertility clinics in Jewish Israeli–majority cities? Where are women's health clinics located within Israel's '48 borders? What borders must Palestinians cross to receive medical services? What language is spoken inside the Israeli hospital, and who is made to feel comfortable and welcome in the Israeli healthcare system? At the core of these questions lies the infrastructure of Israeli settler colonialism and its debilitating effects on Palestinian health and life more broadly.[5]

As architectures of circulation, infrastructures are central to how the modern world works, and their movement, speed, and breaking points reveal who these networks are set up for and how valuable the goods, people, or ideas that circulate through them are under late-stage capitalism.[6] As social, material, and political formations, infrastructures are as critical to everyday life experiences as they are for the imagination of the future.[7] In the Israeli context, the material, political, and ideological dimensions of infrastructure come sharply into focus, as systems of circulation and control are closely intertwined with the logics of settler colonialism. Israeli infrastructure works to fragment historic Palestine into various areas of Israeli jurisdiction, enabling Israeli economies to thrive and Israeli society to flourish. In that sense, Israeli infrastructure is the material site where settler colonial space, life, and future are enabled and imagined. At the same time, it is where Palestinian space is controlled, Palestinian life is slowed down, and Palestinian political futures are hampered.[8] Indeed, as environmentalist scholar Winona LaDuke and geographer Deborah Cowen write for the North American context, "Infrastructure is the *how* of settler colonialism."[9] Israeli health infrastructures are thus a foundational site to explore how the biopolitics of settler colonialism are implemented at the scale of the body, health, and reproduction.

In this chapter, I explore the various ways in which Palestinian women who seek to get pregnant are included in, have access to, are barred from, or cannot reach Israeli health infrastructure. In so doing, I ask what Israeli health infrastructure moves and what gets stuck, what futures the Israeli fertility economy affords, and whose reproductive lives are slowed down or denied. Mapping the organizational logic of Israeli health infrastructure with a focus on women's reproductive and sexual health allows me to articulate the political stakes of infrastructure as both life-provisioning and life-destroying.[10] If, as architect Keller Easterling puts it, "the medium of infrastructure space makes certain things possible and other things impossible," how, then, does Israeli health infrastructure make Palestinian women's reproduction im/possible?[11]

To answer these questions, I revisit various sites of health infrastructure. I approach infrastructures of racialized medical knowledge, the segregation of majority Jewish Israeli cities and Palestinian towns, the scarcity of women's health services in the Naqab, affective infrastructures in East Jerusalem, and racial segregation in Israeli maternity wards as windows into the expansion of Jewish Israeli pronatalism and the strictures of Palestinian reproductive futurity. However, the work of infrastructure is always multiple. Infrastructures are not inherently colonial, but also essential for transformation; sites where the future can be assembled otherwise.[12] I thus also explore how Palestinian healthcare providers are actively assisting, fixing, bridging, and building infrastructure to work toward conditions of reproductive justice for Palestinian women.

I explore Israeli health infrastructure through interviews with Palestinian health scholars like Najwa and Palestinian physicians, healthcare providers, and activists. All of them are women, and they are all concerned with Palestinian women's reproductive and sexual health and rights. Their understanding of Israeli healthcare and reproductive injustice is not only informed by their experience of working in Israeli medical institutions but also by their own experience of this system *as* Palestinian women. Reconstructing the spatiality of reproductive injustice through their narratives about Palestinian health allows me to do two things. First, I show the various ways in which physical health infrastructures are coupled with affective or less visible infrastructures. Second, this focus on the limitations of Palestinian women's reproduction also tells a story about Palestinian resistance against reproductive injustice and my interview participants' refusal to be invisibilized by the structures of the settler state.

Attending to Palestinian counter-infrastructures, such as mobile clinics that cater to remote Palestinian communities in the Northern Galilee or the Naqab, the provision of reproductive and sexual health education in the West Bank, or the recognition of the vulnerability of Bedouin women in Israeli maternity wards demonstrates how Palestinian medical staff and activists reject pessimistic narratives and imaginaries of Palestinian lives as disposable, as epidemiologist Danya Qato puts it in the epigraph. I center their narratives about and experiences of the Israeli healthcare system to focus attention on how female Palestinian medical workers reclaim power in the Israeli medical system and thereby challenge and refuse its settler colonial foundations. Their work demonstrates the foundational principle of reproductive justice: Palestinian reproductive health and freedom are not just about surviving, but also about building the infrastructures needed to make autonomous reproductive decisions.[13]

'48 PALESTINIANS: THE "MINORITY HEALTH" FRAMEWORK AND INFRASTRUCTURES OF KNOWLEDGE

Najwa is a Palestinian health scholar who researches the structural dimensions of health inequalities between Jewish Israeli and Palestinian women. For Najwa, "Health is an outcome and a mirror of what's happening in society." Palestinian women's health lies at the center of an intersectional network of factors that shape not only their actual health and access to health services but also their assertiveness in the healthcare system and their relationship to their bodies.[14] Bringing together these overlapping modes of oppression, Najwa offered a sharp summary of the status of being a Palestinian woman in Israel:

> There are different factors that make the Palestinian woman more sick and less assertive in the healthcare system, and I think it relates to the Arab woman's status in Israel in general, being a woman in the Israeli system, being an Arab in Israel, but also the status for the Palestinian Arab woman inside the Palestinian society, it's also a lower status. Bringing the two together, you see a very complex picture that Arab women's health is poorer than other women's health, and you can see that Palestinian Arab women are less assertive when it comes to interaction with the healthcare system.

To be a Palestinian woman in Israel means she has to navigate both a patriarchal Israeli and Palestinian society,[15] as well as a legal system that relegates her to the site of settler colonial citizenship.[16] In this structure of space, gender, and racialization, Palestinian women are positioned at the periphery on every scale. Sociologist Sarab Abu-Rabia-Queder argues that in the case of Palestinian women, intersectionality and settler colonialism must be thought together. Palestinian women's different positionalities cannot be understood "without the context of the structured apparatus of power and violence in the settlement colonialist system."[17] Palestinian women's health outcomes are thus determined by their social and political status in the settler state and its history *as* a settler colonial endeavor.

Unsurprisingly, a historical and intersectional understanding of Palestinian women's health and health outcomes is not anchored in the majority of Israeli research on unequal health outcomes, despite it clearly reflecting the broader structures of inequality between Jewish Israelis and Palestinians. Palestinian women's life expectancy is 82.3 years compared to Jewish Israeli women's at 85.1 years. The neonatal mortality rate (per 1,000 live births) lies at 5.4 for Palestinian women and 2.4 for Jewish Israeli women.[18] In his analysis of these health outcomes, public health scholar Osama Tanous shows how the hegemonic framing of such differences relegates Palestinians to the status of a "minority" in Israel, comparing them to other groups of Jewish or non-Jewish immigrants, such as Asian migrant workers or Ethiopian Jews. Furthering the epistemological fragmentation of the Palestinians, studies on the health of Palestinians in the West Bank, East Jerusalem, or Gaza operationalize their research through the lens of "health in conflict zones" or migrant or refugee health.[19] Palestinians exist either as an apolitical minority, "on the other side" of the separation wall and barbed wire, or they do not exist at all in studies on health, medicine, and illness in Israel.[20] If Palestinian adverse health outcomes are discussed, they are explained through essentialized cultural, developmental, or behavioral factors or as determined by static and biologized understandings of race and ethnicity.[21] In my research with Jewish Israeli fertility doctors and medical staff, I would often encounter similar modes of explanation. A striking common notion among female fertility doctors was, for instance, to explain Palestinian women's infertility as caused by being overweight and a lack of willpower or interest in losing weight, which they would explain to me through a culturalist lens of otherness (see chapter 3).

This framing disconnects Palestinian health from settler colonialism and structural racism in the Israeli healthcare system. The research economy of Palestinian health invisibilizes Palestinians not only as people with a distinct history of oppression but also how their coercive inclusion in the Israeli state and its institutions is one of the drivers of their health outcomes. On an epistemological level, the "minority health" framing presents the transformation of Palestinians into settler colonial citizens of the Israeli state as a natural, nonconsequential, and completed transformation. On a medical level, it ignores the Nakba, structural racism, and psychosocial trauma as social, political, spatial, and economic determinants of Palestinians' health.[22] Najwa reflected on such ostensibly neutral and apolitical explanations of Palestinian health and their implicated health interventions. The way that Palestinian health was taught when she was in graduate school individualized Palestinians and their health outcomes, blaming them for "unhealthy habits" and refraining from any structural understanding of health, oppression, and marginalization. Najwa remembered:

> I heard how Palestinians are not OK, they are doing this to themselves, they are smoking, they are not eating healthy, they are eating olive oil, olive oil is not healthy—you know that time, twenty years ago. I said OK, I was listening to this, you want to believe, but you know that this is not right. So, coming back to the root causes, people changed their diet because the land was taken from the Palestinians, and they changed their lifestyle from agriculture to semi-industrial. This change was very rapid, very quick, and it was not accompanied by the support of the state.

Najwa connects the history of the Nakba and Palestinians' forced displacement and sedentarization to their changing health. Her reference to a lack of state support is crucial here, flipping the script of the historical narration of Palestinians as uncivilized and thus unhealthy and unhygienic Others.[23] Instead, she foregrounds Palestinians' positionality in Israeli society and their health outcomes as determined by their subordinate legal, political, and geographic status.

However, nothing much has changed since Najwa went to grad school. She shared how she and her colleagues keep addressing the Palestinian health gap and its political and historical root causes. She talked about how, for years, the Israeli Ministry of Health would not acknowledge their reports, papers, and research presentations on Palestinian health disparities. Instead, the official Israeli narrative would either defer to culturalist assumptions about Palestinian habits and lifestyle choices or refer to their places of residency as an individual choice that determined their lack of access to health infrastructure. This ignores the political and historical reasons why there is a lack of health services in these areas, as well as the ongoing active destruction of Palestinian rural and urban space and related health consequences.[24] The Judaization and military control of Palestinian localities both within Israel and the West Bank, as well as the de-urbanization of pre-1948 Palestinian urban centers, have restricted Palestinian rural and urban development.[25] In the south and the north of the country, where most of Israel's 21 percent of Palestinian citizens live today, the Israeli state and public planners actively work to transform Palestinian villages and small towns into enclaves to allow for ongoing Jewish Israeli land grabs and the maintenance of demographic balance on a spatial level.[26] The Israeli state invests in public infrastructure in majority Jewish Israeli areas while Palestinian dispossession and "urbicide" continue at the same time.[27] Palestinian towns in Israel are thus cut off from essential infrastructures such as health and public transport, and Palestinian communities lack access to the resources to provide the services that are needed.

The Israeli circulation of ahistorical and apolitical frameworks of Palestinian health demonstrates how Palestinians are excluded as subjects with a specific history of oppression and related medical needs and health outcomes. This knowledge confirms hegemonic Israeli beliefs of Palestinians as "backward" and "irresponsible." It mirrors similar histories of medical knowledge production in North America, in which white bodies remain the political and epidemiological focus.[28] In the Israeli case, what gets circulated is a Jewish Israeli–centric discourse about health, in which the Palestinian appears as an atavistic Other or does not appear at all. This affects not only how Jewish Israelis approach their Palestinian patients through a unidimensional lens, but also the Palestinian medical staff themselves. Najwa reflected on this as a Palestinian health scholar: "It's about hegemony because, you know, once you read all these studies, you absorb this information, and you start to believe it, and this is a third type of discrimination, you start to discriminate against yourself and against your people." This infrastructure of knowledge production further inscribes anti-Palestinian racism into the Israeli healthcare system and alienates Palestinians from seeking the healthcare services they might need.

INFRASTRUCTURES OF REPRODUCTIVE INJUSTICE

Within Israel's borders, spatial segregation is a major cause of Palestinians' lack of access to healthcare. This affects Palestinian women in particular and further undergirds the need for an intersectional and infrastructural analysis of Palestinian women's reproductive rights and health. For Palestinian women who live in predominantly Palestinian towns with a scarcity of healthcare services, their main point of contact would often be a Palestinian physician they know, or a family relative who works in healthcare. According to Najwa and other Palestinian women who shared their experience of accessing reproductive and sexual health services with me, this lack of healthcare infrastructure means that Palestinian women would feel less comfortable sharing difficult questions or concerns with their primary healthcare physician. A lack of anonymity and a fear of stigma in more conservative parts of Palestinian society shape Palestinian women's self-confidence and agency in navigating reproductive and sexual health services. This lack of choice and the accessibility of appropriate health services entrench Palestinian women's multiple forms of oppression in space.[29] Najwa further explained this by referring to the inaccessibility of women's health services in Palestinian towns:

> Palestinian women live in places far from clinical services. For example, a woman who needs mammography has to travel to another town, a Jewish town, because mammograms are not offered in Arab localities. She needs to pay more money because she has to travel, maybe she doesn't have this money because she's not working, and it is more likely that she's not working in comparison to a Jewish woman. And if she doesn't speak the language,

> then there is another barrier, so all of these barriers come together to form a complex picture that Palestinian women have less access to healthcare services.

An ordering of space that allows for the flourishing and health of Israeli society appears across transportation, work, and language, disallowing Palestinian women's (re)productive mobilities. On the level of health infrastructure, Israel's biospatial politics reveal how reproductive injustice is inscribed into the daily flow of knowledge, resources, and technology.[30]

While Najwa's explanation applies to women's health services in general, an analysis of more specific and technologically advanced reproductive services, such as assisted reproductive technology, further demonstrates what Israeli health infrastructures enable and what they foreclose. Looking at a map of Israel, what is noticeable at first glance is the topography of Israel's fertility economy. Most of Israel's fertility clinics are located in central Israel and West Jerusalem, while one large hospital in Beersheba caters to the populations in the south, and only one large clinic close to Tiberias caters to patients who live north of Haifa. The Northern Galilee areas face a historic scarcity of reproductive health services.[31] The spatial infrastructure of Israel's fertility economy is not coincidental and further disconnects Palestinians from implementing their reproductive choices. Historian Himmat Zu'bi notes how this distance from Israeli hospitals intersects with other factors that marginalize Palestinian women:

> Fertility clinics are located in hospitals at large distances from Arab villages and cities. Women often become dependent on others for transportation and mobility. Usually, this dependence entails courting favor from their husband's side of the family, since they usually reside closer to them.[32]

Salam is a senior physician who works in the IVF department of a large public hospital in the Tel Aviv area and lives in a small town along the border of the occupied West Bank. Among Palestinian and Jewish Israeli medical staff as well as scholars and activists in the field of reproductive and sexual health and rights, Salam was well known, and people I talked to about my research project would always mention her name. Salam and I discussed her Palestinian patients' experiences of undergoing fertility treatment in Israeli hospitals and clinics, and met a few times over the years. During our first interview, Salam explained to me how Palestinians' spatial segregation exacerbates their access to and participation in the Israeli fertility economy:

SALAM: Formally, all are equal, so all are getting the same service, also the same complicated service. However, the accessibility is sometimes problematic. I think that you should have nearby hospitals, nearby clinic units. Sometimes, more sophisticated treatments are not available, or people are not aware of them because what they talk about in Tel Aviv is not the same as somewhere else, which I think is normal, it's just about the main cities, or suburbs, or compared to the countryside, in any other place in the world. But because there's ethnic partition between the people here, it also comes in terms of national and ethnic issues.

GALA: Also, because some people can't afford to live in Tel Aviv.

SALAM: Most of them don't want to live in Tel Aviv. Just to make it clear, most of them don't want to, because there's a personal cost that you don't want to pay, with the education of children, what kind of culture.... Even my son, who is young, twenty years old, it has never crossed his mind that he wants to live in Tel Aviv for good, maybe to study or something, but not for good, because he wants an Arab environment, for his family and children. How you raise your children it's just like ... in general, minorities think in order to protect their own self, their own existence.

In this exchange, Salam makes a broader argument about Israeli health infrastructure, settler colonialism, and reproductive justice. When I offered my reading of racialized housing inequalities between metropolitan and rural areas within Israel's '48 borders, Salam firmly interjected, making it clear that not living in Tel Aviv or other predominantly Jewish Israeli areas is not only a condition of the settler colonial ordering of space but also a Palestinian choice. By connecting the spatio-political and historical reasons for Palestinian women's distance from advanced biomedicine with Palestinian agency and choice in placemaking, she refers to an important dimension of reproductive justice. Reproductive justice is not only concerned with access and the means and resources needed to implement reproductive choices, but also with the right to parent children in safe, healthy, and enabling environments.[33] And this includes, in Salam's words, education, culture, language, and an "Arab environment." In 2018, the Israeli state passed the nation-state law, assigning the Arabic language a "special status" and legalizing the ongoing practice of establishing Jewish-only settlements.[34] The Israeli educational sector is centered around promoting Zionist and militaristic values and actively excludes Palestinian history as well as Palestinian students who challenge the hegemonic Zionist narrative. As a result, the Palestinian and the Jewish Israeli educational (pre-university) sectors are segregated.[35] If

Palestinians are included in Israeli space, institutions, or society, their inclusion is based on their status as a minority, a "stranger" in their own land.[36] Salam thus highlights that Palestinians are not only forcibly dispossessed from their lands and spatially segregated, but to protect their existence, identity, and language, Palestinians also refuse to be included in Jewish Israeli society and its institutions.[37]

Salam's insistence on clarifying this point, and her personal and affective investment in getting her point across—bringing in her own son as an example—offers two interconnected readings of Palestinian practices of refusal. Israeli settler sovereignty relies on and is produced through the continued attempts to erase Palestinians' Indigenous sovereignty.[38] To insist on Palestinian Indigenous sovereignty outside of Israeli hegemonic settler space thus challenges inclusion in a system that is based on Palestinian dispossession, be it legally, spatially, or culturally. Salam's interjection that there is a personal cost for Palestinians if they were to move to Tel Aviv is a refusal to be placed in the framework of settler colonial recognition and reclaims Palestinians' sovereign relationship to the land of Palestine.

I also read this conversation as an ethnographic limit that starkly illuminates my own limitations as a non-Palestinian trying to make sense of Palestinians' access to the Israeli fertility economy. My interjection demonstrates how, in that moment, I only saw moving to Tel Aviv through an economic lens, and reproductive justice as a form of redistribution of resources. However, as anthropologist Audra Simpson reminds us, the "practice of refusal, one of various sorts, revenges the conceit of easy politics, of the very notion that Indigenous peoples had all things been equal would have consented to have things taken, things stolen from them."[39] In this conversation with Salam, my way of approaching Palestinians' access to reproductive technology was limited by the "conceit of easy politics"—that if Palestinians had more resources, they would possibly live closer to medical infrastructures. My point of view in this conversation exemplifies Simpson's argument about the "ruse of consent," that there can be justice within an existing settler colonial structure.[40] Salam's insistence on Palestinian sovereignty, agency, and a refusal of recognition and inclusion demonstrates the multilayeredness of what reproductive justice entails as a concept developed to describe the reality of Black, Indigenous, and women of color. Full reproductive justice for Palestinians would not only include access to culturally, linguistically, and easily accessible reproductive options, but also Indigenous sovereignty and living in a free Palestinian society, one that protects their existence, culture, and identity. In refusing my making sense of what she said, Salam escapes any "easy politics" and, in so doing, challenges my understanding of reproductive justice.

The settler colonial ordering of space and Israeli infrastructures allow simultaneously for the flourishing of settler colonial futurity and expansion and for the destruction of Palestinian life. The fact that Palestinian women cannot easily access advanced reproductive technologies unless they live in or have the means to travel to majority–Jewish Israeli areas illustrates this on two levels. Palestinians' reproductive movements and decision-making are slowed down, interrupted, or barred by spatial segregation, while the reason for their distance to such infrastructure is the historical and ongoing destruction of Palestinian infrastructures at the hands of the Israeli state. Salam's call-in further exemplifies the infrastructural dimension of reproductive justice, not just as a material analysis but also as a way of knowing the world centered in Black and anticolonial feminist thought.

THE BEDOUIN POPULATION OF THE NAQAB AND COUNTER-INFRASTRUCTURES

The relationship between racialization and dispossession, land, sovereignty, and reproductive injustice also appears in the case of the Indigenous Bedouin population in the south of Israel. The Bedouin population is a group within the population of Palestinians in Israel. About two-thirds of the Bedouin population live in townships that the Israeli state built from the 1960s to the 1980s. The remaining third chose to stay on their lands in the Naqab, in villages that the Israeli state refuses to recognize. As a result, their houses and built infrastructures are routinely denied permits or demolished, forcing many to live in tents and other temporary dwellings. There are about thirty-five unrecognized villages that the Israeli state considers illegal. Residents of the unrecognized villages face the constant threat of Israeli eviction and home demolitions, driven by the aim to Judaize the Naqab further and to end Bedouins' claim to their historical land and rights.[41]

Even though Palestinian Bedouins hold Israeli citizenship, they are not entitled to vote or run for political office. A lack of basic infrastructure, such as water, electricity, public transportation, education, and health services, exacerbates their legal exclusion. This lack of basic services and the ongoing demolition of their villages determine the Bedouin population's health outcomes.[42] Bedouin women and mothers bear the gendered brunt of these conditions, displaying high levels of emotional distress, postpartum depression, high levels of infant mortality, and other health conditions.[43]

Layla is a Bedouin physician in her thirties who specialized in internal medicine and volunteers in an organization to promote equality in medical care for Arabs and Palestinians. From a young age onward, Layla worked with organizations supporting Bedouin women to promote their equality both in the Bedouin community as women and in Israeli society as Arabs. Sitting in a sunny café in Yafa in the summer of 2020, Layla shared with me her understanding of Bedouin women's positionality in the settler state. Having worked with Bedouin women in a variety of settings, including in the hospital at which she is currently employed, Layla cares deeply about Bedouin women's health-related struggles and, more specifically, their reproductive and sexual health.

Like Najwa, Layla explained the multilayered and decidedly infrastructural forms of oppression Bedouin women experience: "I'm gonna focus on healthcare, but inequality shows on many levels, from building permits for housing, the water, the electricity, and so on." The Bedouin population's general living conditions are woven into their status as an oppressed Indigenous group. To further exemplify this point, Layla talked about Bedouin women's access to prenatal care and how cultural, linguistic, and geographic factors intersect in their experiences:

> For example, prenatal care and pregnancy screening. One of the things is the lack of awareness of the importance of testing; there are no campaigns in Arabic or campaigns that are accessible, that get to the different sections of Bedouin society. Some of the campaigns or ads are only in Hebrew or are formulated in a way that is only accessible to modern women, Arab women from the north, and so on, and less so to Bedouin women. But they need it even more there, in the Bedouin community. . . . Many of them, most of them, they don't see a gynecologist, they don't have prenatal screening, and not to speak about testing the parents for genetic diseases before trying to get pregnant, as in family planning. But also after that, to get the ultrasound, and the testing, which mostly has to be done in the first trimester, there was research done that compared the prenatal screening between women in recognized towns and women in unrecognized villages, and it was shown that most women in the recognized town did have prenatal screening in the first trimester, which is the most critical one to find if there are any abnormalities and plan for that, while most of the women in the unrecognized villages it happened in the second trimester, sometimes even in the third trimester if at all, so that also proved that it's also a problem of access itself.

Layla foregrounds class differences among Palestinian women. Israeli infrastructures are elastic and adaptable in that sense, providing information that more educated "modern" women from the north can access easily, while Bedouin women with less access to education might struggle to understand. She also attributes differences in accessing prenatal screening to whether Bedouin women live in recognized or unrecognized villages or towns, further stressing the relationship between settler space and reproductive health. These conditions translate into cumulated occurrences of genetic diseases and high rates of infant mortality and morbidity, which, in turn, affect the mothers of these children in a gendered way. Layla explained:

> So, as a result, a lot of genetic diseases exist. There is a very high rate of infant mortality, and there is a very high rate of morbidity among children and infants, which adds a burden on the family, which usually comes from a very low socioeconomic background. So, when it comes to prenatal care, it falls on the women. It falls on the mom to take care of the baby, and a lot of the time, they are also blamed, in society itself, if they have these children.

Understood through the lens of reproductive justice, Bedouin women's rights to have children, safe pregnancies, and the resources to raise their children in a healthy and enabling environment are impeded on several intersecting levels. Bedouin women from the Naqab lack access to and knowledge of proper pre- and postnatal care, which may result in complications during pregnancy and birth and can lead to a gendered burden of responsibility to care for disabled or sick children. Bedouin women are predominantly affected by language barriers, a lack of cultural sensitivity in Israeli healthcare, a lack of access to housing, and outright racism against the Bedouin population.[44]

At the time of my interview with Layla, I had talked to quite a few Palestinian physicians, scholars, or activists like her, who were all working at the interface where the Israeli state and its (health) infrastructure failed to provide for its Palestinian citizens and occupied subjects. We were talking about this deliberate disengagement on the part of the Israeli state, or "vacuum," as Layla called it. I asked her how she felt about intervening and thereby, in a sense, normalizing the settler state's ongoing and organized abandonment of Palestinian and Bedouin communities.[45] Layla said: "When I try to actually think about that, I feel like . . . in a way again, I feel like I'm not angry, I'm not surprised, I'm not disappointed, which is very sad. I'm saying I'm used to it, it's OK in a way, but it's not." Layla's reflective response points to her complicated positionality vis-à-vis Israeli infrastructure. She is aware and critical of how Palestinian (reproductive) health is curtailed, but she also wants to step in to provide relief for Bedouin women.

NGOs such as the group Layla volunteers with, or organizations like Physicians for Human Rights Israel, step in to fill this vacuum, fixing or bridging Israeli health infrastructures where Palestinian reproduction and sustenance are curtailed. Both within Israel's '48 borders, the occupied West Bank, and before October 7, also in Gaza, these organizations provide mobile clinics to offer health services that would otherwise not reach Palestinian populations. "So, a mobile clinic is like, you want to create this solution, but it's really not optimal," Layla reflected. Additional resources need to be mobilized to reach marginalized Palestinian communities, and they rely on medical volunteers to offer their services, many of whom are Palestinian or Bedouin themselves. Their work includes broadening Israeli infrastructure by offering more accessible services or bringing medical technologies closer to Palestinian localities. However, their work also includes mediating between the marginalized and racialized communities and a system they experience as hostile and racist.[46] Layla explained:

> I guess another thing is also that people don't trust a lot of the services that are provided, especially if they don't speak Hebrew well. Israeli hospitals, these places are unknown, unfamiliar to them. So, in a way, it's OK that there are NGOs that are based in local communities and [work with] people that know them, and they talk in the same language and on the same level. But NGOs shouldn't try to replace what is basic, what they should get.

In that sense, these organizations, and volunteers like Layla, also set up "alimentary infrastructures" offering a supportive and transformative network against the organized abandonment the Bedouin community experiences at the hands of the Israeli state.[47] In establishing these counter-infrastructures, Palestinian healthcare providers, activists, and scholars remind us of the slow and transformative work of thinking, building, and fighting for new worlds; new worlds in which Palestinian women's health, well-being, and reproduction are central.

BORDERS, CHECKPOINTS, AND LANGUAGE BARRIERS IN EAST JERUSALEM

The relationship between the settler colonial ordering of space and reproductive injustice also materializes in Palestinian women's lives in occupied East

Jerusalem. In 1967, Israel unlawfully annexed East Jerusalem and legally separated Palestinians living in East Jerusalem from Palestinians in the West Bank by assigning them the status of "permanent residents" (which comes with a blue "Jerusalem ID"). This legal status transforms Palestinian Jerusalemites into stateless foreigners in their own city, who, unlike Jewish Israelis and Jews from the diaspora, cannot easily settle and receive citizenship in Jerusalem. Their residency status is fragile and can be revoked, for example, when a Jerusalemite Palestinian stays abroad for too long or cannot prove that their center of life is indeed Jerusalem. Unlike citizenship, residency status cannot be passed on to children. To be eligible to apply for Jerusalem residency status, Palestinian children must be born in a Jerusalem hospital. Demographic anxieties lie at the core of these policies and continue to legitimize the ongoing efforts to evict Palestinian residents of East Jerusalem.[48]

Being legally defined as a "permanent resident" determines the intimate life of Palestinians living in East Jerusalem and affects Palestinian women in particular. Based on her long-standing research with East Jerusalem Palestinians, feminist legal scholar Nadera Shalhoub-Kevorkian finds that "[s]ituated as foreigners/invaders in their own native lands, a demographically undesirable population, and the reproducers of Palestinians, Palestinian women (and their unborn or newborn children) are made especially vulnerable."[49] Palestinian women in East Jerusalem face particular challenges navigating urban space *as* women. The Israeli military not only regularly invades the private and intimate domains of Palestinian homes but also public spaces such as the Al-Aqsa compound in the Old City, where Palestinian women gather.[50] These normalized and ongoing military interventions are often carried out in a gendered or sexually degrading way and shape Palestinian women's reproductive autonomy and pregnancy outcomes. For instance, a common fear among East Jerusalemite women is an unplanned birth in an area outside of Israel-defined Jerusalem, thereby foreclosing the possibility of applying for a Jerusalem ID for their future child. Pregnant women share how they have restricted their movement during the time of pregnancy, which leads to additional adverse health effects such as anxiety, stress, or elevated blood sugar and pressure.[51] The Jerusalem municipality furthermore denies Palestinians in East Jerusalem building permits, and many families face the constant threat of house demolition. This ongoing reality further exacerbates Palestinian women's freedom of movement and their feeling of security in East Jerusalem and has serious health repercussions.[52]

While East Jerusalemites are denied basic political rights that Israeli citizens have, like voting in the Knesset and holding a passport, they have the right to work in Israel and receive social benefits such as Israeli health insurance.[53] The majority of permanent residents in East Jerusalem study in Palestinian-run educational institutions with a Palestinian curriculum taught in Arabic. Resisting their inclusion in the Israeli educational system centered around Zionism and militarization means that many East Jerusalemites are not fluent in Hebrew.[54] This puts them in a complicated relationship vis-à-vis the Israeli institutions they are included in but not a part of. Indeed, it is precisely the mechanism of precarious inclusion in permanent statelessness that offers Palestinians in East Jerusalem access to more resources than Palestinians in the occupied West Bank, while it simultaneously entraps them in East Jerusalem and curbs any efforts of social mobility.[55]

In one of our conversations, Salam and I talked about the particularity of the situation of Palestinian women undergoing fertility treatment in Jerusalem. Salam summarized their complicated reality:

> They cannot afford private treatment in the West Bank, and they are pushed to the Israeli side, also because of better technology, but part of it because it might be covered, it might be funded, which is very attractive. I think they swallow their feelings and keep going, because it's very complicated, they are poor, they can't afford it, there is no accessibility, even if they want to go to the West Bank, it's not insured there. Then to go to your foe for your treatment, it's against any instinct.

While Palestinian women with a Jerusalem ID are eligible for fertility treatment as part of their insurance plan, they might in fact prefer to undergo IVF or artificial insemination in the West Bank. However, fertility treatment in the West Bank is costly and more difficult to reach due to the separation wall and checkpoints. Furthermore, the Palestinian medical infrastructure in the West Bank is less developed and technically inferior to the Israeli biomedical and healthcare sectors. This is also true for East Jerusalem. In search of Palestinian-administered clinics offering fertility treatment, I visited Palestinian-run medical institutions in East Jerusalem, such as a clinic in Sheikh Jarrah or the Christian Augusta Victoria Hospital. However, in both clinics, I was told that they only provide basic obstetric and gynecological services and do not offer fertility treatment. Palestinian patients will only receive preliminary tests for infertility, such as ultrasounds, follicular tests, and hormonal profiling. For further procedures of fertility treatment, such as sperm count, hysteroscopy, as well as the fertility treatment itself (IVF, ICSI, or artificial insemination), patients at the Palestinian clinics will be referred to one of the major Israeli hospitals, which are staffed with fertility specialists and equipped with advanced biomedical technology.[56] Palestinians in East Jerusalem are thus not only financially incentivized to undergo treatment in Israeli hospitals but are also literally "pushed" to Israeli institutions, given the scarcity and underfunding of Palestinian-run clinics.

Salam, a physician herself who works alongside her Jewish Israeli colleagues in the fertility department in Tel Aviv, also reflected on how the spatial and structural conditions of occupied East Jerusalem translate into medical encounters between patients and doctors. Talking about this topic, she expressed herself carefully, questioning how her Jewish colleagues might approach their Palestinian patients in Jerusalem:

> Even some of the medical staff members, they might not mean it, or there were no bad intentions. I assume there were no bad intentions, really. I want to keep believing that the medical staff are different and that they are committed to their values. They are my colleagues, and I know the material they are made of, but the situation [in Jerusalem] is bad.

Salam does not specify exactly what she thinks her colleagues "might not mean," but her acknowledgment of East Jerusalem women's pain and difficulty in receiving fertility treatment with her Israeli colleagues—their "enemy"—conveys her sentiment clearly. Salam and I met a few times, and while she spoke openly about the difficulties Palestinian patients face across Palestine/Israel, she would always be cautious in talking about her Jewish colleagues and their intentions. In our last interview, during which I told her that I needed to stop doing fieldwork soon and get to writing my PhD, Salam concluded: "It's very hard, it's very hard. I think to talk about East Jerusalem and reproduction is another PhD."

In East Jerusalem, I also interviewed Hanan, the executive director of a sexual and reproductive health and rights nongovernmental organization that mainly serves the Palestinian population in the West Bank and East Jerusalem. To explain the differently fragmented health infrastructures in Jerusalem to me, Hanan also shared her own experience as a resident of East Jerusalem. Hanan speaks English with an American accent and is more fluent than most Jewish Israeli physicians I interviewed. And yet, she reflected on language barriers and how they intersect with a feeling of animosity, similar to what Salam had described:

> Sometimes I do have problems with the language, but because my English is good, it helps, even though it doesn't work all the time. So, it helps, but it's also a burden. Even my insurance company, they have a website and they don't have it in English or Arabic, so they say, "OK, get your test results from the website" or whatever, or you get a call, so I could read the [Hebrew] letters, but I don't understand really.... When you go to really specialized doctors, you feel like they're more on their side than on our side, so when things get tough, it's where [unclear, mumbles] ... but really when things get serious and you'll have to go ...

Hanan describes three levels of exclusion and oppression she experiences as a Palestinian resident of East Jerusalem accessing health services in Israeli medical institutions. First, there is the practical, bureaucratic machinery of the health system, which works in Hebrew, even though, at one of the largest Israeli hospitals in Jerusalem, almost 50 percent of the patients are Palestinians from East Jerusalem or the West Bank.[57] Second, there is the spatial reality of a fragmented and occupied city, forcing some Palestinians to cross checkpoints every time they need to go to the hospital, not to mention the everyday hardship of fearing the revocation of their residency status, house demolitions, and ongoing military violence. And finally, these very material circumstances translate on a more affective level, the complicated "burden" of being part of a system that is based on one's own dispossession. Hanan said that when she needs to see a specialized doctor, "you feel like they're more on their side than on our side." This feeling of not being able to trust your physician, especially in a medical emergency or difficult situation, adds to the already existing structural inequalities Palestinians face in the Israeli health system. It echoes how Salam questioned some of her Jewish Israeli colleagues' conduct and her description of Palestinian women having to "swallow their feelings" if they want to undergo fertility treatment in Jerusalem. Hanan's tentativeness and her incomplete sentences in trying to convey what happens when "things get tough" medically illustrate the difficulty of having trust in a system that declared as its official state policy to keep Palestinians a demographic minority.[58] Undergoing fertility treatment in this system, as Salam has put it, "is against any instinct."

Similar to the work that Najwa and Layla are involved in, the organization that Hanan directs offers regional services such as providing women's health mobile clinics and information events on family planning in the West Bank. They are also advocating and lobbying for changes in policy and law related to sexual and reproductive health and rights, as well as gender-based violence in the occupied territories. The organization's main focus is on "the prevention of unsafe abortions," which Hanan told me was the language they used to refer to abortions and contraception to work within the more conservative parts of Palestinian society.[59] Hanan explained the different services her organization provides or used to provide. In so doing, she illustrates the choppiness of reproductive and sexual health infrastructures across the fragmented Palestinian territories:

> For the West Bank, it might be to broaden Palestinian women's rights and decision-making with respect to sexual and reproductive health, for them to actually make the right choices about family planning methods, and even in accessing services and so forth. In Gaza, we don't provide sexual and reproductive health now. We used to, years back, but the reason we don't anymore is actually because of the situation there, and everyone is going to UNRWA now and receiving services free of charge, so I really don't know right now what the situation is in Gaza, particularly. In Jerusalem, it's a whole different ball game, as you can imagine. We're talking about the Palestinians living in Jerusalem, so me, as a Palestinian living in Jerusalem, I have my Israeli medical insurance, and everything is fine, I should be able to receive resources as any other person in the country. Where you would have problems... are the ones with the [family] reunifications, those who have applied for reunification but their procedure is still in process, so they still don't have medical insurance and medical rights. Sometimes, even traveling, going and coming from the areas with closures and the checkpoints and so forth, is difficult, and they don't even want to go in or out, they're afraid. And to receive services in Jerusalem is extremely expensive if you are not covered by medical insurance.

In the occupied West Bank, her organization's focus is on services, education, and policy, while the situation in occupied East Jerusalem is more ambivalent, echoing Salam's description of Palestinian women's status of liminality and Hanan's own experience. Hanan's description of family reunification in cases in which one of the partners lives on the West Bank side of the separation wall describes the reality of family life under occupation and the ways in which borders and checkpoints are only the materially visible infrastructures of Israeli colonial bureaucracy, surveillance, and control.[60] Women bear the brunt of such policies and architecture, especially if they are in need of medical treatment or in cases of pregnancy.

The case of Jerusalem shows how the patchworking of infrastructures is an intentional effect of Israeli spatial, political, and demographic governance. Israeli health infrastructure in Jerusalem variously includes or excludes Palestinians with different legal statuses vis-à-vis the settler state. Whether or not Palestinians hold Israeli health insurance, their access to Israeli health services is limited, blocked, disconnected, or interrupted by various borders, barriers, or symbolic boundaries, including racism, language, and militarization. Organizations like the one Hanan works for step in to provide sexual and reproductive health services to Palestinians in the West Bank and occupied East Jerusalem. However, the situation on the ground requires them to attend to many issues at the same time, and working across the occupation and within Palestinian society means that these counter-infrastructures are often choppy and incomplete. This reality and the effects it has on Palestinian women who want to get pregnant alert us once more to the spatiality of Israeli settler colonialism.

INTERIOR FRONTIERS AND SOFT INFRASTRUCTURES: AFFECT AND TRUST

In conversations and interviews, Palestinian medical professionals and activists would repeatedly foreground how Palestinian women's lack of reproductive freedom and autonomy; language barriers; and experiences of racism translated into a lack of assertiveness in their medical encounters with the Israeli healthcare system. Recall, for instance, Najwa's observation at the outset of this chapter, that what makes Palestinian women more sick and less assertive is their complicated status as women *and* as Palestinians. Persisting structural inequalities in the settler colonial healthcare system intersect with and reinforce other gendered and racialized structures of oppression in Israeli society.[61] Palestinian women's embodied experiences of trying to get pregnant in the Israeli fertility economy reveal a complex picture of varying forces of oppression. The different materiality of infrastructures is important to recognize here. There are hard infrastructures, such as actual borders, checkpoints, spatial segregation, or no access to public transport (or other means to sustain everyday life), that directly affect Palestinian women's ability to implement their reproductive choices. But in the narratives of Layla, Hanan, and Salam, we can also trace a different quality of infrastructures. Less obvious, differently felt infrastructures centered around affect, accessibility, language, or culture also shape Palestinian women's reproduction and pregnancy outcomes. Infrastructure not only gives immediate material and concrete form to how life is provisioned or curtailed, it is also about how sociality itself is reproduced.[62] Emotions and the affective are important registers through which such soft infrastructures are regulated.[63]

During her time as a doctor in training, Layla, the Bedouin physician of internal medicine, wanted to specialize in gynecology to work with Bedouin women and help them navigate Israeli medical institutions during an already intense experience such as childbirth. However, when it was her turn to undergo rotation to work in the delivery room and the high-risk pregnancy unit, Layla quickly changed her mind. How her Jewish Israeli colleagues treated their Bedouin patients before and during childbirth was too difficult for her to bear:

> One of the things that was an eye-opener for me about how they treat [Bedouin] women was the high-risk pregnancy unit. Often these women's pregnancies are in danger, and they're so scared, so insecure, looking for answers, all the time looking up and like trying to find the security or something to calm them down. The doctors on rotation would come into their room—now, they would talk to a Jewish woman, and they will talk to her, they will explain things to her, they will look into her eyes, and they will be there, and if she will cry, they will hold her hands. And then, when they reach the bed of a Bedouin woman, they will talk above her, as in, they wouldn't talk to her, they will only talk in Hebrew, they wouldn't translate. Often, they wouldn't know that I could translate. I speak Arabic, but they didn't even ask me for help because they didn't even see why it is important to speak to her in Arabic and explain to her what was going on, even when you could see that she's lost and scared and so on. And this, for me, was, I think, one of the reasons why I decided not to go to that department. Maybe it was a mistake, but I found myself at a point where I didn't want to join the rounds because it was so bad. And also, after the rounds were finished, I would go back and speak to the women and try to give them this feeling of familiarity in a way.

Layla's experience in the delivery room and the high-risk pregnancy unit illustrates how discrimination, racism, or medical neglect are articulated on the affective and emotive level.[64] Language, in Layla's description, is not only a material barrier that can be overcome; language is also about *how* physicians talk to their patients. Bedouin women's particular vulnerability in this situation was not a consideration for Layla's Jewish Israeli colleagues. Furthermore, she found that her colleagues' treatment of their Bedouin patients resulted in their devaluation, not taking them seriously, and not attending to them with the same care they would extend to a Jewish Israeli woman speaking Hebrew. Layla tried to mitigate their patients' feelings by attending to them after the daily rounds were done, giving them a "feeling of familiarity" by speaking to them in their language and attending to their needs. This is another form of a counter-infrastructure, or "alimentary infrastructure," that Palestinian medical staff set up to make space for their Palestinian or Bedouin patients.[65]

In these instances, the hard infrastructures of settler colonialism as a social structure translate into soft infrastructures and shape the reproductive experiences of Bedouin women in the Israeli hospital. To capture the affective and corporeal experiences of those borders and barriers that have a more ephemeral quality, anthropologist Ann Laura Stoler introduced the notion of an "interior frontier."[66] Interior frontiers, Stoler writes, readily include some people, while for anyone designated as dangerous or other, interior frontiers become checkpoints and their trespassing becomes a threat. As citizens of the Israeli state, Bedouin women are granted entry to its institutions, such as the hospital, and yet they are made to feel that they will never fully belong. Layla further reflected on these medical encounters and how a distance between Jewish Israeli medical providers and Bedouin patients is maintained. This distance is neither material nor just linguistic or cultural:

> I feel a lot of times the compliance of the patient depends on the way you talk to them, you know, when you talk to them on their own level, when you talk to them in their language, when you use words that you know that are close to them. . . . And also, our health is very affected by how our soul feels. So, when you come to a place where someone is actually holding your hand and is looking into your eyes, and you feel like they're having empathy for you, and you're feeling what they're feeling, you'll get that security and your soul feels better and that affects your health and the process itself, if it's getting pregnant or whatever.

Empathy, kindness, and respect are difficult to measure, yet these factors determine health outcomes in a significant way. Indeed, as research on Palestinian women in the Israeli healthcare system has shown, Maternal Respectful Care (MRC) is an important factor for postpartum PTSD among marginalized women.[67] Components to identify MRC are privacy, dignity, respect, autonomy, and shared decision-making. These components echo Layla's observations. In Israel, the prevalence of postpartum depression is significantly higher among Palestinian women in comparison to the Jewish Israeli part of the population, exposing the relationship between settler colonialism and Palestinian health.[68]

These findings reflect the broader contours of racialized access to health. Structural racism in the healthcare system enables a culture of differential treatment, and more subtle forms of racism have a significant impact on racialized patients' health outcomes, especially in the realm of pre- and postnatal care.[69] Undergoing fertility treatment is a stressful experience in itself, and the success rate of getting pregnant relies on the patient's overall emotional well-being.[70] How Palestinian women are treated by their gynecologists or in the fertility clinic, as well as the (cumulative) stress they might experience on their way to the clinic or in trying to decipher a diagnosis in Hebrew, affects their health and pregnancy outcomes. Layla made that point in particular with fertility treatment in mind: "I think a lot of the time, the process itself is lonely and you go to a healthcare system that is very distant and very foreign to you, and also a lot of the time very discriminating and very patronizing, so the experience itself can become . . . lonely to traumatic even." The hard infrastructures of Israeli healthcare and its frontiers translate into the soft infrastructures of accessibility and emotional well-being. Such interior frontiers, in turn, become checkpoints and barriers that are usually invisible to those in positions of power.

Yara is a Palestinian health scholar who works in an Israeli NGO providing health services to Palestinians in Israel and the occupied West Bank, similar to the organizations Layla and Hanan work with. During one of our interviews, I shared with Yara an observation about some of my interviews with Palestinian women undergoing fertility treatment. When I asked some of the women I had met if they had experienced discrimination or racism in the fertility clinic, they replied that they had never had any such experiences or that they didn't know. I told Yara that I felt like some of my interview participants weren't comfortable enough to respond to my question, or that they didn't know how to convey their experiences of discrimination to me. Yara's response to that further emphasizes the ethnographic limits of my research. She asked me not to expect Palestinians to talk to me about their experiences of racism in the hospital. Reflecting on the particularity of the medical encounter, especially in the fertility clinic, Yara said:

> You want to trust your doctor, it's very important for the process of the treatment and for your own mental state. If you confess that you are not being

> treated like other people, or like Israelis, that you are treated differently because of who you are, I think people will hesitate to even confess this to themselves. You want to trust the doctor who is treating you, and victimizing yourself is not something that you want to do. I think that if there was another Palestinian sitting there, this would probably affect the way they react to the questions. I myself, with all the awareness of the political nuances and the situation, I don't think that I would, you know . . . maybe, maybe not, I'm not sure actually. You are vulnerable in the place that you are in as a patient. If I'm going to be a patient in an Israeli hospital, of course, I would feel vulnerable, simply because I'm a patient, so if you have another layer, like, being an Arab or Palestinian treated by an Israeli Jew, especially if you feel that he has some prejudice because you are an Arab, or he's going in with a kippa or she's a religious woman, then you automatically think that you are different, you will think that she is hostile, you think that she's afraid of you.

Similar to Layla, Yara highlights how important it is to feel safe and trust your physician for a successful medical outcome. Palestinian women are already in a more vulnerable position, as women, as Palestinians, and as patients. Yara describes my interview participants' reluctance to share experiences of racism or discrimination in the hospital as a mechanism of self-defense. Because even admitting to themselves that they might have experienced racist behavior would make it difficult to enter an already overdetermined situation with a medical professional, a professional they depend on to eventually get pregnant. At the same time, her contextualization reveals the emotional and symbolic boundaries that texture Israeli-Palestinian medical encounters. Reflecting on vulnerability and the justified fear that Palestinian patients will be treated differently by a Jewish Israeli doctor, Yara points to the inherent asymmetry in the medical encounter. Her description of the religious signifiers of Jewish Israeli doctors furthermore reveals the complexity of power relations and prejudice in an ethnonational state and a society that structures belonging according to a Jewish/non-Jewish binary.

But Yara's account also speaks to the ethnographic situation itself. She suggests that the women I interviewed are refusing to relive their experiences of racism for me.[71] They don't seek recognition in the interview situation, for recognition is not an antidote to injustice.[72] Some of my interview partners' experiences of injustice in the medical encounter become untranslatable in the research encounter because both situations are embedded in the same asymmetrical structures of power of settler colonialism. In that sense, the "scene of subjection" and the research encounter are structurally similar.[73]

Whether this ethnographic limit is born out of a strategic refusal, a subconscious mechanism of self-defense, or points to a reticence that signals discomfort or disinterest in the narrative forms available in the interview situation, perhaps matters less.[74] As Yara herself puts it, reflecting on how she would have replied to my question: "I don't think that I would, you know . . . maybe, maybe not, I'm not sure actually." This instance reveals less about the inner lives of my interview participants, or Yara's, but points to the uneven power dynamics that structure my intention to record Palestinian women's suffering. And yet, as Yara, Layla, and Salam's accounts illustrate, it is precisely the complicated register of the affective that materializes as another barrier Palestinian women experience on their journey to becoming pregnant.

Affective or soft infrastructures are central to the medical encounters between Palestinian patients and Jewish Israeli medical staff. However, it is precisely in this encounter that such infrastructures and what they circulate—feeling welcome, safe, and taken seriously—are invisible to those who could offer it, like the Jewish Israeli doctors Layla worked with. It is this disconnection of respect or humanity in the patient-doctor encounter that can be described as tender or slow forms of violence.[75] The effects of such violence, or blockage in the infrastructure, are felt by Palestinian and Bedouin women and physicians, but they are out of sight from the hegemonic Jewish Israeli position. Feminist or anticolonial infrastructures of care and attention, such as Layla's rounds after her official shift (and also some of my interview participants' refusal or discomfort to share certain experiences), exemplify the importance of refusing capitalist, extractive, or colonial forms of infrastructures.

MATERNITY WARDS: RACIAL SEGREGATION AND THE COMMODIFICATION OF HEALTHCARE

While the affective landscape and soft infrastructures of reproductive justice are largely invisible to those who are not negatively affected by it, other policies show openly how Israeli settler colonialism and its borders translate in medical space. In Israeli maternity wards, Jewish Israeli medical staff instituted the practice of spatially separating Palestinian (and other non-Jewish) and Jewish Israeli women after they give birth. This practice was established either upon the birthing woman's request or as a preemptive measure implemented by medical staff in Israeli hospitals. The practice of maternity ward segregation was reported as early as 2006 in the Israeli newspaper *Haaretz*. It has since been a topic of ongoing debate. Maternity ward segregation was subject to several investigations and a 2018 class action lawsuit, as well as the topic of a Knesset committee on "the Status of Women and Gender Equality, Segregation in Maternity Wards in Hospitals" in 2016.[76]

Pregnant women with Israeli citizenship are eligible to choose a hospital to give birth in, and, for each birth, the hospital will receive a payment from the National Insurance Institute. Israeli hospitals thus compete for women to come to their delivery rooms and are invested in complying with their patients' requests. Najwa explained this as a development of the neoliberalization of the Israeli healthcare system:

> What happened over the years is that the neoliberal economy in Israel reduced the funding for the healthcare system, including hospitals and maternity wards. The hospitals then found maternity wards and birthing women a good source of funding for them, so they wanted more and more women to give birth at the hospitals. They were willing, and are still willing, to do what a woman asked them to do, including discrimination against other women. So, if you live in a settlement and come to give birth in a hospital and you don't want to stay with a Palestinian woman, or an Ethiopian, or another immigrant woman, Russian, for instance, you'll say I don't want to stay with this woman, I want to stay with other women, and the hospital will allow it. This is how discrimination came into the maternity wards through the back door. The hospitals say we are doing this because we want to be culturally appropriate and sensitive to the women. But this is not about cultural appropriateness; this is about discrimination. You can't do separation without doing segregation in healthcare. You will give different care to different women staying in different spaces, and that's not right.

Requests for separation center around child-rich Jewish Israeli women in an increasingly Jewish supremacist society. Indeed, it is not surprising that Najwa refers to a woman from an illegal settlement in the West Bank to explain this practice. When the public debate about maternity ward segregation took off in 2016, it was the right-wing politician and West Bank settler Itamar Ben-Gvir, today's minister of finance, who tweeted that "it's only natural that my wife would not want to lie next to a woman giving birth to a baby who would want to slaughter her baby 20 years from now."[77] The anti-Palestinian trope that depicts Palestinian babies as future terrorists and thereby robs Palestinian children of their childhood has long since found its way into Israeli hospitals.[78]

In response to the class action lawsuit, in February 2019, three Israeli hospitals admitted that separating Jewish from non-Jewish women in their maternity wards was part of an unofficial policy. Kupat Holim Clalit, the health insurance company two of these hospitals were working with, responded to this revelation by normalizing racial segregation as part of Israeli society. In their statement, they argued that "not respecting the wishes of mothers for specific placement creates an 'enforced communal hospital stay' when both sides are not interested in this. The purpose of their stay is not to create an artificial melting pot."[79] This statement reflects a settler colonial reality that many liberal Israelis disregard. Israel is not a "melting pot," but a settler colonial society in which a mixing of Israeli and Palestinian populations is undesirable.

The categorization and racial hierarchies that structure Israeli society legitimize the practice of maternity ward segregation.[80] In a recorded phone call by a pregnant woman inquiring about segregation in the maternity ward, a nurse from HaEmek hospital in Afula said they would try to separate rooms based on cultural difference, language, and visitation hours.[81] While these indicators do not per se map onto a certain group of the population, their culturalist implications reference racial hierarchies between Jewish Israelis, Palestinians, and other non-Jewish groups in Israel. A recent study shows how such legitimizations are explained by medical staff.[82] The following quotation from a Jewish Israeli hospital director reveals the underlying racial logic of maternity ward segregation under the guise of "cultural sensitivity": "If there is a bed available and a woman wants to move, I will move her, no matter what the reason is: smell, amount of visitors. But if they will talk about other things such as that she is an Arab, ultra-Orthodox or Eritrean, she will be kicked out."[83] The placeholders of "smell" and "amount of visitors" are less overt and carefully formulated references to race and civilizational Zionist discourse, mirroring the transnational shift from biological to cultural racism.[84] The director even admits it themselves: Patients can speak openly in racist terms, but if they name the people they are referring to, they will get kicked out. This, indeed, is how discrimination came into the maternity ward "through the back door."

Racial categories that legitimize maternity ward segregation circulate widely in Israeli hospitals. For instance, in an analysis of a public debate of a Knesset committee on "the Status of Women and Gender Equality, Segregation in Maternity Wards in Hospitals" in 2016, Hadas Ziv, who works for the Israeli NGO Physicians for Human Rights Israel, presents the testimony of a Palestinian doctor, Lina Kassem, who speaks about her internship at the Shaare Zedek hospital in Jerusalem. Dr. Kassem not only experienced open segregation in the hospital's maternity ward but also saw how such segregation is racialized:

> I started my way as an intern in women's health. . . . I wish to reflect [on] what happens in Shaarei Zedek hospital. . . . I was also in Mt. Scopus in my internship where there is clear segregation in the maternity ward, the rooms of the Arabs are not mixed with [the] rooms of Jews. The midwife calls the nurse in the ward after the birth, and tells her I refer you [to] a "speaker" [not a Hebrew speaker] which is a code [for] . . . at least in Mt. Scopus . . . for an Arab. . . . It is true that the policy of the hospital is not supportive of racism, and I did not personally encounter racism, but the general atmosphere among midwives and nurses in the wards is blatantly racist especially in Shaarei Zedek. I invite you to spend a night in the labor rooms and listen to the talks. They do not call a woman by her name at all, they call her: the Ethiopian, the Arab, the Russian—this is the general atmosphere. An Arab woman [who] comes from East Jerusalem to give birth in Shaarei Zedek is [met] with [an attitude characterized by] many stereotypes and [by] prejudice. They assign them to the rooms at the end of the corridor. . . . I wish to share with you an experience: a midwife brings a new Arab baby to the babies' room, and the nurses tell her: what, you brought another terrorist?[85]

The midwives' reference to a Palestinian woman who just gave birth as a (non-Hebrew) "speaker" illustrates how racial categories are encoded. And while Dr. Kassem doesn't recount racist experiences herself, she talks about how racial categories and demographic anxieties shape medical staff's conduct in the hospital's maternity ward. Her testimony also points to how racialization in Israeli society not only produces the settler/native divide but also engenders a wider racial hierarchy in which Palestinian Arabs are at the bottom, but nonwhite Jews or non-Jewish immigrants are also excluded from the category of "the chosen body."[86] Ashkenazi Israelis occupy the structural position of whiteness, while Arabs—and Palestinians in particular—constitute their racialized Other.[87] The midwives' dehumanization of birthing women as "the Ethiopian, the Arab, the Russian" further shows the continuities of anti-Blackness and Palestinian erasure.[88] In that sense, maternity ward segregation can be considered an infrastructure of racializing space. What this infrastructure circulates is settler futurity imagined as Jewish and white. An infrastructure of feelings, attitudes, and ideology is transformed into a material condition of spatial segregation. As Najwa explained, the practice of maternity ward segregation must also be understood in light of the commodification and neoliberalization of the Israeli healthcare system. In the case of Israeli hospitals, medical staff comply with requests or indirect pressure for racial segregation, basing their decision-making process on treating patients as customers and any kind of request as a legitimate consumer demand. At the center of this practice is the Jewish Israeli child-rich (and thus often religious) woman as the desired patient.

This market-driven logic, centered around the ideal Jewish Israeli patient-customer, structures institutional policies and shapes the everyday clinical experiences of Palestinian medical professionals within these hospitals. Meera is a Palestinian doctor in residency at a Jerusalem hospital who lives in East Jerusalem. She did part of her doctor's rotation in the hospital's IVF unit, and, at the time of our interview, Meera was working at the hospital's maternity ward. Reflecting on her current work environment, Meera explained to me how the economic considerations of the hospital determined her daily tasks:

> My delivery room is crazy about advertising itself to a specific population, which is the religious Jewish population, because they have many children. Their idea is that if she has twelve children and the first one is with us, and she likes it, she will come back with all of them [laughs dryly]. I was talking to one of my friends in the States, and I'm like, I told her that I'm embarrassed, all this technology and all this advanced medicine, when in the end, advertising our delivery room means: We have already precut toilet paper so you can use it on a Saturday, so you don't have to cut it. And I'm like, this is embarrassing, it's even embarrassing to tell you, because this is not what I studied for.

Meera's critique of the maternity wards' economic reliance on catering to the ultra-Orthodox population of Jerusalem highlights how the accommodation of Jewish religious norms is part of a broader infrastructure that centers Jewish Israeli women's reproduction while systematically marginalizing and ignoring the reproductive needs and cultural contexts of Palestinian women. Meera's embarrassment of having to precut toilet paper for religious women to feel accommodated does not stem from the practice of cultural sensitivity itself, but from the fact that in the Israeli medical sphere, such cultural inclusivity is reserved for Jewish Israeli women only. This demonstrates how infrastructures are also concrete sites where ideology becomes material. Ruth Wilson Gilmore offers the notion of "infrastructure of feeling" to capture how infrastructures also organize affect, difference, and identification.[89]

Jewish supremacy, in that sense, is an infrastructure of feeling that produces the ideological and affective vocabulary to privilege Jewish Israeli women's reproduction and dehumanize other women's childbearing.[90] At the same time, this infrastructure of feeling is also a material condition that makes racial ideologies visible and felt in medical space.

PALESTINIAN REPRODUCTIVE FUTURITY

From the history of settler colonial dispossession and its present-day traces in the Israeli healthcare system, stratified access to healthcare services, ongoing fights for land in the Naqab, and institutionalized racism and militarization in East Jerusalem to the affective infrastructures of Israeli maternity wards, what unites these different cases is that in each instance, networks, objects, or architectures support and set in motion settler reproduction and futurity. Palestinian women's access to health, reproductive services, and advanced reproductive technologies is slowed down, blocked, choppy, or often outright denied. Palestinian life and reproductive futurity are curtailed and sometimes destroyed. Multiscalar in nature, the Israeli health infrastructures I have explored in this chapter produce Palestinian im/mobilities and limit Palestinian women's access to the resources needed to implement their reproductive choices and carry out healthy pregnancies. The reproductive injustices that Palestinian women experience are thus infrastructurally anchored in Israeli settler colonialism as a political system.

Cultural theorist Lauren Berlant coined the notion of "slow death" to capture "the physical wearing out of a population in a way that points to its deterioration as a defining condition of its experience and historical existence."[91] Slow death refers to a state of being in which "people do live just not very well."[92] An infrastructural reading of Palestinian women's reproductive health and rights shows just this. Palestinian women's reproducing bodies are disconnected and often barred from accessing Israeli health infrastructures, from regular women's health clinics to more advanced fertility clinics. While these forms of blockage might not amount to obvious amounts of violence like genocide in Gaza or the ongoing killings of Palestinians in the West Bank, their cumulative and latent effects are central to understanding the varying ways in which Palestinian women experience reproductive injustice.

Central to my infrastructural reading of the Israeli health system and fertility economy in this chapter has not only been to explore where they hamper Palestinians' reproduction, but also how these disconnections might seem out of sight for the majority of Jewish Israelis who work in the medical sphere.[93] Infrastructures become most visible in their failure, revealing how relational such systems of motility are.[94] However, who notices the failure of Israeli health infrastructures, and what is done to repair them? Berlant's reading of infrastructure is also instructive here. They describe infrastructure as "the lifeworld of structure," as a network or mechanism defined by the patterning of social form.[95] The softer or more affective forms of infrastructure that exclude Palestinian women in the Israeli hospital provide a crucial example of infrastructure as life-sustaining. Jewish Israeli medical staff actively or subconsciously reproduce a patterning of sociality in which Palestinian women only exist as shadows. Their needs, emotions, history, and health outcomes are invisibilized, while their bodies are inscribed into the racial hierarchy that sustains Israeli society and the Israeli state as a settler colonial project.

It is other Palestinian female healthcare professionals, like Najwa, Salam, Layla, Hanan, Meera, and Yara, who do this work of infrastructural repair and model how to build a world in which Palestinian women's reproductive justice would be central. These women also articulate various strategies of refusal against the extractive mechanisms of settler colonialism and the research situation itself. Building such "alimentary infrastructures" and returning the forces of Palestinian life back into infrastructures built on Palestinian dispossession illustrates the transformative work of social reproduction.[96] Material infrastructures are always accompanied by ideas and concepts that are generated to challenge the circuits of power they produce. Mobile clinics that cater to Palestinian women's needs in segregated or occupied territories work in tandem with the affective attunement to the particular vulnerabilities of Bedouin or Palestinian women. Palestinian counter-infrastructures, in that sense, not only enable Palestinian women to access the means to implement their reproductive choices but are, in themselves, infrastructures of Palestinian reproductive futurity.

THREE

Hospitals

> He answers in monosyllables, gives little in the way of explanation, and soon arouses the doctor's impatience. This attitude is not to be confused with the kind of inhibiting fear that patients usually feel in the doctor's presence. We often hear it said that a certain doctor has a good bedside manner. But it so happens that in the colonial situation the personal approach, the ability to be oneself, of establishing and maintaining a "contact," are not observable. The colonial situation standardizes relations, for it dichotomizes the colonial society in a marked way.
>
> FRANTZ FANON,
> *A Dying Colonialism*

> The settler self is an identity category that is first of all a function of territory.
>
> HAGAR KOTEF,
> *The Colonizing Self*

"LISTEN, I THINK THAT FERTILITY, and the medical world in Israel in general, are a small microcosmos, where people really work together. There are no religion or nation-based confrontations." I was sitting in the windowless office of a major public hospital in Jerusalem, listening to Yekutiel, a Jewish Israeli doctor in his sixties and the head of the hospital's fertility department. One year into researching Israeli fertility clinics and Palestinian patients' access to them, I had heard this exact description many times before. The spatial terms medical staff used to describe their work environment varied—Yekutiel calling it a microcosmos—but the story always remained the same: The hospital is different from most other places in Israel. Across the political spectrum, doctors, nurses, and other health workers described it to me as a peculiar place that lies outside of the politics and usual social relations that structure everyday life in the liberal settler state. But the more often I heard this narrative, the less it seemed to be about the actual realities in Israeli hospitals. The ubiquity of this narrative told me a different story, a story about the strong tie between settler identity and control over space.

Indeed, hospitals are peculiar public spaces in Israel. It is here where Jewish Israelis and Palestinians encounter each other on a regular basis. Palestinians with Israeli citizenship and residents of occupied East Jerusalem are included in the Israeli healthcare system and receive treatment in Israeli hospitals and clinics. With 25 percent of Israel's physicians being Palestinian in 2022, the healthcare sector has one of the highest rates of Palestinian employees and has become a relatively accessible sector for Palestinian medical and nursing graduates.[1] Due to the underinvestment in the Palestinian healthcare systems in the West Bank and Gaza, and before October 7, Palestinians from the occupied territories regularly applied to the military authorities to travel to Israel to receive treatment in hospitals there.[2] As "contact zones" between Jewish Israeli staff and Palestinian patients (or vice versa), Israeli hospitals and fertility clinics are social spaces where the power relations of the settler colonial society are inevitable.[3]

The status of hospitals as a cultural and religious meeting ground is reflected in the Israeli public imagination in the same apolitical way Yekutiel described his working environment. Hospitals are depicted as "oases" or "islands" of harmonious coexistence, both by medical staff working in the healthcare sector as well as in everyday conversations. Enthusiastic Israeli and international newspaper articles emphasize the cooperation and "brotherhood" between Palestinian and Jewish-Israeli physicians, while a 2016 report titled *Heroes of Health* praises the "camaraderie" between medical staff as a model for other economic sectors.[4] Osama Tanous summarizes the various functions the Israeli hospital is imagined to accomplish: "The hospital is portrayed as an intimate meeting ground for all, both providers and recipients of medical treatment, and as a peace bridge to Palestinians in the West Bank, Gaza, and even beyond, to the wider Arab world."[5] The hospital is a site to produce and showcase the Israeli state's ostensibly humanitarian character.

In this chapter, then, I examine the imagination of the Israeli hospital as a medically and politically neutral place. Medical staff's relation to space and practices of place-making are instructive here because access to Israeli hospitals and fertility clinics is not only a question of who can enter and receive treatment; the social and spatial relations in medical institutions are shaped by an affective economy that determines the conditions of entering and belonging to the hospital.[6] How Jewish Israeli physicians, nurses, and social workers *feel* about their Palestinian fertility patients, and, as an extension of these feelings, about themselves, is a crucial component in the formation of Israeli demographic anxieties. At the same time, it is Palestinian physicians' inclusion into the Israeli healthcare sector and their navigation of this space that illustrates how Palestinians continue to resist Israeli rule.

However, Israel's genocide in Gaza has revealed the functional construction of and, ultimately, the void of any notion like coexistence, medical neutrality, or Israel's medical humanitarianism. Since October 2023, Palestinian health workers in Israeli hospitals have reported experiences of intimidation, dehumanization, and criminalization if they expressed empathy for the people in Gaza.[7] Meanwhile, the Israeli army has systematically destroyed the Palestinian healthcare system in Gaza. Israel's assault on medical infrastructure was discernible as one of its main military objectives early on, and it has since been documented extensively. Repeated attacks on hospitals and combat in and around them led to the destruction of most hospitals in Gaza, with a healthcare system on the constant brink of collapse.[8] Palestinian healthcare workers from Gaza have been deported to Israeli detention facilities, where Palestinian doctors, nurses, and paramedics who were later released described experiences of humiliation, beatings, cuffing, blindfolding, and the denial of medical care in Israeli custody. Some also reported torture, including rape and sexual abuse by Israeli forces.[9] In March 2025, fifteen Palestinian medics and rescue workers were shot dead by Israeli soldiers who opened fire on their vehicles, even though the men were identifiable as paramedics, moving with flashing ambulance lights.[10] Despite the fact that intentionally attacking hospitals and systematically attacking healthcare infrastructure and workers are war crimes, Western media outlets, politicians, and commentators have been reluctant in their coverage of such assaults. Indeed, as critical health scholars write, Western media and academics are replicating Israel's language of medical neutrality, intentionally supporting and legitimizing the Israeli narrative.[11]

This context of active destruction of Palestinian healthcare and the oppression and dehumanization of Palestinian health workers across Palestine/Israel textures and sharpens the argument I present in this chapter, namely that Jewish Israeli and Palestinian relations, medical neutrality, and humanitarianism in the Israeli medical sphere have always been deeply fragile constructs. The burden to keep this fiction alive has been carried by Palestinian medical staff who have to negotiate their existence in a space founded on their dispossession, exclusion, and annihilation. The narratives and experiences presented in this chapter can thus be read as a prologue to maintain a discourse of Israel as a liberal democracy invested in humanitarianism, even in the face of committing some of the worst atrocities of the twenty-first century. In other words, while Israel's genocidal war on Gaza has completely shattered the image of Israel as a humanitarian actor with "the most moral army in the world," the Israeli state and its Western allies cling to this vision to present the destruction of Gaza as a legitimate war of defense. My presence as an observer in the Israeli hospital and the ways in which medical staff address me as a Western audience and a witness to their benevolent behavior parallels, in a way, what is happening on a world scale today. Consent for an all-out annihilatory war is manufactured in a civilizational conversation Israel has with the West, in which Palestinians stand in as the Arab Other, threatening not only Israel's security but also the West as a whole.[12] This chapter traces the emergence of such a conversation. It shows how the place-myth of the Israeli hospital as neutral and apolitical is quite literally articulated in conversation with a white German like me.

I begin this chapter with an exploration of Jewish Israeli medical staff's gendered and racialized articulation of Palestinians as the civilizational Other. Attending to the ethnographic situation, I analyze how difference is produced in relation to my presence as a German scholar. Next, I trace how Israeli medical staff articulate a critical distance between the everyday of the occupation and ongoing militarization and the hospital where they work. By removing their own involvement in an ongoing system of segregation and structural racism, Jewish Israeli medical staff are able to present the Israeli medical sphere as neutral and apolitical. In an interlude that connects the ethnographic data presented in this chapter with the experiences of Palestinian healthcare workers in an increasingly militarized medical sphere and society post–October 7, I show the long and ongoing history of Israeli hospitals as "frontier" institutions. I then explore the perspective of Palestinian health workers and their difficult positionality vis-à-vis the Israeli hospital and the state at large. In the penultimate section, I explore the affective economy of the Israeli hospital and its reliance on the hegemonic Israeli framework of security, coexistence, and a need for Palestinians to be grateful for their inclusion. The chapter ends with a reflection on the relationship between affect and space-making, and a car ride across Jerusalem.

Jerusalem is where this chapter begins and ends. Arguably, this is a specific place in Palestine/Israel. As shown in the previous chapters, Jerusalem displays varying demographic strategies of Israeli population management and can be described as an active "frontier" of Israeli settler colonialism, where land confiscation, apartheid, occupation, and annexation are openly promoted.[13] These modalities of control connect seemingly disparate and fragmented parts of the Palestinian people and their lands.[14] The unusually intimate "contact zones" of hospitals in Jerusalem and the closeness to the occupied West Bank are important sites to explore the articulation of hegemonic Israeli identity and its relationship to space.

DIFFERENCE, IDENTITY, AND ETHNOGRAPHY IN THE ISRAELI HOSPITAL

Irit was one of the first Jewish Israeli physicians I contacted when I started researching Palestinian women's access to reproductive technology in Israeli hospitals. I emailed her and introduced myself as a German PhD student, interested in Palestinian citizens' and residents' access to reproductive technologies in Israeli hospitals. I also mentioned that I assumed their access to healthcare to be different, more broadly, from Jewish Israelis'. Irit replied promptly. She thanked me for my interest "in this complicated topic" and noted that she did not fully support my hypothesis about unequal access to healthcare, but that she would happily share her views with me. My encounter with Irit would set the tone for how I came to understand the Israeli hospital, but also how I was perceived within this space.

Irit's eagerness to prove my politically inflected assumption of reproductive *in*justice wrong was a thread that wove through most of my following encounters with Jewish Israeli interlocutors working in Israeli hospitals. Doing critical research about Palestinians in the Israeli medical space has proven to be notoriously difficult. As medical anthropologist Guy Shalev shows in his study on Palestinian doctors' experiences in Israeli hospitals, the hospitals' ethics committees would continuously exacerbate his access to medical space if he used terms such as "Palestinian" instead of "Israeli Arab" or talked about the political situation in terms that differed from the usual framework of medical neutrality.[15] Yet, a year after Irit introduced me to the head nurse at the hospital she worked at, I inquired whether I could approach their Palestinian patients in the unit's waiting room and the head nurse remembered me immediately and allowed me to hand out a short description of my research to their Palestinian patients to make an appointment to talk to them outside of the clinic if they agreed to do so. Just like me, the head nurse was a white and blonde woman, and our physical resemblance was commented on a few times by other medical staff and patients. My whiteness, coupled with people's gendered perception of a young, malleable woman, determined my positionality vis-à-vis Jewish Israeli medical staff. There seemed to be a concerted effort among my Jewish Israeli interlocutors to dismantle any misguided political ideas a foreigner like me could have about Israel.[16] It animated them to explain to me that my assumptions about Palestinian women's unequal access to reproductive technology were wrong. This kind of open criticism of Israeli politics and my interlocutors' benevolent and, at times, paternalistic attention is usually not afforded to nonwhite and non-Jewish racialized subjects in Israel. I attribute my interlocutor's eagerness and openness toward me as an effect of the ways in which racial difference shapes Israeli society today.[17]

Irit worked full-time in the fertility department of one of Jerusalem's major hospitals, as well as twice a week in a smaller nearby clinic run by one of Israel's three largest health insurance providers. She welcomed me to her busy office in the women's health clinic and talked to me in between appointments with patients, phone calls, and chats with the women's clinic's Palestinian head nurse. The women's clinic we met at offers general women's health services, while the larger hospital Irit worked at deals with more complex fertility issues and IVF. Patients who wish to undergo fertility treatment after an initial examination at the clinic were usually referred to the hospital but would come back to the clinic do simpler procedures like blood work or ultrasounds. A fifteen-minute walk apart, both medical spaces cater to the Palestinian population of occupied East Jerusalem and Palestinian patients who would cross the border from the West Bank to be treated in the Israeli health sector.

I arrived at the women's health clinic on a spring morning in April. Immediately after I had pressed "record" on my device, Irit started talking about her Palestinian patients. Without me having asked her a question yet, she began telling me how she feels about treating them:

> I learned to be less judgmental. But still, it's hard for me to give fertility treatments to very, very young women. But on the other hand, if I don't give them fertility treatments, I also don't think it's right. Because you know, they have a different culture, different attitudes toward family. Sometimes it's really hard because she still goes to high school, she's married, but goes to high school, and if she has a child, she will stop. So education-wise, maybe it's better to defer the pregnancy. On the other hand, there is also the family of the

husband, who can be very pressing on the issue of pregnancy. So, this is one very, very typical problem that we have here, like very young women, teenagers, who are married and opt for fertility treatments.

From this first moment, and despite her attempt to be "less judgmental," Irit made it clear to me that she views these cultural differences in light of her own superiority. She presented her Palestinian patients as a homogenous group of Others, while she saw herself and, as we shall see, me, as representing Western modernity and its gendered values.[18] In this first instance, Irit offered an argument about the correlation between education and reproduction, proposing that getting pregnant at a younger age would deter Palestinian women from getting an education (which they implicitly urgently need). Such notions of linking reproduction to underdevelopment and education as an implicit contraceptive have been firmly planted in overpopulation discourse in the mid-twentieth century.[19] This discourse of Palestinians as an over-reproducing and undereducated population looms large over Irit's description of her patients and her judgment of their reproductive choices and lives more broadly (see also chapter 1). Irit's description of Palestinian women's reliance on their husbands and their families further strengthens the racialized image she wants to paint about Palestinian women's lack of agency and control over their reproductive decision-making. Irit, like many of my Jewish Israeli interlocutors, immediately felt the need to discuss her patients' perceived Otherness with me.

In the same breath, Irit continued and described another problem "typical" of her patients: Many of them, she explained, were overweight, and this would interfere with them becoming pregnant, which is why they would turn to fertility treatment without actually needing it. In talking about her patients' bodies, Irit drew me into her narrative, and in so doing, constructed an embodied Western—and transparently white[20]—"us," established around racialized notions of what is considered a healthy and attractive female body.

> Secondly, we see here many obese patients, maybe it's again a cultural thing, because the beautiful woman here is more overweight than what I see in Tel Aviv or in Berlin. So again, it has its problems, because if you have an obese woman, she may suffer from irregularities in the menstrual cycle. . . . First of all, I tell them: "You should reduce weight, go to the gym and start to do sport on a daily or a weekly basis. And then come three months after, and we will see." And sometimes they come pregnant. Easy! The easiest treatment ever! OK, so this is again something that is very typical of this place.

Irit is an Ashkenazi Jewish woman in her late forties.[21] In remarking that a beautiful woman in our respective cultural contexts, in "Tel Aviv or in Berlin," is thinner in comparison to what she sees in her Palestinian patients, she constructed us and our bodies as belonging to and engendering the same racialized notion of what constitutes a healthy, attractive, and reproductive body. This illustrates not only her racialized understanding of the relationship between health, reproduction, and fatness but also reveals the patronizing medical gaze through which she approached her patients.[22]

This way of talking about their Palestinian patients was not unusual among the Jewish Israeli doctors I met. In these instances, a patronizing approach toward Palestinian patients is articulated through the categories of race and gender. In Irit's case, this comes to the fore in her reference to female beauty standards and the connection between education and childbearing. As a female person who was socialized as a girl and a woman, I am deeply familiar with such talk among women. This was slightly different when talking to male fertility doctors and listening to versions of the same gendered and racialized script. Consider, for example, the following quote by Eran, the Jewish Israeli head of an IVF center in Tel Aviv, who talked about his male Palestinian patients in the context of male infertility and sperm donation:

> If you have a Muslim patient and you have exhausted all the attempts to find sperm for the man, and he's walking around with aspirated and chopped balls, in his testicles, there is nothing left, he can go to get a sperm donation. We can assure him that nobody will know, and we can always try to find a donor who will be darker. But most of our donors are of European and East European origin, they look like you, they are blonde, and they have blue eyes, but sometimes we have dark hair, dark skin. Some of them find a way to understand that, and some don't and stay childless. Some of them get divorced. It depends on the status; the marriages in these societies are arranged, sometimes in the family, so everybody knows everything. Sometimes it breaks up families because of that, and then in this society, once a marriage is broken, it's always bad because the woman is perceived as something like a secondhand car, and the man, everybody knows he's not, eh, . . . so they will not do very well afterward. Unless they are educated enough to understand that it's only a biological problem. In the Mediterranean culture, sperm donation equals adultery, so you have to explain to them that sperm donation is not adultery.

Eran presents Muslim men who need sperm donation through his own sense of superiority. In his narrative, most Palestinians are not educated enough to understand that they can receive a sperm donation due to their interpretation and adherence to Islamic regulations of assisted reproduction.[23] Even if they agreed to a sperm donation, he remarks that usually donors "look like me," and these gamete donations would thus not be suitable for Palestinians. This comment implicitly racializes all Palestinians as "darker" and also points to the Israeli economy of egg or sperm donations, in which light skin, blonde hair, and blue eyes are indeed desirable traits, reflecting the broader racial hierarchization in society.[24] The patronizing way he talks about his male patients, specifically how he refers to their medical condition, is what I learned over the years to read as a specific Israeli form of machismo. His overly graphic description of the conditions of male infertility references tropes of the ideal male body in a masculinist and militaristic culture.[25] Eran maps his own gendered notions of masculinity on the Arab Other, implying, for instance, that he is perceived as less masculine if he has infertility issues. He presents Palestinian men as the civilizational Other and their women as the victims of their patriarchal culture. In one sweeping breath, Eran ticks all the boxes of gendered anti-Muslim racism ("arranged marriages," patriarchal masculinity, and uneducated). The way Eran explained his patients to me implied that he felt like he was an expert on Muslim or Palestinian society.

This view and treatment of Palestinian patients in Israeli hospitals and fertility clinics is not unusual, nor is it specific to the political context of Palestine/Israel. Scholarship on medical racism, especially in obstetric settings, shows how doctors in the United States are treating Black and other nonwhite patients as irrevocably Other. Black women, and women of color, are treated through the lens of cultural difference, which ultimately translates to inferior.[26] Medical racism, especially in its disguise as cultural difference, leads to misdiagnoses and can cause the patient serious harm.[27] Throughout my research with Jewish Israeli physicians, I encountered narratives like this repeatedly. My presence in the room often served as a catalyst to establish such arguments, either about incommensurable cultural differences, beauty standards, family values, gender, or education. In these instances, Western values of modernity, civilization, and whiteness would be a shared reference point between a doctor like Irit or Eran and me, the unmarked and universal position from which Palestinians, their bodies, and their reproductive behavior would be described and—although Irit assured otherwise—judged.

I begin this chapter with Irit and Eran to demonstrate how racial hierarchy, sometimes hidden in culturalist assumptions but often not hidden at all, shapes how many Jewish Israeli physicians approach their Palestinian patients at the fertility clinic. Similar to the description of a "demographic race" as a normal part of Israeli life and society (as discussed in chapter 1), Jewish Israeli medical staff presented the establishment of cultural and racial hierarchy as a normal point of shared reference between Germans and Israelis. These assumptions are so normalized and taken for granted, as Irit's inclusion of my own appearance and European values indicates, that they don't challenge universalist notions of medical neutrality. In fact, as we will see later in this chapter, notions of difference are often used to highlight the humanitarian character of the Israeli hospital.

MEDICAL NEUTRALITY AND SPATIAL IMAGINARIES

After our morning at the women's health clinic, Irit invited me to join her in visiting the nearby hospital and its IVF unit, where she worked as a senior gynecologist-obstetrician. We drove there by car, which took a mere few minutes, during which we kept chatting about the two different medical spaces. Irit referred to the IVF unit of the bigger hospital as a "weird capsule" and continued to explain to me that, "you know, even if another Intifada would happen, and we are close to all these terroristic sites, where terrible things happen, but this room, it's like an extraterritorial room." She described the IVF unit as opposed to a violent, political, and possibly dangerous "outside" of the hospital, implicitly acknowledging how Palestinians resist ongoing occupation, land grabs, and demographic politics. Yet the peculiar space inside the hospital seemed to be unrelated to this contested geography and, with Irit's reference to its presumed extraterritoriality, perhaps even outside the limits of its jurisdiction, or at least its usual social order.

I encountered this imaginary of Israeli hospitals as fundamentally different in most of my conversations with medical staff in fertility units or clinics, and they all offered similarly interesting spatial metaphors to describe medical space. Lena, a Jewish Israeli senior physician in Irit's IVF unit at the large Jerusalem hospital, told me there was something strange about their workplace. She said: "I think when it comes to health and medicine, you know, it's outside. Maybe I'm naive, but I feel that in a hospital we are just a no-man's-land." These spatial imaginaries, a "no-man's-land" or an "extraterritorial room," uncannily evoke the colonial language of terra nullius, a territory that belongs to no one, readily available for settlement and colonial development.[28] Osama Tanous argues that in the context of Zionism the notion of terra nullius invisibilizes Palestinians under Israeli law and in the public imagination, relegating them to a broad, unspecified, and extraterritorial category of people "originating and belonging nowhere in particular."[29] The description of a no-man's-land references this nonexistence of both land and people.

While it might seem like these feelings and imaginaries about medical space stem from being in such close proximity to Palestinian neighborhoods and heavy Israeli military presence, as Irit's reference to "all these terroristic sites" indicates, these perceptions of medical space as special or weird were not limited to Jerusalem, nor were they only presented by Jewish Israeli medical staff. Irit and Lena referred to the hospital as existing outside the usual social order, whereas others explained how the outside world and, with it, markers of identity and difference, would be actively *kept* outside of medical space. Jeries, a self-identified "Arab Israeli" doctor, described his working environment in the IVF department of a public hospital in Haifa as follows: "We work professionally, you don't bring your politics to the hospital, I mean, everyone should be treated here according to . . . we're human beings, that's what actually conducts us here." "Conflicts outside of this hospital," Jeries explained, were irrelevant in the Israeli hospital: "We definitely wouldn't recognize a person neither by his color, or his sex, or his religion, or his ethnicity. We just help them." Evoking medical professionalism, Jeries narrates the hospital as a place of neutrality and universalism. Ethno-national tensions shape everyday life in the outside world, but, according to medical staff, these realities do not penetrate the inside of the hospital. Remarkably, although physicians acknowledge the political situation and the identities it produces, these circumstances are either actively kept out ("you don't bring them to the hospital," said, notably, by an Arab Israeli), or they seem to ricochet from an invisible wall enclosing "extraterritorial" space that is the hospital. The production of this spatial reality is fragile, and medical staff are constantly investing in it.

When I asked medical staff about the "outside" of the hospital and how it related to what they described as its apolitical inside, their responses indicated that medical neutrality served a strategic purpose for the settler colonial project. The production of medical space as neutral and universal is a purposefully produced status quo that maintains as implicit whose body, health, and reproduction this place was built for. Consider the following quotation about the inside/outside boundary that separates the Israeli hospital from its sociopolitical context. Shimrit is a nurse in the IVF department of the Jerusalem hospital who lives in a nearby Israeli settlement in the West

Bank. I asked her about the fact that a lot of Israeli-Palestinian politics are described through the lens of demography, and if this was tangible in her day-to-day in the IVF unit. She replied, hesitant at first, by describing her working environment in the known spatial grammar as a peculiar "bubble," but she then went on to wonder about how her Palestinian patients might perceive what she feels like is an apolitical space:

> Yeah, it's been a thought, but I've never . . . I mean . . . as I said, I cut off any . . . there's no politics, no nothing, it's just caring for people. You can't involve politics. And I think this whole hospital, not only our unit, is a bubble. I always say, if people would only come and see! How it's nothing like outside, it's very different. . . . I always wonder how our Palestinian patients see us, because I am sure, a lot of them come very intimidated and ask themselves how we're going to treat them. And once they see that, how they take it out to their families and . . . I never asked. I'm curious, really, it's one of the biggest wonders that I wonder about.

For Shimrit, that she "cuts off any politics" means that she perceives herself and her work to be neutral, as well as neutraliz*ing* of her patients' fears and insecurities. As I have shown in the previous chapter, Israeli healthcare infrastructures are centered around the Jewish Israeli body, feelings, and needs. As an affective economy, the hospital works to reproduce settler sociality.[30] It is thus not surprising that Shimrit is convinced that things are different in the clinic, that the care she and her colleagues extend to Palestinians is indeed disconnected from the outside world. Her and her colleagues' emotions and their care for people in what she perceived as a neutral way *do* something in this situation. They align bodily space with social space.[31] It is through this overlap of hegemonic feelings of care and medical neutrality with the space of the hospital that Shimrit can disconnect her Palestinian patients' anticipated intimidation from the broader political context and see their fears resolved within the medical space. The hospital is centered around emotions like Shimrit's.

It is notable that Shimrit lives in an illegal settlement in the West Bank. Coming back to the Fanon epigraph, there is a broader relation at work in Shimrit seeing her patients' discomfort but understanding her work in the hospital as neutralizing any such feelings. If the Palestinian patient, like other patients in (settler) colonial settings, seems disaffected or uncomfortable, this sheds light on the power relations that structure the medical encounter.[32] Indeed, as Fanon notes, "in centers of colonization the doctor is nearly always a landowner as well."[33] This is the case with Shimrit. She, like many of her colleagues in Jerusalem, is, in the most literal sense, the owner of Palestinian land. Even if Shimrit doesn't consider it, this relationship is foundational to the medical encounter.

Rebecca is a Jewish American nurse who moved to Israel twenty years ago because, as she told me, she hated her job in the United States. Employed at the IVF department of the same hospital in Jerusalem, she described their work in similar terms:

> I think on a daily basis, interacting with individuals, there is no conflict. I think it's greater than just, you know, me and you sitting in a room together. I definitely tell people to come and see what the beautiful work that goes on in the hospital is, that, you know, Arab doctors taking care of Jewish patients, Jewish doctors taking care of Arab patients, men, women, you know, there is no separation, everyone's a person, that's it.

Rebecca's enthusiasm for cross ethno-religious caretaking is indicative of its exceptionality. It elicits so much passion simply because there *is* separation outside of the hospital (as well as inside of it, as discussed in the previous chapter). Sympathetic feeling and, in this case, medical care and attention, release the sympathetic nurse from the realm of politics that shapes the world outside. She feels that in the daily encounters at the fertility clinic, "there is no conflict." Shimrit and Rebecca's positive feelings about their working environment are based on their impression that the history and violence of the political situation outside of the hospital can be dissolved through caring relations.

The narratives of Jewish Israeli medical staff like Shimrit and Rebecca point to what Eve Tuck and K. Wayne Yang term "settler moves to innocence."[34] By removing their own involvement in, or even recognition of, an ongoing system of segregation and structural racism, Jewish Israeli medical staff are able to present the Israeli medical sphere as neutral and apolitical. By averting their gaze from the structural conditions of settler colonialism, Jewish Israeli medical staff present the hegemonic narrative of Israel as a liberal democracy, in which Palestinians have access to advanced fertility treatment just like Jewish Israelis. In that sense, they not only relieve themselves of feelings of guilt or of responsibility to give up power, privilege, or land, but, by claiming the hospital as an apolitical and neutral space, they gain credit as sensitive health workers, creating relationships of care in a difficult political situation. Shimrit and Rebecca's insisting that people "come and see" the "beautiful work" they are doing points to their affective investment in this narrative. If only people critical of Israel (like me?) could understand that Palestinians in the Israeli hospital have rights and are treated well. This move to innocence captures what Indigenous studies scholar Glen Coulthard describes as the transition between openly colonial forms of domination "to a mode of colonial governmentality that works through the limited freedoms afforded by state recognition and accommodation."[35] It is precisely this mode of governmentality that appears in medical staff's narratives of the hospital. It is *because* Palestinians have access to state-funded fertility treatment and caring medical staff in a supposedly neutral environment that their actual feelings of discomfort, disaffection, or anger cannot be seen.

The political structure of settler colonial demographic anxieties and a racialized society that centers legally, socially, and affectively around the (white) Jewish body is strategically concealed and thus reproduced by the negation, misreading, or indifference to Palestinian patients' diffidence. The varied spatial imaginaries of the hospital as a sealed-off "microcosmos," a "weird capsule," or a "no-man's-land" in which care, professionalism, and neutrality reign, evoke a broader strategy of Israeli politics and society. Medical neutrality and the hospital's presumed detachment from the social relations and politics of dispossession and securitization of Palestinians endows the hospital with an "aura of politically neutral benevolence."[36] The distance that medical professionals are crossing between what they perceive to be outside of the hospital (politics, history, and violence) and their neutral and professional care for everyone within the clinic is marshaled as evidence of what anthropologist Rebecca Stein has termed Israel's humanitarian alibi: "Israeli care for Palestinian life in the face of fierce and frequent international accusations to the contrary."[37] The affective investment in the making of settler space that structures these medical staff's narratives offers a window into the historical and ongoing practice of not recognizing Palestinians: as owners of the land, as people with feelings, or as actors with political aspirations that challenge the status quo.

However, Israel's genocide in Gaza shattered any such liberal claims to Israel's humanitarian alibi, and the image of neutral coexistence in the hospital was cracked wide open when Palestinian health workers began to express empathy for the people in Gaza in 2023.[38] What has been revealed since is how much the fiction of medical neutrality and humanitarianism has been built on the fragile and limited inclusion of Palestinians, as patients and as colleagues. Central to this is the alignment of the institution of the Israeli hospital with settler colonial statecraft and the affective sociality of what sociologist Areej Sabbagh-Khoury terms a "potentially antagonistic, dispossessory Jewish Israeli society" in a state of exception.[39] The securitization of public space and the militarization of Israeli society are key to understanding this alignment.

INTERLUDE: THE BIOSPATIAL POLITICS AND MILITARIZATION OF ISRAELI HOSPITALS, 1930–2025

Every time I entered the hospital where Shimrit, Rebecca, and Irit work—or any other Israeli hospital or clinic, for that matter—I had to undergo a brief security check. Like most other public spaces in Israel, such as universities, libraries, malls, or government buildings, hospitals are guarded by private security personnel. These everyday practices of securitization include a bag check conducted by security guards (who would usually be armed), walking through a metal detector, or x-raying any bags or jackets one might carry. As a white woman, the security checks I would get were usually conducted sloppily and with a display of ennui. For Palestinians, on the other hand, the "Israeli gaze" represents an ever-present feeling of being watched and surveilled, whether it be at the door of the hospital or the gate of a military checkpoint.[40]

The way different people are able to enter the Israeli hospital easily or experience its racialized securitization reveals something fundamental about the institution of Israeli medical space itself. As Osama Tanous shows, during the time of the British mandate, colonial hospitals and smaller clinics were built strategically at the frontiers of Zionist expansion, like on top of Mount Carmel in Haifa, the Galilee in the north of what would become Israel, or the Naqab desert in the south. As "facts on the ground," hospitals would not only serve the health of the incoming settler population and their reproduction, but also attract much-needed medical personnel from Europe and North America, which helped establish the medical profession as a central pillar of Zionist settlement.[41] For instance, Hadassah Hospital Mt. Scopus was strategically planned and built in the 1930s. A Zionist "Hospital Site Committee" was appointed in 1932 to discuss the pros and cons of the location of the hospital next to the Hebrew University.[42] Built in 1918 at the apex of Mount Scopus, the Hebrew University was central to establishing a collective Jewish-Zionist identity, and its location was chosen as a strategic outpost for the Zionist movement to mark its symbolic and political claim to

Jerusalem.[43] According to archival research into the Hospital Site Committee's decision-making process, Mount Scopus was discussed as having many disadvantages, including being inaccessible and disconnected from Jewish neighborhoods in pre-state Jerusalem, as well as "worries regarding the site's security,"[44] which usually translates to the presence of a Palestinian community who would contest Zionist settlement.[45] However, despite these concerns, the hospital was built in 1939.

After Israel's occupation of the West Bank and East Jerusalem in 1967, the location of Mount Scopus, including the hospital and the university campus, was central to linking West Jerusalem to occupied East Jerusalem and marking the "unification" of Jerusalem as the Jewish capital, both geographically and symbolically.[46] Today, alongside the university, a Jewish settlement, and major highways, the hospital is a central architectural feature that encroaches on the Palestinian neighborhood of Issawiya. Issawiya was illegally annexed by Israel in 1967 and included in the Jerusalem municipality. Since then, its Palestinian residents have lived under Israeli jurisdiction but without full citizenship, facing land confiscations, active urban underdevelopment, and increased securitization. The planning, establishment, expansion, and securitization of Israeli hospitals, clinics, and other medical spaces are thus centrally linked to pre-state Zionist settlement and later to the Israeli state's biospatial politics.

Such strategic planning is ongoing. The establishment of a medical school at Ariel University, located in a major Israeli settlement in the occupied West Bank, is one example of what Ghada Majadli and Osama Tanous term Israeli "medicine's service to colonialism."[47] The settlement of Ariel was established in 1978 on the land of the Palestinian villages of Kifl Hares and Marda. Today, it houses over twenty thousand Israeli settlers. Founded in 1982, Ariel University is part of the process of normalizing the settlement process and further entrenching Israeli presence in the West Bank. The university is home to the Adelson School of Medicine, which was opened in October 2019, sponsored by the American entrepreneur Miriam Adelson and her late husband, Sheldon Adelson. At the opening ceremony, Miriam Adelson spelled out the medical school's spatial, political, and ideological mission: "This institution, in the heart of Samaria [northern West Bank], brings together so much of what is so dear to our hearts: medicine, Zionism, science, Torah, Jewish pride and Jewish and non-Jewish physicians, as well as our love for our country and our love for mankind."[48] Medicine, science, and health are established and normalized as a site for further illegal settlement in the occupied West Bank. While initially refused by the Israel Council for Higher Education, the medical school is now a recognized Israeli educational institution. It holds an agreement with Tel Aviv University to allow medical students from Ariel University to be placed in Tel Aviv University–affiliated hospitals.[49]

The spatial metaphors of a "no-man's-land," a "bubble," or an "extraterritorial room" and the ethos of medical neutrality so often evoked in the hegemonic Israeli imagination allow for Jewish Israelis to overlook, deny, or actively reinterpret the political, spatial, and legal macro-processes that made the establishment of Israeli medical institutions and the healthcare system possible. This language and its underlying ideology demonstrate how medicine, as a profession, and the clinic, as a physical and ideological space, become "a site to contest, suppress, uphold or reproduce political violence presumed to occur outside its boundaries."[50] Such political violence has intensified in the Israeli medical space in recent years, well articulated under the mantle of medical neutrality. The ways in which the 2021 Unity Intifada was dealt with in the Israeli healthcare system offer some insight into the further coproduction of Israeli hospitals and Israeli state politics, and set the scene for the unprecedented dehumanization of Palestinians in the Israeli medical sphere since October 7, 2023.

The Unity Intifada was a wave of popular Palestinian resistance that erupted in May 2021, shortly after I had completed interviewing people for this project. It was sparked by the systematic coordination between settler organizations and the Israeli courts to evict Palestinian families from the Sheikh Jarrah neighborhood in occupied East Jerusalem. At the same time, an increasing number of Israeli police incursions at the Al-Aqsa compound caused not only injuries to Palestinian worshippers at the mosque but also crossed an important symbolic boundary during the month of Ramadan. Following these instances of political violence, clashes between Jewish Israelis and Palestinians erupted across Israel's so-called mixed cities, and an eleven-day war broke out between the Israeli military and Hamas in Gaza. During this escalation, which was at the time the worst outburst of violence since the Israeli military's Operation Protective Edge in Gaza in 2014, 253 people died in Gaza and 12 in Israel.[51] The wave of popular resistance and protest that built up across Palestinian communities was termed the Unity Intifada (sometimes also translated as Dignity Intifada). What set this uprising apart was its unprecedented scope, as protests, strikes, and clashes spread simultaneously across Gaza, the West Bank, East Jerusalem, and Palestinian communities.[52]

These events reverberated in the Israeli medical sphere. A document analysis conducted by health scholars Zvika Orr and Mark Fleming shows how senior figures in the Israeli healthcare system rallied around clashes between Jewish Israelis and Palestinians within the "Green Line," calling on medical staff to unite and work together in the usual framework of medical neutrality and coexistence, while not mentioning any of the violence caused by the Israeli military in Gaza (which had by far greater casualties).[53] The root causes of this outbreak of protest and uprising—Palestinians' political identity, resistance to dispossession, and the circumstances of the Israeli occupation—remained unnamed. This impulse of framing the Unity Intifada as a question of Jewish Israeli and Palestinian coexistence, while failing to acknowledge not only an actual, simultaneous, and directly related military campaign in Gaza but also the long and ongoing reality of oppression, segregation, and dispossession in all of historic Palestine, is symptomatic of the liberal Jewish Israeli understanding of the Israeli state and its institutions. As we've seen in the previous section, it is precisely this simultaneous process of recognizing and disavowing Palestinians in the medical sphere that shapes the conditions of their inclusion.[54] In so doing, and contrary to liberal Jewish Israeli medical staff's understanding of their place of work, these processes demonstrate the healthcare system's alignment with Israeli state violence and the military ideology of expansion and destruction.[55]

This has become more clear since October 7, 2023. In tandem with Israel's military attack on Gaza, Israeli society has seen an increasing institutionalization of the blurred line between combatants and civilians. Shortly after October 7, the Israeli government began encouraging the armament of civilians on an hitherto unprecedented scale, with the number of private gun licenses increased by eighteen thousand.[56] The healthcare system plays an important role here, as family doctors and other medical professionals are the ones to fill out "health declarations" for anyone applying for a firearms license.[57] Promoted by the Israeli minister of public security, Itamar Ben-Gvir, the state's delegation of violence encourages regular citizens to carry semiautomatic weapons in their day-to-day life, has increased the number of armed civilians in the West Bank, and has empowered them to carry out vigilante acts of violence. In the words of Areej Sabbagh-Khoury, it is "as if the pre-state militias (Irgun, Hagganah, etc.) have re-appeared in the wake of a weakened state, as the continuation of the project of creating a Jewish nation-state."[58] While, as she argues, this shift in the monopoly of violence has existed before, and has become more institutionalized during the Unity

Intifada, it has now significantly intensified. It is in this context of an already militarized society that there is a noticeable shift in the ways in which Jewish Israelis closely monitor their Palestinian colleagues, peers, and public Palestinian figures in an attempt to criminalize their perceived silence about Hamas or expressions of empathy for the Palestinians in Gaza.[59]

This shift is particularly visible and felt by Palestinians in the Israeli healthcare system. A qualitative study conducted by health scholar Ghada Majadli shows how, since October 7, Palestinian medical staff have been dismissed from their workplace for expressing solidarity with the victims of the Israeli assault on Gaza. Her research reveals how an increasingly militarized environment shapes the daily experience of Palestinian medical staff, reinforcing preexisting mechanisms of control and surveillance of Palestinians within healthcare.[60] While research participants describe the racist and dehumanizing language their Jewish Israeli colleagues use to talk about Palestinians in Gaza, they simultaneously observe that the Israeli healthcare system does not allow for racism against Palestinian colleagues to become overt.[61] This alignment of an ostensibly liberal and inclusive site with the ongoing killing in Gaza and attacks on Palestinian healthcare infrastructure there reveals the same process of recognition and disavowal so characteristic of Israeli society and institutions. However, after October 7, this two-pronged and fragmenting approach toward Palestinians is not able to cover the foundational structure of a militarized society. Anyone voicing empathy or support for civilians in Gaza runs the risk of being labeled a terrorist, siding with Gaza, and, essentially, an enemy to their Jewish Israeli colleagues.[62] This militarization of Israeli medical space is not only felt by Palestinian staff but also structurally anchored in Israeli society and visible within the realm of hospitals and clinics. Many of the senior staff at the hospital are also permanent army reservists, moving back and forth between Gaza and their work at the hospital. This includes doctors wearing their army uniform while carrying firearms during their work in the hospital. The increasingly prominent display of Israeli flags and military symbols, such as stickers displaying the war motto "Together We Will Win," added to the interviewed Palestinian medical staff's feeling of fundamental alienation.[63]

While these are only some of the first studies recognizing the increasing militarization of Israeli hospitals since the 2021 Unity Intifada and the 2023 genocidal war, they reveal the continuity of Israeli medical space being built and expanded in the name of Israeli settler colonialism. These findings texture the implications of notions such as medical neutrality, coexistence, and humanitarian care for Palestinians. While these narrative frameworks have to be understood as an active attempt to decouple medical space from ongoing state violence pre–October 2023, the dehumanization, securitization, and silencing of Palestinians in Israeli medical spaces afterward reveal that such attempts were flawed to begin with. This particular conjuncture reveals what was less obvious and yet already present when I interviewed Palestinian medical staff in Israeli hospitals, namely that their partial inclusion in the Israeli healthcare system, the successful economic integration into a settler colonial economy, came at the expense of Palestinians' (varied) political identities, struggles for freedom, and practices of survival.

"PLEASE, DRAW ME THE BORDERS OF ISRAEL": PALESTINIAN PHYSICIANS AND REFUSAL

Roughly one-third of the physicians I encountered when conducting research in Israeli hospitals or fertility clinics from 2018 to 2020 were Palestinian or identified as Israeli Arabs. When I asked them about their workplace, many of them, such as Jeries, referred to it in the same spatial narrative as their Jewish Israeli colleagues. Palestinian physicians' position in and vis-à-vis the Israeli healthcare sector is complicated. According to Israel's Ministry of Health, the number of Palestinians in the healthcare system rose from 9 percent in 2010 to 25 percent in 2022, and healthcare has become a relatively accessible economic sector for Palestinians to work in.[64] Before 2023 and through the Unity Intifada, Palestinian physicians' comparatively visible presence in Israeli hospitals, both as patients and as doctors, had been positively noted in health-related news in Israeli media. This further consolidated Israel's humanitarian alibi and the narrative of the universal character of the Israeli medical sector.[65] As Osama Tanous notes, Palestinian medical staff's inclusion in the Israeli healthcare sector advances the imaginary of medical space as a neutral site of universalism and coexistence. Their inclusion, he argues, allows for Israeli hospitals to be portrayed as "oases of sanity [and] equality," a place of not only medical but also political neutrality.[66] Palestinian physicians, nurses, or other medical staff's position of in/visibility in Israeli medical space, as well as their own sometimes complicated understanding of their workplace, further highlights the affective and material infrastructures discussed in the previous chapter and foreshadows the increasing militarization and dehumanization of Palestinians in the healthcare system today.

Salam is a Palestinian senior physician with Israeli citizenship who lives in a Palestinian village close to the "Green Line." She works at a smaller women's health clinic there, but her main employer is a public hospital in Tel Aviv. I first met Salam for an interview in Tel Aviv in 2018, and our relationship developed over the years. She would often explain a medical procedure or fertility problem I encountered during fieldwork, and we were discussing the first year of the Covid-19 pandemic and Israel's planned annexation of the West Bank as they were happening in 2020. Given her positionality as a Palestinian citizen and Muslim, Salam's understanding of her role in providing fertility care and of the Israeli medical system more broadly differed from how her Jewish Israeli colleagues would talk about it. When I first asked her about her colleagues in the IVF unit in the Tel Aviv hospital, Salam chuckled. She said, "They are Tel Aviv people, Tel Aviv country people," referring to the specific kind of liberalism the majority of Jewish Tel Avivians affiliate with. She then specified, more seriously:

> No, I think we are diverse, we have colleagues with different perspectives on life, an interesting group of people. But I think that we are under the same umbrella, and we behave in a way that would not interfere. I assume that I can guess that each of us can give different consultations to the patient, and I think it's legitimate that you can give some of yourself to your patients, because to give some of what you believe is good. I think we all keep the lines that were suggested, and we offer whatever the unit offers, and in the details, there might be some differences. The patients identify that and then try to go with their hearts to the ones that they believe are closer to them.

Two things stand out in Salam's description of her and her colleagues' relationship and approach to offering fertility treatment. First, Salam refers to the different lived experiences she and her Jewish-Israeli colleagues bring to their workplace, and how their different "perspectives on life" inform how they approach patients from a variety of backgrounds. Although everyone at the IVF unit works according to official guidelines, the small details in their approach might, in turn, also help their patients to identify a doctor they want to go to. Salam carefully reflects how difference and affect ("to go with their hearts") in doctor-patient encounters mirror the broader structures of Israeli society and politics. Second, she addresses how the unit's diversity makes them an interesting group of people with a lot to offer to diverse patients, but she alludes to this diversity needing active maintenance. Working under the "same umbrella"—the Israeli hospital—means behaving in a certain way in order to not challenge the status quo. What that meant specifically, Salam never fully addressed.

Like her Jewish Israeli colleagues I spoke to, Salam described staff dynamics at the hospital as unique and different from social relations outside the hospital. Offering another spatio-temporal imaginary, Salam said: "It's a utopia in hospitals, in Israel, relatively, it's a utopia, it's not perfect, but it's a utopia. And the dynamics between the staff members and the colleagues are very different than anything outside the hospitals." Her reference to the utopian quality of the hospital indicates a vision of an ideal future that has momentarily already arrived within the hospital walls. Etymologically, the term utopia derives from the Greek "ou," meaning no, and "topos," referring to place. In that sense, utopia literally describes a nonplace, evoking Lena and Irit's spatial descriptors. In its contemporary use, utopia designates a "place of ideal perfection especially in laws, government, and social conditions," or an "imaginary and indefinitely remote place," according to Merriam-Webster.[67] In Salam's narrative, Palestinian and Jewish physicians working together without conflict is an ideal social condition. It is, however, a condition that requires constant maintenance precisely because it is not yet a fully achieved social condition in the Israeli state and society writ large.

As discussed earlier, making the case for medical neutrality in Israeli hospitals is centered around Jewish Israeli feelings and settler politics. It is, as anthropologist Guy Shalev argues, a fundamental tool of Israeli hegemony, and it is especially reinforced by Jewish Israeli health administrators and professionals.[68] Palestinian physicians' positionality within the healthcare system is thus characterized by various personal and professional strategies to navigate their workplace. Maintaining "utopian" staff dynamics can be a crucial way to ensure one's own safety and well-being, including the performance of "indirect discipline," self-censorship, deference, or the severance of professional title from civic status as a Palestinian citizen of Israel.[69] The last time I met Salam was in June 2020, a few weeks before then-prime minister Benjamin Netanyahu had planned to annex the West Bank, and in the wake of a wave of protests after the brutal killing of George Floyd by police in the United States. The political situation felt extremely tense, and the annexation plans came up in most conversations I had with Palestinians at the time. Salam brought this up as well, saying that "we are going to an interesting time anyway with the annexation in the next two weeks, and the reality is changing." I asked her if the political climate had affected her working environment in the clinic and her relationship with her colleagues. Salam replied in the known spatial vocabulary. But this time, she clearly alluded to medical neutrality and professionalism needing maintenance: "Maybe, but living in a bubble, which is called the medical system, you cannot feel it. I think everyone avoids talking about it, and I believe in that, because, you see, we have good relationships, and everyone wants to keep them, so I'm not sure that I know what everyone thinks about it." This active making of the status quo, however, requires different things from Palestinian and Jewish Israeli staff. Salam made this point carefully, weighing each word with precision:

> My conclusion is that in every situation in the world, in the shadow of what's happening in America, the privileged always think about things in a different way, and even the formal understanding of the other side is not really deep. Either just to protect yourself, and I think part of it is that you are not aware of the privilege you have and who pays the cost. Because it's very uncomfortable, because you perceive yourself as a good person, and I can say that most of the people here are good people, and you just come and throw in their faces that "you are part of a very bad system," that's inconvenient. If someone comes and tells me, "OK, open your eyes" and tells me that I'm privileged because some other people are suffering, it's inconvenient, it's about changing your perception of life. I think the medical system in general is very protected, and people are aware enough to protect their relationship and the status quo, which is good. How long it will hold? I'm not sure.

In her analysis of Israeli medical space, Salam weaves together global and local politics and shifts between different spatial registers and points of view. She takes the political situation of the George Floyd protests and the United States' reckoning with racial injustice and privilege as a starting point to explain how the privileged have a different understanding of politics or injustice and even fail at a basic understanding of the other side. She finds that being challenged about your privilege is uncomfortable, inconvenient, and requires a reckoning with the systemic nature of being part of a "bad system." This is where she interjects with the actual space and people she is talking about: "And I can say that most of the people here are good people," bringing the analysis back to the hospital and her Jewish Israeli colleagues, and in so doing identifying them as the privileged. Salam notes that it is precisely for the difficulties involved in challenging privilege and systemic injustice—which would require no less than a complete change of one's perspective on life—that the hospital is a protected space where these issues are not opened. This, according to her, is a good thing, but it is also a fragile construct that can easily shatter under the current political circumstances.

This quotation demonstrates the complex situation Salam finds herself in as a Palestinian physician and the limited mode of criticism she wants to share with me (or is comfortable sharing with me). In her weaving together of different political contexts of privilege and suffering, and her shifting between various points of view, Salam critiques the Israeli hospital's insistence on medical and political neutrality without directly addressing her colleagues. She slips into different narrative roles precisely to reveal the affective dimensions of Israeli hegemonic feeling, alluding to the fact that the reconciliation between feeling like one is a good person and one's embeddedness in a systemic structure of violence is inconvenient. I also read Salam's articulation as an ethnographic limit that points to the complexities she faces in narrating her complicated situation in an Israeli institution to an outsider like me. Ethnographic limits remind us that not everything can be conveyed, that "rather than stops, or impediments to knowing, those limits may be expansive in their ethnographic nonrendering *and in what they do not tell us*."[70] Like in the above quotation, on record, Salam would always remain vague in her criticism toward the hospital and Israeli politics more broadly, and she might have various reasons for doing so, reasons I can only speculate about. However, I find that what she does not tell me about her critique is powerfully conveyed in how she articulates her opinions in a conversation with transnational politics.

Scholarship on Palestinian nurses, pharmacists, and doctors employed in Israeli institutions foregrounds this tension I felt in Salam's reflection. Palestinian medical staff, on the one hand, perceive their medical training, workplace, and medical knowledge as neutral and apolitical, just like their Jewish Israeli colleagues. Medical education in general rehearses an objectifying gaze, transforming the patient into an ahistorical and apolitical body and different body parts.[71] In Israel, medical and political neutrality produced in and through the hospital has also been identified as one of the main factors why the medical sector has a comparatively high percentage of Palestinian staff. However, it is the very ethos of neutrality that highlights Palestinian medical staff's difference, especially during times of war or heightened political tension, revealing the fragility of the status quo that Salam referred to. Palestinian physicians made it clear that discussing politics at work is not always a safe thing to do and that political beliefs are best kept private to avoid conflict.[72] However, as Salam's analysis demonstrates, Palestinian medical staff also challenge the ostensible spatial insularity of Israeli medical space as a zone of neutrality and refuse to recognize and be recognized by the settler state in various ways.

Amer is a Palestinian gynecologist-obstetrician who has worked in infertility for over twenty-five years. He lives in Haifa, where he both works in a public hospital and runs his own private women's health clinic with a majority Palestinian clientele. Seated on his terrace overlooking the sea on a warm summer evening, Amer told me that he feels like most of the patients he gets at the hospital, 90 percent of whom are Jewish Israelis, already know he is Palestinian by his name, concluding that he would not get "the extremists" anyway. Nonetheless, he explained that his Israeli citizenship would, in the eyes of some of his patients, align him with the Zionist project and Israeli politics. This is something he refuses to accept.

> Many patients think that if I'm Israeli, I do agree with the occupation, or I do agree with what's going on in Gaza. So, they expect me to agree with them, and they don't like it if I say there is an occupation, and there are people under occupation. You know, there are rules in Israel, as an example, if you are Jewish or a relative of a Jew, you can come to Israel and get everything, but if you are Palestinian, it's forbidden for you to come back to your home and to your country. So, they don't even want to see this, the human rights aspect, and if you say it, they will call you an antisemite.

Referring to the Right of Return, and Palestinians' limited rights for family reunification as settler colonial citizens of Israel, Amer refuses his simple inclusion into the state, and the hospital by extension. He actively voices his disagreement with the Israeli occupation and the settler colonial structure of Israeli statecraft. Reflecting on his disagreement with "what's going on in Gaza" (in 2019) furthermore foreshadows Jewish Israelis' incapability or unwillingness to grasp why Palestinian healthcare workers have voiced empathy with the people of Gaza from October 2023 onward. Amer further alludes to Palestinian citizens of Israel's limited modes of expression in the Israeli public sphere, revealing the selective neutrality of public opinion when it comes to Palestinians expressing even modest criticism of the Israeli state. But his critique did not end there. Amer gave me an example of what his refusal looks like, practically:

> AMER: Sometimes I say, "Does Israel really want peace when it continues to build settlements in the West Bank?" So, actually, I sometimes give them a pen and tell them: "Please, draw me the borders of Israel."

GALA: You do? At work?

AMER: Yeah, it happened to me twice, one time with this lady, I said, "OK, you say you want peace, draw me please, where are the borders of Israel." So, you know . . . they don't like this question, because mainly they are not people who believe in a two-state solution.

In this instance, Amer articulates his vision of a political future for Palestine by engaging with its complicated present. In challenging his patients to draw the borders of a deliberately de-bordered state,[73] he refuses his partial inclusion as a settler colonial Israeli citizen by openly speaking back and he also opens up a new political horizon. He brings the contested borders impeding Palestinian lives and movements back into his office at the hospital and provokes his patients' political feelings and vision. Amer not only refuses the status quo of medical and political neutrality in his workplace but also the political horizon of a Jewish supremacist one-state solution, which is being advanced with the permanent occupation and the building of every new settlement in the West Bank.[74]

Amer is a successful and self-confident male doctor in his sixties and a Christian Palestinian. To openly challenge Zionist ideals of Palestinians' docility and to dissent from the official narrative within the hospital is a risk not everyone can take. As anthropologist Amahl Bishara writes, the "environments of expression" for Palestinians across Palestine/Israel vary and crucially determine who can say what, where, and when.[75] And yet, "Please, draw me the borders of Israel" translates Salam's analysis of the inconvenience of being among the privileged in a violent system of power into an imperative. It shatters the expected coproduction of medical space as politically and medically neutral and it also reveals the easy conflation of the occupied Palestinian territory with Israeli space.

Salam, Amer, and other Palestinian physicians' practices of refusing the narrative and spatial imaginaries of medical space show how Palestinians challenge their inclusion in Israeli institutions. Recognizing and carefully negotiating their position as Palestinians within the medical system, their narratives and experiences reveal the fragility of the spatial imaginary of a "bubble" and the various ways in which they both invest in and contest the status quo. The ways in which Amer and Salam addressed Palestinian politics, identity, and dignity before October 2023 offer a window into how Palestinians have always contested their political nonexistence in Israeli space and foreshadow the dangerous inability or unwillingness of Jewish Israelis to see Palestinian suffering in Gaza after October 7.

"INCLUSIVE EXCLUSION": GEOGRAPHIES OF SECURITY AND (NON)BELONGING

Despite the ubiquity of the narrative of medical and political neutrality, Jewish Israeli medical staff also relate to the geographies and social relations beyond the hospital. We can encounter these links to an elsewhere,[76] the porosity of the narrative of medical neutrality, in feelings of fear, anger, and related measures of securitization and surveillance, but also in feelings of care and intimacy. Ziva is a Jewish Israeli social worker in a large public hospital in Jerusalem, whom I met twice for interviews about her work. I was also in an exchange with her throughout the course of doing fieldwork, especially during the first year of the Covid pandemic. Sitting in her windowless office, Ziva reflected on the geographical location of the hospital where she works. Located in one of the "frontier neighborhoods" of Jerusalem, directly next to Palestinian East Jerusalemite neighborhoods and refugee camps under Israeli control, the hospital is both symbolically and geographically surrounded by contested landscapes and a portion of the separation wall.[77] In referencing this geography, Ziva presented the hospital in the usual spatial grammar. However, in her narrative, we can see how the outside world and its social relations do encroach onto the hospital and, paradoxically, further facilitate its making as a neutral space. Her description of the proximity to the West Bank, the separation wall (which she refers to as a fence), and the East Jerusalem neighborhood of Issawiya, a Palestinian neighborhood that is under constant threat from Israeli land grabs and confiscations, reveals the porosity of her colleagues' spatial imaginaries.

> Here by the fence, we have Issawiya village. During some days, they are throwing bottles from Issawiya, that explode, and stones, and after a few minutes, if they need something, they come *whoosh* [imitates with a higher voice] here to the hospital to the emergency room. And you see, you see the fence. Especially when something happens outside, you know, in Gaza or in the West Bank, we will try that this hospital will be an island, that nothing touches it, but it's here. So, you can hear . . . sometimes, the staff, they are not so understanding, and they're saying things like, "How do they have the guts to come here and ask for help when after a few hours they will throw stones at us? They have the chutzpah to come here and ask?" But after you take these words aside, and sit with a woman that cries, that wants children, you forget it. . . . When a woman comes inside, we are closing the door for everything outside. But it's not clear, we can't, we can't and sometimes . . . you can hear, you know, under, behind the door that . . . we're helping them to have, erm, future terrorists.

Ziva describes the hospital as an apolitical space, but she also recognizes that it is not always possible to disentangle affect, politics, and medical neutrality in the fertility clinic.[78] The hospital's relationality to the surrounding political and spatial landscape appears in sharp contours, contrary to the usual imaginaries of medical space as detached from the outside world. Palestinians from the neighboring Issawiya, throwing stones and explosives at the hospital, literally and figuratively shatter any residual belief in the hospital as an extraterritorial no-man's-land. The way Ziva recounts how, after an attack on the hospital, Palestinians from East Jerusalem would come to the emergency room demonstrates how Israeli hegemonic feelings structure medical space. *Whoosh*—as soon as Palestinians act, feel, or appear outside of the docile positionalities they are assigned to by the Israeli state, military, and society, the idea that the "hospital will be an island" falters. Ziva's description, her hesitancy, and her hearing these fears of helping to reproduce "future terrorists" reveals an Israeli structure of feeling in which the Palestinian Other, and their children, are always already perceived within a framework of securitization. The settler colonial management of Palestinian bodies affectively structures space in the fertility clinic, yet these feelings need to be (partly) hidden to maintain the humanitarian alibi of the hospital and Israel as a liberal democracy (at least until October 7).

Ariella Azoulay and Adi Ophir coined the notion of an "inclusive exclusion" to describe the Israeli state's effort to simultaneously separate and rule over Palestinians: "The fantasy of once and for all separating inside from outside, 'security threats' from peaceful citizens, while nonetheless paradoxically containing and ruling the excluded."[79] The ambiguity of this form of governance is present in Ziva's reflection. On the one hand, Palestinians are described as stone throwers and future terrorists. At the same time, when entering the clinic, they need to be treated according to the clinic's universalist imperatives. The Palestinian population is included as an irrevocable Other in order to demarcate and manage that otherness. Anthropologist Sophia Stamatopoulou-Robbins terms this a "möbius strip of separation and control," in which separation and control of the Palestinians flow and fold seamlessly into one another.[80] This is evident in a spatial sense as captured in the above quotation. Palestinians' presence in the Israeli hospital is a foundational register to further manage and control the Palestinian population through their conditional inclusion, no matter if they are citizens, residents, or occupied subjects. Palestinians are only recognized as an exception. The parameters of this exception are subject to Israeli hegemonic feelings and structures of domination.

The fantasy of separating "security threats" from "regular citizens" also unfolds on a gendered register. In Ziva's narrative, Palestinians are affectively and geographically placed on a scale that ranges from future terrorists, security threats, stone throwers, to a woman who cries. Palestinian masculine corporeality serves as the paradigmatic threat here, "the archetype of the terrorist-other of the Israeli military and the larger Zionist national imaginary," as anthropologist Rema Hammami puts it, while Palestinian women are simultaneously victimized and sexualized by the Israeli military and the state's demographic politics.[81] This allows for a partial humanization of Palestinian women in need of support and saving, and the possibility to "close the door for everything outside." The status of the Palestinian woman who cries and wants children, and her essentialized cultural backwardness in relation to Israeli Western and modern values, enables her placement as nonthreatening. But her status as a vulnerable victim is also fragile: The fact that she might potentially give birth to "future terrorists" reveals that she is never outside the realm of Israeli demographic anxieties.[82]

Finally, Ziva's narrative about stone throwers who come to the hospital to seek treatment afterward points to a broader discourse about Palestinians' relationship with the Israeli state and its institutions. When I talked to Jewish Israelis about my research—research participants and regular people alike—there was often a sense that the topic I was interested in was not an issue. After all, Palestinians have access to world-class medical healthcare and the renowned fertility economy, access they don't have in the West Bank, Gaza, or even abroad. This came through when I first contacted Irit (see above) or in Michael's description of the Bedouin population in chapter 1. I could trace this narrative in Jewish Israeli doctors' description of West Bank fertility clinics as a "wild west," and in their disbelief at why Palestinians with Israeli citizenship would seek treatment there.[83] It also crystallizes in Ziva's quotation here. The basic assumption fueling all of these statements is that Palestinians must be grateful for the state-subsidized medical services they receive in Israeli hospitals. How do they have the "chutzpah to come here and ask"? How can Palestinians (or others, like myself) complain about discrimination in the hospital if Palestinians can access free fertility treatment?

This demand for reverence is articulated in two interrelated ways. On the one hand, it is central to the notion of liberal inclusion, whereby the Israeli state's granting of rights and benefits—in this case, access to state-subsidized healthcare—is perceived as a benevolent act that Palestinians should be grateful for. This argument is often made by referring to '48 Palestinians through a minority framework, in which their rights (or lack thereof) can be compared to any other minority in the Jewish state (such as Ethiopian Jews, or Jewish immigrants from Eastern Europe).[84] This narrative disconnects the coercive inclusion of Palestinians into the liberal settler state and disregards their status as strangers in their own homeland.[85]

On the other hand, this demand is extended to Palestinians with a Jerusalem ID and Palestinians from the occupied West Bank who might seek medical treatment in an Israeli hospital in Jerusalem. In this iteration, Palestinians' gratitude is requested even more forcefully, as they are located on the other side of the border; they are associated with "the enemy." In Ziva's reflections, these are Palestinians who are being treated in an Israeli hospital *even after* they had attacked said hospital (or performed any other act of resistance). Here, the expectation of gratitude stems from a perceived Israeli humanitarianism, even in the face of acts of violence. In both cases, however, the reason why Palestinians end up in an Israeli hospital (or why they have to cross a border or checkpoint to get there, or why they might throw a stone at an Israeli soldier, or why the Israeli police are invading their neighborhood) is occluded. Gender studies scholar Mimi Nguyen's notion of the "gift of freedom" is useful here.[86] Nguyen develops this formulation to capture how Vietnamese refugees who have been resettled to the United States are interpellated as having received the liberal empire's "gift of freedom" twice, first through imperial war and then through the granting of refuge and liberal rights in the United States. However, being the target of the "gift of freedom," she argues, places them in a relationship of debt to empire, as they are expected to perform gratitude to the same powers that necessitated their seeking refuge. In that sense, the gift of freedom is a core function of colonial violence and power. Liberal war and liberal peace, Nguyen argues, are not distinct from each other.[87] This characterizes Palestinians' existence across the territory of historic Palestine. While in the Palestinian case, the option of resettlement has been completely foreclosed since 1948, they are still placed in a perpetual cycle of either having to be grateful for their mere existence in an Israeli institution, or being labeled as untrustworthy, dangerous, a terrorist, or the enemy more broadly. Being Palestinian and receiving (reproductive) health care in an Israeli hospital is framed within the debt of gratefulness; this gift of freedom is an "imperial remains that preclude the subject of freedom from being able to escape a colonial order of things."[88] Demanding this debt fails to recognize that Palestinians never sought to become citizens, residents, or subjects of the Israeli state.

Demanding gratefulness based on inclusion has changed since October 7. While I was conducting research for this project, Palestinians' existence in Israeli medical space was still possible, albeit as an "inclusive exclusion," never fully belonging there. But once Israeli society had entered a militarized state of emergency, being grateful for their inclusion was not enough anymore. This conjuncture exposes the limits of the gift of freedom. Once the target of liberal inclusion is labeled as the key figure of a "security threat," no matter if they are civilians or militants, no performance of gratitude will relieve them from this fundamental dehumanization. Future research will show what kind of demands Jewish Israelis will place on Palestinians to prove that their existence does not threaten them, their institutions, and the Jewish state.

HEGEMONIC FEELINGS AND THE MAKING OF SETTLER SPACE

Israeli hegemonic feelings, fears, and resulting structures of securitization and spatial enclosure are felt by Palestinian patients and physicians alike. Meera is a Palestinian doctor in residency at a Jerusalem hospital who lives in East Jerusalem. Meera and I are the same age, and I remember being impressed when she texted me where she would pick me up with her "black Audi 🙂." As part of her residency, she spent a year in the hospital's IVF department and was based in the delivery room at the time we met. Having worked with Palestinian patients from the West Bank, East Jerusalem, and Israel, Meera noted a big difference between them and her Jewish Israeli patients: While "the Jewish ladies" got on the internet to research their doctors and the process of fertility treatment beforehand, her Palestinian patients seemingly showed less interest and were not as informed as their Jewish counterparts. Meera described their attitude as follows: "Arab ladies come in and they're like 'OK, I get whatever I can.'" They would not ask questions about who the best doctor was or what the side effects of the hormone treatment were. But more than that, again evoking Fanon's description of the colonial doctor-patient relationship, Meera explained to me: "When Arabs come into a Jewish hospital, they take it like: 'I can't ask for anything, I have to be very good because I'm not in my territory.'" Oppression and exclusion are felt on a bodily and affective level just by entering medical space.[89]

In Meera's observation, her Palestinian patients' behavior of taking up less space, not asking for guidance or support, and feeling that they must be "good" in an Israeli hospital indicates an alignment of bodies in social space according to the Israeli politics of fear.[90] Impediments to Palestinians' mobility, agency, and assertiveness in medical space are imposed onto their bodies by the broader structures of Israeli demographic anxieties. A sliding scale of rights and varying modalities of rule differentiate Palestinians in the West Bank and Gaza from Palestinians in East Jerusalem and from Palestinian citizens of Israel and determine their mode of inclusion into the Israeli healthcare system. However, Meera's description of her patients' feelings illustrates that even if included structurally (as most of her patients are, as Palestinians with residency status or citizenship), they are made to feel that racialized hierarchies and essentialized cultural differences exceed the level of formal access or legal equality. Full belonging to state institutions and legal categories such as citizenship or residency are reserved for those whose affective disposition aligns with the right feelings for the state, nation, or political community—a structure of feeling Palestinians are categorically excluded from as settler colonial citizens of a Jewish state or subjects under occupation.[91]

Towards the end of our conversation, I asked Meera how she experienced her Jewish Israeli colleagues' sentiments toward their Palestinian patients, but also toward herself. Like other Palestinian physicians, Meera spoke a lot about the importance of language and culturally appropriate services at the hospital. She noted that the more her colleagues understand their Palestinian patients, both culturally and in terms of a shared language, "the more they can look at them as equals" and not just as "a chart." Meera specifically remembered one of her colleagues who does not speak Arabic and who told her that he did not want to see Palestinian patients because he felt like he was unable to communicate with them. With a deeper voice, Meera imitated him in their conversation: "It's like giving me a stuffed animal or something like that. I can't express myself. I can't explain stuff to them." Meera's colleague acknowledged that his patients need to understand him in order to be adequately treated. But without a shared language, her colleagues' patients appear to him as innate objects: stuffed animals without a voice or agency. Palestinians' deservingness and respectability depend on their proximity to Jewish Israeli physicians, both linguistically and culturally. Yet the factors of their recognition are not fixed. They might be found in a Palestinian woman who dresses "like us" or a Palestinian citizen's accent-free Hebrew and integration into the labor force, but these attributes can signify danger to the settler colonial state and its institutions at any time.

After her doctor's rotation in the IVF department, Meera got offered a position there because they needed an Arabic-speaking person to cater to their East Jerusalemite and West Bank patients. But Meera did not want to be treated as a token. She explained to me:

> I'm like, you know, I like IVF, but I like it if I can do what I want to do and what interests me. And I don't want to be just there as a translator. I don't want to be put in this box. And if there's one thing I kind of had to explain in every place that I worked in, it's that I don't want to be looked at as the person who, you know . . . "just tell the Arab ladies to be quiet."

Meera's own presence as a physician in the Israeli fertility clinic illustrates the limited range of options it affords Palestinians who exist in this space, whether as patients or as staff. Her status in the hospital exemplifies what it means to be included as an exception. She is needed to translate in the IVF department to facilitate a basic understanding between Jewish Israeli medical staff and Palestinian patients, but she is also needed to discipline Palestinian patients. The bounds of Meera's professional inclusion are constantly being renegotiated; she is simultaneously needed as a cultural and linguistic broker, but she is never fully accepted in a way that would enable her to pursue her career in a self-determined way beyond her role *as* a Palestinian physician.

Meera is well aware of this conundrum. She knows the limits of her affective and settler colonial status vis-à-vis her colleagues, the institution, and the state. Meera spoke a lot about her colleagues' racism, which was capacious but never immediately directed against her (an English speaker with a North American accent who was educated abroad). For example, Meera told me about one of her colleagues, a nurse in the IVF department, pointing out her own complicated positionality across class and gender divisions: "I know she has this tendency to be racist. Now, if she sees me, she will kiss me from my head to my toes. Like, she's so in love with me. But I know she has this tendency, especially with the patients who are, you know, from lower classes." It is precisely in these intimate and even tender encounters that the violence of the Israeli hospital as a spatial and affective unit comes to the fore. Meera, an educated Palestinian woman who dresses "modern," can receive such love and appreciation from her colleagues, but she is limited in her professional choices in a settler institution. At the same time, a sliding scale of rights differentiates her from other Palestinian women: more religious, lower-class, and non-Hebrew speaking women, as well as noncitizens from the West Bank or from resisting Palestinian neighborhoods.

In the Israeli medical space, Palestinians move on shifting and slippery grounds, always one step away from doing something wrong. This is evident in how their Jewish Israeli colleagues feel about Palestinians, both as colleagues and patients. In one of my conversations with Ziva, she remembered an encounter with a Palestinian woman from the West Bank. She was waiting for her appointment together with her young son, who was playing in the waiting room. Once her appointment came up, Ziva observed how the woman called for her son, who didn't follow her immediately. According to Ziva, the woman then started hitting him. Ziva told me:

> I couldn't be quiet, and I went there and told her, "Please, don't touch the child, don't do that." She told me, "You want to tell me that after you're killing our children in Gaza? Here, you can be so hypocritical, and there you can say that you are really afraid of my child?" And I told her, you know, "Leave the outside outside now." So she told me, "I'm here. I paid for this appointment. And you will take care of me as much as I like and don't talk to me more than that."

In Ziva's retelling of this instance, the Palestinian woman called her out precisely on the imagined separation of the hospital from the violence linking this place to the broader circumstances of the settler state. She noted the different criteria Jewish Israelis use to differentiate those children whose lives matter and those who are considered collateral damage.[92] But for Ziva, Israeli military and state violence are perceived as an abstract, faraway elsewhere, whereas this woman's violence against her child calls for immediate intervention. In retelling this story to me to make her point about medical staff's practice of "leaving the outside outside" and Palestinians' failure to do so, Ziva told me a much more powerful story: that of Palestinians' refusal to be interpellated according to the disciplinary gaze of the settler state and their relegation to a place of docility and respectability, a refusal of the role of the "perfect victim."[93]

In these instances of intimate encounters and practices of care, the relationship between Israeli territory, hegemonic feelings, security, and Palestinians' identity crystallizes clearly. Notions of belonging, deservingness, and respectability make up the architecture of the Israeli hospital. Despite spatial imaginaries of extraterritoriality, the hospital as a place is constructed in close articulation with social relations shaping Israeli society and its structure of feeling, and the political and geographical landscapes surrounding the hospital itself. The notion of the hospital as "an island" becomes a porous fantasy in service of narratives of benevolence and humanitarianism that distract from Israeli atrocities as a foundational structure, not an event.[94]

. . .

While my meeting with Irit and our short drive from the women's health clinic to the larger hospital marked the beginning of doing fieldwork with medical staff, my encounter with Meera almost marked its end in August 2020. I did a few more interviews that year, but due to the worsening of Covid-19 conditions in Palestine/Israel, I conducted the remainder of them online. After our meeting at a café overlooking the nearby Palestinian neighborhood Wadi al-Joz with a panoramic view of the old city of Jerusalem, Meera offered to drive me back to the central bus station of Jerusalem since it had gotten late. On our way there, we drove through Mea She'arim, an insular neighborhood known for its majority ultra-Orthodox community. While we had been chatting about our lives as women at the end of their twenties—where we had traveled, how Covid had affected our routines—Meera became more serious once we saw more of the traditionally Haredim in their discernible black clothes. She told me that the navigation app she was using had chosen this route for us, but that she would usually prefer not to drive through this neighborhood. "I hate it, emotionally," she said. Residents of this neighborhood had thrown stones and spat on her hijab-wearing mother as she had once passed through there. Since then, Meera wouldn't allow her to drive or walk through this part of the city. The spatial politics of the hospital not being her patients' territory, as she had explained to me just an hour earlier, folded into her personal affective reaction to the city's geography. Her remark indexes the continuum of attachment, rejection, and dispossession from space that structures Palestinian women's everyday lives in East Jerusalem.[95] Her remark also encapsulates the key point of this chapter, that the Israeli hospital, despite its spatial imagination as separate, exists in close articulation with the world beyond itself.[96] As our drive evidenced, the supposedly vast distance hegemonic Israeli narratives erect between the hospital and a violent outside world could be covered in less than fifteen minutes.

The spatial distribution of security practices, such as the military rule over the occupied territories and the policing of its borders, might seem far away from the Israeli hospital (and, as we have seen, this is also what many Jewish Israeli physicians feel), and yet what happens there is foundational for the very *need* of a narrative of the hospital as an island of coexistence. Meera's experiences and her stories about her colleagues might seem like they are normal stories of a diverse workplace with its micro-aggressions and language issues, yet they fold into the city and Meera's fear for her mother. The maintenance of the status quo of the hospital as an apolitical place works at the expense of Palestinian physicians' freedom of expression and derives from pressures Palestinians must contend with to be good and respectable patients. These processes and their formation make up the place-myth of the Israeli hospital and situate it firmly as a spatial entity in larger settler colonial structures.

The imaginary of the Israeli hospital as a special place is in articulation with the broader identity categories available for Palestinians—deservingness, respectability, Western values, and the impossibility of full belonging to the settler colonial state. Palestinians and their bodies arouse feelings of fear, guilt, anxiety, and discomfort.[97] Their foundational nonbelonging sits uncomfortably and inextricably with the fertility clinic's proclaimed medical neutrality. Palestinians in the Israeli medical space, either as doctors or as patients, are constructed in relation to settler identity as a function of territory.[98] It is in the everyday encounters in the fertility clinic, often intimate and caring, that Palestinian women's reproductive rights and freedom are negotiated. These are sites not of spectacular violence and outright control but of small gestures, tender violence, affects, and sentiments often expressed unconsciously. And yet, these processes are foundationally informed and sanctioned by Israeli demographic anxieties.

FOUR

Intimacies

> Here I ask whether a privileging of sexual politics may not adequately capture the colonial and postcolonial forms of governance that manage the carnal, intimate, and affective relations to which people are subjected and by which they, in turn, reorder what most immediately presses on their movements, constrains their choices and manages the politics of their intimate lives.
>
> ANN LAURA STOLER,
> *Duress: Imperial Durabilities in Our Times*

> The denationalized malaise and anxiety women express about love and birth contrast with the notions of politics, resistance, identity, negotiations, and strategies, which blind us to the sneaky violence that the distribution of rights exercises on the fabric of intimacy.
>
> LIVIA WICK,
> *Sumud: Birth, Oral History, and Persisting in Palestine*

ON THE TERRITORY BETWEEN THE River and the Sea, the Israeli state and military directly and indirectly manage and control Palestinian women's most intimate decision-making and reproductive lives. Israel's impact on the Palestinian health sector serves as one example of this control. The siege on Gaza and the military occupation of the West Bank have severely undermined the Palestinian healthcare system by restricting the movement of medical personnel, equipment, and patients, and by limiting access to essential infrastructure and resources. These constraints have led to a fragmented and under-resourced Palestinian health sector, with limited capacity to provide specialized or advanced medical care, including in the field of reproductive medicine and care.[1] Yara is a Palestinian health scholar who works in an Israeli NGO providing health services to Palestinians in Israel and the occupied territories. The organization supports Palestinians in the West Bank and Gaza (pre–October 7) to apply for health-related permits to enter Israel to receive treatment in an Israeli hospital. While this mainly concerns cancer patients and others who require lifesaving treatments, Yara told me that, sometimes, they also receive requests from women in the West Bank to enter Israel or women in Gaza to enter the West Bank, both seeking access to fertility treatment at clinics in Israel or the West Bank:

> I know that we had several cases where we tried to help couples leave the Strip for treatments in the West Bank in private clinics or in Israeli hospitals, and we succeeded a few times. Later, we learned that the Israeli army has certain criteria regarding which patients can obtain the permit and leave the Strip for treatments that are unavailable in their place of residence, and IVF is not one of these treatments. IVF is not perceived as lifesaving treatment and also not as a treatment or medical problem that, if you don't treat it, can affect your well-being and your life, so it was very difficult for us.

In addition to deciding which health-related issues Palestinians from Gaza would get a permit for, the Israeli authorities also have insight into the Palestinian applicants' lives. This includes whether a woman applying for a permit already has children. The military would use this information to judge whether she would receive a permit to undergo fertility treatment. Yara explained:

> We had this kind of problem when I spoke with the Israeli coordination at the Erez crossing [Israel-controlled border crossing between Israel and Gaza]. I discussed one of the cases with a soldier over the phone, and he looked into the data that he had, and he said, "Yeah, but they do have children already," and I said, "Yeah, OK, I myself didn't know that they had children." . . . So, it's like the Israeli authority can even plan for Palestinians how many children they are eligible to have. If you have one kid, then that should be enough.

The bureaucratic and military machinery that the Israeli state has set up to monitor Palestinians' movement across its borders reveals the vast biopolitical reach the Israeli state has into families' most intimate decisions. Israeli soldiers can simply "look into" the data of a Palestinian woman's life and decide whether the treatment she is applying for would affect her well-being and life, and if she is deserving of such treatment. Not only is the Palestinian population's overall health dependent on Israeli governance, but Israel also determines what kind of medical treatment Palestinian women are eligible to receive. Since Israel's genocide in Gaza, this biopolitical management has become necropolitical at its core. Israel has destroyed the vast majority of Palestinian health infrastructure in Gaza, including its few existing fertility clinics, and the conditions of destruction and constant relocation that

Palestinians in Gaza experience severely impact Palestinian women's health, including their reproduction.[2]

Palestinian women's reproductive health, choices, and pregnancy outcomes were thus bound up with the settler state, its military, and demographic politics before October 7, and even more so after.[3] Whether it is pregnant Palestinian women in the occupied West Bank who have to cross checkpoints and highly militarized borders, Palestinian residents in East Jerusalem who have to give birth in an Israeli hospital for their children to receive residency status, Palestinian citizens of Israel who are barred from reuniting with their spouses and families from the West Bank, or Palestinian women surviving Israel's annihilatory assault in Gaza—the Israeli state and its policies overtly or subtly structure their reproductive options and futures. Thinking with Chicana theorist Gloria Anzalduá, Palestinian women's bodies "grate" against the various borders erected to control, manage, and surveil their (reproductive) movement.[4]

Indeed, this points to a central feature of being Palestinian across the territory of historic Palestine. As political theorist Nasser Abourahme puts it, "Crossing barriers is perhaps the single most definitive experience in contemporary Palestinian life." This crossing not only modulates and defines Palestinians' freedom and speed of movement but is also "constitutive of people's experiences of time and space."[5] While this is a formative experience for all Palestinians, the border crossings that Palestinian women who want to become pregnant must perform are specifically complex and defining of their pregnancy journey. Entering Israeli medical institutions (and getting there) presents a particularly intense and gendered interface with Israeli policies, Zionist ideology, and Jewish Israeli professionals. In her study of Palestinian women's experience of undergoing fertility treatment in the Israeli fertility economy, historian Himmat Zu'bi notes that entering Israeli medical space means entering a distinct spatial and temporal reality.[6] For many Palestinian women, their decision to undergo fertility treatment means making first contact with the Israeli healthcare system. Once Palestinians from across Palestine/Israel enter an Israeli hospital, they have to navigate their status vis-à-vis the Israeli state, especially if they seek reproductive treatment. Zu'bi thus writes that Palestinian women's access to Israeli healthcare is contingent on their "historical and contemporary position as Zionism's ultimate other."[7] Feminist legal scholar Nadera Shalhoub-Kevorkian similarly points out the spatial specificity of Palestinian women's reproduction, which constitutes "a specific type of 'conflict zone' within the larger, prevailing colonized zone. Not only do pregnant and birthing women suffer very specific effects as a result of the occupation, but the particular childbirth experiences of Palestinian women are indelibly tied to the politics of the conflict."[8]

This chapter, then, explores how Palestinian women's crossing of various borders, or borders crossing their bodies,[9] shapes the most intimate part of their lives: their reproduction, sexuality, kin-work, and family planning. It asks: How do Palestinian women make sense of the various barriers they experience on their pregnancy journeys? And how does their intimate interfacing with Israeli borders shape their reproductive movement, politics, and agency? Based on the narratives of three Palestinian women from different geographies of Israeli jurisdiction—Celine from the occupied West Bank, Reem from occupied East Jerusalem, and Christeen, who holds Israeli citizenship—this chapter reveals the various borders and interior frontiers the Israeli state sets up to control and manage the Palestinian population across Palestine/Israel. It also attends to the difficult and at times ambivalent strategies that Palestinian women deploy to navigate their enforced inclusion or subjugation to the Israeli state. These include women's everyday practices to manage, contest, and overcome the borders and barriers they have to cross; the various temporal, spatial, and political horizons this border crossing engenders; as well as Reem, Christeen, and Celine's different understandings of Israeli demographic anxieties and the political context of their reproduction.

To fully grasp how these reproductive journeys are shaped by Israeli borders, policies, and institutions, it is essential to situate them within a broader feminist and anticolonial understanding of intimacy as a key site of colonial power and governance, as anthropologist Ann Laura Stoler's epigraph invites. Control of the reproductive body, surveillance of people's sexualities and relationships, and questions of who is regarded as a legitimate parent were foundational to the transatlantic slave trade and plantation slavery, colonialism, and imperialism, and continue to shape today's border and immigration regimes.[10] Reproductive control is a central mechanism that binds together the "intimacies of four continents" on a transnational level.[11] Yet reproduction itself is characterized by the intimate in its more common-sense understanding as relating to closeness and proximity, the registers of touch and care, as well as complicated emotions and feelings like desire, disgust, or love.[12] In this chapter, I argue that it is precisely in the meeting of Palestinian bodies and Israeli borders, in which one crosses the other, that we can discern how the intimate plays out across its two registers. On the macro level, the

Israeli state decidedly regulates the intimate by way of targeting Palestinian women's bodies, reproduction, sexuality, and forms of kinship.[13] On the micro level, in the everyday, it is intimate encounters—the proximity between a Palestinian patient and an Israeli doctor, mediated through care, touch, emotion, or sensibility—that crucially shape the outcome of Palestinian women's fertility treatment.

To capture this duality of how the intimate shapes Palestinian women's reproduction, this chapter explores intimacies in various ways. First, it focuses on intimate decision-making and the bodies of Palestinian women who seek to get pregnant as an analytic to understand the workings of Israeli settler colonial demographic anxieties and policies. Paying attention to Palestinian women's intimate decision-making, reproductive movements, and practices of resistance points to the ways in which the everyday is a space for the making and subversion of settler colonial power structures.[14] Second, this chapter traces the intimate relations and proximities Palestinian women voluntarily or coercively enter as part of their pregnancy journey in Israeli fertility clinics. It shows how meeting Jewish Israeli nurses or doctors can be both a site of hope as well as an experience of racism, violence, and pain. Focusing on these different and often arbitrary levels of intimacy furthers an understanding of how vast and fine-grained settler colonial governance can be. And finally, this chapter also allows the reader to meet Reem, Christeen, and Celine. My own relationship with these women, two of whom I spoke to in English, allows for a more intimate and detailed recounting of their stories. This includes attending to the ethnographic and linguistic limits of such encounters. The intimate is thus mirrored formally and methodologically, inviting the reader into these women's lives while foregrounding the intimate entanglement of undergoing a process as difficult and private as fertility treatment and the broader logics of settler colonial politics, as well as the ways these experiences are narrated.

CELINE: THE OCCUPIED WEST BANK, SETTLER TIME, AND REPRODUCTIVE FUTURITY

Celine is a thirty-four-year-old medical professional who lives with her family in Bethlehem in the occupied West Bank. I met Celine in the crowded waiting room of the fertility unit of a hospital in Jerusalem. Celine was waiting to do a blood test and ultrasound to determine whether she was ready for her egg retrieval, to then undergo a cycle of IVF. With a letter explaining my research in English and Arabic, I introduced myself and asked if she would be interested in talking to me about her experience in the hospital. Celine was eager, and we started chatting in English. As usual, I offered to meet properly with Najla, my research assistant and interpreter at the time, but Celine said she was happy to practice her English. I also suggested visiting her in Bethlehem or meeting somewhere more private in Jerusalem. But Celine politely declined and said that if we were to talk, we would have to do it at the hospital before or after her appointments because she was keeping undergoing IVF a secret back home in Bethlehem. She also explained that she wouldn't have much time because every time she is at the hospital for an appointment, a taxi waits downstairs to take her back to the West Bank. We thus agreed to set up another meeting for the next time she had an appointment at the fertility unit.

A week later, Celine texted me that she would be at the hospital again, and we met up in the waiting room, which was especially noisy this time around. Celine is soft-spoken and carefully weighs her words. Sometimes she would turn to her husband, a thirty-six-year-old accountant, to discuss in Arabic an aspect of my question or a topic we were talking about. Despite the serious tone of our interviews, Celine would often foreground a funnier or more hopeful experience of her pregnancy journey, and the audio transcripts are full of shared laughter. Celine and her husband already have three children: two daughters, aged nine and seven, and a four-year-old son. All three of them were conceived via IVF in the Jerusalem hospital. For Palestinians living in the occupied West Bank, undergoing fertility treatment in a hospital in Jerusalem is a difficult, time-intensive, and expensive endeavor. The couple's story of navigating their complicated situation and their simple quest for a family reveals how Israeli control and domination penetrate Palestinians' most intimate decision-making and everyday lives. While their experience illustrates the intimate entanglement of politics and reproduction, it also points to the limits of this particular narrative. Capital-P politics was a topic Celine would be apprehensive of, echoing anthropologist Livia Wick's work on Palestinian women's complex narration of struggles of pregnancy, birth, and love under occupation.[15] Hers is a story of living on or getting by in a situation of ongoing duress, shaped by the politics of a military occupation but also her agency in telling her story outside of the prescribed politicized script of what it means to be Palestinian.

Celine's husband suffers from a serious genetic illness that causes infertility. His illness was discovered upon birth, and he has had to be treated in a specialized hospital since. From the age of three onward, Celine's husband was treated in the hospital where we met in Jerusalem, and he had a close relationship with his attending doctor. The couple explained that West Bank hospitals are not technically equipped to treat his condition and that the medical staff there lacked specialized knowledge. Celine told me: "In the West Bank, they can't treat patients like here, never," and explained: "Why? The knowledge. They conducted a lot of studies about the illness here, they come up with new methods and new treatment procedures for him that aren't available in the West Bank." Celine's husband's case points to Israel's disregard of its duty as an occupying power under international law to provide healthcare services to the Palestinian population and its deliberate obstruction and underdevelopment of the Palestinian healthcare system.[16] Due to the lack of resources, medical knowledge, and health infrastructures in the West Bank, it is not unusual for Palestinians from the occupied territories to seek treatment in hospitals in Israel or East Jerusalem. Most Palestinians receive care in a Palestinian-run hospital in East Jerusalem. However, these hospitals are managed by Palestinian nongovernmental organizations or charitable societies and rely on international funding, donations, and the Palestinian Authority's financial support, while their operation is overseen by Israeli authorities.[17] This means that for more complicated procedures, including fertility treatment, Palestinians would usually have to go to an Israeli hospital. As outlined at the outset of this chapter, this is also true for Palestinians from Gaza, who would either enter Israel to be treated in the West Bank or also seek treatment in an Israeli hospital. Since October 2023, Palestinians from both Gaza and the West Bank have faced significant challenges in obtaining medical permits to enter Israel for treatment. Approval rates for medical permits have drastically decreased in the West Bank, while the Israeli authorities have imposed stringent restrictions on the movement of Palestinian civilians from Gaza into Israel or Egypt.[18]

Because of his chronic illness, Celine's husband has an ongoing health-related permit, which he must renew every three months. Celine is registered to accompany her spouse to the hospital. When I asked the couple whether Celine's husband's parents also had to apply for a permit when they found out about their child's disease, he laughed, either at my bad math skills or lack of historical knowledge: This was thirty-three years ago. At the time, Palestinians from the West Bank didn't need a permit to enter Jerusalem. The separation barrier between Israel and the West Bank was only built in 2002 to control and monitor Palestinians' movements into Israel in the wake of the Second Intifada.[19]

When her husband was old enough for this information to be relevant, his doctor at the Jerusalem hospital told him that if he got married and wanted children, fertility treatment would be his only option. Celine and her husband thus decided to use his ongoing permit to enable Celine to undergo fertility treatment at the same hospital. They didn't want to apply for Celine's own permit because it would have to go through both the Israeli and Palestinian authorities for approval. The couple doesn't want any information about his genetic illness and the resulting infertility to be known. While how Celine and her husband spoke about this indicated that this was simply a matter of privacy—only their closest friends and family know about the couple's infertility—it is worth noting that the Israeli army and intelligence routinely use Palestinians' intimate information, such as sexual orientation, family life, or health status, to pressure Palestinians into cooperation.[20] The couple's reproductive health issues thus reveal the dependency of Palestinians, in both the West Bank and Gaza, on the Israeli health system and military authorities, and how this dependency is woven into intimate decision-making. The everyday violence of Israel's military occupation is present at the scale of Celine's family, her partner's health, and her own body.

Celine has had a lot of experience with fertility treatment. In addition to the hospital in Jerusalem, she underwent IVF cycles in fertility clinics in Hebron and Ramallah. However, eventually, all of her children were conceived in the Jerusalem IVF unit where we had met. Celine told me that treatment in the Israeli hospital has proven to be "more specific, more scheduled . . . everything is in order," contrasting this to her experience in clinics in the West Bank. This echoes other Palestinian women's experiences with both healthcare systems, as well as how Palestinian physicians working in Israeli hospitals described West Bank fertility clinics. Her experience in the Israeli fertility unit is an overall positive one. Celine described the doctors in Jerusalem as "absolutely perfect" and continuously expressed her gratitude to them. They would usually talk in English, and sometimes, the doctors knew a few words in Arabic. But Celine speaks English fluently, and not all Palestinians can easily converse with Israeli doctors like that. As a medical professional, she is also well versed in medical terminology and knows how to navigate a medical setting. But despite her relatively easy access to assisted reproduction in Jerusalem, as a non-citizen, Celine is not entitled to state subsidies for fertility treatment. This means that the couple pays for their treatment privately. At the time, this amounted to approximately 30,000 shekels or $8,700 per IVF cycle, including costs for transportation from

Bethlehem to Jerusalem. The couple receives financial support from Celine's husband's parents, further indicating the couple's class status in the West Bank.

Celine's border-crossing pregnancy journey entails a personal, medical, and political choreography. While her three children were conceived in vitro in Jerusalem, Celine would only travel back and forth in the first stages of the pregnancy, until a pulse could be detected through ultrasound. She would then continue her pregnancy and give birth in Bethlehem, where her gynecologist is aware of their situation and receives all relevant medical records from his colleagues in Jerusalem via Celine. Each drive from Bethlehem to Jerusalem takes around forty-five minutes if checkpoints are open. For each cycle of IVF, the couple needs to travel back and forth around ten times. The IVF cycle begins by taking hormones for the oocytes to grow, which then need to be monitored two to three times through blood tests and ultrasounds to check on the progression of the follicles and the thickness of the uterus. The next step, the oocyte retrieval, is the most invasive one, a procedure that requires anesthesia and for Celine to rest in the daycare unit of the hospital. The extracted oocytes are then fertilized with a sperm sample, which needs to be provided by the husband. After that, they are either frozen or implanted immediately. Two weeks after the implantation, Celine comes back for a blood test to check if a pregnancy occurred. In case the test is positive, she needs to do another ultrasound and then continue to travel to Jerusalem for checkups for about two months. Celine will only be able to complete her pregnancy in Bethlehem if all of these steps are successful.

Considering that Celine had already had four miscarriages from earlier attempts to get pregnant through IVF, had given birth to three children, and was in another IVF cycle at the time we met, these experiences accumulated to a considerable amount of border crossing, many of them already at the early and critical stages of pregnancy. Several studies have addressed pregnant women's experiences at Israeli military checkpoints.[21] I asked Celine if she had difficulties crossing checkpoints so frequently to become pregnant. Celine thought about this for a moment and then said, chuckling: "Sometimes, not always . . . depending on the political situation at that time. If everything is stable, they are happy to help and let us pass." However, thinking about my question further, she specified that she had been lucky so far, which might have been because she only traveled to the Jerusalem hospital up until the end of the second trimester. "So, you know, I don't cross the borders when I'm really pregnant and my belly is out," she said. While Celine doesn't mention any direct experiences of violence at the checkpoint, she refers to her dependence on Israel's arbitrary rule at the checkpoint and the oppression of Palestinians' freedom of movement writ large. Celine's passage depends not only on her husband's permission to enter Israel but also on the checkpoint soldiers, whose disposition and opinion of the political situation can vary from day to day.

The arbitrariness of the Israeli checkpoint and the soldier who guards it is intimately linked to Celine's quest to become pregnant and her husband's health. Celine's experience of constant border crossing exemplifies what gender and Indigenous studies scholar Mark Rifkin terms "settler time." As an analytic, settler time describes how sovereignty over temporality serves to normalize and cement a settler state's occupation, hegemony, and control of land.[22] In his book *The Time Beneath the Concrete*, Nasser Abourahme applies this understanding of settler time to Palestine, arguing that time looms large over Palestinians' experience of Israeli governance; it is also central to understandings of Zionism as settler colonialism.[23] The Palestinian condition is centrally shaped by settler time: at the checkpoint, through closure, in waiting.[24] Jasbir Puar terms the temporal modality of Israeli rule "slow life," capturing the arbitrariness and uncertainty that Palestinians experience across time and space.[25] The temporality of Israeli settler colonialism is particularly obvious in the wider reproductive sense of Celine's case. It is not only that Celine's whole pregnancy journey needs to be choreographed according to the material realities of settler time—when will the checkpoint be open, how long is the wait going to be, will the soldiers let her pass—but settler time also reaches into her reproductive future. How will her pregnant body react to the constant border crossing, waiting, and potential closure? Every time the border crossing came up in our conversation, Celine would present it as an almost normal, or normalized, condition of the couple's situation. The power of settler time to shape her future is already part of Celine's narrative, and the temporality of physical enclosure is accounted for in her reproductive journey. Or, in Puar's words, "the uncertainty of the indefinite is countered only by the certainty of a dictated future."[26]

However, even though settler time circumscribes Celine's reproductive life and future, she also refuses to be confined by the parameters of Israeli spatial and temporal control. I interviewed Celine twice, once right before the oocyte retrieval and a second time shortly after the transfer. Our second interview took place in the daytime care unit of the hospital in Jerusalem, located in its windowless basement, closed off by an automatic door, and only accessible to patients, spouses, and visitors. The beds in the daytime care unit were separated by curtains, and one could hear people talking in the next bed over; from time to time, a nurse would come in to check on Celine. When the nurse started talking in Hebrew, she politely asked, "In English please." Celine explained the procedure to me: "Today is the day of the transfer, which means they transfer the fertilized eggs into the uterus. They took the eggs last Thursday, they fertilized them the same day, and waited until the eggs grew to get more cells until today." Celine also told me that she was really hopeful it would work this time around because they used "fresh" oocytes that had only been retrieved the week before and were fertilized immediately after. Her previous miscarriages all occurred when she had used frozen oocytes. I was impressed by her knowledge of the process from a biomedical point of view and told her that she is basically an expert now. She laughed and proudly agreed.

The intimacy of sitting with Celine and her husband right after the oocyte transfer in the shabby basement of the hospital gave me a sense of Celine's endurance and *sumud* (steadfastness in Arabic). To come to this hospital, where she and Palestinian women like her are perceived through the one-dimensionality of the Israeli medical gaze, and to cross a militarized border for every blood test or ultrasound, require an immense amount of determination and strength. Celine's experience is deeply political in that sense. But at the same time, her quest to get pregnant and have the family she has always dreamed of ("two boys and two girls") was also indicative of something outside of a clear and readily available political script of Palestinian resistance. Celine's story of getting pregnant and the way she shared it with me points to a different grammar of politics. Similar to what anthropologist Livia Wick describes in her book *Sumud: Birth, Oral History, and Persistence in Palestine*, Celine's story of getting pregnant and the way she shared it with me points to a different language of politics articulated in Palestinian women's birth stories. Wick writes, "These personal anecdotes regarding care and love seem to be more important than what is political or nonpolitical, and yet deeply connected to the political and the distribution of life."[27] Celine's tactics of enduring the Israeli occupation were articulated on a different scale, focusing on overcoming the interruption of her everyday life and the spatial and temporal barriers that the occupation places on her and her husband.

Celine's capacity to focus on endurance for the sake of a normal family life demonstrates the dynamic and fluid nature of resilience in the face of violent living conditions.[28] She framed her family life and reproductive decision-making as simultaneously shaped by the political conditions of Israeli rule, as well as by her determination to provide for her children as best as she could. This became particularly clear when we talked about how she imagined their future. I remarked that I imagined growing up in the West Bank to be extremely difficult, to which she replied: "Life is getting harder, even. I guess they have to be strong enough, well-educated, to have self-esteem, so they can manage every trouble, get through, and live a good life after all." Celine hopes to instill this same sense of *sumud*, of perseverance, into her children, so they will "get through" this tough life like her and her husband. This response to the Israeli occupation, a mode of "getting by," is neither synonymous with complacency nor resistance in its politicized grammar. Instead, as Wick points out, it denies the very logic of occupation by simply focusing on the management of life in a situation of ongoing duress.[29]

My ethnographic encounter with Celine also reveals a broader question of studying the experience of colonial power relations through people's everyday lives. As anthropologists Ann Laura Stoler and Karen Strassler point out, the assumption that there are hidden counter-narratives about the colonial experience that can be easily "decoded" by the ethnographer presumes that subaltern knowledge always contains a political critique that can be shared and narrativized. This disregards how memories or experiences of colonial power might not appear in the form of compelling plots about nationalism, anticolonial heroes, or violent struggle.[30] Whenever I tried to talk to Celine about the political reasons for her and her husband's situation, she would patiently but decidedly refrain from speaking in political terms or openly criticizing the Israeli regime. For instance, when I inquired more about the political situation in the West Bank and how it might impact the less effective treatment she had received in clinics there, Celine told me that she only sees these differences "from a scientific point of view, not a political one." Similarly, when I asked her about the politics of reproduction, both from the point of view of the Israeli regime as well as how reproduction is framed as resistance in Palestinian society, Celine reflected: "I don't know [speaks to husband in Arabic], I think the Arab population is bigger than the Israeli one, but the Israeli one is stronger [laughs], but in general, I don't like to speak in politics." While Celine reflected on the importance of demographic questions under settler colonialism, she also declined to speak about politics. In this situation, my insistence on discovering the political in her pregnancy journey is precisely what overdetermines our encounter, and my inability to listen to what she told me. Celine's way of sharing her experience with me neither resists nor conforms to available scripts of living under settler colonialism. My encounter with Celine challenges the assumption that the colonial is always present in Palestinians' everyday lives and can be retrieved through ethnography, that there is resistance in every small gesture (or lack thereof), and that all retelling of the colonial has a therapeutic function.[31]

Celine and her husband's experience might be presented as an outlier in how Palestinians from the West Bank navigate the Israeli healthcare system and fertility economy. After all, they continue to receive a permit and have the financial means to travel and receive treatment in an Israeli hospital, which they perceive to be mainly hospitable and friendly. However, I find the couple's case to be instructive in revealing the less visible and less overt forms of Israeli domination that shape their reproduction and health. In Celine's narration of her pregnancy journey, the occupation, with all of its personal, medical, economic, temporal, and spatial effects, has become normal. Celine schedules her appointments according to how long it will take her to cross the checkpoint, and her bodily functions are intimately synced up with her border crossing. Considering how much time she must spend traveling, waiting at the checkpoint, waiting at the fertility clinic, and traveling again, her reproductive futurity is tied up with Israeli time. "Time thus is the meter of power; it is one form that physical enclosure takes on," writes Puar.[32] The cumulative effect of Celine's pregnancy journey is hard to measure, but Celine's reproductive future is linked to the temporality of a military occupation. Her pregnancy outcomes are directly or indirectly shaped by this political reality. However, for Celine, what matters is her family and her (future) children. Her focus is on getting pregnant and to provide for her children so they will become as steadfast as she is. And yet, the arbitrariness of Israeli occupation has real consequences on Celine and her husband's family planning. When I asked her about the outcome of the egg transfer two weeks later via WhatsApp, she told me that a pregnancy did not occur.

REEM: REPRODUCTIVE POLITICS AND INJUSTICE IN EAST JERUSALEM

Reem is a forty-year-old woman, born and raised in East Jerusalem. She left the city to pursue graduate studies, obtaining a PhD in history from a prestigious university in the UK. Reem now works as a high school teacher in Jerusalem and lives with her husband, a fifty-year-old nurse, in their house in the Old City. The couple got married when Reem was thirty-eight years old, and, for a few months, tried to get pregnant "naturally." After having had two miscarriages, Reem decided to see a doctor to do some checkups, because "the fertility of a woman declines over time," and she knew that she wanted to have children. Ever since, Reem has been trying to get pregnant by way of IVF in a large hospital in Jerusalem, which is where I first met her. As an East Jerusalemite, Reem is acutely aware of the politics of reproduction. In our interview, which took place in a small park near Damascus Gate on a hot day in May, Reem eloquently spelled out the interconnections between reproduction, family-building, the occupation, settler colonialism, and resistance. Hers is a story about the Palestinian fight for reproductive justice.

As usual, I opened our interview by asking Reem to describe how she came to undergo fertility treatment. After telling me about her age and how long she has been trying to get pregnant, Reem immediately connected her experience to living under occupation in East Jerusalem. Referring to the fragmentation of Palestinians' access to (reproductive) health across Gaza, the West Bank, and East Jerusalem, and the limitations this has on their freedom of choosing the right doctor and hospital, she explained:

> Here in Jerusalem, we are covered by the Israeli insurance. So, you know, if you think about undergoing IVF and paying for it yourself, you can go for another area in the West Bank, but you will not be covered there, and anyway, we are paying here, a lot. So, I used to go to my doctor, and he gave me some tests, some medications, and after two unsuccessful attempts [of getting pregnant naturally], I suggested that I wanted to go for IVF.

Because of her status as a Jerusalem resident, Reem is included in the Israeli healthcare system, which she pays for through her employer, like all citizens and residents. However, despite being covered by Israeli health insurance, Reem immediately brings up the West Bank and the possibility of trying to get pregnant in a Palestinian fertility clinic. Her remark echoes how Palestinian gynecologist Salam talked about Palestinian women's experiences in East Jerusalem, explaining that against all affective and political instincts, East Jerusalem fertility patients "are pushed to the Israeli side" (chapter 2). Their inclusion in the Israeli system as permanent residents incentivizes them financially to go where treatment is state-subsidized.

Reem's experience of starting the process with her health insurance company was time-consuming. After she told her family doctor that she wanted to try IVF, she had to undergo a variety of blood tests, ultrasounds, and cardiological tests. These took place in clinics run by her Israeli health insurance company, facilitated by Jewish Israeli medical staff in Hebrew. It seemed like wherever she went, the doctors forgot to tell her which tests were needed, where and when she could access the results, what they meant, and how to continue the process. It took almost one year until she was able to begin the actual process of fertility treatment. This was an upsetting experience for Reem, for, as she explained, at her age, "time runs." Reem speaks English with a British accent, but, like many other East Jerusalemites, she doesn't speak Hebrew—a fact she connects to the politics of living under occupation in East Jerusalem, in a society and educational system that is not hers: "I have never been in their schools and their universities, I studied outside. So, I speak English." As illustrated in the previous chapters, language barriers are one of the major limits Palestinian women, doctors, and activists refer to when describing the accessibility of reproductive health services. Given that the timing and chronology of hormonal treatment, blood work, and the female cycle are crucial in getting pregnant, language is another way in which settler time shapes Palestinian women's chances to get pregnant as well as their pregnancy outcomes. An Israeli monopoly over political, legal, and interpersonal time characterizes the political geography of the occupied Palestinian territories.[33]

After a year of waiting, testing, and not really understanding what was going on, Reem was finally able to start IVF in a large hospital in Jerusalem. With most of her Jewish Israeli doctors and nurses, Reem felt welcome. Only the recurring encounters with the nurse who would do her ultrasounds and the nurse who would draw her blood were markedly unpleasant, especially since she had to see the two of them regularly for these checkups in the early stages of the fertility treatment. Reem described these encounters as "a matter of discrimination." From the beginning, Reem recounted, she wouldn't feel comfortable with the ultrasound nurse. She told me that she never had any issues with the other medical staff for not speaking Hebrew, except for this nurse, who shouted "Arabic, Arabic" at her when they first met, indicating that she didn't speak Arabic. Reem said she remained calm, but she reflected, laughingly, "I said it's no problem for me, but why are you shouting?" From then on, her experience became painful. Reem remembered: "She would never give instructions, that you can cover your body, for your privacy, she never said 'take a deep breath' for the ultrasound, she never gives you tissues to clean yourself after using the gel." Once, when this nurse was on holiday, Reem was treated by a different person. This nurse conducted the ultrasound more gently, explaining every step and guiding her through the process in a dignified way. Reem compared the two experiences: "The experience was so different, so different, even the pain is different, I felt the pain so severely with her [her regular nurse], it was not nice at all." What Reem describes as discrimination translates on the bodily level and into her perception of pain. The relatively noninvasive procedure of receiving an ultrasound became painful and uncomfortable.

Her regular nurse would also not hide her dislike of Reem when she entered the examination room: "Even when you come, and you are Israeli, she smiles at you and says 'good morning,' but if you are an Arab, she does not look at you once, and when I had two IVF cycles, they were both unsuccessful." Reem notices such subtle ways of expressing racism toward herself and other Palestinians and connects her experiences of two unsuccessful cycles of IVF to the affective treatment she experienced at the hands of this nurse. One night, during her second cycle of IVF, Reem felt severe pain and went to the hospital the next morning. She told the nurses who took her in first that the pain was gone, but they found that she was bleeding. She was then sent to do an ultrasound with the nurse in question, and Reem remembered her shouting:

> "Why should I do that, you told me that you don't have pain now?" and I found myself really stressed, I was bleeding heavily and I was really under stress, because the estrogen was not developing properly and there was the risk of stopping medications, so you have an abortion, and then I started just crying, I did nothing but cry, because that was really bad . . .

The aggressive treatment in an extremely vulnerable situation of the IVF cycle affected Reem enormously. She was scared she would have to stop this cycle and have a miscarriage, which eventually also happened. When she went back to the other nurses, they soothed her, but the nurse in question did not apologize. Reem summarized: "It's that kind of discrimination, I can see how she acts with the other patients," noting—only half-jokingly—that every time she goes to the hospital now, she hopes that a different person will do the ultrasound. After the incident, Reem felt like she could have complained about the way she was treated: "I think that at that time I had the right even to make a complaint, but I really did not want to distract myself." To complain about abuses of power in asymmetrical situations might seem pointless to begin with. As feminist theorist Sara Ahmed points out, complaints against racism are easily dismissed by institutional structures, and "making a complaint is never completed by a single action: it often requires you to do more and more work. It is exhausting, especially given that what you complain about is already exhausting."[34] For Reem, it was easier to focus on what she wanted to achieve—to become pregnant—than to "distract" herself by going through the process of making a formal complaint.

In her work on the reproductive outcomes of Black women in the United States, anthropologist Dána-Ain Davis coined the term "obstetric racism" to analyze the historical and ongoing stigmatization of Black women in reproductive care and how Black women recount their encounters with medical staff. Davis proposes this notion to foreground the particularity of the experiences of Black women's pregnancies and births. While medical racism is part of this experience, Davis argues that the gendered nature of reproduction requires a more intersectional reading. Obstetric racism, then, comprises four dimensions: "critical lapses in diagnosis; being neglectful, dismissive, or disrespectful; causing pain; and engaging in medical abuse through coercion."[35] Obstetric racism offers a crucial lens from which to understand intimate clinical encounters beyond medical racism, taking into account the specificity of the obstetric setting. Reem experienced at least two of these dimensions: neglectful, dismissive, or disrespectful treatment, and pain at the hands of the ultrasound nurse.

In comparison to encounters with the ultrasound nurse, Reem described—in her deadpan humor—the nurse who would usually do the bloodwork as "very nice, she does not say good morning, but at least she does not deal differently with you, you don't feel the pain, you don't feel any difference, it's very professional." This experience captures the infrastructure of the Israeli fertility clinic. Oppression and exclusion are felt on a bodily level in an affective economy centered around some bodies, while others are feared, excluded, and marked as Other. Considered cumulatively, it is at these micro-nodes of governance that Palestinian lives and reproduction are worn down and aggravated. Intimate and everyday encounters and proximities are sites where fears, anger, and frustration are produced and negotiated, and it is at the scale of dismissive and disrespectful behavior where racialized women's experience of reproductive care is shaped.

In addition to these difficult experiences and painful encounters, Reem also talked about the structural level of the politics of reproduction in Palestine/Israel. Reem shared with me how the everyday condition of racism in militarized Jerusalem exacerbated her pregnancy journey. I asked her how this experience shaped the importance and meaning that having a family under occupation has for her. Reem replied:

REEM: Actually, I do believe that it's very difficult to live under occupation, all the families are affected badly by the occupation. Yes, I do believe that we are getting the advantage of the positive sides, but it is compulsory of course.

GALA: What do you mean, what are the positive sides?

REEM: For example, having the medical services, but it is compulsive of course, you know when you live under occupation, it is a struggle, even when you go there, you feel that there is a gap, especially when you remember, for example, a week ago, or a few weeks ago, they arrested my brother, they arrested my neighbor, or they bomb Gaza, yes . . . there's a struggle and definitely, it's even clearer from the Israeli side, that there is a demographic struggle, or challenge. That's why the Jewish women bring so many children, and they announce it. Maybe Arab women don't have this awareness up until now, that it is a matter of demographic struggle. I can't be part of it, because I don't have this chance. I feel that they [Israeli women] have the awareness [laughs], but we are the owners of the land, our ancestors have lived here, and many of us were expelled to the refugee camps, so it is us who should reproduce and bring children!

The constant, intimate presence of the Israeli occupation is felt by all Palestinian families in East Jerusalem.[36] Even in situations in which Palestinians experience "the positive sides" of inclusion into the institutions of their occupation, such as the healthcare system and fertility economy, living under occupation is an everyday struggle. This struggle, or the "gap" that opens when Reem enters Israeli institutions, is felt and points to the structural function of settler colonialism. The inclusive exclusion that settler colonialism offers to Palestinian residents or citizens can never cover its underlying function of a demographic struggle for the population majority. The Israeli side has already understood that—"that's why the Jewish women bring so many children." Israel's pronatalism and the country's so-called wars of the wombs, in which non-Jewish women's fertility is perceived as part of a "demographic threat," are well documented.[37] Reem finds that many Palestinian women lack the same awareness of the politics of reproduction, even though, as indigenous to the land, it should be Palestinians "who reproduce and bring children" as a means of resistance.

Reproduction, for Reem, is political. Her understanding of settler colonialism as a question of demographic control echoes Rhoda Ann Kanaaneh's analysis of Palestinians' deployment of the comparative political arithmetic through which the Israeli state interpellates them. "The focus of Zionism on the ratio of Jew to Arab" is mirrored by Palestinians, "to the extent that ethnic-based political arithmetic has come to play an important role."[38] While Reem herself remarks that she can't be part of the demographic struggle (presumably because of her age), I asked her why she thinks other Palestinian women don't have that same political awareness. Her response illustrates the importance of a reproductive justice lens to reproduction in Palestine.

> I don't blame the Palestinian women, their lives are really difficult, and they don't have the same financial support. For example, settlers in Beitar Illit [a fast-growing Israeli settlement in the West Bank] are paid a lot, they don't work, maybe one of the parents might have a part-time job, they have a house, they are supported. Palestinian women do struggle financially, many are working mothers, and this burdens them a lot. . . . Imagine, they are supported politically! We are not supported politically, nor financially, nor emotionally [laughs].

Reem's explanation for the Palestinian woman's lack of political consciousness is rooted in her understanding of their material conditions. Comparing them to Jewish Israeli women in illegal settlements in the West Bank and in East Jerusalem, where they pay cheap rent and are supported by the state, Palestinian women struggle with the everyday conditions of their lives under occupation. Palestinian women in East Jerusalem fear evictions, dispossession, losing their residency status, and the military violence of the occupation.[39] Having more children might simply not be feasible under such circumstances. Their right to have a family and to raise their children in a dignified and healthy environment is limited by settler colonial governance, which, in turn, also shapes their political awareness. Reem further explained that their experience of trying to get pregnant in an Israeli fertility clinic also intersects with their material resources. While she was able to take time off work during the cycles of IVF she has already done, the experience might be "hard for a working lady," because "you need to take an hour from your work, you need to ask for permission, and when you come in again, you need to show documentation of having been at the hospital. Also taking the medication on time restricts you and your movements." Being a Palestinian woman living and working under Israeli occupation not only shapes Palestinian women's political consciousness but also their actual chances of successfully conceiving via IVF. According to Reem's analysis, the politics of reproduction in Palestine are material, affective, and political.

However, similar to my other Palestinian interlocutors, Reem also noted a methodological issue. When she shared with me her sense of a lack of reproductive resistance among Palestinian women, I told her I had also been surprised that few women spoke about that. To that, Reem responded: "Many women don't want to talk about it. Because sometimes your speech will be elaborated, and you will be brought to prison so easily. So, I do believe they are afraid of politics and talking about politics." Not feeling safe to discuss the political aspects of reproduction with a foreign researcher—or, in general, in public—points to the question of freedom of speech in an increasingly authoritarian Jewish supremacist state. It also points to questions of trust, safety, and refusal in the interview setting, and to what happens when a Western researcher travels with these stories across the highly securitized borders of the Israeli state. However, while this might be the case for some, other Palestinian women, Reem continued, might retreat to the private. Their intimate and family life remains one of the only sites not touched by politics and the occupation. For Reem, however, this position is untenable because politics permeate every aspect of her life in East Jerusalem.

> But they will still dominate us. If I don't submit documents that I still live within the municipality of Jerusalem, I pay taxes, and I don't have any other property in the West Bank, and [I] pay for the state like those who have high salaries, then I will lose my right to live here. And this happens every day in Jerusalem for the Jerusalemites. You live in Jerusalem, grow up in Jerusalem, and then get married in Jerusalem, and then you don't have 1.5 million to buy or 3,000 [shekels] to rent a house, so if you move just to the West Bank you lose your rights. So, it's not only family that gives you security, they dominate it. How can you make this family life secure if you can't rent a house here and keep them in here?

Furthering her materialist analysis, Reem asked how can the family be a space of freedom and security if Palestinians lack the financial means to buy or rent a house in East Jerusalem or live freely and securely on their land? Reem continued: "What will a family do for me? Family will not secure me." If the material conditions to live a life that is not under constant threat of eviction and dispossession are not given, the family will never be a private retreat to intercept these conditions. Living in occupied East Jerusalem and experiencing this context intimately informs Reem's analysis of how sexuality, reproduction, kinship, and the body are not only not protected from state violence but are indeed crucial to govern and control colonial and racialized subjects.

Reem's experience at the fertility clinic as well as her analysis of the politics of reproduction demonstrate the interconnected scales of oppression and reproductive injustice that Palestinian women experience in East Jerusalem. On a structural level, Israeli military occupation shapes Palestinian intimate lives from birth to death, including marriage, childbirth, and kin relations. These structural conditions translate to the affective level. Reem's experiences of subtle and overt obstetric racism are a concrete outcome of Israeli settler colonialism and its function to destroy and replace. And finally, these politics, policies, and sentiments register on a bodily and even microscopic level. Reem feels how the broader circumstances of her (coerced) inclusion in the Israeli healthcare system shape her experience in fertility treatment, and she registers the pains of knowing that her Palestinian brothers and sisters are being killed and bombed while she is trying to conceive. These different experiences, or gradients of violence, might affect Reem's reproductive outcome. When I contacted Reem a year after our interview, when Covid-19 had just begun to affect nonelective procedures in Israeli hospitals, Reem was still not pregnant. At the time, she described the disruption that the pandemic introduced to her fertility treatment as a much-needed break for her mental health.

CHRISTEEN: SPATIAL SEGREGATION, RACISM, AND THE ISRAELI FERTILITY ECONOMY

Christeen is a thirty-year-old woman who studied alternative medicine and lives in a small village in the north of Israel with her husband, a thirty-four-year-old pharmacist. They are both '48 Palestinians (or, Palestinian citizens of Israel). At the time of our interview, which took place at her mother's house together with my translator Mary, Christeen had just given birth. Three weeks before, her daughter Mia, who, as she proudly stated, has "an American name," had been born. The long story of Mia's conception and birth illustrates the hardship of undergoing fertility treatment for an extended period—in this couple's case, for almost five years. It shows how some of the difficulties Christeen and her husband faced were caused by their status as Palestinians with settler colonial Israeli citizenship and the experience of medical racism. But Christeen's experience also speaks to the myriad ways in which Palestinian citizens of Israel contest and challenge their unequal and coerced inclusion in the Israeli state and its institutions, navigating their class position as Palestinians in a settler state as well as the spatio-temporal conditions of their dispossession.[40]

Most of Israel's 21 percent of Palestinian citizens live either in the Northern Galilee area (like Christeen and her husband), the Triangle area, or in the Naqab desert in the south of the country. Palestinian citizens of Israel are those Palestinians who stayed inside the newly established borders of the Israeli state after they were expelled, dispossessed, or transferred from their homes by Zionist militia forces leading up to 1948. Successively, these internally displaced Palestinians were granted Israeli citizenship and included in the liberal settler state.[41] However, Israel defines itself as the nation-state of the Jewish people and effectively bifurcates "nationality" and "citizenship" based on racialized categories and demographic concerns.[42] One must be Jewish to be a full and legitimate citizen, and only being Jewish grants citizens of the state access to good jobs, healthcare, and education. Palestinian citizens of Israel are subjected to more than sixty Israeli laws that discriminate against them, ranging from political participation to housing, education, culture and language.[43] In her five-year journey of trying to get pregnant, Christeen encountered many of these inequalities. Living farther away from large hospitals with well-equipped fertility units and access to advanced medical knowledge was one of the main factors that slowed down Christeen's pregnancy journey. However, as a well-educated middle-class woman, Christeen was able to harness certain resources—such as knowing a Jewish Israeli IVF specialist and being able to access the financial means to get treated in a private clinic—to overcome the structural barriers that Israeli settler colonialism imposes on Palestinian citizens. Her story broadly exposes the political economy of Israel's fertility complex and how racism and ethnonational segregation limit Palestinian women's reproductive health and choices.

Christeen and her husband have been married for eight years. They didn't try to get pregnant for the first few years of their marriage, because Christeen was still studying for her degree. After she had finished her studies and a pregnancy didn't occur "naturally," the couple underwent some tests and examinations. This process revealed that her husband's low sperm count and motility were the cause of their infertility. Christeen asked her doctor what to do, and he suggested undergoing fertility treatment. First, the couple started the process with artificial insemination, where sperm is directly inserted into the womb. This, however, didn't work, and Christeen began to undergo IVF treatment in a public health-insurance-run clinic in Afula, a town thirty minutes from where they live.[44] Christeen told me that they "tried a lot": She underwent several cycles of IVF, but most of the oocytes that were retrieved couldn't be fertilized because the sperm was not strong enough. After a while, the couple got discouraged and took a year off, recovering from the emotional and psychological stress the fertility treatment brought about. Their next attempt was equally unsuccessful, and Christeen suffered from ovarian hyperstimulation syndrome (OHSS), a complication that can occur as a side effect of the hormonal treatment stimulating the production of egg cells. While most cases of OHSS are mild, Christeen suffered from an unusually severe case. She remembered: "They started to extract ovules again, the last time they extracted twenty-seven, and I had an overstimulation that was life-threatening, I almost died. It results in the inflammation of the ovaries." Despite this traumatic experience, the couple continued with the IVF treatment, and she underwent another four cycles of egg retrieval, none of which successfully led to a pregnancy.

As a result of the exhaustion this situation caused her, Christeen decided to take another few months off. During that time, the couple began thinking about finding a private clinic to continue the fertility treatment. As a citizen of the Israeli state, Christeen is entitled to up to two fully subsidized IVF cycles leading to a live birth. However, after being treated at the local health-insurance-run clinic for over four years, she felt discouraged by the lack of success and questioned the quality of the treatment she had received in the clinic: "I saw no results, and then you get bored of the place, and you start to see the doctors as ghosts [laughs]. And it was the *kupat holim* [health insurance], we would pay only for the things we needed to." The treatments in the public clinic in Afula would only cover the bare minimum, which in her case was not enough to get pregnant. Beyond that, her doctors appearing as "ghosts" points to the lack of attentiveness and engagement of medical staff at the local clinic. The process had become routine for her. The couple decided to continue their treatment in a private clinic in Tel Aviv, a two-hour (or longer) drive by car from their small village. They had found this particular clinic through Christeen's expanded network of friends. A Jewish Israeli acquaintance had given her a recommendation to see the Jewish Israeli doctor who works at that clinic and who was supposed to be a specialist in IVF treatment and had been "dealing with reproductive technology since they started the whole IVF process in Israel." Christeen recounted:

> The one I heard it from is not an Arab, she's Jewish. And she told us about it, and if we will do it at a private clinic, there will be payments. We went there, and he said that sperm is indeed not strong enough, but we'll do it step by

> step. He gave me a very different process from what I had in Afula after he saw that they extracted so many eggs, and he was shocked. It's a shame. The eggs go for nothing.

For Christeen, it felt like she had misused her time in the public clinic; her eggs and her time were "wasted." This experience echoes Palestinian physician Salam's analysis of Palestinian citizens' distance from reproductive infrastructures in Israel, both in terms of geographic accessibility and knowledge (chapter 2). In addition to geography, class, both within and across the settler/native divide, is a crucial factor in accessing advanced reproductive technology.[45] To be able to receive information about a good private clinic, as well as being able to pay for it, highlights the stratification of reproduction along class and ethnonational divides.[46]

Christeen's experience exemplifies Palestinian citizens' complicated relationship vis-à-vis the settler state as well as their internal class structure. Since the establishment of the State of Israel, Palestinians' inclusion in the state's institutions—the labor market, education, or healthcare—relied on their status as settler colonial citizens, an Indigenous minority that threatens the establishment and maintenance of a Jewish population majority. The transfer of Palestinian private land into Israeli state control transformed a primarily agricultural Palestinian economy into a cheap labor force for the Israeli economy. This can be seen in Palestinians' limited inclusion in the Israeli labor market as well as the underdevelopment of local Palestinian economies.[47] While Israel's Judaization process of the majority-Palestinian areas in Israel is ongoing—as exemplified by urban planning and other spatial politics in the Galilee, the Naqab, and in so-called mixed cities—some '48 Palestinians like Christeen and her husband enjoyed upward class mobility, forming a growing middle class. However, despite these developments, Palestinians in Israel still live in highly segregated and stratified societies. Within Israel today, Palestinian citizens' income is 55 percent less than that of their Jewish counterparts.[48] '48 Palestinians face higher levels of poverty, unemployment, lack of participation in the labor force, politics, and education, as well as a lack of development in the local Palestinian economy and urban planning. As evident in Christeen's experience, Palestinian sociopolitical relations are linked to their place of residency in segregated Palestinian localities.[49] Due to her relative privilege as an educated middle-class woman, she found a better, private clinic, run by one of Israel's leading IVF specialists. Christeen can afford both the two-hour drive to Tel Aviv and the treatment itself.

The change of clinic and treatment method was exactly what she needed. The specialist would retrieve fewer egg cells at once and assess their quality before fertilizing them. Christeen finally got pregnant with her last frozen egg cell from the first cycle at the private clinic. She reflected on her experience there:

> When you have money, the whole attitude changes. That's what I've come to believe. For every treatment, he would take 2,500–3,000 [shekels] [around $775–930]. Every insertion back to the womb was 2,000 [around $620]. . . . But the treatment is personal, he welcomes you directly. It's different with the private clinic. They were great in Afula but there were a lot more people. By the way, most of the people treated in Afula are Arabs.

Christeen points to how the socioeconomic resources and spatial segregation of Jewish Israeli and Palestinian patients determine who is found in each clinic: In Afula, it was "mostly Arabs," while in Tel Aviv, "mostly Jews." Being able to afford private fertility treatment not only enabled her to get pregnant within weeks but also changed her whole experience of the process. The fertility treatment was much more personal, and the doctor welcoming. For Christeen, the private clinic "would convey a different feeling." This remark echoes Himmat Zu'bi's findings on Palestinian women's experience of the Israeli fertility economy.[50] Palestinian women's general sense of invisibility in Israeli medical space is reinforced in public hospitals, while being included as a private customer removes at least one layer of discrimination.

Differential treatment at the private clinic illustrates once more how settler time shapes Palestinian reproductive futurity. While at the local clinic in Afula, wait time averaged around three hours for each appointment; in the private clinic in Tel Aviv, patients were received immediately. The wait time at the local clinic affected Christeen physically and mentally, possibly determining her IVF outcomes: "Every time I went, I'd wait God knows how long. It would take a lot for the results of the blood test. This affects you strongly. Boredom on top of the treatments and the hormones, going nuts." I asked her if she thought that the long wait time and her general emotional state due to the hormonal injections affected her pregnancy outcomes. She said, unmistakenly: "Yes, I began to despise that place." While Palestinians' lives within the "Green Line" are less disrupted and slowed down than what Palestinians experience in the occupied territories, settler time still shapes their everyday lives and movement. Israeli hegemony over Palestinian time affects Palestinians in the different jurisdictions between the River and the

Sea differently. But it is Israeli authorities and local actors (the military, doctors, bureaucrats) who are usually in power and can implement different temporal regimes.

Christeen similarly spoke about the internal stratification of the Palestinian population and how Palestinian class position shapes Jewish Israeli forms of racism. Phrased carefully at first, when I inquired about the different experiences at the local and the private clinic, Christeen said: "In Afula, I sensed a bit of racism toward Arabs," and then went on to explain:

> They would let others in before us. This kind of disgusting thing was happening. And when speaking to us! They didn't dare with me, but if a simple woman would come, from Umm al-Fahm, for example, wearing, you know, this clothing [imitates wearing the hijab], they would immediately start to harass her and shout: "Didn't you understand?!" and stuff like that. It comes down to the person, at the end.

In the local clinic, Palestinians' internal class position is hierarchized according to racist and civilizational assumptions. Palestinian women from more traditional backgrounds and more remote majority-Palestinian villages experienced racism and harassment. Witnessing this treatment, Christeen also reflected on the fact that all Palestinian patients were made to wait longer and spoke about their experience in the plural, including herself, despite her class position and receiving slightly more respectful treatment. While settler colonial structures of apartheid rule are evident in the differential governance of the fragmented Palestinian body politic, racialized hierarchy also structures internal division among Palestinian groups, articulated through the modality of class.[51] Geographer Oren Yiftachel finds that Palestinians

> are divided into the following main groups, ranked according to their rights: Druze; Palestinians Arabs in the Galilee and Triangle region; the Bedouins in the Negev; Palestinians in Jerusalem; Palestinians in the West Bank other than Jerusalem; residents of Gaza; and refugees not under Israel's control whose claims for residency and reclamation of property are rejected out-of-hand.[52]

Within Israel and in the public Israeli imaginary, Palestinians in the Galilee and Triangle region are considered more "modern" than Palestinian Bedouins or other previously nomadic or agricultural communities, echoing the long colonial history of divide and conquer. The number of children and family size is often cited as a gendered indicator of assessing what it means to be a modern, educated Palestinian woman.[53]

Despite racialized class difference and the fragmentation of the Palestinians across Israel's different jurisdictions, for Christeen, Palestinians' experience of racism at the hands of Israeli medical staff was easy to identify: "I mean, how the nurse is treating a Palestinian woman, that's an indicator if she's being racist or not." Often, Christeen remembered, the first question a nurse would ask was "if you're Arab or Jewish." Revealing a Palestinian identity would mean that medical staff would assume that they didn't speak Hebrew well and yell stuff like "'Didn't you understand?! Give me the paperwork.'" Christeen said that this affected all Palestinian women in the clinic strongly, especially at a time "when the hormones go crazy." This "mentality," she found, also determined whether fertility treatment would be successful or not, exacerbating the already exhausting side effects of the hormone treatment, such as depression, fatigue, anxiety, irritability, or restlessness.

This treatment also led to the spreading of rumors at the local clinic. Christeen told me that she would hear from other Palestinian fertility patients that the doctors "would fail the process for Arabs on purpose so that they won't reproduce more." As discussed in chapter 1, these fears mirror Israeli demographic anxieties from the standpoint of its victims.[54] However, for Christeen, "medicine is medicine, they are not allowed to do that, and I didn't pay any attention to it." Christeen's view on these rumors reminds me of how health scholar Yara talked about Palestinian patients' vulnerability in the medical setting of an Israeli clinic (chapter 2). As a Palestinian patient in the Israeli medical sphere, "you want to trust your doctor, it's very important for the process of the treatment and for your own mental state." The stories Christeen heard and her own reaction to them illustrate this vulnerability and the strength it takes to receive such an intimate and invasive, possibly long-term, treatment in a hostile environment.

During her numerous stays at the local clinic, Christeen would often intervene if the Jewish Israeli nurses treated women in more traditional attire or with less Hebrew skills badly. As a medical professional, she was also able to explain the procedure and translate from Hebrew. However, after five years of experiencing or witnessing this sort of treatment and the mental toll it took on her, she also felt like she was getting angrier at the medical staff in the local clinic. Eventually, this contributed to her wanting to change to the private clinic. Her story illustrates the internal stratification of Palestinian patients along racial and class lines, as well as how racialized and social presumptions are produced in the fertility clinic. Embedded in the larger structures of medical racism in the Israeli healthcare system, the experience of racism and discrimination in Israeli fertility clinics affects Palestinian women's pregnancy outcomes in different ways. While Christeen was eventually able to avoid the medical racism she witnessed and seek more advanced treatment in an accommodating private clinic, this privilege is only afforded to Palestinians with the respective social, cultural, and economic capital.

To some degree, the commodification of biological processes such as IVF seems to temporarily suspend structural racism in the Israeli healthcare system. Legal sociologist Dorothy Roberts analyzes the inclusion of Black women into the "market and cultural imaginary of the new reprogenetics" in the United States and shows how the extension of choice to select from a variety of reproductive options was made available to a small and elite contingent of Black women and women of color who would be able to afford reproductive technologies.[55] However, their inclusion in the neoliberal bioeconomy only broadened the exclusion of less resourceful women and relegated their reproductive health and decision-making to the private market. This change facilitates a shift from the state's responsibility to offer accessible reproductive technology and to foster reproductive and sexual health and rights for all to private responsibility, as exemplified in Christeen's case.[56] This "neoliberal reification of market logic" places (some) Palestinian women in the Israeli fertility economy at a complicated nexus of being included as a client but never fully as a citizen.[57] The Israeli/Palestinian divide does not cease to exist in the Israeli fertility economy; if anything, it is reinforced through further stratifications that determine who can afford to receive the most advanced reproductive technology and who must endure racist and less developed treatment at local clinics.

Christeen's case also demonstrates the limit of a choice-centered approach to reproductive justice. The fact that she can choose from the most advanced private fertility treatment and will momentarily be treated as a client and not *just* as a Palestinian doesn't mean she will be able to raise her children in a safe and healthy environment or live a self-determined life in her homeland. As her long pregnancy story shows, her partial inclusion in the Israeli fertility economy is still strictly circumscribed by the conditions of Israeli settler colonialism, determining her access to healthcare and her place of residency. Christeen is well aware of this conundrum. Toward the end of our interview, Mary asked Christeen how she sees her baby girl's future as a Palestinian living in Israel and her opportunities at school, education, and the job market. Christeen replied: "Not that great. In the context of education, school, of course, there's a bit of racism." She later added that "the conditions of education in the Arab schools are not like those in the Jewish schools. Everything is different." While Celine understands her class position and navigates Israel's fertility economy according to her social and financial resources, she knows that her daughter will face similarly unequal conditions in the realm of education and the labor market. Reproductive justice means not only full autonomy over the process of (assisted) reproduction but also extends to the future and the next generations' chances in a deeply unequal settler society. Even if partial openings or inclusions exist, the Israeli state intimately interfaces with Palestinians, their bodies, reproductive decisions, and futures.

INTIMACIES: TIME, SPACE, AND RESILIENCE

I opened this chapter with Yara's reflection on how Israeli borders, policies, laws, and soldiers determine "how many children Palestinians are eligible to have." The militarization of Palestinian women's (reproductive) health might be most obvious when Palestinian women cross highly surveilled borders, and it culminates in the destruction of Palestinian lives in Gaza today, but Israel's biopolitical reach into Palestinian reproductive lives and family planning also occurs at various other borders and barriers. Central to the experiences of Reem, Christeen, and Celine is how their bodies interface with borders of various shapes and forms, including checkpoints and walls, language barriers, affective boundaries, and interior frontiers.[58] These various crossings reveal the multilayered intimate relations these borders introduce into Palestinian women's lives. Intimacies, defined by anthropologist Aslı Zengin as "affective and physical proximity," shape and expose the relationship between power, space, bodies, and affect.[59] Varying degrees of closeness to Israeli institutions and varying intensities of how these proximities shape Palestinian women's reproduction—from looking for a new doctor to syncing up one's reproductive bodily capacity with a militarized border—characterize Reem, Christeen, and Celine's encounters with Israeli borders. A sense of trust and closeness afforded by Reem, Christeen, and Celine toward me and my research project allowed me to closely recount their stories, including where we encountered the limits of ethnography. The varying registers of intimacies that appear in this chapter expose how Israeli demographic anxieties configure the reproductive lives of Palestinian women.

The lens of the intimate also attunes us to its co-constitutive relationship with violence.[60] Close proximities and relations of care can become violent and shape the most intimate parts of lives, bodies, and subjectivities. Reem's experience of living under militarized occupation in East Jerusalem, one of the active frontiers of Israeli settler colonialism, informs her materialist analysis of reproduction. The intimate ways in which her body interfaces with the Israeli state and its institutions simultaneously cause her more pain but are also a site to recover her insurgent spirit. Reem's refusal to accept her inclusion in the settler state and her affirmation of the politics of reproduction constitute what Saidiya Hartman beautifully terms "a revolution in minor key."[61] Here, violent intimacies take on creative and rebellious forms in Palestinian women's everyday lives. In Celine's case, the Israeli state's borders are imposed on her and her husband's lives and health. But more than that, Celine's reproductive body is intimately synced with the spatial architecture of a military occupation as well as with its temporality. But this violent intimacy doesn't break Celine's steadfastness and her dreams of a good life for her children. Celine's intimate experience of the Israeli border also opens a window into the ethnographic encounter and challenges the assumption that the violence of the colonial is always readily available as a political script shared by those who experience such violence, and as ethnographic data interpretable by the ethnographer. Instead, Celine's pregnancy journey alerts us to the ways in which asymmetrical power relations might be recounted differently, outside and against readily available political interpretations of resistance, resilience, and endurance. As a Palestinian citizen of Israel, Christeen is structurally most included in the liberal settler state. Christeen experiences a particular configuration of power, space, bodies, and affect as both Zionism's Other as well as being a well-educated middle-class woman. This intimate inclusion and exclusion from a system based on her dispossession allows Christeen to harness her class status to be treated by one of Israel's IVF specialists and to escape the racism and time-consuming treatment she experienced in a public health clinic. However, while Christeen is socially mobile and thus enjoys the full benefits of Israel's repro-economy, her case illustrates the fine-grained stratification of access to assisted reproduction in Palestine/Israel.

Time and space are crucial registers for the mediation of the intimate. Understanding the structural gradients of how Israeli governance interferes with Palestinian's freedom, their bodies, and their family lives is crucial to working against the common Israeli perception of a fragmented and disconnected Palestinian body politic.[62] These three cases demonstrate how Israeli hegemony over space and time across the territory between the

River and the Sea affects Palestinian women's reproductive futurity. As media scholar Helga Tawil-Souri writes, "Prolonged and unpredictable waiting has become part of the structure of Israel's rule."[63] But it is not only checkpoints, roadblocks, segregated highways, or the separation wall that slow down Palestinian lives. For Reem, Christeen, and Celine, the fertility clinic and the Israeli healthcare sector at large are places where Palestinians are made to wait. Their homes are located at a distance, or across a border, from the Israeli fertility economy, and they rely on all sorts of private and public transport to get to the fertility clinic. Celine faces prolonged and unpredictable waiting periods on her way to Jerusalem and back, depending on the soldier's evaluation of the political situation on any given day. Reem's experience of beginning the process of IVF treatment was slowed down by different doctors and medical staff, who were unable to communicate properly which tests to take and where to get the results. She describes how Palestinians' individual time as well as the Palestinian life-course are entangled with Israeli surveillance and control. In Christeen's experience, Palestinians' being made to wait longer hours than Jewish Israelis in the public clinic, only thirty minutes from her home, made her move to the private clinic, accepting the two-hour drive as a necessary price to pay to get pregnant. The three women might have different "packages of rights" afforded by the settler colonial state,[64] but Israeli hegemony over time and space shapes their reproduction across varying registers.

What unites Reem, Christeen, and Celine across these different materializations of settler colonial rule in their everyday lives is their ways of coping with these intimate interruptions. Himmat Zu'bi shows how Palestinian women deal with the "paradox of being a Palestinian woman who is at once subject and object of Israeli treatment and suspicion" by developing a variety of complex and multifaceted coping mechanisms and strategies of survival and resistance.[65] Reem, Christeen, and Celine all find their own way to engage less with the racism, discrimination, or oppression they experience to be able to focus more on their goal to get pregnant, have a family, and provide a good life for their children. Surviving and resisting settler colonization, as Nasser Abourahme writes, "is about refusing temporal orders as much as it is about clinging to what's left of geography."[66] Palestinian women's reproduction does both. As Reem, Christeen, and Celine inhabit and navigate what remains of their homeland, they are also refusing their material and corporeal confinement by settler time. They are not just overcoming and disavowing settler time and colonial borders, but their acts of love, care, and (social) reproduction *are* the future of Palestine. Whether their pregnancy journeys, and Palestinian women's reproduction as such, are framed and narrated as political, or whether reproductive lives are placed outside the often masculinist narrative of national and heroic anticolonial resistance, is less relevant.[67] Rather, these women's experiences and their overcoming of the strictures of Israeli time and space give insight into the production of Palestinian reproductive futurity. Giving birth, as Wick argues, is "as transformative as joining political parties and working in public politics, often more so."[68] Reem, Celine, and Christeen's pregnancy journeys are testament to this. They teach us about the various forms, strategies, and refusals that Palestinian women's reproductive and everyday resistance might take.

FIVE

Bodies

ON A HOT SUMMER DAY in July 2018, Mary, the Palestinian interpreter I was working with, and I sat in the office of a Palestinian prisoners' rights organization in Jenin in the occupied West Bank. We were waiting for our contact person from the organization to drive us to the homes of three Palestinian women and mothers (to be) whose detained husbands had managed to smuggle a sperm sample out of Israeli prison to subsequently enable their wives to undergo IVF in fertility clinics in the West Bank. The walls of the small office were plastered with old newspaper cuttings that I looked at while waiting. Due to the nature of our endeavor, the illustration of the pregnant woman stepping on the jagged-edge wall or road caught my eye immediately. I took a photo with my phone. Later, in the car, I showed Mary the photo and she translated it from Arabic to English. The illustration's top corner contained a single phrase, "On the road to give birth / to be born." "The United National Government" was printed over the pregnant woman's belly. Although probably much older than the practice of sperm smuggling itself, which first successfully led to the birth of a child in 2012, the yellowed illustration captures the fundamental relationship between Palestinian women's bodies and the Israeli state. The visibly pregnant woman tries to step over a spiky wall, reminding me of the heavily surveilled and militarized borders and checkpoints that impede Palestinian women's already scarce access to reproductive health services in the occupied West Bank. The illustration evokes how Israeli borders interfere with Palestinian women's reproductive movement and rights. From the perspective of Israeli population politics, the pregnant Palestinian body becomes a site of surveillance, control, and containment. At the same time, this interpellation enables Palestinians to harness reproductive technologies in order to challenge the Israeli carceral

FIGURE 1: Wall plastered with newspaper cuttings, Jenin. Source: Author.

regime and military occupation through new modes of border-crossing kin-work.

In August 2012, Dalal al-Ziben gave birth to her son Muhanned, the first baby conceived with smuggled sperm, in a fertility clinic in Nablus in the occupied West Bank. Muhanned's father, Ammar, a Palestinian prisoner who was sentenced to twenty-five years in Israeli prison, managed to smuggle a sperm sample out of prison and into the Razan Center for Infertility in Nablus. Once the sperm sample had arrived at the fertility clinic and its origin was confirmed by family members on both sides, it was immediately frozen to enable Dalal to undergo IVF treatment. In summer 2019, ninety-six babies had been conceived by sperm that had been smuggled out of Israeli prisons and into Palestinian fertility clinics, a number that is probably much higher by now.[1] The practice of conceiving with smuggled sperm in the West Bank and in Gaza has been discussed extensively in local Palestinian media, North American and European newspaper articles, a recent film (*Amira*, 2021), and in scholarly articles. Feminist historian Sigrid Vertommen contextualizes the practice of sperm smuggling as a co-product of Israel's settler colonial population politics, which aims to control Palestinian women's fertility to maintain a Jewish population majority across Palestine/Israel.[2] Vertommen provided the groundwork to theorize sperm smuggling as a tool of biopolitical resistance for Palestinian women and men who want to continue their family life after incarceration. Other scholars have since approached the phenomenon from a literary or ethical perspective, and they demonstrate how sperm smuggling produces gendered identities and an affirmation of Palestinian life in the face of settler colonial social and political death.[3] Elsewhere, I have shown how sperm smuggling is embedded in the racial geographies of the Israeli occupation and how Palestinian families embrace and normalize sperm smuggling as an everyday practice of social and biological reproduction.[4]

Central to the workings of this practice is the (reproductive) body. As the sperm sample crosses the prison walls and Israeli borders and checkpoints, bodily matter becomes agentive and challenges the various forms of carcerality Palestinian bodies are enclosed by. In the fertility clinic, the sperm sample is received and prepared to be used in IVF, requiring a variety of different material, technological, social, and religious infrastructures and protocols. In this process, the sperm sample crosses, unmakes, and remakes various borders, (bodily) boundaries, and embodied states. Palestinians' bodies and bodily matter thus constitute a crucial lens from which to analyze the multiscalar registers of Israeli securitization and militarization as well as the embodied practices of resistance that emerge in this context. Focusing on Palestinian bodies and their gendered and racialized materiality as contested sites[5] is key to understanding how settler colonial power not only materializes in and through bodies but also how oppression and resistance produce, signify, and modulate the matter of bodies.[6]

The body is not external to political processes but constitutes a crucial site for politics and is, in turn, constitutive of politics itself.[7] Bodies are produced by and are productive of social and political relations; they are politically constituted as well as *constituting*.[8] It is precisely because bodies and body parts are "discrepantly enrolled, altered, and announced as alterable by processes and structures that exceed the body proper" that they matter as an entity of analysis.[9] Different bodily materialities are made disposable or productive at the various intersections of race, class, gender, and sexuality.[10] Egg cells, fetuses, embryos, sperm, and other forms of vital matter appear as animate actors in current politics as they index belonging, denote kinship relations or relatedness, stand in for sexed and gendered forms of embodiment, or figure as threats to biosecurity.[11] In Palestine/Israel, a recent turn to bodies reveals them to be a crucial yet understudied site for settler colonial oppression and Palestinian practices of resilience.[12]

Conceiving with smuggled sperm points to the complex interplay between biopolitical and necropolitical forms of power, acts of resistance, and people's everyday lives. In this chapter, I examine the tension between oppression and resistance, governance and matter(ing), by analyzing Israeli settler colonialism and Palestinian practices of resistance through a matter-oriented approach. I explore how bodies and bodily matter figure as actors in the counter-infrastructures that Palestinians have established to enable the smuggling of sperm out of Israeli prisons and into Palestinian fertility clinics. To draw out the relationship between oppression and resistance in the practice of sperm smuggling, I specifically focus on the body and bodily matter not as passively awaiting cultural inscription, but as active entities, recognizing that "matter and meaning are not separate elements."[13] I illustrate how this oscillating movement between matter reflecting social structures and matter itself matter*ing* is reconfigured by biological processes and social or institutional forces.[14] This understanding of matter as active and activated allows me to examine the multiple scales and actors that are constitutive of the practice of sperm smuggling.

To this end I present fieldwork I have conducted in the West Bank together with two Palestinian collaborators and interpreters, Mary, a Palestinian with Israeli citizenship, and Rafa, who lives under Israeli occupation in the West Bank. To understand the political, social, and gendered meaning of sperm smuggling, we met nine Palestinian women and their families, whose husbands (or son, in one case) had smuggled their sperm out of Israeli prisons. We mainly reached out to these families through a prisoners' rights organization, as well as with the help of fertility doctors in the West Bank. The women we interviewed were keen on telling their stories, and I later recognized some of them in other studies and newspaper articles. The families we met welcomed us warmly, and we would usually spend an hour or two drinking tea together or snacking on green almonds and sweets. We began each interview by asking the women how they came to know about the practice of sperm smuggling, what was their decision-making process in trying to conceive like this, and how they experienced getting pregnant and giving birth in such a novel way. We also asked about which other actors or institutions were involved and supported them, how sperm smuggling was socially and religiously perceived, and how they felt about its political implications. These encounters were rather social, with me, Rafa or Mary, and other family members, friends, or neighbors being present. While we mainly spoke to the women and were interested in learning about their experiences, others would also participate in these conversations, which sometimes complicated translation and the women's abilities to speak freely. To understand the institutional and biomedical perspective of sperm smuggling, I also conducted interviews with the spokesperson of the Razan Center for Infertility in Nablus and the director of a fertility clinic in Ramallah.

Drawing from these interviews, field notes, and English-language newspaper articles on sperm smuggling published between 2012 and 2022, I approach sperm smuggling as an assemblage, taking seriously how the interplay between different actors, institutions, and technologies is relevant to how this practice works and to how it is narrated.[15] I first demonstrate how sperm smuggling in the West Bank is organized communally. I show how bodies, technology, infrastructures, religion, and settler colonialism converge, shape, and are being shaped by the practice of sperm smuggling. I then turn to the political and affective meaning that marriage, pregnancy, and childbirth have for Palestinian women in the West Bank. Third, I explore how Palestinian women and their families conceive of sperm smuggling as a material, embodied form of resistance against the settler colonial regime. I show how in the practice of sperm smuggling, bodily matter is assigned evidentiary status to signify resistance, both by the Israeli military authorities and by Palestinian families. I then complicate this narrative by asking whose body and gametes figure as central political actors in the practice of sperm smuggling, illustrating how Israeli militarization, securitization, and incarceration reinforce sexual and political difference in a patriarchal society. In the penultimate section, I come back to my argument about sperm smuggling as an assemblage and discuss how the work of translation and a critical politics of location are central to understanding sperm smuggling. I conclude with some reflections on the political work that different bodies do, and I argue that it remains imperative to acknowledge Palestinian women as the producers of knowledge about the various ways of unruly and convivial forms of Palestinian resistance I present in this chapter.

ISRAEL'S CARCERAL PROJECT AND A COMMUNAL PRACTICE OF PALESTINIAN RESISTANCE

The story of Muhanned al-Ziben, the first IVF baby conceived with smuggled sperm in 2012, was broadcast widely once the baby was born in the Razan Center for Infertility in Nablus. Everyone I interviewed in the West Bank knew about them or mentioned their case, as do most other scholarship or media coverage of the practice. Suhad, a thirty-six-year-old mother of five who lives in a refugee camp in Nablus, got pregnant with her youngest child, two-year-old daughter Huriye, with sperm that her imprisoned husband Samir had succeeded in smuggling out of prison. Suhad explained how the story of Muhanned's birth changed the situation of all the wives of long-term prisoners: "He was the first to shake the feelings of motherhood in all mothers. He renewed their identities." Muhanned's origin story was framed by the hardship of Palestinian women who had been deprived of motherhood due to their husbands' incarceration. This first case of a successful pregnancy with smuggled sperm points to how sentiments of hope and excitement are attached to the novel possibilities presented by IVF with smuggled sperm. This new way of conception resolved a social and political problem. Couples separated by the ongoing occupation and Israel's carceral regime were now able to continue having biologically related children. Sameer, the director of a fertility clinic in Ramallah, referred to how reproductive technology shapes and is shaped by the society in which it is embedded.[16] He explained how utilizing IVF in Palestine responds to the social relations and political realities created by the Israeli occupation:

> There are some cases where a couple cannot have children because they don't have money. They don't have money because, for example, the occupation affects the husband, they don't allow him to work or to go outside, or he's in prison, and when you separate families from each other for years, for example, if she is in prison or he in prison, you should find some new technologies to have children.

As a reaction to incarceration, the economic effects of the occupation, and Israel's severing of families, Palestinians challenge and resist their subjugation through various embodied ways and find novel strategies for using and further developing existing reproductive technology. In the occupied West Bank, medical professionals, religious authorities, Palestinian media, and civil society organizations have worked together to set up the necessary infrastructures and social and religious protocols to enable more women to get pregnant like this.

While the practice of sperm smuggling originates in a couple's wish to procreate, the actual need to smuggle semen out of prison is caused by the discrepant treatment Palestinian prisoners receive in Israeli jails. According to figures from Palestinian NGO Addameer Prisoner Support and Human Rights Association and the Israeli NGO B'Tselem, as of September 2025, the total number of Palestinian prisoners is around 9,500.[17] The Israel Prison Service (IPS) classifies prisoners incarcerated in Israel into two categories: "criminal" and "security" prisoners. These classifications are the result of internal decisions made by the IPS. Unsurprisingly, most of Israel's security prisoners are Palestinians. As a result, thousands of Palestinians are categorically transformed into a single group, who then pose a singular threat to the Israeli state. Palestinian NGOs such as Addameer thus refer to security prisoners as political prisoners.

Palestinian political prisoners are deprived of some of their basic rights, including access to medical care or a fair trial. They are subject to stricter conditions of confinement, including the rejection or limitation of family visits as well as the prohibition of conjugal visits by their partner. In contrast to that, Jewish Israeli security prisoners are allowed to receive such visits. The most well-known case in this context is Yigal Amir, convicted of murdering then-Prime Minister Yitzhak Rabin. Amir was caught smuggling sperm out of prison in 2006, which resulted in an official ruling by the Israeli Supreme Court in favor of conjugal visits from his wife. This case was echoed in my interview with the official spokesperson of the Razan Center for Infertility who summarized the disparate treatment of Palestinian and Jewish Israeli security prisoners: "But if you look at Yigal Amir, he killed Rabin, he killed the 'King of Israel!' . . . Yigal Amir was more than a terrorist and had children from within the prison. But because he's Jewish, it's not a security issue. It's only related to: 'Are you an Arab or not? Jewish or Muslim?'" The Israeli state and its military authorities actively support human and reproductive rights for their Jewish citizens, while they control Palestinians' reproductive lives and restrict their rights.

Detention and imprisonment are key to the structure of the Israeli occupation in the Palestinian territories as well as to its rule over the Palestinians within Israel. This carceral regime targets Palestinian society in myriad ways.[18] The carceral state's reach has vastly increased since December 2022, when right-wing and ultranationalist politician and settler Itamar Ben-Gvir became minister of national security, overseeing the police and the IPS.[19] The long history of Israel's carceral and military domination in the occupied West Bank affects the social fabric of Palestinian society and shapes Palestinian identity and modes of resistance.[20] Salem Abu Khaizaran, director of the Razan Center for Infertility in Nablus, summarized this in a newspaper interview about sperm smuggling:

> We have had more than 800,000 people in and out prison since 1967. Do you know what that means for a population of 4 million? That means every one of us has spent part of his life in prison, and if not himself then his brother, or his neighbor. It's a highly emotional issue for the Palestinian people.[21]

Israel's carceral regime affects every Palestinian in the West Bank and shapes relationships, kinship, and everyday life. Against the vast reach of Israeli carcerality, Palestinians' practices such as sperm smuggling or letter writing with imprisoned friends, family members, or partners can be considered material expressions of care, love, and hope, everyday practices that deal with the settler colonial reality of living under occupation.[22] In that sense, sperm smuggling is embedded in Palestinian society and is a practice of both social and biological reproduction. As this chapter shows, Palestinians try to conceive with smuggled sperm for a variety of reasons and assign meaning to it in contingent ways. However, at the same time, sperm smuggling also derives its political efficacy because the Israeli authorities deem it successful. Sameer talked to me about the politicization of sperm smuggling:

> I think the Israelis don't want us to do this political IVF in Palestine because it is a success on two levels, in politics and medicine. If they don't want to, or if they don't see it as a success, let the prisoners have some normal life with their wives and have children, it will not affect Israel and it will not affect the security of Israel if they grant permission for the prisoner to sleep with his wife in the prison for a few hours.

He points not only to the biomedical innovation of sperm smuggling but also to the politicization of Palestinian reproduction. Sameer's sober account of Palestinian children not posing a security risk for Israel reveals the importance that the Israeli state assigns to Palestinian birth rates and its development of tactics to surveil a population deemed inherently dangerous. This form of settler colonial political arithmetic produces a political situation in which the reproduction and affirmation of life, love, sexuality, and family become a site of both oppression and resistance.

To enable the practice of sperm smuggling, the Razan Center for Infertility in Nablus and other fertility clinics in the West Bank are offering "free help" to the wives and families of Palestinian prisoners. The IVF treatment, which would otherwise cost around $3,400, is offered free of charge or at a reduced rate. If a couple decides to try and conceive like this, the Palestinian prisoner smuggles a sperm sample out of prison and into a cooperating fertility clinic in the West Bank or Gaza, where the sample will be cryopreserved immediately.[23] The Razan spokesperson described the process as follows:

> The women bring the samples. The wife of a prisoner comes to us and tells us that she just came from a visit, or that "I have a sample from my husband, how do I do that?" "When you arrive at Nablus or Ramallah or Bethlehem, call this number. An employee will receive you." And she needs to bring two certificates, from her and his parents, IDs, and the official marriage papers. The sample will be examined. If the sample is good, we sign that this sample is her husband's, and we'll freeze it at -197 degrees.

The practice of sperm smuggling constitutes a concerted effort that includes various actors and travels across different scales and borders. The fertility clinic is the most important biosocial infrastructure, mediating between the prisoner, his family, and their wish to procreate. Although it is theoretically possible to undergo artificial insemination with smuggled sperm without medical assistance, it is technically difficult. Medical staff at the fertility clinic are thus central to facilitating the procedure of receiving, examining, and freezing the sperm sample, performing IVF cycles, and treating the women during pregnancy and birth. In addition to that, medical staff have also established a socially accepted protocol to verify the semen's origin and legitimize the process while considering religious and social issues that could arise if a woman whose husband is known to be imprisoned for over a decade becomes pregnant.

After facilitating the first few successful cases and before fully advertising it to more families of detainees, Razan staff discussed the practice with religious authorities. This led to multiple fatwas officially approving artificial insemination for women married to Palestinian long-term prisoners. Specific conditions of Islamic law determined this approval. The intended parents must be married, and the desired pregnancy must be agreed on by the wife, her husband, and their respective families. These religious rulings were an important reference point for all the women I spoke to. Although reproductive technologies are generally widely used and embraced in the Muslim world,[24] the women I interviewed expressed relief that there were official guidelines to embed this (at the time) novel practice in the fabric of society. Establishing social and religious protocols helped women and their families navigate fears regarding accusations of adultery and the resulting illegitimacy of the child according to Islamic law.

Some women developed their own strategies for making sure that the practice was accepted and announced publicly to prevent any suspicions. Marwa, thirty-nine years old, lives in a village close to Jenin with her two teenage children and her nine-month-old son, Majd. Her husband, a thirty-nine-year-old political prisoner sentenced to twenty-one years, smuggled his sperm out of the Israeli prison, which resulted in the birth of their son. Marwa described her pregnancy as very emotional, not only because she was pregnant with twins and lost one of them after three months, but also because she was generally skeptical and scared about conceiving in such a complicated and novel way. Her friends and family supported her and accompanied her throughout the different stages of the pregnancy, and she pointed out how supportive and resourceful the Razan medical staff was. It was through their support that she was finally able to enjoy the pregnancy, despite her traumatic experience of losing one of her twins. Like the other women, Marwa also mentioned the 2013 fatwa. But in addition to that she also obtained personal fatwas for herself, for her "internal satisfaction," she said, continuing:

> If I walked on the street when my husband is in jail and everyone would see me pregnant . . . I saw that this thing could be difficult for me. People might see it as *haram*. We are religious. *Alhamdulillah*, we are preserving our ways of life and our prayers, so I wanted to be certain that it's not *haram*. So, I went to the mufti to get the approval. I have three: one from Nablus, Ramallah, and Jenin.

Marwa made sure getting pregnant with smuggled sperm was religiously approved. She also remembered publicizing her pregnancy: "We declared it in the village and almost everyone knew that I'm implanting fertilized ova. On the day of the birth, we announced it on TV and the internet and explained how I did the smuggling." Embedding sperm smuggling in her religious life and publicizing it on several channels demonstrates not only how Palestinian women have become actively involved in shaping this form of conception, but also how new forms of assisted reproduction create new forms of social relations and practices.[25]

Palestinian women's active engagement in normalizing and embedding sperm smuggling in society was successful in many ways. Salam, thirty-one years old, lives in a small village close to the "Green Line" in the northwest West Bank, together with her mother Kifaya, her three older daughters, and her son Sharif (two and a half years old), who was conceived with smuggled sperm. When Salam's husband, who faces twenty years in Israeli prison, had the idea to smuggle sperm, Salam and her mother had similar fears. However, soon thereafter, they were convinced that the pregnancy would be accepted. Kifaya recounted: "I was thinking, how would the people around us accept this? But actually, people were encouraging us to do something like this!" Similarly, Suhad expressed how she had feared her community's judgment of being the first woman in the refugee camp to conceive like this, yet was met with support instead:

> This period was really difficult for me. First of all, after thirteen years, having another child. But what happened was that people started treating me well in the community. During the nine months, different refugee families, men, young, old—my family members. Sweethearts! They made me feel reasonable and comfortable, and I was not scared after all.

The communal acceptance of the practice of sperm smuggling was an important factor for the women's general well-being and status in society and helped these women to conceive safely and give birth to healthy children.

In the practice of sperm smuggling, several actors, institutions, and technologies converge. They are activated, implemented, and supported by fertility clinics and their staff, religious authorities, the couples' families, friends, and communities, as well as by the women themselves. An assemblage approach helps to identify how this multiplicity of actors, affects, relations, and temporalities constitutes the phenomenon of conception with smuggled sperm and its different forms of emergent agency.[26] The practice of assisted reproduction is not only *engendered by* the circumstances of the Israeli carceral regime and military occupation but also *acts as* an assemblage that allows for a new organization of everyday life and kin-work. Sperm smuggling emerged as a communal counter-infrastructure that challenges the militarized geographies of the occupation, such as borders, checkpoints, and prisons. As a concerted effort, pregnancy and childbirth with smuggled sperm enable a temporal passage through the fissures and cracks of the infrastructures of military oppression and control.

REPRODUCTION AND POLITICS: FAMILY AGAINST THE OCCUPATION

In the West Bank, marriage, pregnancy, and childbirth take place amid the everydayness of life, even as they are shaped by the occupation and Israel's politics of fear and securitization. As such, reproduction and kin-work both mirror and contest power structures and thereby become constitutive of Palestinian identity.[27] Palestinian leader Yasser Arafat has been famously quoted referring to the womb of the Palestinian woman as the strongest weapon of the Palestinian people, later making similar references to Palestinian women's reproductive behavior. As a response to settler colonial reproductive politics, reproduction is also central to Palestinian popular resistance.[28] In the West Bank, local Palestinian political leaders have endorsed the practice of sperm smuggling, and in Palestinian public discourse, children born from it are described as "ambassadors of freedom"[29] or "babies against imprisonment."

Fatiha, a thirty-seven-year-old woman who lives in a village near Nablus, got pregnant with her now two-year-old son with smuggled sperm. Fatiha's husband was sentenced to twenty years in prison only eighteen days after they got married, and after hearing about the story of Muhanned, he suggested the idea to Fatiha. Fatiha shared that when her son was born, many people came to visit her at the hospital, including the then-governor of Ramallah. However, even though her son's birth was celebrated politically, for Fatiha, this was just a personal decision. She remembered: "Was I thinking about the Israeli government? Not at all." As anthropologist Livia Wick explores in her book *Sumud: Birth, Oral History, and Persistence in Palestine*, Palestinian women's birth stories in the West Bank are often framed outside the realm of politics while at the same time revealing the myriad ways in which care, reproduction, and love are connected to the political and the unequal distribution of life under settler colonialism.[30] Sameer described this simultaneity and ambivalence of politics and reproduction:

> Human reproduction or infertility treatment is a field full of human feelings. And politics should not be there. But in Palestine, there is nothing without politics and everything, from medicine, love, to having kids, to everything, you will find some politics in that. This is not good, but it's a fact here in Palestine.

The practice of sperm smuggling is characterized by jumping various collective, individual, and institutional scales, being celebrated as a political victory, while at the same time also being a normal and normalized part of women's everyday lives and reproductive decision-making.

The range of meanings family and reproduction take on in the narratives of Palestinian women in the West Bank is reflective of the various ways the occupation, directly and indirectly, interferes with their lives. While for some women, like Fatiha, reproduction is not connected to politics or occupation, others describe the impact of the political situation on their family life and reproductive behavior as ever-present. Iman, thirty-nine years old, lives in a small village near Jenin with her two older daughters, her family, and her four-year-old son Bahaa. Bahaa was conceived with smuggled sperm after his father had already been imprisoned for eleven years. Iman told us with pride that she was the fourteenth case of conceiving with smuggled sperm in the West Bank. At first, when her husband suggested the idea, she was hesitant, although she had seen and heard about it in the local media. But after being encouraged by her family and because she felt lonely at home with her husband "waiting" for her in prison, she decided to give it a try and got pregnant during her first cycle of IVF. Iman explained the importance of family in her situation: "Of course, the family helps to continue going and bear up life under the occupation, and if something happens, there's the family to help with everything. Even if you have good neighbors, there is no replacement for the family." For her, the family is a safe space, offering protection and helping her get on with life under the occupation. Besides providing hope, stability, and support, kin-work enables a sense of belonging and co-constitutes a part of Palestinian identity. In a similar conversation about the role the family plays in Palestinian society, Marwa shared:

> It's nice that every person has a sense of belonging to his family home, his homeland, and his parents. Some people don't even have a sense of belonging to their families. But we, *Alhamdulillah*, do have that, and that's the most important thing that we have in our country, that everyone has a sense of belonging to his home, parents, and his family.

The family stands in for the home/land, and vice versa, offering a sense of identification and belonging. It is precisely through this process of signification that building a family and kin-work challenges settler colonial rule. Conceiving with smuggled sperm can be understood as an assisted extension of this relationship.

Having children and a big family is also a way to challenge and reverse the settler colonial logic of elimination. The Israeli state and military authorities are invested in producing statistical and population-level knowledge about Palestinians in the occupied territories, obsessing over "the intimate details of who is sleeping with whom, who is marrying whom, who is giving birth, and whose children will be recognized, or not."[31] Palestinian women conceiving with smuggled sperm are keenly aware of how their bodies, their children, and their families are subjected to intimate surveillance. Amal, thirty-eight years old, lives with her teenage son and daughter in a village near Jenin. When her husband was imprisoned, her daughter was only eighteen days old. From the first time Amal had heard that couples could conceive with smuggled sperm, she wanted to do it. Her husband was not enthusiastic about it at first. However, when the practice became more popular, he agreed to it, and when we met Amal, she was visibly pregnant. Reflecting on having a family and being Palestinian, Amal said, "It's a big thing when we build a family because they don't want us to have a family and children, to build our lives." Amal intimately knows Israel's demographic anxieties and reproductive politics and affirms how Palestinians are defying them by reclaiming their "right to life"[32] and "right to family."[33] As she stated dryly, "We as Palestinians are becoming more and we're having children." For her, the family and reproduction are sites of resistance, simply because the restriction of Palestinian reproduction is so central to Israel's settler colonial project. Amal's framing of the family evokes what Rhoda Ann Kanaaneh has termed a "reverse calculus among Palestinians."[34] She argues that Israeli population politics have had unintended consequences. By organizing demographic policies and institutions around a distinction between Jews and Arabs, Israeli state policies came to be mirrored and deployed by Palestinians themselves.

While this narrative was expressed openly by some women, such as Amal, Marwa alluded to a "reverse calculus" in a more ambiguous way. Mary, the interpreter, asked her what she thinks about the role of reproduction in her society. Marwa said: "The mortality rate is high because there's a lot of killing and death here, and although I don't like the idea, in contrast to death, we have new lives. There's reproduction, and babies are being born." Marwa refers to the relationship between oppression and reproduction but points to the necropolitical register of the occupation.[35] Palestinians produce new lives as a response to constant death. Reproduction is an everyday practice of responding to the Israeli military's ongoing presence and incursion into Palestinian life. The Palestinian family exists simultaneously as a "counterspace,"[36] enabling women to survive and envision a different future, and it also exists as a tool of resistance against the occupation, taking up Israel's demographic interpellation in numbers. As Sameer put it, in Palestine, whether women frame reproduction as political resistance, a private space of support and protection, or as an individual decision outside of capital-P politics, "you will find some politics in that."

ENGENDERING RESISTANCE: BODIES THAT MATTER

We were sitting in Iman's living room along with her sister and Bahaa, who was watching a children's program on TV. Spread out on the floor were all the documents Iman had kept from undergoing IVF with her husband's smuggled sperm, such as letters from the prison authorities and birth certificates. Iman described sperm smuggling as a practice supported by her community and the Razan Center for Infertility, but also as a form of resistance against the occupying power. She said, "The most important thing is to beat the Jews. This is against them. This is one way to beat them. Although he's in prison, we'll have children." Later in our conversation, Iman came back to this point and elaborated further, referencing the material and bodily conditions that sperm smuggling challenges: "Even though we are in chains and imprisoned, there is nothing to prevent us from having children, to have a family, a society. That's the most important thing." In Iman's narration, the incarceration of her husband and other Palestinians, their bodies being confined and "in chains," is overcome by their mere continuation of life through reproduction and kin-work, and by growing as a society. The settler colonial regime has the power to decide which bodies matter and which bodies need to be contained, but, in so doing, it also signifies *how* these bodies come to matter.[37]

Carcerality is an important site for the relationship between oppression and signification. As sociologist Ashjan Ajour shows, the Israeli prison is set up not only as an institution to punish Palestinian political prisoners but also to contain their activism and political identity. However, for many Palestinians, Israeli incarceration is not the end but rather the beginning, or a reconfiguration of their strategies of resistance against settler colonialism and occupation.[38] Anthropologist Esmail Nashif discusses how, in a dialectical process between the settler colonial regime and Palestinian society, political captivity assigns imprisonment the status of a rite of passage and enables Palestinian political prisoners to regain a sense of national belonging and community. In that sense, the space of the Israeli prison produces "Palestinian bodily matter."[39] The Israeli prison system and settler colonial securitization engender the imprisoned Palestinian body and bodily matter as a site of national belonging, community, and resistance. Palestinian bodily matter, then, matters precisely because of its imprisonment behind "bars" and "metal." In the case of sperm smuggling, the connection that is established across the borders, walls, and chains of the prison is enabled through sperm as a materiality that challenges and overcomes carcerality. As a substance deriving yet being separated from the body, smuggled semen becomes biopolitically relevant precisely because it constitutes an active bounded (if temporal) entity. The sperm sample's movement reveals the porosity of the borders that the Israeli state and military set up to slow down or impede Palestinians' (reproductive) movement.[40] In that process, the Palestinian prisoners' very material confinement is temporarily suspended through the sperm samples' animacy.[41] Carrying the prisoner's status across the walls of the prison and into embodied futures, the sperm sample figures as an active entity of Palestinian reproductive futurity.

Salam explained her husband's reasoning for wanting to smuggle sperm, evoking Nashif's analysis of the dialectic of political captivity:

> You know, a prisoner, he considers this an opportunity, an opportunity to go against the authorities, in that he is locked in a room and his wife cannot visit him. So, he had the idea that he wanted to have a boy and also break the rules.... The Israelis are not going to stop us; they have locked him in, and they have forbidden me and his daughters to visit.

Like Iman, Salam referred to the materiality of power through the lens of the embodied status of being imprisoned ("locked in a room"), which, once overcome, turns into an act of resistance. For Salam's husband, smuggling his semen out of prison constituted an opportunity to engage in the Palestinian liberation struggle while at the same time allowing him and his wife to continue having children. Salam and her daughters are prohibited from visiting their husband and father, but by conceiving with smuggled sperm, they suspend the family's material separation.

Salam remembered that what "drove the Israelis mad" was when she and other mothers who had conceived with smuggled sperm applied for permits to visit their husbands with their newborn babies. Palestinians living in the West Bank cannot freely travel across the "Green Line" without applying for a permit, and some Israeli prisons are located within Israeli territory. The Israeli prison authorities would refuse to acknowledge that the prisoner in question was the legitimate father of the child they were applying for, noting that he had been imprisoned during the time the child was born. Fatiha explained to me that this led many of the so-called new mothers to carry out DNA tests to prove their husbands' paternity. Once they applied to visit again, this time showing proof of paternity, the prison authorities began to prohibit visitation for the wives and children of the prisoners in question and established further punitive measures, such as prolonging the prisoners' sentences or sentencing them to a fine for their involvement in the practice of sperm smuggling.

This was the case with Lydia, a thirty-eight-year-old woman from the village of Beit Rima, whose story has been published in several newspapers. After Lydia's son Majd, conceived with his father Abdel's smuggled sperm, was born, Lydia tried to bring Majd with her to the prison to visit his father. The IPS denied them their visitation rights for eight months and asked for a DNA test to prove Abdel's paternity. After producing the necessary paperwork and demonstrating Abdel's paternity, he was interrogated and confessed to the sperm smuggling. This led to the IPS sentencing him to eight more months on top of his twenty-five-year sentence, as well as a 5,000-shekel fine (almost $1,500).[42] IPS spokesperson Sivan Weizman has been quoted as doubting that the practice of sperm smuggling happens successfully due to the strict security protocols of the prisons and the longevity of sperm.[43] Yet, by requesting DNA tests and punishing prisoners and their families on the grounds of smuggling sperm, the prison authorities acknowledge the existence and success of sperm smuggling. In this process, the IPS charges Palestinian bodily matter with political meaning; bodily matter becomes evidence.[44]

Salam framed the evidentiary status of Palestinian bodies and bodily matter as a response to Israeli demographic anxieties: "Our children, they fear them!" Salam's son Sharif was denied an entry permit to Israel, which they had also applied for to travel to the Israeli prison and visit Salam's husband. Salam reflected, chuckling: "When they gave him the letter stating that Sharif cannot enter Israel, he brought joy to this family and the father! In that his son is still a baby and already wore them out. His son became a threat to Israel." In denying Sharif entry, the Israeli authorities not only impeded the babies' freedom of movement but also granted the little boy something else. Imbued with the power to be a threat to Israel, Sharif's body resisted by merely existing. Salam's son embodies the relationship between Palestinian bodily resistance and Israeli practices of targeting Palestinian bodies, sexuality, and reproduction. Sharif's body is evidence to his family and imprisoned father that Palestinian bodies matter.

The evidentiary status assigned to gametes breaching the prison's walls makes the semen even more "sacred."[45] Palestinian bodies are made, and bodily matter emerges, in interaction with the Israeli carceral system, which, in turn, further hones its security apparatus by inventing and implementing modes of surveillance and control. DNA tests to prove paternity, sperm crossing the walls of the prison and the "Green Line," or the children conceived with smuggled sperm—these are all actors or bearers of resistance in and through their relationship with the Israeli carceral system. Palestinian bodies are *made*, and bodily matter *matters* in a multiscalar system of state violence, communal counter-infrastructures, reproductive technology, and social and religious protocols.

THE ABSENCE OF THE FEMALE BODY

The reproductive body is central for sperm smuggling to lead to a pregnancy and the birth of a child. To ensure their pregnancies with smuggled sperm would be successful, the women I met recounted various precautionary measures they applied. Iman remembered that she refrained from visiting her husband while she was pregnant. Echoing the broader effects the architecture of the occupation has on women's bodies,[46] she said, "One does get scared at the checkpoints when undergoing fertility treatment because there might be things that can affect the embryo. So, when I was pregnant, I didn't visit him at all." Others reported side effects from the hormonal treatment as part of the IVF procedure, general fatigue associated with the pregnancy, or concerns about whether the fertility treatment would work out. As these instances suggest, the female body, gestational labor,[47] and women's experiences of conceiving with smuggled sperm are key to understanding this phenomenon. However, while male bodies, bodily matter, and the children conceived with smuggled sperm take center stage as *political* actors in the process of sperm smuggling, the bodies of Palestinian women are strikingly absent in how the practice of sperm smuggling is narrated. This absence is remarkable, considering the temporal, social, and bodily uncertainties of fertility treatment, the process of giving birth and raising a child without the husband/father present, as well as dealing with the everyday worries and social burden sperm smuggling can have for Palestinian women. Instead of talking about their own corporeal experience in the sperm smuggling process, the women I interviewed tended to sideline themselves in several narratives that centered around their absent husbands. In other words, while conceiving with smuggled sperm reveals the entanglement of technology, bodily matter, and practices of resistance, it also points to how this entanglement is gendered in a patriarchal society.

In her work about the wives of Palestinian prisoners in the West Bank, anthropologist Lotte Buch Segal describes how the absence of their detained husbands translates into emotional, financial, and social labor these women have to perform. In that process, the wives of prisoners are inclined to become "exemplary," a particularly gendered performance of being a Palestinian woman in which the burden of continuing life with a detained husband needs to be hidden.[48] Buch Segal shows how, in order to fulfill these societal and national requirements, women mute their feelings of loneliness, anxiety, or fear while foregrounding motherhood and care as a primary source of identity and pride.[49] In the case of smuggled sperm, becoming exemplary entails finding and applying strategies to normalize the unusual conception of the child, pregnancy, and birth, and the ensuing family situation. In these attempts to perform an ordinary family life, both under the occupation and without the active involvement of a husband, the emotional and social burden falls on the wives' shoulders. The following passage, in which Marwa talks about how she deals with her husband's absence, is demonstrative of this:

> Our family hasn't lived as a normal family, we're not complete, and we're missing the most important part of the family, which is, of course, the father. I tried to make my children not to be influenced by his absence. The mother can be really strong, bold, and a protector of the house, but the most important thing is that the father is missing. His absence is present and clear, not only for his children but also for the stranger coming from the outside, it is noticeable that the father figure is not present. . . . So, we lived this prison life on holidays, at events, parties, at weddings of brothers-in-law, and so on. We would do all of that as if he was present. But on the inside we would feel his absence, and on the outside we'd convey the message as if everything is normal.

To live what Marwa calls "this prison life" is to fill the gap the imprisoned father left in their household. To deal with this absence, Marwa pretends to continue a normal family life, "as if he were present." Yet, on the inside, she strongly feels his absence, and in conveying that everything is OK, she mutes these feelings. Marwa carries the gendered burden of living alone, and her reflection centers around the husband as the main figure of the household.

In most houses of the wives of prisoners I visited in the West Bank, the women or other family members proudly showed us colorfully adorned altars or little shrines they had set up for their detained husband or son. Usually located in their living room, these sites consisted of family photos, huge portraits of the prisoner, and photos showing the prisoner together with national figures such as Yasser Arafat or symbols like the Dome of the Rock. The celebration of the prisoner as a national hero and his importance as the head of the household materialized in these living room settings and how they were included and presented in my encounter with the family. These gender roles reflect Buch Segal's findings on the everyday lives of the wives of prisoners. While their detained husbands are praised as national heroes, Palestinian women's sacrifices and hardships due to their husbands' absence are left undisclosed. Palestinian women's womanhood and subjectivity are reduced to motherhood.[50]

For some women, conceiving with smuggled sperm was not their choice or desire in the first place, and the absence of their bodies can be traced in the biosocial decision-making process of undergoing IVF with smuggled sperm. Some participants shared a recurring argument leveraged by their husbands or other family members, referring to the fact that their "biological clock was ticking." Fertility clinics in the West Bank only subsidize IVF with smuggled sperm for couples where the husband faces a long-term sentence of at least fifteen years. For most wives of long-term prisoners, they would not be able to get pregnant again after their husbands' release. Islamic law allows for the wives of prisoners who have been incarcerated for a prolonged period to get divorced on these grounds. However, due to the heroic reputation of long-term political prisoners, women would usually not make use of this regulation. In a 2013 interview, Salem Abu Khaizaran referred to this dilemma:

> The women here are loyal and want to stand by their husbands, but by the time the men are out of prison, many of these women will be too old to have children. When the man eventually leaves prison, there can be a lot of pressure on him to remarry to have children with a younger wife—and of course, leave his loyal wife. There are certainly cases in which this has happened.[51]

This fear of their husband marrying another woman to have a new family was echoed in all interviews, whether it was the woman's wish to undergo IVF with smuggled sperm or not. Salam remembered how her husband used the "biological clock" argument to convince her to undergo fertility treatment with smuggled sperm, cautiously at first and more seriously later:

> When he gets out of jail after the twenty years, he will be in his fifties, and I will be in my forties, and I will not be able to give birth. "So, this is a blessing that you can still have children," and he said, "I don't want to marry another woman to have another child. I consider that a betrayal." . . . He was scared when I refused, he started saying sweet things like "my Sweetheart" and "my Love." After that, he said, "You are getting older, and you will stop having children." I told him it's not a problem for me. Last thing he said was: "This means that you don't want me anymore, and I see you when I see you" [laughter].

Although Salam refers to this episode jokingly, it reflects how the "biological clock" argument is coupled with the threat of divorce or marrying a second wife. Different embodied temporalities play out in this scenario. On the one hand, the woman's reproductive capacities are addressed, and the importance of motherhood and having children "in time" is emphasized.[52] On the other hand, the period of absence from regular life and the prisoner's desire for continued fatherhood are considered. In the "biological clock" argument, the latter is balanced against women's bodies. Marwa recounted a similar conversation with her husband:

> He said, "I didn't have the chance to live with small children. When I'll be back home, I want to have a small child. Where should I get one if you didn't give birth to one?" I said, "You got imprisoned. It was out of my and your control." He said, "But see, people are implanting and having children, is there a possibility for us to have a kid, and when I come back, I'll get to live and see what I couldn't?"

Either implicitly or explicitly, the women's reproductive capacities are used as an argument in favor of undergoing fertility treatment with smuggled sperm. In part to enable her to have a family and children, and, in doing so, fulfilling her role of being an "exemplary" Palestinian woman, but also for the imprisoned husband to be able to pick up life where imprisonment cut it off. The carceral horizon of Israeli settler colonialism thus affects Palestinian women and their reproductive decision-making and reinforces patriarchal intimacies. Long-term incarceration and the prohibition of conjugal visits for Palestinian political prisoners position Palestinian women's bodies at the threshold for a Palestinian future while simultaneously reinforcing their political invisibility.

This is not to say that Palestinian women are not engaged in the Palestinian liberation struggle. Palestinian women are actively resisting settler colonialism in various capacities: political mobilization, strikes, participating in demonstrations, urban disobedience, and raising international awareness, as well as challenging the occupation through embodied forms of resistance.[53] While fewer in numbers, Palestinian women are also among political prisoners in Israeli prisons, where their experience of incarceration is particularly gendered.[54] Some of the women we spoke to recounted publicizing the practice of sperm smuggling by giving interviews or appearing on TV to encourage others to follow their example. Salam told us that as the third woman to undergo IVF with smuggled sperm, she considered herself a role model to other women, gave them advice, and shared her experience with them. Indeed, as literary scholar Mohammed Hamdan argues, in being the main narrators of the practice of sperm smuggling, "the wives of Palestinian prisoners reclaim power as active agents of history in which their published written stories of sperm smuggling on media challenges the Israeli colonial narrative and decolonizes the oral male history of resistance."[55] However, a matter-oriented approach reveals how the Palestinian body of resistance is gendered in complex ways. Sexual difference is political difference[56] and shapes knowledge about bodies according to a binary logic, and it also determines what kind of political work different bodies do.[57]

In the case of sperm smuggling, many Palestinian families use the opportunity to opt for nonmedical sex selection. Nonmedical sex selection is done either through sperm micro-sorting according to the gametes' chromosomal bearing, or the embryos produced in vitro are selected by their genetic (chromosomal) makeup through preimplantation genetic diagnosis (PGD).[58] Sperm smuggling requires the freezing of gametes and conception via IVF and thus introduces nonmedical sex selection as an optional biomedical procedure, reflecting traditional gender roles and patriarchal structures in the West Bank and beyond.[59] According to the spokesperson of the Razan center in Nablus, the center generally facilitates sex selection if the couple already has two daughters and has obtained a fatwa from a mufti stating that they are eligible for sex selection.

In our interviews, almost all the women stated that they had opted for nonmedical sex selection and had given birth to a son. Their reasoning for doing so varied. Some mentioned their husband's wish for a son or societal expectations, while others referred to economic considerations of a life under occupation. Iman, for instance, explained that "with us, the *fellaheen* [farmers], there is no situation where we don't have a boy. The boy is an essential need. That's the reason the father wanted a boy." Preference for a son is not unique to Palestinian society, but patrilineality in Islamic family law produces specific biopolitical categories of belonging and determines questions of inheritance and caring responsibilities.[60] Anthropologist Laura Ferrero thus argues that nonmedical sex selection needs to be understood as a strategy Palestinian women deploy in their daily struggle for security and subsistence.[61] Preference for a son is also reflected in the history of Palestinian national discourse, where women's contribution to the resistance movement is often focused on their role of giving birth to sons to become fighters and martyrs.[62] On a microscopic level, then, son preference illustrates how the specific parameters and possibilities of embodied resistance are modulated along with sexual and political difference but are also inflected by the social, political, and economic situation of a society under occupation.

Palestinian women's presence as the narrators of the practice of sperm smuggling and their way of narrating it (remember Salam's chuckling in her recounting of her husband's wish for a son), as well as their everyday struggle to survive Israeli settler colonialism, illustrate their centrality in this form of resistance. However, on the material level of the body and bodily matter, their reproductive capacities, desires, and everyday practices of resistance seem to be harnessed for the social and biological reproduction of a patriarchal society under occupation. The Israeli settler colonial regime has a long history of exploiting uneven gender relations in Palestinian society by using military strategies intimately targeted at women's bodies, mobilities, sexuality, and their role in society.[63] A series of T-shirts produced by Israeli battalion members for tourists in Jerusalem reveals the normalization of such militarized sexual violence and its embodied effects. These T-shirts depict pregnant Palestinian women with captions such as "One Shot, Two Kills," "Better Use Durex," or "Bet You Got Raped," illustrating how, from the perspective of an Israeli soldier, the pregnant woman becomes a target of military violence first and foremost for her reproductive capacities.[64] Israel's racialized politics of the womb expose the ambiguous status of the female Palestinian body.[65] It either needs to be saved from a patriarchal system or be contained in its capacity to give birth. If the Israeli prison engenders the male Palestinian body as a figure of resistance, then Israeli settler colonialism and its pornotroping of female Palestinian bodies situate them as a liminal figure in the realm of agentive politics.[66] It is precisely in this context where militarized state violence and sexuality merge that the female Palestinian body is simultaneously dehumanized, ungendered, and hypervisibilized as a site of domination and a threshold to a Palestinian future.

ASSEMBLAGE AS METHODOLOGY: TRANSLATION AND THE POLITICS OF LOCATION

Sperm smuggling constitutes a particular kind of kin-work, established by Palestinian families in the West Bank to resist the Israeli occupation. This practice is embedded in and produced by different systems of power and regimes of knowledge production—settler colonialism, sexual difference, religion, the family, and technology. Understanding sperm smuggling as an assemblage helps to underscore the interplay between different actors, institutions, and technologies that make up this form of conception.[67] As a response to the social problem that incarceration poses for Palestinian families, sperm smuggling developed as an experimental practice, responding to social, political, religious, and technological inputs, such as the novel possibilities opened up by reproductive technology. Palestinian medical staff work together with the families of Palestinian detainees to establish socially accepted protocols, such as the requirement to testify about the origin of a sperm sample and the parents' intention to procreate. By obtaining a fatwa, medical staff found a solution to embed sperm smuggling in Islamic law and to protect Palestinian women from the accusation of adultery. Palestinian women themselves participate as main narrators in this process to further stabilize the different elements and events that make up the practice of sperm smuggling and to adjust it to their own lives and needs. However, Palestinian society and Israeli militarized heteropatriarchy are both a part of this assemblage and pose particular challenges to foregrounding Palestinian women and their bodies as central to this form of resistance.

Another part of understanding sperm smuggling as an assemblage of various elements and processes is to analyze the conditions that allowed me to listen to Palestinian women narrate their experiences to me in the first place. Central to enabling me to relay these stories here is another group of Palestinian women, Maya and Rafa, the interpreters I worked with. Both helped me navigate the West Bank, pointing out and explaining to me the geography of the occupation and contextualizing what we saw through their own lived experience as Palestinian women. Their translation work during the interviews was crucial not only for me (and for the non-Arabic-speaking reader) to be able to listen to what our research participants were saying, but also for the women we interviewed and their families to trust a German PhD researcher who didn't speak their language with some of the most intimate details of their lives. Rafa and Mary's translation work adds another layer of meaning to these encounters[68] and illustrates the nature of "language-in-and-as-translation."[69] On our way back from the interviews, Mary and I would often discuss what we had experienced, and her cultural and political explanations of the families' different class backgrounds, political affiliations, or affective reactions to me allowed me to get a much more nuanced understanding of these women's lives. This is not to say that I believe a full representation of their lives is possible in my recounting of the practice of sperm smuggling. As Black feminist scholars have long argued, such extractive forms of knowledge production, or "knowing-to-prove" are inherently limited and often reinforce the power structures that produce them.[70] Instead, as Black studies scholar Katherine McKittrick suggests, I understand the stories that Palestinian women have trusted me with as part of a framework in which we share "information and stories and resources to build the capacity for social change."[71] And part of these resources includes the cultural, political, and affective translation work that Mary and Rafa did to enable me to listen and understand our interview participants.

These translation practices went both ways. As part of our encounters with the wives of Palestinian detainees, Mary and Rafa also introduced and translated my identity to them. For instance, by the end of our interview with Suhad in a refugee camp in Nablus, Rafa explained to Suhad why we were asking her all of these questions, some of which might have seemed obvious to her:

> So, it's her first time in Palestine. She knows that the situation is messy here. Like they are abroad and they see something different when they come here. So, I wanted to explain to her our nature here, our ways. How our society is. It is important that you stay alive. I will tell you, I am really impressed by you and the Palestinian girls who are like this, we have to be this way. The grandmothers and mothers in Palestine must be this way.

Being touched by the stories Suhad had told us, Rafa expressed her admiration for Palestinian women, mothers, and grandmothers, and their strength. She emphasizes why "staying alive" has a different meaning in Palestine, reinforcing an affirmation of life in the face of a constant threat of Israeli settler or military violence. This, I believe, is what political theorist Sumi Madhok means when she writes about "feminist debt," a proposition that highlights the generative epistemological and methodological interventions that a critical and reflexive politics of location enables.[72] Rafa engages in an ethics of responsibility that opens up new ways of thinking and expresses how she, and, by extension, I, am indebted to the women we interviewed for calibrating our frames of reference.

In a different instance, after our interview, Kifaya, the mother of Salam, wanted to learn more about my background, where I was from, and whether I was married and had children. At the time, I was not married but in a relationship and had no kids. Rafa explained to Kifaya:

> Look, the story here is that in European society, they don't believe in marriage. They are not a religious society, they used to believe in marriage when it was a largely Catholic society. They consider themselves not religious, so they consider marriage something really complicated. They don't get married to have children, and sometimes they have children in relationships. They consider this, a girl who lives with a boy and has a child, the child is accepted in society. They don't believe in marriage. . . . The idea of a family, they are scared of it. How can you be a mother when your freedom is taken away?

Rafa painted this very accurate portrait of how a Western millennial sees marriage and having children and, in so doing, translated my identity to Kifaya and Salam. This also reveals the various frames of reference that appear in relation to family life and occupation. For a Western woman, marriage and childbirth can signify a loss of freedom, whereas, in the case of sperm smuggling and living under military occupation, the continuation of family life is what constitutes freedom. Rafa further explained to them that when I was in Palestine for the first time (during the time these interviews were conducted), I was shocked by the conditions of the Palestinians. She correctly pointed out that "the Germans don't talk about the country of Israel, they don't consider it a place that is a conflict zone, they consider it a normal place." Rafa captured and translated not only my own political awakening to Palestine but also explained the ideological erasure of Palestine in the German public, political, and academic context.[73]

After looking at some photos of my then-partner and my parents, Kifaya and Salam wanted to know how I came to research this particular topic. Rafa shared with them that I had read about the practice of sperm smuggling in an English-language newspaper article:

> So, she wanted to know why people were doing this. She went to her department head, just like how we do our master's program. So, when she passed the idea to her, the professor asked if she was willing to go to Palestine to do further research, and she was told to continue this study. So, this is what she did. She was able to freely go to Palestinian families, so we started to talk about political affairs.

In explaining to Kifaya and Salam why I was interested in their stories, Rafa made an additional point about the politics of location.[74] As a holder of a German passport and as a culturally Christian and white woman, I was indeed free to travel to the West Bank and interview Palestinian families. This freedom of movement is not granted to everyone. Implementing specific regulations on obtaining visas or restricting travel from several Muslim-majority countries, the Israeli state determines who can enter the country to do research there or in the occupied territories. Palestinian or other Arab scholars face significant limitations in obtaining visas and experience violent and invasive searches and interrogations at the border if they are granted a visa. This shapes what kind of research can be done on Palestine and Israeli settler colonialism, and by whom.[75] Such practical concerns illustrate how settler colonial borders enable or foreclose possibilities of building and maintaining certain relationships, such as my relationships with Rafa, Mary, and the women we spoke to, as well as being able to travel and visit them at their homes.

In addition to Rafa and Mary's translation work, the affective intimacies that they introduced in our encounters with Palestinian women in the West Bank, as well as Israel's border management, are another crucial element of understanding the practice of sperm smuggling and how I relay these stories here. A critical politics of my location—what my passport and whiteness enable me to do—and my relation to the Palestinian women I worked with and met reveals how the ongoing coloniality of knowledge production, as well as the material circumstances of settler colonialism, determine the conditions of social theory itself.[76] Sperm smuggling becomes a meaningful practice through these complex, multi-sited, and multitemporal technologies of translation and relationality, as well as the (im)mobilities that shape the material politics of location of doing research in Palestine. Sperm smuggling reveals both the materiality and entangled nature of oppression and resistance and what this practice, as an assemblage, does to our understanding of the relationality of power and bodies and the way we analyze and narrate them.

RESISTANCE AS EPISTEMOLOGY

Focusing on the body as a central site of Israeli oppression and Palestinian resistance in the practice of sperm smuggling reveals how bodies and body parts are both constituted and constitutive of politics and political processes. Political theorist Banu Bargu, writing about hunger strikers in Turkish prisons, states that what lies at the core of the weaponization of life, central to hunger striking, "is a tactic in which the body is utilized as the conduit of a political intervention."[77] Ashjan Ajour similarly demonstrates this in the case of Palestinian hunger strikers, foregrounding how dispossession gives rise to new forms of subjectivity that center the body as a site of anticolonial resistance.[78] The practice of sperm smuggling can be understood as a political intervention directed at the weaponization of life through reproduction, through the affirmation of life, family, and kinship. It responds to Israeli demographic anxieties and fears of Palestinian population growth, which result in the circumstances of Israeli carcerality and the containment of Palestinian reproduction and fertility writ large.

Sperm smuggling focuses our attention on the co-constitutive relationship between oppression and resistance. Following anthropologist Lila Abu-Lughod, we can understand Palestinian embodied resistance as "diagnostic of power."[79] Instead of simply signifying resilience or a failure of Israeli population politics, Palestinians' reproductive resistance reveals the forms of oppression that Palestinians are subjected to. These include interlocking systems of power, such as the Israeli carceral system, kin-work and the importance of family, Palestinian resistance, and militarized heteropatriarchy. An analysis that considers these intersecting forms of oppression sheds light on Palestinian women's complex positionality as actors of resistance and as mothers, and it allows for a better understanding of the reproductive and emotional labor they perform.

The molecular scale of taking seriously the sperm sample as an entity of analysis further undergirds this argument. Conceiving with smuggled sperm is an embodied form of resistance in which matter and meaning converge on a bodily level and modulate who or what counts as a political body and what kind of political work bodies do.[80] While the right to a body that matters is not distributed equally in the biopolitical and necropolitical context of Israeli settler colonialism,[81] the practice of sperm smuggling reveals how certain bodies are overburdened with meaning. What crosses the walls of the prison, borders, and, ultimately, engenders resistance is the male prisoner, his body, his semen, and the (preferably XY-chromosomal) child to be born. These actors are doing political work, both from the point of view of the Israeli state and Palestinian society. Palestinian women's bodies and reproductive capacities are central to conceiving with smuggled sperm, and Palestinian women are the main narrators of this practice. However, their bodies are situated ambiguously, as a site of Israeli domination and as a threshold to a Palestinian future. Recognizing this, Palestinian women's bodies do a different kind of political work. They urge us to reckon with the manifold ways in which bodies become a target for contested and intersecting forms of power and the embodied indeterminacy of meaning-making.

This connects to my methodological argument about what it means to study assemblages of bodies, borders, translation, technology, and settler colonial violence. Taking seriously all material, collective, and discursive actors constitutive of sperm smuggling also implicates how we come to produce knowledge about this form of resistance. The material context of Palestine and its politics of location crucially shape how I narrate the practice of sperm smuggling in this book. It remains imperative to acknowledge not only Palestinians' embodied forms of resistance against Israeli settler colonialism but also to recognize the specific kind of knowledge about bodies and the materiality of power that emerges when we study *from* Palestine. As historian Sherene Seikaly puts it, "In the age of catastrophe, Palestine is a paradigm." Palestine can not only teach us "about our present condition of the permanent temporary," but also holds an "abundance of lessons about persisting in the looped and looping time of the present."[82] As shown in this chapter and across this book, Palestinian women are central interlocutors to understanding the present moment of ongoing catastrophe. Their labor of narrating various unruly, convivial, and embodied forms of Palestinian resistance[83] reconfigures what counts as political, where it takes place, and how it is known.

Conclusion

> "At this point, there's nothing that can be added to what everyone saw."
>
> YARA,
> *Palestinian health scholar*

IN DECEMBER 2023, AN ISRAELI shell hit one of the largest fertility clinics in Gaza City, the al-Basma IVF center. Possibly provided by the United States, the shell caused an explosion that blasted the lids off five nitrogen tanks that held frozen egg cells, sperm, and embryos to be used in IVF treatments. The explosion destroyed more than four thousand embryos and one thousand more specimens.[1] Thousands of potential future lives and hopes were ended in a single strike. This number and the notion of "potential future lives" might seem abstract, especially in light of the number of actual Palestinians who have been killed during the Israeli genocide. However, for the intended parents who were patients at the al-Basma IVF center, these numbers represent a dream, an investment, or a long journey to a normal family life. Just like the Palestinian women in this book, women in Gaza might have suffered from infertility for years and have gone through the tiring process of fertility treatment with the hope of getting pregnant. But unlike Palestinians with Israeli citizenship and Palestinians from East Jerusalem, Palestinian women in Gaza cannot easily access a fertility clinic in Israel, the West Bank, or neighboring Arab countries. Fertility treatment in a Gaza clinic is costly, and some families had been saving up for years. This number—four thousand potential future lives—thus alerts us to Palestinian reproductive futurity and living a normal life despite the Israeli siege and dire conditions in the Gaza Strip, way before October 2023. It alerts us to the manifold ways in which Israel's genocide in Gaza is also a question of reproductive justice.

At the beginning of the genocide, 250 women had gotten pregnant via IVF in the al-Basma IVF center.[2] Many of them, like some of the women I have interviewed for this book, were at higher risk of a difficult pregnancy and birth due to their age or other complicating factors. Since Israel started bombing Gaza in October 2023, these women had to manage air strikes, evacuation orders, displacement, and a lack of food, clean water, and medical supplies, all while carrying out a high-risk pregnancy. In October 2023, the UN Population Fund estimated that there were fifty thousand pregnant women in Gaza, around five thousand of them due to deliver in the next month. In October 2024, they estimated that around 46,300 women were pregnant in Gaza.[3] For two years, pregnant women in Gaza have faced the destruction of the healthcare system, overcrowded hospitals or makeshift medical settings, and a complete lack of prenatal and antenatal care.[4] Many women were forced to give birth in tents, or via C-sections without anesthesia, and miscarriage numbers have risen over 300 percent.[5] Many of the children who are born despite these circumstances have lost their parents shortly after, and Palestinian women have lost their newborn babies and toddlers in Israeli air strikes.[6]

Israel's practices of mass killing, destruction of infrastructure, forced displacement, exposure to toxicity and waste, and starvation point not only to genocidal intent but also to the specific ways in which Israel prevents and limits the social and biological reproduction of the Palestinian people in Gaza. Anthropologist Sarah Ihmoud terms this condition "reproductive genocide."[7] The material, psychological, and embodied effects of Israel's annihilatory assault on Gaza will affect and shape future generations of Palestinians. However, Ihmoud also focuses on narratives of resilience and survival. Like the women in this book, women in Gaza refuse their elimination and invisibilization by telling their stories and representing their cause. Listening to women in Gaza is crucial to understanding the gendered effects of Israeli state-sanctioned reproductive injustices and to theorizing reproductive justice as a pillar of Palestinian freedom.

. . .

In October 2023, the Israeli news website Ynet began an article about Palestinian healthcare workers' increasing experiences of racism in Israeli hospitals like this: "The Israeli healthcare system has long been a bastion of coexistence, where Jews and Arabs work seamlessly with each other. Sadly, since the horrific events of October 7 this no longer seems to be the case."[8] Rehearsing the common Israeli depiction of the healthcare system as a harmonious, humanitarian, and apolitical place, it also states that this apparent "bastion of coexistence" shattered after October 7. The article reports on various Palestinian healthcare workers' experiences of racism and discrimination. It cites a Palestinian nurse from central Israel who has been targeted for expressing empathy for civilians in Gaza and who has been called a terrorist sympathizer despite condemning the Hamas attack. It also features Dr. Odi Ibrahim, a doctor in a hospital in Ramat Gan in central Israel. He discusses how interactions with colleagues and patients have changed, impacting him emotionally.

A similar case unfolded in a hospital in the central city of Petah Tikva, where Dr. Abed Samara, director of the cardiac intensive care unit, was forced to leave what had been his workplace for fifteen years. After being suspended for unfounded accusations of supporting terrorism on social media, he saw himself left with no other option than to fight his case in labor court. He finally settled with the hospital and left his job in December after months of facing threats to himself and his family.[9] While there is not yet complete data on such cases of harassment, hearings at disciplinary committees, and suspensions and dismissals from work, according to the public health scholar Nihaya Daoud, there are more than fifty recorded cases, with many Palestinian healthcare workers not reporting on their experiences.[10] A study conducted by health scholar Ghada Majadli discusses how these incidents instilled a collective fear in Palestinian doctors, nurses, and other medical staff. Enforced silence, intimidation, and the criminalization of empathy led to widespread self-censorship, with medical staff fearing threats to their careers and reputations.[11] These cases reveal the fragile material conditions of working for a militarized Israeli institution as a Palestinian citizen and point to the affective dimension of being included in a political system centered around the proliferation of only one ethnonational group—Jewish Israelis.

The Ynet article is right, though, in stating that the Hamas-led October 7 attack was a turning point insofar as it shattered Israel's image as the Middle East's ultimate security state and subsequently harnessed the Jewish Israeli population's pain and fear to manufacture consent for an all-out annihilatory war of expansion and domination.[12] However, the affective economy that Israel's politicians and military generals tapped into was not new at all. It is precisely Israel's "security theology" and demographic anxieties that harness fear to legitimize domination.[13] As the experiences of Palestinian medical staff in Israeli hospitals and fertility clinics recounted in this book reveal, such affective, material, and political relations have long structured the Israeli healthcare sector. Israeli hospitals, and fertility clinics in particular, are sites not only for healing and the reproduction of life but also institutions to consolidate settler colonial power relations and implement demographic goals.[14] Palestinian physicians and other medical staff's inclusion in this project has always been conditional. The symbiotic relationship between limited inclusion and outright violence against health workers can be seen in the context of Gaza today. Palestinian doctors and nurses from Gaza have been deported to Israeli detention facilities, where they experienced humiliation, torture, sexual abuse, and the denial of medical care.[15] In March 2025, fifteen Palestinian medics and rescue workers were shot dead by Israeli soldiers who opened fire on their vehicles, even though they were identifiable as paramedics.[16] Israel's genocide in Gaza exposes such continuities between everyday mechanisms of control within its healthcare system and the broader project of settler colonial control of Palestinian lives and health.

. . .

Right before Israel's 2014 war on Gaza, Ayelet Shaked, a far-right politician and then-Knesset member, wrote on social media that the entire Palestinian people are enemy combatants, including "the mothers of the martyrs who send them to hell with flowers and kisses." The post continued with a call to action: "They should follow their sons, nothing would be more just. They should go, as should the physical homes in which they raised the snakes. Otherwise, more little snakes will be raised there."[17] This dehumanizing statement presents all Palestinians as complicit in terrorism and calls for their destruction, with a particularly gendered and sexual focus on the home and reproduction.

Such racializing and dehumanizing language has also been deployed to justify Israel's genocide in Gaza. From Israeli defense minister Yoav Gallant, who has gone on record to state that Israel is fighting "human animals" and is acting accordingly, to Prime Minister Benjamin Netanyahu's countless racist remarks, including dehumanizing Palestinians, the "children of darkness," as inherently evil (a post that has now been deleted), to President Isaac Herzog, who clarified that the war on Gaza is a war "intended to save Western civilization."[18] Drawing out the historical dimension of the use of zoological language to racialize and dehumanize, media scholar Nabil Echchaibi writes that "those who were dehumanized and exterminated as 'rats' yesterday bomb and annihilate others as 'human animals' today."[19] The transnational and historical racial logic of dehumanization is central for the Israeli state to legitimize its annihilatory project.[20] And yet, this logic is not new. The State of Israel, as social theorist Theo Goldberg has argued, has been thought of and thinks of itself as a racially configured state, representing modernization, progress, and hard work. Palestine—Israel's constitutive other—represents the past, antique lands barely cultivated, continuous failure of governance, a prehistoric place characterized by its racial immaturity.[21] As this book shows, reproduction, health, and notions of overpopulation are central to the production and circulation of such racial grammars.

Racialization under settler colonialism oscillates between the visibility and invisibility of the Indigenous other.[22] In the preceding chapters, I have illustrated this fluctuation across many instances that deal with Palestinian women's reproductive health, rights, and decision-making. The Palestinian population is hypervisible but only on the aggregate level, a mass of people, a "dangerous problem" prone to "overpopulation" that needs to be managed and surveilled.[23] Palestinian women are either represented as (Muslim) women in need of saving from their backward religion and tradition, subjects without agency or political will, or as hyper-fertile mothers of Palestinian "terrorists." Palestinian women's reproductive health, and Palestinian health in general, only exists as "minority" health, neglecting structural racism and settler colonialism as crucial health determinants.[24] The Israeli hospital constitutes one of the foundational sites to produce this in/visibility, in which Palestinian patients' and workers' feelings, politics, and agency are invisibilized and sanctioned. As this book demonstrates, it is in the Israeli hospital, the fertility department, or the maternity ward, across medical encounters and infrastructures of care, where such Orientalist and racist sentiments are articulated and circulated. It is here—in the intimate—that the consolidation of settler colonial power happens alongside, in tandem with, and sometimes contrary to the extreme and spectacular forms of violence and destruction Israel deploys against the Palestinians.

TENDER VIOLENCE: MEDICAL ENCOUNTERS AND THE LIMITS OF INCLUSION

These three scenes and sites of Israeli settler colonialism—reproductive genocide, the Israeli healthcare system, and the racial character of the Israeli state—demonstrate the continuum of Israeli structures of domination and oppression from the time when I conducted research for this book to finalizing the manuscript in 2025. They capture how *Demographic Anxieties* sets the scene for understanding how the escalation that Israel's genocide in Gaza presents is not a rupture or a single event but part of an ongoing structure of settler colonial statecraft and its affective economy.[25] Israel's reaction to the Hamas-led attack on October 7 saw the intensification of core facets of the Israeli state and society, such as its reliance on military force and the militarization of society, the dehumanization of Palestinians, and its demand for absolute loyalty to Israel as a Jewish nation-state.[26] As I have discussed in the preceding chapters, the roots of this ideological orientation of the Israeli state can be traced back to the Zionist project in the late nineteenth century, which relied on ethnic cleansing, territorial expansion, the implementation of Jewish organizing structures (schools, hospitals, labor markets), and Orientalizing and racist tropes of the Indigenous Palestinian population. However, the expressions of hatred, mistrust, and dehumanization of Palestinians that currently shape the status quo in Israeli society are unprecedented.[27]

I set out to write *Demographic Anxieties* to shed light on the less spectacular and disastrous forms of Israeli violence that shape Palestinian women's reproductive decision-making and reproductive outcomes, not knowing that I would soon be faced with some of the worst atrocities committed by the Israeli state against the Palestinians. Necessarily, this led me to question my argument about the need to focus on slow and tender forms of violence.[28] However, as anthropologist Ann Laura Stoler notes, to examine the less openly violent forms of the encounter between colonizer and colonized is not to turn away from structures of dominance and obvious instances of violence but to trace how they are made possible in the first place. While sentiments of outrage, hatred, and disgust are easy to decipher as political feelings, it is "an understanding of the affective heavily weighted to the 'tender'" that may lead to a deeper understanding of the making and persistence of settler colonial or racialized identities and structures of dominance.[29] This book opened a window into the production and circulation of demographic anxieties in the everyday encounter between Jewish Israeli medical staff, Palestinian healthcare providers, and Palestinian fertility patients before (and after) they erupt into disastrous and spectacular forms of violence.

American studies and gender scholar Laura Wexler proposed the notion of "tender violence" to explore how marginalized subjects are framed as objects of (white, or settler) sympathy and care while maintaining power over them; a form of violence that is characterized as being protective or caring while ignoring its structural conditions.[30] In this book, I have traced how such forms of tender violence reproduce state-sanctioned reproductive injustice in Israeli hospitals and fertility clinics. My interviews with Jewish Israeli medical staff show how conditions of care and benevolence also produce dominance and oppression. It is precisely the making of Palestinian fertility patients into objects of sympathy and care that allows Jewish Israeli medical staff to maintain power over them and their representation. Wexler calls this the structural conditions of the "averted gaze."[31] The fact that Jewish Israeli medical staff can uphold the fiction of the hospital as an apolitical place of coexistence relies on them averting their gaze from the structural conditions that made Palestinians into Israeli citizens, residents, and patients in an Israeli hospital in the first place. Only if Palestinians' inclusion into the Israeli state and its institutions is understood as disconnected from the dispossession and violence that precluded their inclusion can the hospital be presented as a site where "politics don't count," as one Jewish Israeli doctor put it. Such "settler moves to innocence"[32] allow Jewish Israeli medical staff to present the hegemonic narrative of Israel as a liberal state in which Palestinians have access to advanced fertility treatment just like Jewish Israelis. In this view, Palestinians' inclusion in the Israeli hospital and fertility economy is measured against a liberal vision of inclusion and access;[33] discriminatory experiences become a simple feature of such systems.

However, this liberal understanding of Israeli institutions masks what they are predicated on: the normalization of domination and Israeli sovereignty, producing racialized difference, classifying populations, and maintaining a Jewish population majority. Jewish Israeli fertility doctors and nurses thus not only avert their gaze. In conversation with me—a white German researcher—Jewish Israeli medical staff felt comfortable sharing their deeply dehumanizing, gendered, and racialized views of their Palestinian patients.[34] For instance, when doctors such as Michael lament that the Israeli state "supports" what he perceives as Bedouin men's extraordinary virility by "letting them have three wives" and allowing them access to state-subsidized fertility treatment. Or when Jewish Israeli social worker Ziva recounts with a certain discomfort that, mere minutes after throwing bottles at Israelis, Palestinians come to an Israeli hospital in East Jerusalem and ask for help. Or that behind closed doors, fertility doctors discuss how they are helping

Palestinians to reproduce "future terrorists." Jewish Israelis' conviction that such statements are not racist exposes the centrality of racialized eugenicist thought to a state built on population control. It is in these instances that Palestinians' status as Israel's civilizational Other appears most powerfully and where Israeli demographic anxieties are produced and circulated.

REPRODUCTIVE JUSTICE AND PALESTINIAN LIBERATION

Palestinian medical staff working in Israeli hospitals have no difficulty deciphering such hegemonic Israeli feelings, oscillating between recognition and disavowal.[35] Remember, for instance, how Meera talks about one of her colleagues in a Jerusalem hospital, who adores her, a well-educated young Palestinian physician who speaks English with an American accent, but "has this tendency to be racist" when she meets patients from different Palestinian class backgrounds. The Palestinian doctors and healthcare providers I have met offer a nuanced and rigorous analysis of how their inclusion in the Israeli healthcare system requires them not to cross certain political lines at the workplace. But Palestinian healthcare professionals, scholars, and activists not only offer their insight into the internal workings of the settler colonial medical sphere, but also actively work to set up counter-infrastructures of health, care, and support for Palestinian women who seek reproductive services. Some of them work in fertility clinics, maternity wards, or delivery rooms and bridge the cultural and linguistic gap between their Palestinian or Bedouin patients and the Israeli system. Others work in or volunteer with Israeli or Palestinian NGOs that offer reproductive and sexual health services that Palestinian women would otherwise not be able to access. Despite their own struggles as workers in the Israeli system, these Palestinian healthcare professionals demonstrate what it means to work toward conditions of reproductive justice for Palestinian women on the ground. In a political system founded on Palestinians' dispossession and elimination, this work challenges the material conditions of reproductive rights and health and points to building a just future in which Palestinians enjoy the right to have children, make a family, and raise their children in a healthy and peaceful environment.

Reproductive politics always oscillate between extending reproductive control to women and controlling women's reproduction.[36] The stories of

Reem, Christeen, Celine, and the other Palestinian women trying to get pregnant in Israeli fertility clinics exemplify this contradiction. While Palestinian women have access to advanced fertility and biotechnology, they live in a state or under the jurisdiction of a state that historically, structurally, and affectively considers their reproduction a "demographic threat." The militarization of everyday life, experiences of subtle and open racism in the fertility clinic, or the psychological stress of being in a vulnerable medical setting and having to rely on their doctor's sympathy in the face of structural oppression are forms of "slow violence" that sustain the uneven geographies of reproduction in a settler colonial state.[37] It is precisely Palestinian women's closeness to Israeli institutions and staff and their crossing of material and symbolic borders on their pregnancy journeys that reveal the contours of the contradiction of their inclusion in the Israeli healthcare system, fertility clinic, and settler state. These less visible forms of reproductive injustice that Palestinian women experience are central to understanding how Israeli demographic politics and sentiments shape Palestinian (reproductive) lives.

However, the Palestinian women I have met contest their "inclusive exclusion" into Israeli institutions as they fight against racism and open up new forms of reproductive futurity. Palestinian women in the West Bank are getting pregnant with sperm their husbands smuggled out of prison, thereby forging new forms of kinship and forms of resistance. East Jerusalemite women like Reem or Rima articulate how living under occupation constitutes a form of state-sanctioned reproductive injustice and call on Palestinian women to reproduce and raise their children to challenge the Israeli political arithmetic and resist Israeli demographic politics. Palestinian women with Israeli citizenship, such as Celine, Leen, Douha, or Haya, inhabit the complex positionality of being included in the Israeli state and deriving some benefit from this inclusion, but also navigating a system in which they never enjoy full (reproductive) rights. Through education and investing in their (future) children's future, navigating and challenging racism, and solidarity with other Palestinians, they work toward securing their right to have a family while also challenging Israeli institutions and their status within them. Palestinian women's pregnancy journeys, their resilience, and their analyses of life under settler colonialism reveal both what it means to be perceived as a "demographic threat"—"a stubborn *problem*"—and what it means to be *a people* fighting for freedom and liberation.[38] Contesting this space of subordination enables the women on the pages of this book to resist, reframe, and challenge the reproductive injustices they experience and to fight for their right to a (reproductive) future.

REPRODUCTIVE IN/JUSTICE: A TRANSNATIONAL PERSPECTIVE

Reproductive politics have always been global in nature. Eugenic thought and practice, reproductive technologies, and reproductive resistance have traveled across various sites—over the Black Atlantic, from the United States to Puerto Rico, Bangladesh, India, the United Kingdom, and South America.[39] These circuits of reproductive oppression inform the central paradigms through which nation-states understand reproduction as a problem and a site for intervention. And while location matters, certain factors, themes, tropes, and notions appear across these sites and within this book. These include, for instance, the fear of overpopulation, demographic "otherness," scientific and sexual experimentation, economic underdevelopment, lack of access to healthcare, and poverty.[40]

In this book, I have posited Palestine as a site to investigate the shared conditions and histories of reproductive oppression and violence, as well as the forms of resistance and solidarity that reproductive injustice engenders. Building on existing links between Black feminist thought and decolonial or anticolonial Palestinian feminism has allowed me to take the reproductive justice framework to Palestine.[41] Palestinian women's experiences of having access, albeit limited, to Israel's fertility economy while knowing that their children, friends, or family members might routinely get killed by the Israeli army echo similar experiences of Black women's access to assisted reproduction in the United States.[42] Palestinian women might have access to advanced reproductive technologies and can implement their reproductive choices, but their children will remain settler colonial citizens in a state built and expanded on their dispossession and expulsion. Their experiences are characterized by the Möbius strip of Israeli biopolitics and necropolitics in an increasingly neoliberal bioeconomy.

The genocide in Gaza has put this simultaneity of making life and death into sharp relief. It also further exposes the transnational dimension of Palestinian women's experience of reproductive injustice and genocide. One of the key characteristics of settler states is their targeting of reproduction, kin-work, and care to achieve their own selectively pronatalist goals. As gender studies scholar Nadine Naber puts it,

> As perfect allies, the US and Israel depend upon violating mothering and caregiving to accelerate the progress of settler-colonialism—positioning Black, Indigenous (including Palestinian) and people of color mothers/caregivers in a dual struggle to protect themselves from the same state apparatus which they are fighting to protect their loved ones.[43]

The experiences, narratives, and strategies that Palestinian women, as well as Palestinian doctors and medical staff, shared with me highlight the paradox Naber draws out. The settler colonial structures of governance that Palestinians must confront to survive are the same structures they rely on to access healthcare, education, or safety for their families. It is in this context that I understand Palestinian women's struggle for reproductive autonomy and freedom, and Palestinian healthcare workers' and activists' provision of alternative health and care infrastructures, as part of a global struggle for reproductive justice. Importantly, this shared political struggle and vocabulary do not disregard different histories and realities of oppression in Israel and the United States, but reveal imperialism, colonialism, and white supremacy as global phenomena that firmly entrench reproductive injustice in settler states' political structure. Rather than collapsing these differences, such resonances invite a deeper understanding of how reproductive governance functions across borders and how Zionism and anti-Blackness converge in biopolitical control over who is allowed to reproduce the nation.

The shared analytical and historical horizon between the United States and Israel allows me to foreground the central argument of *Demographic Anxieties*, namely, that liberal paradigms like citizenship or recognition are an insufficient lens to understand the obstacles Palestinian women face if they want to undergo fertility treatment and give birth in an Israeli hospital. Approaching the question of reproductive justice from the perspective of Palestinian women exposes the futility of (settler) states as political systems that can grant reproductive justice. In other words, the theoretical work that this book does is to trace how access to the resources to implement reproductive decisions is materially linked to the demographic interests of the nation-state form and affectively articulated through ideologies of difference. Thinking with reproductive justice across these contexts thus opens a shared space for dismantling settler colonial, racist, and patriarchal statecraft and shifts our focus to building infrastructure care and alternative futures.

ON OPACITY AND SOLIDARITY

Central to recounting Palestinian women's experiences of reproductive injustice in this book has been an interrogation of the conditions to do so. These include being able to enter Palestine/Israel, cross its borders, access Israeli institutions without fear, as well as being able to listen to Palestinian women. Halfway through conducting research for this project, I started working with Najla Fawwaz, who would become my research assistant, interpreter, and long-term collaborator. On a hot summer day in 2019, two of our interviews in Jerusalem got canceled at the last minute, as is so often the case when doing qualitative research. I had already traveled to Jerusalem, so Najla and I decided to still meet up. In my field notes from June 4, 2019, I wrote about our meeting:

> Yesterday, I met up with Najla in Jerusalem to conduct two interviews, but unfortunately, both got canceled, so we had a conversation about the research instead. Najla told me that she felt a little uncomfortable after our interview with Riham and Israa, two weeks ago in East Jerusalem. She said she felt uncomfortable because we came into their home, they were welcoming and hospitable (as everyone always is when they invite us to their house) and shared so much information with us. They even gave us a gift—beautiful night-blue shawls that had Jerusalem written on them, "so that we wouldn't forget about us," as Riham said. But can we give back to them in return? Of course, Najla said, the research is important, but it doesn't go directly to the participants, it doesn't directly make their lives better. We enter their house, leave with the knowledge, and we'll never really be able to give anything back. What does it mean to do research like that, she asked me.

This question has stayed with me, and I never have forgotten about Riham and Israa, and our long conversation, smoking cigarettes until midnight. If there is one thing that I hope this book can give back, it is to open a framing of Palestinian women that challenges the Israeli and Western gaze, and firmly centers Palestinian liberation as a feminist issue.[44] Indeed, a framing that is no framing at all. This means to take Riham and Israa and the other women's stories and experiences as a starting point to challenge the ways in which the Israeli state traps Palestinian women in a system of binary logic (liberal inclusion/terrorism, "overpopulation"/Muslim women in need of saving, educated and modern/savage and backward) and to write against Palestinians' physical and narrative erasure.[45] This means to illustrate the many ways in which the Israeli state limits their reproductive choices, dreams of the future, and everyday lives. And this means to insist on reproductive justice as not just a framework that asks for equal rights, but as a transformative framework that changes the conditions under which people make reproductive decisions.

This approach is inspired by anthropologist Sarah Ihmoud's invitation to think with Palestinian feminism and take Palestine seriously as a "microcosm of all the internal and external survivors of Europe's racist imperialist nationalist project."[46] In that sense, this book has necessarily been a transnational project, attending not only to how these relations of European colonialism and racial hierarchy inscribe reproductive injustice into the settler colonial state's political and affective structure but also to how these relations shape my encounter with Palestinians and Jewish Israelis. Practically, this meant working and thinking alongside my interlocutors without imposing static and preconceived categories of identity, nationality, or gender onto them. Indeed, as the Caribbean writer and poet Édouard Glissant reminds us, solidarity does not rely on transparency. Instead, he calls for "a right to opacity" to allow the other to be unknowable. This opens a different infrastructure of forging solidarity: "To feel in solidarity with him or to build with him or to like what he does, it is not necessary for me to grasp him."[47] A transnational vision of (reproductive) justice and solidarity relies on a heterogeneous understanding of people's desires, actions, and practices, recognizing the historically interlinked processes that shape the anti-Palestinian world we live in. In having shared the stories, narratives, and experiences of reproductive injustice, medical encounters, and reproductive resistance, I center Palestine as a crucial site to propose reproductive justice as a transnational framework and to recognize how our history and present relate to the injustices we are currently witnessing. If theory can do anything, then this is my "feminist debt."

AFTERWORD

The following is part of a lightly coedited conversation I had with the Palestinian health scholar Yara on Zoom in September 2024. I asked Yara to reflect on political changes in Palestine/Israel since we first met in 2020 and how her experience as a Palestinian working in Israeli institutions has changed since October 7. Yara's insights offer a perspective on many of the topics I have discussed in this book, reframing themes such as Palestinian health workers' and patients' experiences in Israeli hospitals, the militarization of medical space, Zionism and decolonization, and reproductive health through the lens of the genocide in Gaza.

ON PALESTINIANS WORKING IN ISRAELI (HEALTH/HUMAN RIGHTS) ORGANIZATIONS

When we met in 2020, on a professional level, I was a year into my new role as the manager of the department [of an Israeli health organization], and the years that followed were very challenging for me professionally. Specifically, how to manage the work and how to decide on the topics that we should focus on. And how to adapt to the political situation, because it has changed a lot during these years. We had a couple of emergencies in 2020, and then with the Dignity Uprising in May 2021 and the war, and then another war. Three Palestinian women who worked with me in 2020 left two years later, and this is usually the period of time for Palestinians in the organization. It was challenging and emotionally difficult to understand that people are leaving because of the political situation and because it's been a burden for them to continue doing this work for more than two years. This was something that we discussed a lot in the organization. Palestinians come, and they can't handle all of this *because* they are Palestinian. It's not something that we saw with the Israeli teams. So, we had to be more aware of the Palestinian staff and what's happening to them, because it wasn't only because of what's happening to Palestinians and the work that we as Palestinians do on Palestine but there's also all the internal issues in the organization and "Israelis versus Palestinians," which added more to this experience of frustration or powerlessness. When I think about it, to have Palestinians advocating for the rights of other Palestinians, and doing this in the framework of Israeli organizations, I think it's an inherent conflict. This conflict was kind of managed until October 7, when everything exploded. I won't say much about my experience in the organization because I would be emotionally charged when I talk about this, but I would at least say that what I thought could be managed or could be changed, I learned after October 7, this is something that would never be resolved. I was even more extremist, and I concluded that Israeli organizations should stop working on issues related to Palestinians. But I know this wouldn't be realistic because they want to, and second, they still also have tools that no other organizations have because they have access to things.

ON DECOLONIZATION AND ZIONISM

I'm more and more convinced that it's not even decolonization. There is a lot of talk about decolonization in Israeli society—not within all Israeli society, of course, but at least Mizrahi activists and other collectives. They may have spoken about decolonization before October 7. But I'm more convinced that it's not even decolonization, but it's dismantling Zionism. Much of how I understand what happened after October 7, much of what happened within the organization and other NGOs, is an emotional reaction that is very much connected to Zionism and what Zionism made of Jewish Israelis. And I do believe that without Israelis "de-Zionizing," or whatever the term might be, I don't see how they can ever genuinely and fully work for Palestinians. And when I say this, I tell myself, "Wow, that's too much that you're asking. That's a lot. You sound delulu, like someone very delusional." But I swear, that's what I felt and experienced. What I saw after October 7 meant that there is no hope for Israelis to be true allies for Palestinians unless they become anti-Zionist. They can, of course, continue doing their work. B'Tselem is doing its work, and they're doing good work, but it will still always be limited. If there were another October 7, we would see the same thing again and again.

ON AFFECT AND DEHUMANIZATION

The Israelis I worked with, the ones who took a large part in all the changes that we implemented recently in the organization in terms of framing our work on health in the occupied territories from a lens of settler colonialism and apartheid, were also the ones who wrote about Israeli victims and Palestinian victims after October 7 in different languages. Without even noticing. Because even when I said, "That's a double standard," they were shocked and apologized. It's to that extent. This dehumanization is deeply rooted and unrecognized by Israelis, even those who have been covering and documenting violations against Palestinians for many, many years. For me, it was insane. I was also very sad and angry to see this. I say it's emotional for them because what they felt after October 7 was an existential crisis. It was "we and our children and our spouses and our parents, we're threatened," and it doesn't matter if they understood the context. And it doesn't matter if they knew that Israel was founded after the Nakba or that there has been a military occupation for fifty-something years. All of this logical knowledge was there, somewhere in their awareness, but this was only an emotional reaction. And I don't want to say it's only an emotional reaction because an emotional reaction would be for two weeks, three weeks, one month, but five and six and seven months into this, while still having a double standard when you talk about Israeli victims versus Palestinian victims, this is not an emotional reaction. It should be called something else. But it's when those Israelis who have been advocating and doing work and being activists for Palestinian rights would prefer their own existence at the expense of the existence of Palestinians. Not that I agree with that—that the situation we are in means "your existence at the expense of our existence"—but they made this the only option.

ON PALESTINIANS IN ISRAELI HOSPITALS

I will start with my own experience. I participated in one of the demonstrations in Haifa, and I was kicked by one of the police officers. I got hurt and I didn't know what it was, but it was difficult for me to sit because I had not only pain, it changed from pain to not being able to sit comfortably, or lay back on my back. So, I thought that might be something more serious. I was planning to go to an orthopedic, and a friend of mine said, "You need to say that you were in the demonstration, and you were kicked by a police officer, because this should be documented." And I was like, I don't know if I want to do this. I don't know if I want to go to an Israeli doctor now, after October 7, and say that I was in the demonstration against the war in Gaza, and I was kicked by one of the officers. And with all my awareness, and with all my political activism and understanding of the power dynamics, and that this is my right, and I haven't been doing anything illegal—blah, blah, blah, blah—I chose not to go to, not to have this checkup because I didn't want to be in this situation. And then two months later, I had an injury while doing sports, and this time it was very serious. I couldn't not go to the hospital, so I went. I had an appointment at the hospital, here in Haifa. I went, and then I saw all the Israeli flags everywhere, all "together, we will win" everywhere, on the screens, stickers, everywhere. And I constantly see the Israeli flags everywhere, right? But seeing this in the hospital, in the place where you should be taken care of, is something that I couldn't reconcile. It was very, very difficult to be there. I think this is something that I said in the interview (see chapter 2), and I will say it again this time. I felt even more vulnerable being there after October 7, needing a physician to check up on me and be there to listen to me so I could also ask all the questions and address all my concerns. It always felt difficult for me because physicians aren't always that tolerant and nice. They give you three minutes and then tell you to go home. So, to add to this October 7. Hospitals were always militarized, but there was an intensification of the militarization in these spaces. That's my own experience of not wanting to go to the hospital because I don't want to feel even more vulnerable than I already feel as someone with a medical problem. I can only imagine what's happening to other patients who are not going because they have a problem with their shoulder, but because they need an oncology treatment or a more serious medical condition. They're probably more vulnerable, and they need to have a good relationship with their doctors and then be there with all these warfare symbols. It's something that I can't really articulate in words. What does that do to you? How does it feel for patients now in Israeli hospitals after October 7?

ON INCLUSION

But it's even more complicated. On the one hand, there's this ethos that hospitals are places where everyone—physicians and patients—is seen as equal. Everyone will receive the medical treatment they deserve. But then we also had examples where we saw racism within the Israeli healthcare system against Palestinians, and you would find this voice within the healthcare system, usually from people who are high in the hierarchy, saying that this is not acceptable. And then you have this feeling of, "Oh, they see us as human beings. We are not being dehumanized as we thought we would." And for people who are oppressed, this is something that you really want and need, and you can be very appreciative of this kind of statement. And you might also be in a hospital where you get special treatment, by a very knowledgeable surgeon, Israeli, Ashkenazi probably, and you will feel very good. And then it would be even harder for you as a patient to go against that and say something about your experience there because you also had these moments of being appreciated and seen and cared for. But then on the other side, the Israeli healthcare system isn't something that is operating in a vacuum. The Israeli healthcare system and physicians in the Israeli healthcare system see themselves as an integral part of Israel's diplomacy efforts. They are also part of the military. And these are militarized places. And that's where it becomes more complicated. This physician might go to Gaza and might be part of the war efforts. And here you find this separation between the political and the experience as a patient. Perhaps the doctor can separate it, but other people can't. And saying anything against Israel's war in Gaza is something that isn't tolerated. For me, it's very difficult to do this separation. Yet I know that if I am in a very vulnerable situation and I am in a hospital, probably I don't want to think about all these political things, and I only want to be seen as a human.

ON GAZA, HEALTH, AND REPRODUCTIVE JUSTICE

What's happening in Gaza in terms of the destruction of the healthcare system—if some people are still convinced that this is not systematic and intentional, then I think there is a huge problem with their morality. And then for me, these are not people that I'm going to argue with or try to convince. At this point, there's nothing that can be added to what everyone saw. There is plenty of information and documentation, and if you don't think that this is something that should be amplified, then, for me, that equates to not seeing Palestinians as deserving of humanity. But for other people who kind of understand and do see what's happening in Gaza, then health offers an important lens. You have to be delusional not to see that the Palestinian body is targeted and that the infrastructure that is essential for the survival of the population is also targeted. There's a direct connection between this and the question of reproductive justice, fertility, demography, and all the themes that you are addressing. Because if you want to eradicate people, then you don't want them to exist as a large group. You want to diminish them, and you want them to be less than what they are. And this has everything to do with the topic that you are dealing with. So that's why I think health, especially today, is very important to address.

NOTES

INTRODUCTION

1. Dána-Ain Davis, "Obstetric Racism."

2. Berda, "Managing 'Dangerous Populations.'"

3. Robinson, *Citizen Strangers*; Sabbagh-Khoury, "Citizenship as Accumulation by Dispossession"; Tatour, "Citizenship as Domination."

4. Noura Erakat, "Whiteness as Property in Israel," 3.

5. See the Palestinian NGO Adalah's database for discriminatory Israeli laws: https://www.adalah.org/en/law/index.

6. Except for some of my interlocutors in chapter 5, who are also engaged in public forms of speaking about the case of sperm smuggling and specifically wanted to be named, I'm not using people's real names. All pseudonyms have been chosen together with an Arabic or Hebrew native speaker from Palestine/Israel to somewhat reflect the person's class, religious, or ethnic background. This can obviously only capture parts of people's multifaceted identity and family histories. Hopefully, however, this adds a layer to the interpretation I offer in the text. For instance, both Celine and Christeen are Christian Palestinians, but Palestinian religious affiliation was not central to how most of my interview partners described their pregnancy journey, which is why it is not included in my analysis.

7. Shalhoub-Kevorkian, *Security Theology*.

8. Kanaaneh, *Birthing the Nation*.

9. Du Bois, *The Souls of Black Folk*.

10. Benjamin, "Black Afterlives Matter," 56.

11. This is not to argue that these structures of racial hierarchy and violence are the same. I am drawing here on decolonial feminist research that illustrates the interplay between logics of anti-Blackness and Palestinian oppression in settler states through the lens of reproduction: Ihmoud, "Born Palestinian, Born Black"; Abusneineh, "Who Is Entitled to Bear Children."

12. Shalhoub-Kevorkian, *Security Theology*.

13. Du Bois, *The Souls of Black Folk*, 2.

14. Simpson, *Mohawk Interruptus*; Audra Simpson, "The Ruse of Consent"; Sumi Madhok, "A Critical Reflexive Politics of Location."

15. Ihmoud, "Countering Reproductive Genocide in Gaza," 44.

16. Khatib et al., "Counting the Dead in Gaza." Since the genocide began in 2023, whenever I revisit this manuscript, I have to delete and retype the number of reported dead. Every time I retype this number, I am unable to continue writing. It seems impossible to translate the affective charge of such unspeakable violence, of lives and worlds lost, onto the page. This is the most recent UNRWA report I am including: UNRWA, "UNRWA Situation Report #203."

17. UNRWA, "UNRWA Situation Report #172."

18. UNRWA, "UNRWA Situation Report #203."

19. Keane, "Gaza Subjected to Forced Starvation"; UNRWA, "UNRWA Situation Report #191."

20. Hazkani and Sorek, "Yes to Transfer"; Burke and Borger, "Gaza Will Be Entirely Destroyed."

21. Gowayed, "On Parenthood and Genocide"; Lama Z. Khouri, "Gaza's Broken Lullaby"; Ihmoud, "Countering Reproductive Genocide in Gaza"; Jemima Repo, "Genocide and the Destruction of the Means of Social Reproduction in Gaza."

22. Irfan et al., "Will There Be a Future for Newborns in Gaza?," 1726.

23. UN Women, "War on Women's Health in Gaza."

24. Hamamra et al., "Surviving Trauma."

25. Dardona et al., "Health and Environmental Impacts of Gaza Conflict."

26. Perugini and Gordon, "Medical Lawfare"; Turfah, "Israel Has Created a Medical Apocalypse in Gaza"; Amnesty International, *Israel/ OPT: Investigate Killings of Paramedics and Rescue Workers in Gaza*; United Nations Office of the High Commissioner, *Thematic Report: Attacks on Hospitals During the Escalation of Hostilities in Gaza*.

27. United Nations Human Rights Council, "'More Than a Human Can Bear.'"

28. Rudrappa, "No Reproductive Justice," 1.

29. As I finalize the manuscript in October 2025, the Trump-brokered ceasefire is imminent. As many observers have noted, this might mean the end of the genocide, but it doesn't mean the end of Israeli occupation, apartheid, and the killing of Palestinians. While I am slightly hopeful and incredibly relieved to see an end to the genocide in Gaza, there is currently no indication of Israeli reparations, demilitarization, legal accountability, and a reckoning within Israeli society. In addition to these uncertainties, Israel's long history of breaking ceasefires they had agreed to does not elicit trust. For a critical assessment of this point in time, see Buttu, "A 'Magic Pill' Made Israeli Violence Invisible." For an insightful historical account of how Israel treated negotiations with the Palestinians, and Hamas specifically, see Baconi, *Hamas Contained*.

30. Sabbagh-Khoury, "Turning Theory to Practice"; Gunaratnam, "Explosive Legacies"; Burawoy, "Why and How Should Sociologists Speak Out on Palestine?"

31. Rexer, "Social Theory after* Gaza?"

32. Salamanca et al., "It's Been 164 Days."

33. As Sarah Ihmoud writes: "I argue that Israel's genocidal project, hypervisible now in the intensification of warfare against the occupied and besieged Gaza Strip, but also unfolding across occupied Palestinian territory since the 1948 Nakba, should be understood centrally as reproductive genocide, a systematic assault on Palestinian reproductive health, and an attempt to prevent the reproduction of present and future generations of Palestinian lives." Ihmoud, "Countering Reproductive Genocide in Gaza."

34. Goldberg, "Racial Palestinianization"; Kemp, "'Dangerous Populations'"; Shalhoub-Kevorkian, "At the Limits of the Human"; Razack, "Race and Palestine." Future work on the genocide in Gaza and Israeli settler colonialism will inevitably also have to address how internal Israeli politics have shaped decision-making in this war and how Israel has made Israeli and Jewish suffering into a weapon to be harnessed to unleash a genocide against the Palestinians, see Klein, "How Israel Has Made Trauma a Weapon of War"; Flaschenberg and Itzhaky, "How October 7 Transformed Israeli Society."

35. Wolfe, "Settler Colonialism and the Elimination of the Native."

36. Aziza, "The Work of the Witness."

37. Sa'di, *Thorough Surveillance.*

38. See Amnesty International, "Israel's Refusal to Grant Palestinian Refugees Right to Return has Fuelled Seven Decades of Suffering," press release, May 15, 2019, https://www.amnesty.org/en/latest/press-release/2019/05/israels-refusal-to-grant-palestinian-refugees-right-to-return-has-fuelled-seven-decades-of-suffering/.

39. Hammoudeh et al., "Beyond the Physicality of Space."

40. Asi, "Israel Sees Palestinian Family Reunification as a Demographic 'Threat.'"

41. Kanaaneh, *Birthing the Nation*, 35.

42. Quoted in Kanaaneh, *Birthing the Nation*, 35.

43. Quoted in Yuval-Davis, "National Reproduction and 'the Demographic Race' in Israel," 92.

44. Zikri, "Bedouin Birthrate in Israel Is 'Bomb' That Needs Defusing."

45. Tanous, "Israel and the Palestinian 'Womb.'"

46. Article II of the Genocide Convention names the intent of "(a) killing members of the group; (b) causing serious bodily or mental harm to members of the group; (c) deliberately inflicting on the group conditions of life calculated to bring about its physical destruction in whole or in part; and (d) imposing measures intended to prevent births within the group" as dimensions of the intent of destruction. See International Court of Justice, "Summary of the Order of 26 January 2024," https://www.icj-cij.org/node/203454.

47. Rapoport, "The 'Second Nakba' Government Seizes Its Moment."

48. Sokol, "Ben Gvir."

49. Birenbaum-Carmeli, "Thirty-Five Years of Assisted Reproductive Technologies in Israel."

50. Keshet and Popper-Giveon, "Neutrality in Medicine and Health Professionals from Ethnic Minority Groups."

51. Tanous, "Covid-19 Fault Lines"; Shalev, "Helsinki in Zion"; Shalev, "A Doctor's Testimony."

52. Majadli, "Silenced Voices and Militarized Spaces."

53. Wexler, *Tender Violence.*

54. Stoler, *Haunted by Empire.*

55. Stoler, "Tense and Tender Ties."

56. Nixon, *Slow Violence and the Environmentalism of the Poor*, 2.

57. Atshan and Galor, *Moral Triangle*; Rexer, "How Race, Nationality, and Gender Shape Fieldwork and Data Collection."

58. Erakat, "Geographies of Intimacy."

59. Rothberg, *Multidirectional Memory.*

60. Nasser Abourahme usefully differentiates between the first and second wave of settler colonial studies in the context of Palestine, of which the last two decades form the second wave, see Abourahme, *Time Beneath the Concrete*, 20.

61. Salamanca et al., "Past Is Present: Settler Colonialism in Palestine"; Sayegh, "Zionist Colonialism in Palestine (1965)"; Veracini, "Israel-Palestine Through a Settler-Colonial Studies Lens"; Busbridge, "Israel-Palestine and the Settler Colonial 'Turn'"; Bhandar and Ziadah, "Acts and Omissions"; Sabbagh-Khoury, "Citizenship as Accumulation by Dispossession"; Sabbagh-Khoury, "Tracing Settler Colonialism"; Khalidi, *Hundred Years' War on Palestine.*

62. Wolfe, "Settler Colonialism and the Elimination of the Native"; Shalhoub-Kevorkian, "Sacralized Politics," 136.

63. Veracini, *Settler Colonialism*, 176.

64. Bhandar, *Colonial Lives of Property*; Kotef, *The Colonizing Self*; Todorova, *Decolonial Solidarity in Palestine-Israel.*

65. Williams, *Marxism and Literature.*

66. Masalha, *Bible and Zionism.*

67. Bhandar, *Colonial Lives of Property*, 82.

68. Boehm, *Haifa Republic*, 99–102; Masalha, *Palestine Nakba*; Sabbagh-Khoury, "Memory for Forgetfulness."

69. Citing former Israeli prime minister Levi Eshkol, Lana Tatour succinctly notes that "Israel wanted the dowry (the land) but not the bride (the Palestinian people)." See Tatour, "Citizenship as Domination," 8.

70. Khalidi, *Hundred Years' War on Palestine.*

71. Ariella Azoulay, for instance, suggests a chronology from 1492 and the discovery of the "new world" to 1948 and the expulsion of the Palestinians from their homeland. See Azoulay, *Potential History.*

72. Said, "Zionism from the Standpoint of Its Victims," 2.

73. Erakat, "Whiteness as Property in Israel."

74. Hirsch, "'We Are Here to Bring the West, Not Only to Ourselves.'"

75. Lentin, *Traces of Racial Exception*, 85.

76. Goldberg, "Racial Palestinianization," 33.

77. Wolfe, "Settler Colonialism and the Elimination of the Native," 388.

78. Bhandar and Ziadah, "Acts and Omissions."

79. Masalha, *Palestine Nakba*, 38.

80. Sabbagh-Khoury, "Tracing Settler Colonialism," 51.

81. Tanous, "Covid-19 Fault Lines."

82. Bishara, *Crossing a Line*; Salamanca et al., "Past Is Present."

83. Schultz, "Reproducing the Nation"; Deutscher, "Foucault's History of Sexuality"; Stoler, *Race and the Education of Desire.*

84. Bhambra, *Connected Sociologies*; Lowe, *Intimacies of Four Continents.*

85. Saidiya Hartman makes this connection painfully clear, opening her foundational essay "The Belly of the World" like this: "*The slave ship is a womb/abyss.* The plantation is the belly of the world. *Partus sequitur ventrem*—the child follows the belly. The master dreams of future increase. The modern world follows the belly. Gestational language has been key to describing the world-making and world-breaking capacities of racial slavery." See Hartman, "The Belly of the World," 166; Morgan, *Laboring Women*; Weinbaum, *The Afterlife of Reproductive Slavery.*

86. Roberts, *Killing the Black Body.*

87. Angela Davis, *Women, Race, & Class.*

88. Owens, *Medical Bondage*; Spillers, "Mama's Baby, Papa's Maybe"; Snorton, *Black on Both Sides.*

89. Stoler, *Carnal Knowledge and Imperial Power*; Balani, *Deadly and Slick*; McClintock, *Imperial Leather.*

90. Davin, "Imperialism and Motherhood."

91. Schoen, *Choice and Coercion*; Lira, *Laboratory of Deficiency*; Sánchez-Rivera, "From Preventive Eugenics to Slippery Eugenics"; Vergès, *Wombs of Women*; Washington, *Medical Apartheid*; Murphy, *Economization of Life*; Briggs, *Reproducing Empire.*

92. Brown, *Breathing Race into the Machine*, 83–109; Murphy, *Economization of Life;* Schoen, *Choice and Coercion.*

93. Kalpana Wilson, "In the Name of Reproductive Rights"; Murphy, *Economization of Life.*

94. Abdo, "The Palestine Exception, Racialization and Invisibilization"; Morgensen, "Theorising Gender, Sexuality and Settler Colonialism"; Morgensen, "Biopolitics of Settler Colonialism"; Rifkin, *When Did Indians Become Straight?*; Abdo, *Women in Israel.*

95. Theobald, *Reproduction on the Reservation.*

96. Stevenson, *Intimate Integration.*

97. Dána-Ain Davis, *Reproductive Injustice*; Bridges, *Reproducing Race.*

98. Vergès, *Wombs of Women*, 49.

99. Naber writes: "From Turtle Island to Palestine, we can no longer separate contexts like the Oakland cops in riot gear who evicted houseless moms from the abandoned home where they were staying with a SWAT team and tanks in 2022; the United States's forced hysterectomies of migrant and Puerto Rican women; police killings of Black mothers like Korryn Gaines; and the invisible histories of US medical violence against Black mothers, which take us back to the rape and sexual assault of enslaved women as a means of reproducing enslaved people in

service of white capital." See Naber, "Reproductive Justice from Turtle Island to Palestine."

100. Shohat, "Rupture and Return."

101. Yuval-Davis, *Gender & Nation.*

102. Balibar, "Racism and Nationalism."

103. Fezehai, "Disappeared Children of Israel."

104. Ziv, *Racism in Medicine*, 11.

105. Weiss, *Chosen Body*, 61; Ziv, *Racism in Medicine.*

106. Ohayon, "'Ragged Rats.'"

107. Shohat, "Rupture and Return." Fittingly, the operation to airlift Yemenite Jews out of Yemen in 1948 and onward held the Orientalist title "Operation Magic Carpet."

108. Hirsch, "'We Are Here to Bring the West,'"; Madmoni-Gerber, "From Mainstream to Social Media."

109. Abdo, "Palestine Exception"; Moses, *Genocide and Settler Society*; Stevenson, *Intimate Integration*; Theobald, *Reproduction on the Reservation.*

110. In the 1990s, a targeted campaign pushed thousands of Black women in the United States to receive long-acting contraceptives such as Depo-Provera or Norplant. See Roberts, *Killing the Black Body.* For a history of how Depo-Provera unevenly "traveled" globally and contributed to the creation of the Global South as a coherent spatial and epistemological category, see Callaci, "'Injectable Development.'"

111. Ziv, *Racism in Medicine*, 18.

112. Abusneineh, "(Re)producing the Israeli (European) Body," 101.

113. Weiss, *Chosen Body.*

114. Anthropologist Sarah Ihmoud writes that "the racialized politics of birth at the center of the Zionist project's ongoing colonization of Palestine is imbricated with the foundational gendered logics of antiblackness." See Ihmoud, "Born Palestinian, Born Black," 307.

115. Ihmoud, "Born Palestinian, Born Black." See also Ihmoud, "Palestinian Feminism."

116. Vertommen, "From the Pergonal Project to Kadimastem."

117. Birenbaum-Carmeli, "Thirty-Five Years of Assisted Reproductive Technologies in Israel"; Birenbaum-Carmeli and Carmeli, *Kin, Gene, Community.*

118. Nahman, *Extractions*; Zu'bi, "Palestinian Fertility in the Israeli Sphere"; Portugese, *Fertility Policy in Israel.*

119. Nahman, *Extractions*, 17.

120. Vertommen, "Towards a Political Economy of Egg Cell Donations," 176.

121. Mitra et al., *Cross-Cultural Comparisons on Surrogacy and Egg Donation*; Yurdakul et al., "Contested Authorities over Life Politics."

122. Some of the few scholars who specifically consider Palestinian women's experiences in Israeli hospitals include Michal Nahman, Sigrid Vertommen, Larissa Remennick, and Himmat Zu'bi. This also reflects the fact that doing critical research on Israel and in Israeli institutions is limited by the state's visa regime and

border management, as well as who gets access to do critical research on Palestinians in the Israeli healthcare sector. See Shalev, "Helsinki in Zion"; Bishara, "My Impossible Ethnography."

123. Birenbaum-Carmeli, "Cheaper Than a Newcomer"; Birenbaum-Carmeli and Carmeli, *Kin, Gene, Community*; Donath, "Regretting Motherhood"; Gooldin, "'Emotional Rights.'"

124. Steinfeld, "Wars of the Wombs," 2.

125. Zu'bi, "Palestinian Fertility in the Israeli Sphere," 160.

126. Franklin, *Biological Relatives*, 1.

127. Roberts, "Reproductive Justice, Not Just Rights,"

128. Ross and Solinger, *Reproductive Justice*, 19.

129. Ross and Solinger, *Reproductive Justice*, 9.

130. Abusneineh, "(Re)producing the Israeli (European) Body"; AlRifai, "Abortion as a Contested Right"; Elia, *Greater Than the Sum of Our Parts*; Hamayel et al., "Reproductive Health and Rights in East Jerusalem"; Hammoudeh et al., "Beyond the Physicality of Space"; Ihmoud, "Born Palestinian, Born Black"; Shalhoub-Kevorkian, *Militarization and Violence Against Women*; Shalhoub-Kevorkian, "Terrorism and the Birthing Body in Jerusalem"; Shalhoub-Kevorkian, "Politics of Birth"; Shalhoub-Kevorkian, *Incarcerated Childhood and the Politics of Unchilding*; Hasso, *Buried in the Red Dirt*.

131. Naber, "Reproductive Justice from Turtle Island to Palestine"; Rudrappa, "No Reproductive Justice with no Ceasefire in Palestine"; Khouri, "Gaza's Broken Lullaby"; Ihmoud, "Countering Reproductive Genocide in Gaza"; Shoman et al., "Feminist Silences"; Repo, "Genocide and the Destruction of the Means of Social Reproduction"; Qutami et al., "Genocidal Assault on Palestine"; Sigle et al., "What Reproductive Justice Brings to and Requires of the Feminist Economics Project"; Vertommen, "Surrogacy at the Fertility Frontier."

132. Hammami, "Destabilizing Mastery and the Machine"; Shalhoub-Kevorkian, "Palestinian Women and the Politics of Invisibility"; Alasah, "Palestinian Feminist Movement and the Settler Colonial Ordeal."

133. Abu-Lughod, *Do Muslim Women Need Saving?*; Mikdashi, "Can Palestinian Men be Victims?"

134. Abdulhadi, "Israeli Settler Colonialism in Context; Erakat, "Whiteness as Property"; Said, *Orientalism*.

135. Elia, *Greater Than the Sum of Our Parts*; Lugones, "Toward a Decolonial Feminism"; Vergès, *A Decolonial Feminism*; Vergès, *Wombs of Women*; Altay et al., "Crossing Borders"; Korteweg and Yurdakul, "Liberal Feminism and Postcolonial Difference."

136. Ihmoud, "Palestinian Feminism," 294.

137. Sophie Lewis's work on enemy feminisms chronicles the histories of white, liberal, or Zionist feminism and charts the uncomfortable territory of what it means to be part of and to challenge exclusionary feminist projects. See Lewis, *Enemy Feminisms*.

138. Rothberg, *Multidirectional Memory*.

139. Madhok, "A Critical Reflexive Politics of Location," 396.

140. Trouillot, *Silencing the Past.*

141. Abu-Rabia-Queder, "Dissipation of the Green Line in Palestinian Women's Research in Israel," 21.

142. Puar, "'I Would Rather Be a Cyborg Than a Goddess'"; Spivak, "Politics of Translation."

143. Here, I draw on the important lessons developed by Black feminists, that to tell stories and analyze social inequality from the perspective of the most marginalized reveals important insight into how power and oppression work. See hooks, *Feminist Theory from Margin to Center*; Angela Davis, *Women, Race, & Class;* Hayes et al., "Nothing About Us, Without Us."

144. Ali Meghji has termed this form of social theory "reverse tutelage," spelling out what learning from anticolonial and antiracist movements means for sociologists. See Meghji, "From Public Sociology to Sociological Publics."

145. Rexer, "Words Failed Us."

146. Robinson, *Citizen Strangers*; Sabbagh-Khoury, "Citizenship as Accumulation"; Rouhana and Sabbagh-Khoury, "Settler-Colonial Citizenship."

147. Azoulay and Ophir, *One-State Condition.*

148. Abu-Rabia-Queder, "Biopolitics of Declassing Palestinian Professional Women"; Shalhoub-Kevorkian, *Militarization and Violence*; Shehadeh and Alayan, "Between Colonialism and Patriarchy."

149. Abdulhadi, "Israeli Settler Colonialism in Context"; Schulman, *Israel /Palestine and the Queer International*; Shafie, "Pinkwashing."

150. Lubin writes that what connects their experiences "is not merely the recognition of shared histories of racial violence and exclusion; rather, it is the recognition across continents, across national borders, and across religious beliefs of contending with shared conditions of colonial violence, even while local and regional differences in language and power ultimately make the comparisons appear arbitrary." See Lubin, *Geographies of Liberation*, 7.

151. Erakat, "Geographies of Intimacy."

152. Angela Davis, *Freedom Is a Constant Struggle*; Salih et al., "'From Standing Rock to Palestine We Are United.'" For a transnational ethnographic perspective on Palestine, see, for example, Kelly, *Invited to Witness*; Rabie, *Palestine Is Throwing a Party.*

153. Of particular interest for the relational argument I develop in this book is Nassar's analysis of the Palestinian poet and essayist Mahmoud Darwish's column in the communist newspaper *al-Ittihad* titled "Letter to a Negro," in which Darwish expressed a sense of connection and an acknowledgment of shared forms of oppression with Black Americans, particularly addressing the writer James Baldwin. In his second installment of "Letter to a Negro," Darwish highlights similarities in governmental structures in the United States and Israel, and how they affect Palestinian citizens like himself and Black Americans, respectively. He wrote: "But I won't mislead you—I will tell you that we can't go everywhere we want to in our own country! And we can't farm our land because it is, as they say, not for us. And the

[policymaker] in the current government here is much smarter than [the policymaker in] your government when it comes to the job of oppression. For he sees but is unseen. He tries to take the land under our feet without us feeling his smooth hands." This last part of his letter, written in 1966, precisely refers to those forms of "tender" or "slow" violence that I explore in this book. The idea that the Israeli state governs its Palestinian citizens without them feeling the state's "smooth hands" offers an evocative historical analytic of the contemporary conditions that Palestinian women experience in Israeli fertility clinics today and that shape their reproductive choices writ large. See Nassar, "Palestinian Engagement with the Black Freedom Movement," 28.

154. Feldman, *A Shadow Over Palestine*; Kelley, "From the River to the Sea"; Lubin, *Geographies of Liberation*.

155. Erakat and Hill, "Black-Palestinian Transnational Solidarity." For a discussion of specifically Afro-Palestinian forms of solidarity and political imaginaries, see Azeb, "Epilogue"; Hill, "From Ferguson to Palestine."

156. Naber, "'The US and Israel Make the Connections for Us.'"

157. Clarno, "The Thorns That Exist and Resist."

158. Feldman, *A Shadow Over Palestine*, 187–91.

159. Clarno, "The Thorns that Exist and Resist."

160. Erakat, "Geographies of Intimacy"; Erakat and Hill, "Black-Palestinian Transnational Solidarity."

161. Qutami et al., "Genocidal Assault on Palestine"; Naber, "'The US and Israel Make the Connections for Us'"; Naber, "Arab and Black Feminisms."

162. Elia, *Greater Than the Sum of Our Parts*; Ihmoud, "Born Palestinian, Born Black"; Ihmoud, "Palestinian Feminism"; Mikdashi and K. Puar, "Queer Theory and Permanent War"; Qutami, "Why Feminism?"

163. Barakat intends not to "remove Lorde from her own social and political contexts as a black lesbian feminist," but to help her "understand where we as Palestinians are in our own locations; I want to show how she helps us think with her." See Barakat, "Reading Audre Lorde in Palestine."

164. Cited in Feldman, *A Shadow Over Palestine*, 185.

165. Cited in Feldman, *A Shadow Over Palestine*, 186.

166. Feldman, *A Shadow Over Palestine*, 216.

167. Sarah Ihmoud makes that link as well in her essay "Born Palestinian, Born Black," discussing the political imaginaries of solidarity in Jordan's writing in the context of Israel's reproductive politics.

168. Atshan and Galor, *Moral Triangle*.

169. Erakat, "Geographies of Intimacy," 479.

170. Rich, "Notes Towards a Politics of Location."

171. Adrienne Rich herself identified with Zionism in her early work and activism in the 1980s. In her article on the correspondence of June Jordan and Audre Lorde, and Black feminism and anti-Zionism more broadly, writer Marina Magloire chronicles how this led to a four-year gap in Rich's and Jordan's friendship. Today, Rich is known as an anti-Zionist poet, having been active in anti-Zionist Jewish

organizing in the 1980s and endorsing the academic and cultural boycott of Israel in 2009. Magloire suggests that Jordan's uncompromising commitment to Palestinian liberation and her willingness to lose friendships over the question of Israel led to, or influenced, Rich's eventual turn to anti-Zionism. While this important historical dissection of feminist movement formation over Zionism and the question of Palestine is relevant for my theorizing of Black–Palestinian relationality and the intimacies of transnational solidarity more broadly, Rich is also a meaningful figure for myself—a non-Jewish German whose education was modeled around a particularly German strand of liberal Zionism centered around the importance of a *Jewish* state, inflected by German Holocaust guilt. When I started research on this project and traveled to Palestine/Israel for the first time in 2015, I was already critical of the occupation and driven by wanting to understand how Palestinians experience Israel's fertility economy, but I was far from spelling these questions out through the lens of settler colonialism or anti-Zionism. Indeed, my own political trajectory mirrors, in a way, Rich's own shift from Zionism to anti-Zionism. It was through my research and my engagement with Palestinian and anti-Zionist Jewish and/or Israeli thinkers, activists, comrades, and friends, that I was challenged to reflect on my own politics when it came to Israel. In that sense, taking Rich seriously, and starting with one's own body and its relation in the world, is central to contextualizing the "we" of feminist theory and to understanding the different ways we arrive at certain "we's," or coalitional politics. See Magloire, "Moving Towards Life." See also Lober, "Adrienne Rich's 'Politics of Location.'"

172. Stoler, *Haunted by Empire*; Zengin, "Violent Intimacies."

173. Lowe, *Intimacies of Four Continents*, 18.

174. Wekker, *White Innocence*.

175. Ziv, "A Cognitive Dissonant Health System; Ziv, *Racism in Medicine*; Wispelwey et al., "Because Its Power Remains Naturalized"; Tanous et al., "Structural Racism and the Health of Palestinian Citizens of Israel"; Yara Asi et al., "Reassembling the Pieces."

176. Bishara, "My Impossible Ethnography."

177. Rich, "Notes Towards a Politics of Location," 224.

178. Nixon, *Slow Violence*; Wexler, *Tender Violence*; Stoler, "Intimidations of Empire."

179. Nixon, *Slow Violence*, 2.

180. Plonski, *Palestinian Citizens of Israel*, 9.

181. McKittrick, *Dear Science and Other Stories*, 45.

182. Peteet, "Language Matters," 26.

183. Helga Tawil-Souri, "Uneven Borders, Coloured (Im)mobilities"; Erakat, *Justice for Some*. I also thank one of my book's reviewers for asking me to clarify this.

184. On the delusion of the two-state solution absent a reckoning with the Nakba and the 2023 genocide, see Eghbariah, "The Two-State Solution Is a Delusion."

185. Peteet, "Words as Interventions."

186. Abourahme, *Time Beneath the Concrete*, 17.

187. El-Kurd, "Jewish settlers Stole My House."

188. For some critical engagements on the relationship between Zionism and Judaism, and anti-Zionists and Zionism, see Angel, "On Loving Jews"; Danforth-Appell, "Against Zionist Realism."

CHAPTER ONE

1. Palestinians with Israeli citizenship are the descendants of the 156,000 Palestinians who remained in Israel after their expulsion, dispossession, or internal transfer in 1948. Characterized by racial hierarchy and demographic classifications, Palestine scholars term their civic rights in Israel "settler colonial citizenship," a status that makes them a minority in their own homeland. See Sabbagh-Khoury, "Citizenship as Accumulation"; Rouhana and Sabbagh-Khoury, "Settler-Colonial Citizenship"; Tanous, "'You, as of Now, Are Someone Else!'"; Robinson, *Citizen Strangers*.

2. The word "Palestinian" doesn't appear in Israeli statistical records. Usually, Palestinians are counted with reference to their religious affiliation. Only in 1995 did the word "Arab" first appear in Israeli demographic documents. Before that, Palestinians were grouped under "non-Jews." Cohen and Gordon, "Israel's Biospatial Politics," 203. Famously, then-prime-minister of Israel Golda Meir said in a 1969 interview that "there is no Palestinian people." Razack, "Race and Palestine."

3. Erakat, *Justice for Some*, 62.

4. Bishara, *Crossing a Line*; Tawil-Souri, "Uneven Borders."

5. Elsewhere, I have written about Israeli medical staff's confusion about the treatment of '48 Palestinians in West Bank clinics, see Rexer, "Borderlands of Reproduction". For further reporting on '48 Palestinians' choice to use West Bank fertility clinics, see Amun, "Israel Offers Free IVF Treatment."

6. On the long history of Palestinians' distrust of Israeli medical staff and institutions, see Kanaaneh, *Birthing the Nation*, 74.

7. Giacaman et al., "Health Sector Reform in the Occupied Palestinian Territories (OPT)"; Majadli, "Healthcare in the Occupied Territory During Covid-19"; Rosner and Majadli, *Responsibility Shirked*.

8. Birenbaum-Carmeli, "Thirty-Five Years of Assisted Reproductive Technologies"; Vertommen, "From the Pergonal Project to Kadimastem."

9. Zu'bi, "Palestinian Fertility in the Israeli Sphere."

10. Foucault, *Society Must Be Defended*.

11. See also Zu'bi, "Palestinian Fertility in the Israeli Sphere."

12. Mbembe, "Necropolitics."

13. For a discussion on the role of reproduction in Foucault's biopolitics, see Deutscher, "Foucault's History of Sexuality." On women's interpellation as mothers of the nation or the national collective, see Yuval-Davis, *Gender & Nation*.

14. Kanaaneh, *Birthing the Nation*, 24.

15. Cohen and Gordon, "Israel's Biospatial Politics"; Ihmoud, "Policing the Intimate"; Ihmoud, "Born Palestinian, Born Black"; Sabbagh-Khoury, "Citizenship

as Accumulation"; Shalhoub-Kevorkian, *Security Theology*; Vertommen, "From the Pergonal Project to Kadimastem"; Wind, *Towers of Ivory and Steel*; Yiftachel, "Deepening Apartheid."

16. Briggs, *How All Politics Became Reproductive Politics*.

17. Murphy, *Economization of Life*, 64.

18. Murphy, *Economization of Life*; Dow and Lamoreaux, "Situated Kinmaking."

19. Mikdashi, *Sextarianism*.

20. The politicization of the population and investments in population politics are by no means unique to the Israeli state. Since the late eighteenth century, modern states and nation-building projects have produced political knowledge about their populations, such as statistics, demography, or markers of global health. Biopolitics depends on knowledge about "the ratio of births to deaths, the rate of reproduction, the fertility of a population." See Foucault, *Society Must Be Defended*; Lemke, *Biopolitics*.

21. On the relationship between Zionism and demography, Rhoda Ann Kanaaneh writes: "The very definition of the Zionist state, as of most other nationalisms, is based on demography and numbers, but the settler colonial history of the state of Israel heightens this obsession, as well as its consequences." See Kanaaneh, *Birthing the Nation*, 28; Zureik, "Colonialism, Surveillance, and Population Control"; Zureik, "Demography and Transfer."

22. Yuval-Davis, "National Reproduction," 92.

23. Abulof, "Deep Securitization"; Rouhana and Sultany, "Redrawing the Boundaries of Citizenship."

24. Gooldin, "'Emotional Rights.'"

25. Steinfeld, "Wars of the Wombs"; Birenbaum-Carmeli, "Thirty-Five Years of Assisted Reproductive Technologies"; Birenbaum-Carmeli and Carmeli, *Kin, Gene, Community*; Birenbaum-Carmeli, "Cheaper Than a Newcomer."

26. Hashiloni-Dolev, "Effect of Jewish-Israeli Family Ideology"; Sperling, "Commanding the the 'Be Fruitful and Multiply' Directive."

27. Gooldin, "'Emotional Rights.'"

28. Murphy, *Economization of Life*, 7.

29. Murphy, *Economization of Life*, 12.

30. In Israel, the population-reproduction nexus revolves around the settler /native dichotomy, but it also fans out across other registers. Depending on the context, Black Jews, Mizrahi Jews, migrant laborers, and other racialized non-Jewish minorities are also grouped, counted, and interpellated as those always already too many, reproducing too fast. See, for example, Ihmoud, "Born Palestinian, Born Black"; Abusneineh, "(Re)producing the Israeli (European) Body."

31. Wolfe, "Settler Colonialism and the Elimination of the Native."

32. Sabbagh-Khoury, "Settler Colonialism and the Archives of Apprehension."

33. Sa'di, *Thorough Surveillance*, 5–8.

34. Sa'di, *Thorough Surveillance*, 18.

35. Sa'di, *Thorough Surveillance*; Erakat, *Justice for Some*; Robinson, *Citizen Strangers*.

36. Kemp, "'Dangerous Populations.'"

37. Erakat, "Whiteness as Property"; Tatour, "Citizenship as Domination."

38. Kemp, "'Dangerous Populations,'" 80.

39. Berda, "Managing 'Dangerous Populations.'"

40. Cohen and Gordon, "Israel's Biospatial Politics"; Kanaaneh, *Birthing the Nation.*

41. Sa'di, *Thorough Surveillance.*

42. Shalhoub-Kevorkian, *Security Theology*; Zureik, "Colonialism, Surveillance, and Population Control."

43. Murphy, *Economization of Life.*

44. Murphy, *Economization of Life*, 135.

45. The framing of the Bedouin Palestinian population in the Naqab as Indigenous has been critically contextualized by Lana Tatour. She argues that while Bedouins are indeed indigenous to the Naqab, and to Palestine more broadly, the classification of their indigeneity relies heavily on a culturalist understanding. Their recognition has been premised on their cultural distinctiveness, resulting in understanding Bedouin Palestinians as separate from Palestinians across historic Palestine (and relatedly, understanding non-Bedouin Palestinians as non-indigenous), tying their status of indigeneity to a "premodern" or sufficiently traditional way of life, and, perhaps most importantly, sidelining settler colonialism as the root cause of their political struggle for land. See Tatour, "The Culturalisation of Indigeneity."

46. Tanous and Eghbariah, "Organized Violence and Organized Abandonment"; Tanous et al., "Structural Racism and the Health of Palestinian Citizens of Israel"; Nasasra, "The Ongoing Judaisation of the Naqab."

47. From an anticolonial feminist perspective, this state-sponsored preservation of religious law in the Israeli legal system reinforces the multiple forms of oppression Bedouin women experience, as women in a patriarchal state, as Palestinian women in a settler state, and as Bedouin women in a religious and traditional society. Aburabia, "Law on the Books."

48. Aburabia, "Redefining Polygamy."

49. Aburabia, "Law on the Books," 638.

50. Aburabia, "Law on the Books," 653.

51. Asi, "Israel Sees Palestinian Family Reunification."

52. Aburabia, "Law on the Books," 639; Abu-Lughod, *Do Muslim Women Need Saving?*

53. This collapse of territory, population, and racialization has been described as a feature of the making of the Palestinians in Israel into a "dangerous population," see Kemp, "'Dangerous Populations.'"

54. Kedar et al., *Emptied Lands.*

55. Sufian, *Healing the Land and the Nation*; Hirsch, "'We Are Here to Bring the West, Not Only to Ourselves.'"

56. Michael's excitement and disbelief reminded me of Paul Ehrlich's description of the Indian population in his 1968 book *The Population Bomb.* For a critical feminist discussion of Ehrlich, see Schoen, *Choice and Coercion.*

57. Said, *Orientalism.*

58. Murphy, *Economization of Life*, 6–7.

59. The "initial" failure of Israeli population politics after the state of Israel was founded in 1948 can be traced in the archives. In 1952, Israeli political leaders and trade unionists were debating what to do with the 156,000 of 900,000 Palestinians who remained in Israel after the 1948 war. To discuss these questions, then-prime-minister David Ben-Gurion summoned a group of so-called Arabists, politicians, soldiers, and others who had gained knowledge about the Arab population as part of their work in different institutions. One of them was Reuven Barkatt, an "Arabist" and trade unionist. In a meeting in the summer of 1952, he admitted to the failure of Zionist population politics, a failure that characterizes the fate of the state until this day: "I am afraid that today the Arabs number [200,000]. This means that all the measures we undertook to decrease their number in the country were unsuccessful. The majority of the Arabs do not think of leaving the country. And the Arabs surrounding us [i.e., the refugees] are still attracted to it. . . . Today we don't have much choice. . . . The Arabs attained rights and various political and economic achievements. We cannot turn the clock back. We cannot go back to square one and plan our policy towards the Arabs. We cannot withdraw what we have already granted." See Sa'di, *Thorough Surveillance*, 25.

60. Mbembe, "Necropolitics," 14. On the day I wrote about this for the first time, in summer 2021, as part of my PhD, four Palestinian men were killed in Jenin in the West Bank. Living in Palestine/Israel and consuming local news was startling; almost every day and every week, more Palestinians were killed, usually framed in the well-known Israeli framework of securitization that normalizes the ongoing killing of Palestinians. Israel's genocide in Gaza has reshaped Israel's necropolitical repertoire to a hitherto unknown level. As of May 2025, the Israeli army has killed at least 53,000 people in Gaza, leaving the population on the brink of starvation.

61. Luna, "Black Celebrities, Reproductive Justice and Queering Family," 89.

62. Roberts, "Reproductive Justice, Not Just Rights."

63. On the concept of settler colonial citizenship, see Sabbagh-Khoury, "Citizenship as Accumulation"; Rouhana and Sabbagh-Khoury, "Settler-Colonial Citizenship."

64. Abu-Rabia-Queder, "Biopolitics of Declassing Palestinian Professional Women"; Rouhana and Sultany, "Making of an Underclass."

65. Kanaaneh, *Birthing the Nation*, 60–64.

66. Kanaaneh, *Birthing the Nation*, 107.

67. Importantly, both modes of Palestinian subjectification and categorization of reproductive behavior are a response to Israeli demographic politics and political arithmetic. Kanaaneh, *Birthing the Nation*, 107.

68. Ironically, Israeli government officials similarly debated the question of "quality" versus "quantity" in Palestinian family size and translated those debates into educational policy. During the time of the military rule over Palestinian citizens of Israel, Israeli politicians and advisors discussed whether access to education

would strengthen Palestinian resistance and should thus be discouraged, or if it would encourage "cultural assimilation" into the Jewish state, including lower Palestinian fertility rates, a common argument of demographers and even feminists at the time. In a 1968 meeting, Shmouel Tolidano, then advisor to the prime minister on Arab affairs, posed the question of what would be preferable, "a large Palestinian population with a low [national] consciousness" or a "small population, more educated and more nationalistic"? Cited in Wind, *Towers of Ivory and Steel*, 149. This question cut to the core of Israeli demographic anxieties, as it pronounced the well-known Western logic of access to education as a form of birth control. Ultimately, Israeli policy gave priority to the "demographic issue." Sa'di, *Thorough Surveillance*, 44.

69. Jefferis, "Institutionalizing Statelessness"; Jefferis, "The 'Center of Life' Policy."

70. Shehadeh and Alayan, "Between Colonialism and Patriarchy."

71. Naber, "Reproductive Justice," 545.

72. Tanous, "Israel and the Palestinian 'Womb.'"

73. Ihmoud, "Born Palestinian, Born Black"; Steinfeld, "Wars of the Wombs."

74. It is important to note here that patients and physicians construct medical narratives differently. These different modes of communication and experience are often at odds with one another, and the meaning of medical technologies or diagnoses can be interpreted differently. As Johanna Schoen cautions, we should thus be careful not to privilege medical or scientific accounts of medical encounters over personal ones, but we must also be mindful of understanding health and disease as social constructs. Schoen, *Choice and Coercion*, 16–18.

75. Dána-Ain Davis, "Obstetric Racism."

76. Popper-Giveon, "Preferring Patient–Physician Concordance"; Ziv, "A Cognitive Dissonant Health System:"; Ziv, *Racism in Medicine*.

77. Theobald, *Reproduction on the Reservation*, 163. Johanna Schoen similarly discusses how Black nationalists have used the notion of genocide to refer to sterilization abuses and family planning targeting Black women in the United States throughout the twentieth century. See Schoen, *Choice and Coercion*, 46.

78. Such fears, rumors, and stories are not new. Rhoda Kanaaneh's 2002 study of Israel's provision of family planning for Palestinians shows how similar fears circulated about sterilization, bolstered by a general suspicion that Jewish Israeli doctors might not have Palestinian women's best interests in mind. Frantz Fanon also writes about the ways in which fear and suspicion shape the encounter between colonized and colonizer in medical settings, see chapter 3 and Fanon, *A Dying Colonialism*; Kanaaneh, *Birthing the Nation*.

79. Rexer, "Borderlands of Reproduction," 14.

80. Abu-Rabia-Queder, "Biopolitics of Declassing Palestinian Professional Women"; Abu-Rabia-Queder, "Dissipation of the Green Line."

81. Wind, *Towers of Ivory and Steel*.

82. Abulof, "Deep Securitization"; Amit, "Israel, Zionism and Emigration Anxiety."

83. On the notion of haunting in colonial or racist contexts, see Gordon, *Ghostly Matters*.

84. Shalhoub-Kevorkian, *Security Theology*, 145.

85. Shalhoub-Kevorkian et al., "Secret Penetrabilities."

86. Majadli, "Silenced Voices." See also Masarwa, "Israeli Doctor Compared Killing Palestinians."

87. Murphy, *Economization of Life*, 60.

88. Shalhoub-Kevorkian, *Security Theology*.

89. Murphy, *Economization of Life*, 64.

90. Shalhoub-Kevorkian, *Security Theology*, 56.

CHAPTER TWO

1. First quotation from Najwa is from a 2020 interview. The second is from Qato, "Introduction," 15.

2. Cohen and Gordon, "Israel's Biospatial Politics"; Plonski, *Palestinian Citizens of Israel*; Yiftachel and Yacobi, "Urban Ethnocracy."

3. Naser-Najjab, *COVID-19 in Palestine*.

4. Shalhoub-Kevorkian, *Security Theology*.

5. Puar, *Right to Maim*; Puar, "Spatial Debilities."

6. I am drawing from anthropologist Brian Larkin here, who defines infrastructures as "built networks that facilitate the flow of goods, people, or ideas and allow for their exchange over space. As physical forms they shape the nature of a network, the speed and direction of its movement, its temporalities, and its vulnerability to breakdown. They comprise the architecture for circulation, literally providing the undergirding of modern societies, and they generate the ambient environment of everyday life." Larkin, "Politics and Poetics of Infrastructure," 328. See also Attewell et al., "Inscribing New Infrastructural Relations into the World."

7. Anand et al., "Introduction."

8. Gunaratnam, "Infrastructures of Racial Violence, Health and Debility"; Plonski, "Mobile and Carceral Logics of Haifa Port"; Salamanca, "Assembling the Fabric of Life"; Stamatopoulou-Robbins, *Waste Siege*.

9. LaDuke and Cowen, "Beyond Wiindigo Infrastructure," 245.

10. Attewell et al., "Inscribing New Infrastructural Relations into the World," 18.

11. Easterling, *Extrastatecraft*, 14.

12. LaDuke and Cowen, "Beyond Wiindigo Infrastructure," 246.

13. Murphy, *Seizing the Means of Reproduction*.

14. Qato, "Introduction."

15. Alasah, "Palestinian Feminist Movement and the Settler Colonial Ordea"; Shehadeh and Alayan, "Between Colonialism and Patriarchy."

16. Sabbagh-Khoury, "Citizenship as Accumulation"; Rouhana and Sabbagh-Khoury, "Settler-Colonial Citizenship"; Tatour, "Citizenship as Domination."

17. Abu-Rabia-Queder, "Dissipation of the Green Line in Palestinian Women's Research in Israel," 32.

18. Tanous, "'You, as of Now, Are Someone Else!,'" 69.

19. Tanous, "'You, as of Now, Are Someone Else!,'" 69.

20. The Israeli literature on Palestinian women in the Israeli fertility economy, reproduction and childbirth, and biomedicine more broadly adapts a similar perspective. In Susan Martha Kahn's foundational study, *Reproducing Jews*, she states that her ethnography does not focus on "non-Jewish Israeli minorities or on Palestinians living in the Occupied Territories," even though she does encounter Palestinians in the clinics she studies. Kahn makes clear that when she is referring to Israelis, she only refers to Jewish Israelis. Similarly, in Tsipy Ivry's book *Embodying Culture*, Palestinians are not considered as research participants in Israeli hospitals (due to their different culture and religion, according to the author). They are, however, mentioned with regard to the "demographic race." The edited volume *Kin, Gene, Community: Reproductive Technologies Among Jewish Israelis* references its main research participants in its title. However, a notable exception is Larissa Remennick's contribution, which also features the voices of some Palestinian IVF patients. In the introduction to the edited volume on *Bioethics and Biopolitics in Israel*, Palestinians also only appear as Palestinians in the West Bank or the diaspora, with two contributions (Himmat Zu'bi and Hadas Ziv) also offering a perspective on Palestinian experiences in Israel. Birenbaum-Carmeli and Carmeli, *Kin, Gene, Gommunity*; Ivry, *Embodying Culture*; Boas et al., *Bioethics and Biopolitics in Israel.*

21. Tanous et al., "Structural Racism and the Health of Palestinian Citizens of Israel."

22. Asi et al., "Reassembling the Pieces"; Daoud et al., "Internal Displacement and Health Among the Palestinian Minority in Israel"; Wispelwey et al., "Because Its Power Remains Naturalized"; Saabneh, "Health Inequalities Between Palestinians and Jews in Israel"; Tayara, "Health and Humanitarianism."

23. Hirsch, "'We Are Here to Bring the West.'"

24. Yacobi and Milner, "Beyond 'Causes of Causes.'"

25. Blatman and Sabbagh-Khoury, "Presence of the Absence"; Pasquetti, "Experiences of Urban Militarism"; Yacobi, *Jewish–Arab City*; Yiftachel and Yacobi, "Urban Ethnocracy"; Yacobi and Pullan, "Geopolitics of Neighbourhood."

26. Kedar et al., *Emptied Lands*; Nasasra, "Ongoing Judaisation of the Naqab"; Cohen and Gordon, "Israel's Biospatial Politics."

27. Abujidi, *Urbicide in Palestine.*

28. Bridges, *Reproducing Race*; Wailoo, *How Cancer Crossed the Color*; Owens, *Medical Bondage.*

29. Abdo, *Women in Israel.*

30. Cohen and Gordon, "Israel's Biospatial Politics."

31. Kanaaneh, *Birthing the Nation.*

32. Zu'bi, "Palestinian Fertility in the Israeli Sphere," 172.

33. Ross et al., *Radical Reproductive Justice*, 19.

34. Tatour, "Citizenship as Domination."

35. Wind, *Towers of Ivory and Steel*; Abu-saad, "Separate and Unequal."

36. Robinson, *Citizen Strangers*.

37. Nadim R. Rouhana and Areej Sabbagh-Khoury show how Palestinian citizens of Israel understand their citizenship in the settler state as a direct consequence of the Nakba and are thus calling for full citizenship and historical justice. This "return of history" in the Palestinian political discourse and consciousness is guided by insisting that full citizenship rights cannot be granted in an ethnonationalist settler colonial state like today's Israel. Rouhana and Sabbagh-Khoury, "Settler-Colonial Citizenship."

38. Nabulsi, "Reclaiming Palestinian Indigenous Sovereignty."

39. Simpson, "Ruse of Consent and the Anatomy of 'Refusal,'" 29.

40. Simpson, "Ruse of Consent and the Anatomy of 'Refusal,'" 29.

41. Nasasra, "Ongoing Judaisation of the Naqab."

42. Contreras et al., "Racial and Ethnic Disparities in Access to Safe Water and Sanitation"; Yacobi and Milner, "Beyond 'Causes of Causes'"; Tanous, "'You, as of Now, Are Someone Else!'"; Tanous and Eghbariah, "Organized Violence and Organized Abandonment"; Shibli et al., "Perceptions About the Accessibility of Healthcare Services."

43. Marey-Sarwan et al., "Blurring the Borders"; Alfayumi-Zeadna et al., "Direct and Indirect Predictors of Postpartum Depression"; Berger-Polsky et al., "Polygamy and Birth Outcomes"; Abu-Kaf et al., "Emotional Distress Among the Bedouin Arab"; Shibli et al., Aharonson-Daniel, and Feder-Bubis, "Perceptions About the Accessibility of Healthcare Services."

44. Tanous and Hagopian, "Locations of Palestine and the US in the Global Map of Homelessness"; Tanous, "Israel and the Palestinian 'Womb.'"

45. Ruth Wilson Gilmore proposed the notion of organized abandonment to describe the intentional disinvestment in communities by the state and capital. Osama Tanous and Rabea Eghbariah draw from Gilmore to examine the forms of "organized abandonment" that Bedouins experience. This is one of the many examples in which the context of Black Americans' systematic oppression is made productive for an analysis of Palestine. This transnational perspective on global structures of power is foundational to my exploration of Palestinians' experiences of reproductive injustice. Gilmore, *Abolition Geography*; Gilmore, *Golden Gulag*; Tanous and Eghbariah, "Organized Violence and Organized Abandonment."

46. Shibli et al., "Inequalities in Trust Levels."

47. LaDuke and Cowen, "Beyond Wiindigo Infrastructure," 246.

48. Khamaisi, "Jerusalem Demography"; Ihmoud, "Mohammed Abu-Khdeir and the Politics of Racial Terror"; Tanous et al., "Beyond Statelessness."

49. Shalhoub-Kevorkian, "Politics of Birth and the Intimacies of Violence," 1189.

50. Ihmoud, "Murabat"; Shalhoub-Kevorkian and Ihmoud, "Exiled at Home."

51. Shalhoub-Kevorkian, "Politics of Birth and the Intimacies of Violence."

52. Bouquet et al., "Housing Precariousness and Health."

53. For an extensive review of the legal and health implications of Israel's annexation of East Jerusalem, see Tanous et al., "Beyond Statelessness."

54. Abbas and Mendel, "Hebrew Studies Amongst Palestinians in East Jerusalem."

55. Tanous et al., "Beyond Statelessness," 94.

56. Birenbaum-Carmeli and Kochman-Haimov, "Fertility Treatments Under Semi/Occupation."

57. Birenbaum-Carmeli and Kochman-Haimov, "Fertility Treatments Under Semi/Occupation," 39.

58. Tanous, Wispelwey, and Muhareb describe the condition of Jerusalem as "the most active Zionist settler colonial frontier," where the investment into settler futurity and construction and Indigenous elimination happen on a daily basis and are openly inscribed into policy and law, which translates into the ongoing forcible expulsion of Palestinian neighborhoods from the city. Tanous et al., "Beyond Statelessness," 90.

59. AlRifai, "Abortion as a Contested Right"; Shahawy, "Unique Landscape of Abortion Law and Access"; Shahawy and Diamond, "Perspectives on Induced Abortion Among Palestinian Women."

60. I met Hanan in the summer of 2019. In March 2022, Israel passed a law that denies family reunification in cases where one partner lives in the occupied territories and the other one is an Israeli citizen or resident. Family unifications are also barred for couples where one of the spouses lives in an "enemy country," such as Lebanon, Syria, or Iran. Asi, "Israel Sees Palestinian Family Reunification as a Demographic 'Threat.'"

61. Shehadeh and Alayan, "Between Colonialism and Patriarchy"; Abdo, *Women in Israel.*

62. Berlant, "The Commons."

63. Billy Holzberg's notion of affective bordering is useful here to understand how affect animates and segregates space. Holzberg, *Affective Bordering.*

64. Bonilla-Silva, "Feeling Race." See also Bridges, *Reproducing Race*; Davis, *Reproductive Injustice*; Underman, *Feeling Medicine.*

65. LaDuke and Cowen, "Beyond Wiindigo Infrastructure."

66. Stoler engages with this notion via the German philosopher Johan Gottlieb Fichte, who coined the term "interior frontiers" in 1808, which has then been reanimated in various works of the French philosopher Étienne Balibar. See Stoler, "Interior Frontiers."

67. Abu-Hamad and Daoud, "Maternal Respectful Care and Post-Traumatic Stress Disorder."

68. Shwartz et al., "Postpartum Depression Among Arab and Jewish Women in Israel."

69. Slaughter-Acey et al., "Skin Tone Matters"; Davis, "Obstetric Racism."

70. Rooney and ADomar, "Relationship Between Stress and Infertility."

71. For a discussion on Palestinians' refusal to perform subjection and suffering for the Western gaze, see Kelly, "Subjection and Performance." Similarly, Yara's

reflection here also speaks to the question of what sort of emotions can be made visible in the recounting of violent events, and how the affective structuring of memory and experience might render them unavailable for ethnographic interpretation. See Stoler and Strassler, "Castings for the Colonial." I have also discussed similar methodological questions elsewhere, see Rexer, "Words Failed Us."

72. Simpson, *Mohawk Interruptus*, 29.

73. Hartman, *Scenes of Subjection*; Smith, *Decolonizing Methodologies*.

74. On the notion of reticence in ethnographic work that seeks to understand the everyday intimacies of colonial relations, see Stoler and Strassler, "Castings for the Colonial," 10.

75. Nixon, *Slow Violence and the Environmentalism of the Poor*; Wexler, *Tender Violence*.

76. Ziv, "Racism in Medicine."

77. Regev, "Israeli MK Calls for Hospital Segregation."

78. Nadera Shalhoub-Kevorkian coins the term "unchilding" to refer to the practice and ideology whereby Palestinian children's childhood is included in the strategic calculus of Israeli settler colonialism and militarization. Unchilding works as a racial ideology that constructs Palestinian children as dangerous entities. This ideology, in turn, allows Israel to expose children to violence and humiliation and serves as a legitimization to disregard international humanitarian law. Shalhoub-Kevorkian, *Incarcerated Childhood and the Politics of Unchilding*, 16.

79. Hovel, "Israeli Hospitals Admit to Segregating Jewish and Arab Women at Maternity Wards."

80. Goldberg, *Threat of Race*; Abu El-Haj, "Racial Palestinianization and the Janus-Faced Nature of the Israeli State"; Shalhoub-Kevorkian, "At the Limits of the Human."

81. Hovel and Efrati, "In Israeli Maternity Wards, Jewish and Arab Segregation Is the Default."

82. Daoud et al., "Mechanisms for Racial Separation and Inequitable Maternal Care."

83. Daoud et al., "Mechanisms for Racial Separation and Inequitable Maternal Care," 4.

84. Goldberg, *Threat of Race*, 372.

85. Cited in Ziv, "A Cognitive Dissonant Health System," 91.

86. Weiss, *Chosen Body*.

87. Goldberg, *Threat of Race*; Shohat, "Rupture and Return"; Weiss, *Chosen Body*.

88. Abusneineh, "(Re)producing the Israeli (European) Body"; Ihmoud, "Born Palestinian, Born Black."

89. Gilmore, *Abolition Geography*, 490.

90. Cowen and LaDuke offer a similar reading of Gilmore's infrastructures of feeling, applying it to white supremacy in the United States. See LaDuke and Cowen, "Beyond Wiindigo Infrastructure."

91. Berlant, *Cruel Optimism*, 95.

92. Berlant, *Cruel Optimism*, 95.

93. For a critical meditation on slow violence being "out of sight," see Davies, "Slow Violence and Toxic Geographies."

94. Star, "Ethnography of Infrastructure."

95. Berlant, "The Commons."

96. LaDuke and Cowen, "Beyond Wiindigo Infrastructure."

CHAPTER THREE

1. Keshet and Popper-Giveon, "Neutrality in Medicine and Health Professional"; Majadli, "Silenced Voices."

2. Majadli, *Responsibility Shirked*; Kinani et al., "Challenges in Accessing Care for Palestinian Cancer Patients."

3. Mary Louise Pratt coined the notion of "contact zones" to capture social spaces "where disparate cultures meet, clash, and grapple with each other, often in highly asymmetrical relations of domination and subordination—like colonialism, slavery, or their aftermaths as they are lived out across the globe today." Pratt, *Imperial Eyes*, 4.

4. Rosner, *Heroes of Health*, 37; Tanous, "Covid-19 Fault Lines."

5. Tanous, "Covid-19 Fault Lines," 39.

6. Ahmed, *Cultural Politics of Emotions*.

7. Majadli, "Silenced Voices."

8. United Nations Office of the High Commissioner, *Thematic Report—Attacks on Hospitals During the Escalation of Hostilities in Gaza (7 October 2023–30 June 2024);* Perugini and Gordon, "Medical Lawfare"; Turfah, "Israel Has Created a Medical Apocalypse in Gaza."

9. Human Rights Watch, *Israel: Palestinian Healthcare Workers Tortured*.

10. Amnesty International, *Investigate Killings of Paramedics and Rescue Workers in Gaza*.

11. Majadli et al., "Why Is the New England Journal of Medicine Promoting 'Health Bridges' While Gaza's Hospitals Burn?"; Turfah, "World's Top Medical Journal Is Giving Cover to Genocide."

12. Rexer, "Social Theory After* Gaza?"

13. Tanous et al., "Beyond Statelessness."

14. Yacobi and Pullan, "Geopolitics of Neighbourhood"; Salamanca et al., "Past Is Present."

15. Shalev, "Helsinki in Zion." Since I did not intend to do ethnographic observations with medical staff *in* Israeli hospitals but met them privately outside of their working hours to understand how they think about their working environment, I did not have to apply for ethics approval with the hospital, and my access to medical staff and patients was purely mediated by whether they decided to talk to me or not.

16. Their desire to show me that peace and coexistence do exist has probably also been reinforced by me being from Germany, a state whose nationalized guilt

prevents any critique of the Israeli state for a fear of moral condemnation. Atshan and Galor, *Moral Triangle.*

17. Lentin, *Traces of Racial Exception*; Goldberg, *Threat of Race.*

18. Lugones, "Toward a Decolonial Feminism"; Said, *Orientalism.*

19. Murphy, *Economization of Life.*

20. Silva, *Toward a Global Idea of Race*, 8.

21. During Zionist settlement in Palestine, Jews of European descent—Ashkenazim like Irit—were framed as bringing modernization to the barren and backward land and making up the elite of the state to be founded in 1948. The racial order of Israel's historical foundation as an outpost of European civilization, its alliance with global white supremacy, and its goal of legally achieving the supremacy of Jewish nationality led to whiteness structuring Jewish Israelis' proximities to power in Israeli society. Erakat, "Whiteness as Property," 132; Shohat, "Rupture and Return"; Ihmoud, "Mohammed Abu-Khdeir and the Politics of Racial Terror." Theo Goldberg writes: "The Europeanness of politically and religiously dominant Israelis renders the Promised Land and its members . . . as normatively white. [Ashkenazi] Israelis occupy the structural positions of whiteness in the racial hierarchy of the Middle East." Goldberg, *Threat of Race*, 116–17.

22. For a discussion of a patronizing medical gaze in relation to women's bodies, health, and weight, see Valdez, *Weighing the Future*; Dame-Griff, "Future is Brown."

23. For a discussion of Sunni and Shia perspectives on gamete donation, see Inhorn and Tremayne, *Islam and Assisted Reproductive Technologies.*

24. For a discussion of the transnational and racialized circuits of egg donation, see Michal Nahman's work: "Repro-Migration"; *Extractions*; "Reverse Traffic."

25. Weiss, *Chosen Body.*

26. Owens, *Medical Bondage*; Washington, *Medical Apartheid.*

27. Bridges, *Reproducing Race*; Dána-Ain Davis, "Reproducing While Black" and "Obstetric Racism."

28. Bhandar, *Colonial Lives of Property.*

29. Tanous, "Covid-19 Fault Lines," 39.

30. On infrastructures as sociality, see Berlant, "The Commons." What I also hear in Shimrit's reflection on her Palestinian patients' feelings is what Nasser Abourahme terms "settlerness," a concept that describes a political mode of existence that can appear anywhere where large-scale population replacement occurs. "Settlerness describes life in the shade of an uneasy domination. It describes a form of restless inhabitation." This uneasiness, a sense of knowing that something, if *off*, can be traced in the nurses' narrative. Abourahme, *Time Beneath the Concrete,* 22.

31. Ahmed, *Cultural Politics of Emotions*, 69.

32. On disaffection and unfeeling, see Yao, *Disaffected.*

33. Fanon, *A Dying Colonialism*, 133.

34. Tuck and Yang, "Decolonization Is Not a Metaphor."

35. Coulthard, *Red Skin, White Masks*, 15–16.

36. Shalev, "Helsinki in Zion," 3.

37. Stein, "Impossible Witness," 147.

38. Majadli, "Silenced Voices."

39. Sabbagh-Khoury, "On the Monopoly of Violence," 18.

40. Zureik, "Strategies of Surveillance," 14.

41. Tanous, "The Hospital as a Place of Labor." On the importance of healthcare and the establishment of Jewish hospitals for the Zionist movement, see also Sufian, *Healing the Land and the Nation*.

42. Rotem, "'A Never Ending Source of Wonder,'" 127.

43. Wind, *Towers of Ivory and Steel*, 13.

44. Rotem, "'A Never Ending Source of Wonder,'" 128.

45. This fear was not unfounded. In 1948, a medical convoy en route to Hadassah was ambushed by Palestinian forces, killing seventy-eight Jewish doctors, nurses, patients, and Haganah militants. Rotem, "'A Never Ending Source of Wonder.'"

46. Yacobi and Pullan, "Geopolitics of Neighbourhood."

47. Tanous and Majadli, "A Medical School in the Service of Colonialism."

48. Cited in Tanous and Majadli, "A Medical School in the Service of Colonialism."

49. Tanous and Majadli, "A Medical School in the Service of Colonialism." For an extensive study on the militarization of the Israeli educational system, see Wind, *Towers of Ivory and Steel*.

50. Benton and Atshan, "'Even War Has Rules,'" 153.

51. Sabbagh-Khoury, "On the Monopoly of Violence," 9–10; Orr and Fleming, "Medical Neutrality."

52. This moment came to represent, in the words of sociologist Areej Sabbagh-Khoury, "the contiguity in *a single moment* of the colonization process against *all* Palestinians." Sabbagh-Khoury, "On the Monopoly of Violence," 10.

53. Orr and Fleming, "Medical Neutrality," 10.

54. On recognition and disavowal, see Sabbagh-Khoury, "Memory for Forgetfulness."

55. Majadli, "Silenced Voices."

56. Ziv, "Medicalization of Armament," 2.

57. Ziv, "Medicalization of Armament," 7.

58. Sabbagh-Khoury, "On the Monopoly of Violence," 11.

59. Sabbagh-Khoury, "On the Monopoly of Violence," 11.

60. Majadli, "Silenced Voices."

61. Majadli, "Silenced Voices," 14.

62. Majadli, "Silenced Voices," 15.

63. Majadli, "Silenced Voices," 21.

64. Keshet and Popper-Giveon, "Neutrality in Medicine"; Majadli, "Silenced Voices," 7.

65. Birenbaum-Carmeli, "Health Journalism in the Service of Power."

66. Tanous, "Covid-19 Fault Lines," 38.

67. References to utopia abound in social theory. The double signification of utopian social relations referring to an ideal status as well as the need for substantial transformation for utopian circumstances to exist are foundational to this notion in

its political and philosophical iterations. Paul Gilroy has written about this extensively in *The Black Atlantic*. His interpretation furthermore suggests that utopian social relations between subaltern groups and their oppressors need to change in a twofold way: "The invocation of utopia references what, following Seyla Benhabib's suggestive lead, I propose to call the politics of transfiguration. This emphasises the emergence of qualitatively new desires, social relations, and modes of association within the racial community of interpretation and resistance *and* between that group and its erstwhile oppressors." Gilroy, *Black Atlantic*, 37.

68. Shalev, "A Doctor's Testimony."

69. Tanous, "Covid-19 Fault Lines," 39.

70. Simpson, *Mohawk Interruptus*, 133.

71. Davenport, "Witnessing and the Medical Gaze"; Taylor, "Confronting 'Culture'"; Underman, *Feeling Medicine*.

72. Shalev, "Helsinki in Zion."

73. Tawil-Souri, "Uneven Borders."

74. Erakat, *Justice for Some*.

75. Bishara, *Crossing a Line*, 29.

76. Massey, "Places and Their Pasts."

77. Yacobi and Pullan, "Geopolitics of Neighbourhood." The neighborhood the hospital is located in, as well as Jerusalem as a whole, are considered an active "frontier" of Israeli settler colonialism because they exemplify the twinned strategies of Jewish Israeli settlement and Palestinian dispossession via land confiscations, eviction, and legal battles. The location of this hospital in East Jerusalem symbolizes its strategic placement at the expanding frontier of a city under occupation since 1967.

78. During the years I was in contact with Ziva, many Palestinians brought into this hospital were injured by Israeli border police after raids of Issawiya and the violent attempts to end Palestinians' demonstrations against dispossession and land grabs in East Jerusalem. I am grateful to Sophia Goodfriend for asking me to clarify the political background of Ziva's narrative.

79. Azoulay and Ophir, *One-State Condition*, 97.

80. Stamatopoulou-Robbins, *Waste Siege*, 13.

81. Hammami, "Destabilizing Mastery."

82. Nadera Shalhoub-Kevorkian writes about Palestinian women's complex political status: "Palestinian women's passage, their daily border crossings—from being frontliners, 'security threats,' mothers of martyrs, icons of the nation, and protectors of the society into the weakest members of that society and so requiring protection or deserving punishment if 'transgressing the limits'—has transformed their bodies and lives into a colonial weapon, a marker of colonization and military oppression." Shalhoub-Kevorkian, *Militarization and Violence Against Women*, 205.

83. Rexer, "Borderlands of Reproduction," 1665.

84. Tanous, "'You, as of Now, Are Someone Else!'"

85. Robinson, *Citizen Strangers*.

86. Mimi Thi Nguyen, *Gift of Freedom*. Sociological work on racialized refugees in North America makes similar arguments. See, for instance, Vinh Nguyen, *Lived Refuge*; Gowayed, *Refuge*.

87. Nguyen, *Gift of Freedom*, x.

88. Nguyen, *Gift of Freedom*, 5.

89. Puwar, *Space Invaders*; Ahmed, *Cultural Politics of Emotions*; Bonilla-Silva, "Feeling Race."

90. Shalhoub-Kevorkian, *Security Theology*.

91. To capture such affective dispositions vis-à-vis various national projects, political sociologist Bilgin Ayata suggests the term "affective citizenship." Ayata, "Affective Citizenship."

92. Puar, *Right to Maim*.

93. On the notion of the "perfect victim," see Erakat, "Grieving Palestinian Life"; Mikdashi, "Can Palestinian Men be Victims?"; El-Kurd, *Perfect Victims*.

94. Wolfe, "Settler Colonialism and the Elimination of the Native."

95. Ihmoud, "Murabata."

96. Massey, "Places and Their Pasts."

97. I am drawing here from Black Studies scholar Jackie Wang's analysis of the function of white space, which I see working in similar ways as settler space in Palestine/Israel, despite its own distinct racial hierarchies: "The urban landscape is organized according to a spatial politics of safety. Bodies that arouse feelings of fear, disgust, rage, guilt, or even discomfort must be made disposable and targeted for removal in order to secure a sense of safety for whites. In other words, the space that white people occupy must be *cleansed*. The visibility of poor Black bodies (as well as certain nonblack people of color, trans people, homeless people, differently abled people, and so forth) induces anxiety, so these bodies must be contained, controlled, and removed." Wang, *Carceral Capitalism*, 270–71.

98. Kotef, *Colonizing Self*, 73.

CHAPTER FOUR

1. Asi, "Palestinian Dependence on External Health Services; Majadli, *Responsibility Shirked*; Kinani et al., "Challenges in Accessing Care for Palestinian Cancer Patients."

2. Perugini and Gordon, "Medical Lawfare"; Masarwa, "Israeli Doctor Compared Killing Palestinians in Gaza to 'Eliminating Cockroaches.'"; Rudrappa, "No Reproductive Justice"; Ihmoud, "Countering Reproductive Genocide in Gaza."

3. Ihmoud, "Countering Reproductive Genocide in Gaza"; Naber, "Reproductive Justice from Turtle Island to Palestine."

4. Anzaldúa, *Borderlands/La Frontera*; Rexer, "Borderlands of Reproduction."

5. Abourahme, "Spatial Collisions and Discordant Temporalities," 453.

6. Zu'bi, "Palestinian Fertility in the Israeli Sphere," 171.

7. Zu'bi, "Palestinian Fertility in the Israeli Sphere," 177.

8. Shalhoub-Kevorkian, *Security Theology*, 146.

9. Mbembe, "Bodies as Borders."

10. Morgan, *Laboring Women*; Stoler, *Carnal Knowledge*; Balani, *Deadly and Slick*; Roberts, *Killing the Black Body*; Hartman, "Belly of the World"; McClintock, *Imperial Leather*; Rifkin, *When Did Indians Become Straight?*

11. Lowe, *Intimacies of Four Continents.*

12. Stoler, "Intimidations of Empire"; Zengin, "Violent Intimacies"; Stoler, *Haunted by Empire.*

13. Shalhoub-Kevorkian, *Security Theology*; Shalhoub-Kevorkian, "Terrorism and the Birthing Body in Jerusalem"; Ihmoud, "Policing the Intimate"; Abusneineh, "(Re)producing the Israeli (European) Body"; Puar, *Right to Maim.*

14. Shalhoub-Kevorkian, *Security Theology*, 3; Pell, "Reproductive Cecisions in the Lives of West Bank Palestinian Women; Rexer, "Materiality of Power."

15. Wick, *Sumud*; See also Buch Segal, "Burden of Being Exemplary"; Abu-Duhou, "Motherhood as a Script for Nationhood."

16. Majadli, "Healthcare in the Occupied Territory."

17. Kinani et al., "Challenges in Accessing Care for Palestinian Cancer Patients"; Majadli, *Responsibility Shirked.*

18. WHO, "Hostilities in the Occupied Palestinian Territory"; Solaimane, "Palestinians in Gaza Desperate to Travel Abroad."

19. Bishara, "Mobilizing Resistance".

20. Goodfriend, "Algorithmic State Violence"; *The Guardian*, "Any Palestinian Is Exposed."

21. Griffiths and Repo, "Women and Checkpoints in Palestine"; Hamayel et al., "Reproductive Health and Rights in East Jerusalem"; Hammami, "Destabilizing Mastery."

22. Rifkin, *Beyond Settler Time*, 9.

23. Drawing from Rifkin, Abourahme argues that time itself is a foundational question *and* site in settler states. He shows how Israeli settler colonialism is and was centrally occupied not only with the conquest of land, but also with the conquest of time. For Zionism, and for the Israeli state today, what began in the late nineteenth century was characterized by both the racialization of historical time (in which Palestinians either didn't exist, or existed as some anachronistic primitives) as well as an ontologically new temporality (the beginning of "civilizational time" in Palestine). Abourahme, *Time Beneath the Concrete*, 16.

24. Peteet, "Closure's Temporality"; Tawil-Souri, "Checkpoint Time"; Wick, "Practice of Waiting"; Yiftachel, "Deepening Apartheid."

25. Puar, "Spatial Debilities."

26. Puar, "Spatial Debilities," 404.

27. Wick, *Sumud*, 44.

28. Giacaman, "Reflections on the Meaning of 'Resilience'"; Nguyen-Gillham et al., "Normalising the Abnormal."

29. Wick, *Sumud*, 37.

30. Stoler and Strassler, "Castings for the Colonial," 8.

31. Stoler and Strassler, "Castings for the Colonial," 38.
32. Puar, "Spatial Debilities," 404.
33. Yiftachel, "Deepening Apartheid."
34. Ahmed, *Complaint!*, 5.
35. Davis, "Obstetric Racism," 562.
36. Shalhoub-Kevorkian and Ihmoud, "Exiled at Home"; Shalhoub-Kevorkian, "Terrorism and the Birthing Body"; Shalhoub-Kevorkian, "Politics of Birth."
37. Steinfeld, "Wars of the Womb"; Abusneineh, "(Re)producing the Israeli (European) Body"; Birenbaum-Carmeli, "Thirty-Five Years of Assisted Reproductive Technologies"; Vertommen, "From the Pergonal Project to Kadimastem"; Vertommen, "Babies from Behind the Bars."
38. Kanaaneh, *Birthing the Nation*, 58.
39. Shalhoub-Kevorkian, "Birthing in Occupied East Jerusalem"; Shalhoub-Kevorkian, "Politics of Birth"; Shalhoub-Kevorkian, *Security Theology*; Shalhoub-Kevorkian, "Terrorism and the Birthing Body."
40. Plonski, *Palestinian Citizens of Israel*; Rouhana and Sultany, "Making of an Underclass"; Rouhana and Sabbagh-Khoury, "Settler-Colonial Citizenship."
41. Robinson, *Citizen Stranger*; Sabbagh-Khoury, "Citizenship as Accumulation."
42. Erakat, "Whiteness as Property," 3.
43. Adalah Discriminatory Law Database: https://www.adalah.org/en/law/index.
44. Health-insurance-run clinics are small, public clinics offering basic services. Services like IVF or other fertility treatments will be offered in designated women's clinics, affiliated with one of the three large health insurance providers in Israel.
45. Nahman, *Extractions*.
46. On the notion of stratified reproduction, see Colen, "Like a Mother to Them."
47. Shehadeh and Raja Khalidi, "Impeded Development"; Rouhana and Sultany, "Making of an Underclass."
48. Yiftachel, "Deepening Apartheid," 10–11.
49. Yacobi, *Jewish–Arab City*.
50. Zu'bi, "Palestinian Fertility in the Israeli Sphere," 168.
51. I am borrowing from Stuart Hall here, who proposed that race is the modality through which class is lived. Hall, "Race, Articulation, and Societies," 314.
52. Yiftachel, "Deepening Apartheid," 10.
53. Kanaaneh, *Birthing the Nation*.
54. Said, "Zionism from the Standpoint of Its Victims."
55. Roberts, "Race, Gender, and Genetic Technologies," 786.
56. For an analysis of this shift more broadly, see Rose, *Politics of Life Itself*.
57. Roberts, "Race, Gender, and Genetic Technologies," 799.
58. Stoler, "Interior Frontiers."
59. Zengin, *Violent Intimacies*, 8.
60. Zengin, *Violent Intimacies*, 8.
61. Zengin, *Violent Intimacies*, 9; Hartman, *Wayward Lives*.

62. Salamanca et al., "Past Is Present"; Bishara, *Crossing a Line*.
63. Tawil-Souri, "Checkpoint Time," 403.
64. Yiftachel, "Deepening Apartheid."
65. Zu'bi, "Palestinian Fertility in the Israeli Sphere," 172.
66. Abourahme, *Time Beneath the Concrete*, 17.
67. Abu-Duhou, "Motherhood as 'an Act of Defiance.'"
68. Wick, *Sumud*, 39.

CHAPTER FIVE

1. See Ftouni, "'They Make Death.'"
2. Vertommen, "Babies from Behind the Bars."
3. Hamdan, "'Every Sperm Is Sacred'"; Ferrero, "Palestinian Sperm-Smuggling"; Vardit Rispler-Chaim, "Ethical Aspects Concerning Sperm Smuggled"; Ftouni, "'They Make Death.'"
4. Rexer, "Borderlands of Reproduction."
5. Ihmoud, "Born Palestinian, Born Black"; Abusneineh, "(Re)producing the Israeli (European) Body."
6. Mikdashi, *Sextarianism*, 180.
7. Agard-Jones, "Bodies in the System"; Harcourt et al., "Introduction."
8. Wilcox, *Bodies of Violence*.
9. Murphy, *Seizing the Means of Reproduction*, 26.
10. Chen, *Animacies*.
11. Paige Marie Patchin, "Thresholds of Empire"; Carsten, "Substance and Relationality"; Newman and Nahman, "Nurture Commodified?"; Fortier, "Blood, Sperm and the Embryo"; Martin, "Egg and the Sperm." Almeling et al., *Seminal*.
12. Daher-Nashif, "Colonial Management of Death"; Ajour, *Reclaiming Humanity*.
13. Barad, *Meeting the Universe Halfway*, 3.
14. Pitts-Taylor, *Mattering*, 9. Almeling et al., *Seminal*.
15. Collier and Ong, "Global Assemblages, Anthropological Problems," 4. For an in-depth discussion of the concept of the assemblage, bodies, and resistance, see Bargu, *Starve and Immolate*, 52.
16. Franklin, *Reproducing Reproduction*; Franklin and Inhorn, "Introduction."
17. When I first wrote about this as part of my PhD in April 2021, this number was 4,500, with numbers almost doubling from 2023 to 2024 with Israel's genocidal war in Gaza and its increasingly extremist government and police force. Adameer, see https://addameer.ps/statistics; B'Tselem, "Statistics on Palestinians in Israeli Custody," https://www.btselem.org/statistics/detainees_and_prisoners.
18. Hajjar and Farraj, "Israel Is Waging War on Palestinian Prisoners"; Khalidi, "Israel: A Carceral State."
19. Not only have incarceration rates almost doubled since October 2023, but Israeli violence against Palestinian prisoners has been described as reaching unprec-

edented levels of violence. See Hajjar and Farraj, "Israel Is Waging War on Palestinian Prisoners."

20. Ajour, *Reclaiming Humanity*; Giacaman and Johnson, "'Our Life Is Prison'"; Shwaikh, "Prison Periods"; Shwaikh, "Engendering Hunger Strikes."

21. Dawber, "Babies Behind Bars."

22. Ftouni, "'They Make Death'"; Ihmoud, "On Love, the Palestinian Way."

23. Most of the women I interviewed asked me to not disclose details about the actual procedure of how sperm samples are smuggled out of prisons. I will thus not address this practicality here.

24. Inhorn and Tremayne, *Islam and Assisted Reproductive Technologies*; Fortier, "Religious and Non-Religious Issues."

25. Franklin, *Embodied Progress*, 7.

26. Ghoddousi and Sam Page, "Using Ethnography."

27. Johnson, "Living Together."

28. Abu-Duhou, "Motherhood as a Script for Nationhood"; Abu-Duhou, "Motherhood as 'an Act of Defiance.'"

29. Ftouni, "'They Make Death,'"105.

30. Wick, *Sumud*, 44.

31. Shalhoub-Kevorkian, "Terrorism and the Birthing Body," 47.

32. Ftouni, "'They Make Death.'"

33. Shalhoub-Kevorkian, *Security Theology*, 64.

34. Kanaaneh, *Birthing the Nation*, 56.

35. Mbembe, "Necropolitics."

36. Shalhoub-Kevorkian, *Militarization and Violence*, 187.

37. Butler, *Bodies That Matter*; Wilcox, *Bodies of Violence.*

38. Ajour, *Reclaiming Humanity*, 315.

39. Nashif, "Attempts at Liberation," 46.

40. Rexer, "Borderlands of Reproduction."

41. Chen, *Animacies.*

42. Alsaafin, "Sperm Smuggling by Palestinian Prisoners."

43. Vertommen, "Babies from Behind the Bars," 215.

44. Maguire and Rao, "Introduction."

45. Hamdan, "'Every Sperm Is Sacred.'"

46. Hamayel et al., "Reproductive Health and Rights in East Jerusalem"; Hammoudeh et al., "Beyond the Physicality of Space"; Hammami, "Destabilizing Mastery."

47. Lewis, *Full Surrogacy Now.*

48. Buch Segal, Bburden of Being Exemplary."

49. Buch Segal, *No Place for Grief*, 144; Buch Segal, "Burden of Being Exemplary."

50. Buch Segal finds that "reducing womanhood to motherhood becomes a means of sustaining the Palestinian struggle for a nation-state through nurture and support, making sure that violence does not fragment the Palestinian collective." Buch Segal, "Burden of Being Exemplary," 42.

51. Dawber, "Babies Behind Bar"

52. Abu-Duhou, "Motherhood as a Script for Nationhood."

53. Abdallah, *A History of Confinement in Palestine*; Hawari, "Political Marginalization of Palestinian Women in the West Bank"; Kayali, *Palestinian Women and Popular Resistance*; Shwaikh, "Prison Periods"; Shwaikh, "Engendering Hunger Strikes"; Ihmoud, "Murabata."

54. Meari, "Re-Signifying 'Sexual' Colonial Power Techniques."

55. Hamdan, "'Every Sperm Is Sacred,'" 537.

56. Pateman, *Sexual Contract.*

57. Wilcox, *Bodies of Violence*, 13.

58. Whittaker, "Reproduction Opportunists."

59. Bhatia, "Figuring India and China."

60. Abu-Duhou, "Motherhood as a Script for Nationhood"; Mikdashi, *Sextarianism*; Inhorn and Tremayne, *Islam and Assisted Reproductive Technologies.*

61. Ferrero, "Palestinian Sperm-Smuggling," 221.

62. Johnson and Kuttab, "Where Have All the Women (and Men) Gone?"; Shwaikh, "Engendering Hunger Strikes."

63. Medien, "Israeli Settler Colonialism," 14–19; Shalhoub-Kevorkian, *Militarization and Violence.*

64. Sharif, "Bodies, Buses, and Permits."

65. Ihmoud, "Born Palestinian, Born Black."

66. Ihmoud, "Mohammed Abu-Khdeir"; Spillers, "Mama's Baby, Papa's Maybe."

67. Following anthropologist Aihwa Ong, assemblages are "experimental systems, that is, open-ended and responsive to unfolding elements and events, so that solutions to particular challenges are not given in advance." Ong, "Scales of Exception," 121. See also Collier and Ong, "Global Assemblages, Anthropological Problems."

68. Temple et al., "Grasping at Context"; Temple and Young, "Qualitative Research and Translation Dilemmas."

69. Spivak, "Politics of Translation," 184.

70. McKittrick, *Dear Science and Other Stories*, 4.

71. McKittrick, *Dear Science and Other Stories*, 16.

72. Madhok, "A Critical Reflexive Politics of Location."

73. Taher and Younes, "Lebensraum, Geopolitics and Race."

74. Rich, "Notes Towards a Politics of Location."

75. Bishara, "My Impossible Ethnography."

76. Mikdashi and Puar, "Queer Theory and Permanent War."

77. Bargu, *Starve and Immolate*, 16.

78. Ajour, *Reclaiming Humanity*, 316.

79. Abu-Lughod, "Romance of Resistance," 42.

80. Wilcox, *Bodies of Violence.*

81. Puar, "Spatial Debilities."

82. Seikaly, "Nakba in the Age of Catastrophe." See also the Scholars for Palestinian Freedom's open letter, "Palestine & Praxis," in which scholars from a variety

of different disciplines affirm: "Approaching Palestine as a field of knowledge, rather than a case study or site of theoretical extraction, demands engaging with the intellectual labor of its people as a genealogy of subjugated knowledge in praxis. Resisting their erasure from the historical record requires a citational practice that both names Palestinians as intellectual subjects and challenges the very intellectual discourse that relegates them to the margins." See Scholars for Palestinian Freedom, "Palestine & Praxis," https://palestineandpraxis.weebly.com/.

83. Puar, "Spatial Debilities"; Salih and Corry, "Displacing the Anthropocene."

CONCLUSION

1. Mahdawi, "An Israeli Bomb Destroyed 4,000 Embryos."
2. Mousa and Graham-Harrison, "War Halts IVF Treatment in Gaza."
3. United Nations Population Fund, "Women of Gaza."
4. Perugini and Gordon, "Medical Lawfare"; Elnakib et al., "Pregnant Women in Gaza."
5. Cheung, "Miscarriages in Gaza Have Increased 300%."
6. Rajvanshi, "What Pregnant Women Face in Gaza."
7. Ihmoud, "Countering Reproductive Genocide."
8. Yanko, "'She Asked No Arab Come Near Her Daughter.'"
9. Efrati, "Arab-Israeli Doctor Leaves Job."
10. Cited in Zu'bi, "Since the War: Unprecedented Persecution of Arab Medical Workers."
11. Majadli, "Silenced Voices and Militarized Spaces."
12. Goodfriend, "Israel's Security Theater."
13. Shalhoub-Kevorkian, *Security Theology*.
14. Tanous, "Hospital as a Place of Labor."
15. Human Rights Watch, *Israel: Palestinian Healthcare Workers Tortured*.
16. Amnesty International, *Israel/ OPT: Investigate Killings of Paramedics and Rescue Workers in Gaza*.
17. Cited in Shalhoub-Kevorkian and Ihmoud, "Two Letters from Jerusalem," 8.
18. *Middle East Monitor*, "Israeli President Herzog Says."
19. Echchaibi, "A Scream for Gaza," 1023.
20. Rexer, "Social Theory After* Gaza?"
21. Goldberg, *Threat of Race*, 108–9.
22. Shalhoub-Kevorkian, "At the Limits of the Human," 2253.
23. Kemp, "'Dangerous Populations'"; Sa'di, *Thorough Surveillance*.
24. Wispelwey et al., "Because Its Power Remains Naturalized"; Tanous, "'You, as of Now, Are Someone Else!'"
25. Wolfe, "Settler Colonialism and the Elimination of the Native."
26. Flaschenberg and Itzhaky, "How October 7 Transformed Israeli Society."

27. A 2025 representative poll shows that 82 percent of Jewish Israeli respondents support the expulsion of Gaza's residents. Fifty-six percent of respondents favored expelling Palestinian citizens of Israel. See Hazkani and Sorek, "Yes to Transfer."

28. Stoler, *Haunted by Empire*; Wexler, *Tender Violence*; Nixon, *Slow Violence.*

29. Stoler, "Intimidations of Empire," 14.

30. Wexler, *Tender Violence.*

31. Wexler, *Tender Violence*, 56.

32. Tuck and Yang, "Decolonization Is Not a Metaphor."

33. On liberalism, inclusion, and recognition under settler colonialism, see Coulthard, *Red Skin, White Masks.*

34. Rexer, "How Race, Nationality, and Gender Shape Fieldwork and Data Collection."

35. Sabbagh-Khoury, "Memory for Forgetfulness." Sabbagh-Khoury, *Colonizing Palestine.*

36. Schoen, *Choice and Coercion.*

37. Puar, "Spatial Debilities"; Nixon, *Slow Violence.*

38. Benjamin, "Black Afterlives Matter," 56.

39. Theobald, *Reproduction on the Reservation*; Schoen, *Choice and Coercion*; Patchin, "Thresholds of Empire"; Murphy, *Economization of Life*; Hartman, "Belly of the World"; Briggs, *Reproducing Empire*; Sánchez-Rivera, *Slippery Eugenics*; Roberts, *Killing the Black Body.*

40. Schoen, *Choice and Coercion*, 8.

41. Naber, "'The US and Israel Make the Connections for Us'"; Barakat, "Reading Audre Lorde in Palestine"; Ihmoud, "Born Palestinian, Born Black"; Azeb, "Epilogue."

42. Luna, "Black Celebrities, Reproductive Justice and Queering Family"; Roberts, "Race, Gender, and Genetic Technologies."

43. Naber, "Reproductive Justice from Turtle Island to Palestine," 546

44. Shoman et al., "Feminist Silences."

45. Kelly, "Subjection and Performance," 102.

46. Ihmoud, "Palestinian Feminism," 294.

47. Glissant, *Poetics of Relation*, 193.

BIBLIOGRAPHY

Abbas, Fahima, and Yonatan Mendel. "Hebrew Studies Amongst Palestinians in East Jerusalem: Not 'Language of Success' but 'Language of Access.'" *Hebrew Studies* 63 (2022): 221–43.

Abdallah, Stéphanie Latte. *A History of Confinement in Palestine: The Prison Web.* Palgrave Macmillan, 2022.

Abdo, Nahla. "The Palestine Exception, Racialization and Invisibilization: From Israel (Palestine) to North America (Turtle Island)." *Critical Sociology* 49, no. 6 (2022).

Abdo, Nahla. *Women in Israel: Race, Gender and Citizenship.* Zed Books, 2011.

Abdulhadi, Rabab. "Israeli Settler Colonialism in Context: Celebrating (Palestinian) Death and Normalizing Gender and Sexual Violence." *Feminist Studies* 45, no. 2/3 (2019): 541–73.

Abourahme, Nasser. "Spatial Collisions and Discordant Temporalities: Everyday Life Between Camp and Checkpoint." *International Journal of Urban and Regional Research* 35, no. 2 (2011): 453–61.

Abourahme, Nasser. *The Time Beneath the Concrete: Palestine Between Camp and Colony.* Duke University Press, 2025.

Abu-Duhou, Jamileh. "Motherhood as 'an Act of Defiance': Palestinian Women's Reproductive Experience." *Development* 46, no. 2 (2003): 85–89.

Abu-Duhou, Jamileh. "Motherhood as a Script for Nationhood." In *Reproduction, Childbearing and Motherhood: A Cross-Cultural Perspective,* edited by Pranee Liamputtong. Nova Science Pub, 2007.

Abu El-Haj, Nadia. "Racial Palestinianization and the Janus-Faced Nature of the Israeli State." *Patterns of Prejudice* 44 (2010).

Abu-Hamad, Sirat, and Nihaya Daoud. "Maternal Respectful Care and Post-Traumatic Stress Disorder Among Postpartum Mothers in Israel." *European Journal of Public Health* 23, no. 3 (2022).

Abujidi, Nurhan. *Urbicide in Palestine: Spaces of Oppression and Resilience.* Routledge, 2014.

Abu-Kaf, Sarah, Ora Nakash, Tsachi Hayat, and Michal Cohen. "Emotional Distress Among the Bedouin Arab and Jewish Elderly in Israel: The Roles of Gender, Discrimination, and Self-Esteem." *Psychiatry Research* 291 (2020).

Abulof, Uriel. "Deep Securitization and Israel's 'Demographic Demon.'" *International Political Sociology* 8, no. 4 (2014): 396–415.

Abu-Lughod, Lila. *Do Muslim Women Need Saving?* Harvard University Press, 2015.

Abu-Lughod, Lila. "The Romance of Resistance: Tracing Transformations of Power Through Bedouin Women." *American Ethnologist* 17, no. 1 (1990): 41–55.

Aburabia, Rawia. "The Law on the Books Versus the Law in Action: Muslim Women in Polygamous Marriage Under the Jewish State." *Social Politics: International Studies in Gender, State and Society* 29, no. 2 (2021): 634–57.

Aburabia, Rawia. "Redefining Polygamy Among the Palestinian Bedouins in Israel: Colonialism, Patriarchy, and Resistance." *Journal of Gender, Social Policy and the Law* 19, no. 2 (2011): 459–93.

Abu-Rabia-Queder, Sarab. "The Biopolitics of Declassing Palestinian Professional Women in a Settler-Colonial Context." *Current Sociology* 67, no. 1 (2019): 141–58.

Abu-Rabia-Queder, Sarab. "The Dissipation of the Green Line in Palestinian Women's Research in Israel: Production of Ethical Knowledge and Research Justice." In *70 Years of Nakbah*, edited by Mohanad Mustafa. Mada al-Carmel–Arab Center for Applied Social Research, 2018.

Abu-saad, Ismael. "Separate and Unequal: The Role of the State Educational System in Maintaining the Subordination of Israel's Palestinian Arab Citizens." *Social Identities* 10, no. 1 (2004): 101–27.

Abusneineh, Bayan. "(Re)Producing the Israeli (European) Body: Zionism, Anti-Black Racism and the Depo-Provera Affair." *Feminist Review* 128, no. 1 (2021): 96–113.

Abusneineh, Bayan. "Who Is Entitled to Bear Children: Discourses of Race and Eugenics in the Law of Return." *Critical Ethnic Studies Journal* 9, no. 1 (2024).

Agard-Jones, Vanessa. "Bodies in the System." *Small Axe: A Caribbean Journal of Criticism* 17, no. 3 (2013): 182–92.

Ahmed, Sara. *Complaint!* Duke University Press, 2021.

Ahmed, Sara. *The Cultural Politics of Emotions*. Edinburgh University Press, 2004.

Ajour, Ashjan. *Reclaiming Humanity in Palestinian Hunger Strikes: Revolutionary Subjectivity and Decolonizing the Body*. Palgrave Macmillan, 2021.

Alasah, Eman. "The Palestinian Feminist Movement and the Settler Colonial Ordeal: An Intersectional and Interdependent Framework." *Meridians: feminism, race, transnationalism* 23, no. 1 (2024): 110–32

Alfayumi-Zeadna, Samira, Huda Abu Ghalion, Norm O'Rourke, Zuya Azbarga, and Nihaya Daoud. "Direct and Indirect Predictors of Postpartum Depression Symptoms Among Indigenous Bedouin Mothers in Israel." *Research in Nursing and Health* 47, no. 2 (2023): 114–24.

Almeling, Rene, Lisa Campo-Engelstein, and Brian T. Nguyen, eds. *Seminal: On Sperm, Health, and Politics*. New York University Press, 2025.

AlRifai, Ayesha. "Abortion as a Contested Right in Occupied Palestine." *Journal of Middle East Women's Studies* 14, no. 3 (2018): 384–89.
Alsaafin, Linah. "Sperm Smuggling by Palestinian Prisoners Swimmingly Successful." *Middle East Eye*, February 13, 2015.
Altay, Tunay, Gökce Yurdakul, and Anna C. Korteweg. "Crossing Borders: The Intersectional Marginalisation of Bulgarian Muslim Trans*Immigrant Sex Workers in Berlin." *Journal of Ethnic and Migration Studies* 47, no. 9 (2021): 1922–39.
Amit, Hila. "Israel, Zionism and Emigration Anxiety: The Case of Israeli Academia." *Settler Colonial Studies* 9, no. 1 (2018): 6–21.
Amnesty International. *Israel/OPT: Investigate Killings of Paramedics and Rescue Workers in Gaza*. April 1, 2025.
Amun, Fadi. "Israel Offers Free IVF Treatment. So Why Do Many Palestinian Israelis Prefer West Bank Clinics?" *Haaretz*, April 8, 2024.
Anand, Nikhil, Akhil Gupta, and Hannah Appel. "Introduction: Temporality, Politics, and the Promise of Infrastructure." In *The Promise of Infrastructure*, edited by Nikhil Anand, Akhil Gupta, and Hannah Appel. Duke University Press, 2018.
Angel, Arielle. "On Loving Jews." *Jewish Currents*, September 13, 2021.
Anzalduá, Gloria E. *Borderlands/La Frontera: The New Mestiza*. Aunt Lute, 1987.
Asi, Yara. "Israel Sees Palestinian Family Reunification as a Demographic 'Threat.'" Arab Center Washington DC, February 2, 2023.
Asi, Yara. "Palestinian Dependence on External Health Services: De-Development as a Tool of Dispossession." *Middle East Law and Governance* 14, no. 3 (2022): 366–87.
Asi, Yara, Weeam Hammoudeh, David Mills, Osama Tanous, and Bram Wispelwey. "Reassembling the Pieces: Settler Colonialism and the Reconception of Palestinian Health." *Health and Human Rights* 24, no. 2 (2022): 229–35.
Atshan, Sa'ed, and Katharina Galor. *The Moral Triangle: Germans, Israelis, Palestinians*. Duke University Press, 2020.
Attewell, Wesley, Emily Mitchell-Eaton, Richard Nisa, Deborah Cowen, and Laleh Khalili. "Inscribing New Infrastructural Relations into the World: Deborah Cowen and Laleh Khalili in Conversation." *Radical History Review* 147 (2023): 13–34.
Ayata, Bilgin. "Affective Citizenship." In *Affective Societies: Key Concepts*, edited by Jan Slaby and Christian von Scheve. Routledge, 2019.
Azeb, Sophia. "Epilogue: From Antigua to Algérie: The Particularity and Promise of the Afro-Arab." *Post45*, November 9, 2020.
Aziza, Sarah. "The Work of the Witness." *Jewish Currents*, January 12, 2024.
Azoulay, Ariella. *Potential History: Unlearning Imperialism*. Verso, 2020.
Azoulay, Ariella, and Adi Ophir. *The One-State Condition: Occupation and Democracy in Israel/Palestine*. Stanford University Press, 2013.
Baconi, Tareq. *Hamas Contained: A History of Palestinian Resistance*. Stanford University Press, 2018.

Balani, Sita. *Deadly and Slick: Sexual Modernity and the Making of Race.* Verso, 2023.

Balibar, Étienne. "Racism and Nationalism." In *Race, Nation, Class: Ambiguous Identities*, edited by Étienne Balibar and Immanuel Maurice Wallerstein. Verso, 1991.

Barad, Karen. *Meeting the Universe Halfway: Quantum Physics and the Entanglement of Matter and Meaning.* Duke University Press, 2007.

Barakat, Rana. "Reading Audre Lorde in Palestine: Exploring Differences Between Generative and Extractive." *Kohl: A Journal for Body and Gender Research* 9, no. 1 (2023).

Bargu, Banu. *Starve and Immolate: The Politics of Human Weapons.* Columbia University Press, 2014.

Benjamin, Ruha. "Black Afterlives Matter: Cultivating Kinfulness as Reproductive Justice." In *Making Kin, Not Population*, edited by Adele Clarke and Donna Haraway. Prickly Paradigm Press, 2018.

Benton, Adia, and Sa'ed Atshan. "'Even War Has Rules': On Medical Neutrality and Legitimate Non-Violence." *Culture, Medicine, and Psychiatry* 40, no. 2 (2016): 151–58.

Berda, Yael. "Managing 'Dangerous Populations': How Colonial Emergency Laws Shape Citizenship." *Security Dialogue* 51, no. 6 (2020): 1–22.

Berger-Polsky, Alexandra, Nihaya Daoud, Ruslan Sergienko, Eyal Sheiner, Ilana Shoham-Vardi, and Natalya Bilenko. "Polygamy and Birth Outcomes Among Bedouin Women of the Negev: The Contribution of Social Determinants and Pregnancy Complications." *Health Care for Women International* 41, no. 1 (2020): 54–74.

Berlant, Lauren. "The Commons: Infrastructures for Troubling Times." *Environment and Planning D: Society and Space* 34, no. 4 (2016): 393–419.

Berlant, Lauren. *Cruel Optimism.* Duke University Press, 2011.

Bhambra, Gurminder K. *Connected Sociologies.* Bloomsbury, 2014.

Bhandar, Brenna. *Colonial Lives of Property: Law, Land, and Racial Regimes of Ownership.* Duke University Press, 2018.

Bhandar, Brenna, and Rafeef Ziadah. "Acts and Omissions: Framing Settler Colonialism in Palestine Studies." *Jadaliyya*, January 14, 2016.

Bhatia, Rajani. "Figuring India and China in the Constitution of Globally Stratified Sex Selection." *Asian Bioethics Review* 13 (2021): 23–37.

Birenbaum-Carmeli, Daphna. "Cheaper Than a Newcomer: On the Political Economy of IVF in Israel." *Sociology of Health and Illness* 26, no. 7 (2004): 897–924.

Birenbaum-Carmeli, Daphna. "Health Journalism in the Service of Power: 'Moral Complacency' and the Hebrew Media in the Gaza–Israel Conflict." *Sociology of Health and Illness* 36, no. 4 (2014): 613–28.

Birenbaum-Carmeli, Daphna. "Thirty-Five Years of Assisted Reproductive Technologies in Israel." *Reproductive Biomedicine and Society Online* 2 (2016): 16–23.

Birenbaum-Carmeli, Daphna, and Yoram S. Carmeli, eds. *Kin, Gene, Community: Reproductive Technologies Among Jewish Israelis.* Berghahn Books, 2010.

Birenbaum-Carmeli, Daphna, and Ronit Kochman-Haimov. "Fertility Treatments Under Semi/Occupation: The Case of East Jerusalem." *F, V & V IN OBGYN* (2010): 35–42.
Bishara, Amahl. *Crossing a Line: Laws, Violence, and Roadblocks to Palestinian Political Expression*. Stanford University Press, 2022.
Bishara, Amahl. "Mobilizing Resistance: Israel's Racist Walls of Separation." *Anthropology Now* 9, no. 3 (2017): 38–46.
Bishara, Amahl. "My Impossible Ethnography: Gaza's Great March of Return." Insaniyaat Society of Palestinian Anthropologists, July 2023.
Blatman, Naama, and Areej Sabbagh-Khoury. "The Presence of the Absence: Indigenous Palestinian Urbanism in Israel." *International Journal of Urban and Regional Research* 47, no. 1 (2022): 119–28.
Boas, Hagai, Shai Lavi, Yael Hashiloni-Dolev, Dani Filc, and Nadav Davidovitch, eds. *Bioethics and Biopolitics in Israel: Socio-Legal, Political and Empirical Analysis*. Cambridge University Press, 2018.
Boehm, Omri. *Haifa Republic: A Democratic Future for Israel*. New York Review of Books, 2021.
Bonilla-Silva, Eduardo. "Feeling Race: Theorizing the Racial Economy of Emotions." *American Sociological Review* 84, no. 1 (2019).
Bouquet, Ben, Manal Massalha, Juliana Nassar, Bashaer al-Natsheh, and Rita Giacaman. "Housing Precariousness and Health: A Mixed-Methods Study into Households Affected by Displacements and Demolitions in East Jerusalem." *The Lancet* 399, no. S35 (2022).
Bridges, Khiara M. *Reproducing Race: An Ethnography of Pregnancy as a Site of Racialization*. University of California Press, 2011.
Briggs, Laura. *How All Politics Became Reproductive Politics: From Welfare Reform to Foreclosure to Trump*. University of California Press, 2017.
Briggs, Laura. *Reproducing Empire: Race, Sex, Science, and US Imperialism in Puerto Rico*. University of California Press, 2003.
Brown, Lundy. *Breathing Race into the Machine: The Surprising Career of the Spirometer from Plantation to Genetics*. University of Minnesota Press, 2014.
Buch Segal, Lotte. "The Burden of Being Exemplary: National Sentiments, Awkward Witnessing, and Womanhood in Occupied Palestine." *Journal of the Royal Anthropological Institute* 21, no. 1 (2015): 30–46.
Buch Segal, Lotte. *No Place for Grief: Martyrs, Prisoners, and Mourning in Contemporary Palestine*. University of Pennsylvania Press, 2016.
Burawoy, Michael. "Why and How Should Sociologists Speak Out on Palestine?" *Sociological Review* 73, no. 2 (2025): 49–260.
Burke, Jason, and Julian Borger. "Gaza Will Be Entirely Destroyed, Israeli Minister Says." *The Guardian*, May 6, 2025.
Busbridge, Rachel. "Israel-Palestine and the Settler Colonial 'Turn': From Interpretation to Decolonization." *Theory, Culture and Society* 35, no. 1 (2018): 91–115.
Butler, Judith. *Bodies That Matter: On the Discursive Limits of Sex*. Routledge, 1996.

Buttu, Diana. "A 'Magic Pill' Made Israeli Violence Invisible. We Need to Stop Swallowing It." *The Guardian*, October 6, 2025.
Callaci, Emily. "'Injectable Development': Depo-Provera and Creation of the Global South." *Radical History Review* 131 (2018): 82–104.
Carsten, Janet. "Substance and Relationality: Blood in Contexts." *Annual Review of Anthropology* 40 (2011): 19–35.
Chen, Mel Y. *Animacies: Biopolitics, Racial Mattering, and Queer Affect*. Duke University Press, 2012.
Cheung, Kylie. "Miscarriages in Gaza Have Increased 300% under Israeli Bombing." *Jezebel*, January 17, 2024.
Clarno, Andy. "The Thorns That Exist and Resist: Black-Palestine Solidarity in the Twenty-First Century." *Middle East Report* 282 (2017): 2–7.
Cohen, Yinon, and Neve Gordon. "Israel's Biospatial Politics: Territory, Demography, and Effective Control." *Public Culture* 30, no. 2 (2018): 199–220.
Colen, Shellee. "Like a Mother to Them: Stratified Reproduction and West Indian Childcare Workers and Employers in New York." In *Conceiving the New World Order: The Global Politics of Reproduction*, edited by Faye D. Ginsburg and Rayna Rapp. University of California Press, 1995.
Collier, Stephen J., and Aihwa Ong. "Global Assemblages, Anthropological Problems." In *Global Assemblages: Technology, Politics, and Ethics as Anthropological Problems*, edited by Stephen J. Collier and Aihwa Ong. Blackwell Publishing, 2005.
Contreras, Jesse D., Haneen Shibli, Marisa C. Eisenberg, et al. "Racial and Ethnic Disparities in Access to Safe Water and Sanitation in High-Income Countries: A Case Study Among the Arab-Bedouins of Southern Israel." *Journal of Water, Sanitation and Hygiene for Development* 13, no. 9 (2023): 611–24.
Coulthard, Glen Sean. *Red Skin, White Masks: Rejecting the Colonial Politics of Recognition*. University of Minnesota Press, 2014.
Daher-Nashif, Suhad. "Colonial Management of Death: To Be or Not to Be Dead in Palestine." *Current Sociology* 69, no. 7 (2020).
Dame-Griff, E. Cassandra. "The Future Is Brown . . . And Fat: Population Control, Latina/O/X 'Health' and Protecting the Future Nation-State." *Fat Studies* 9, no. 3 (2020): 220–33.
Danforth-Appell, Jon. "Against Zionist Realism." *Jewish Currents*, April 9, 2025.
Daoud, Nihaya, Sirat Abu-Hamad, Alexandra Berger-Polsky, Nadav Davidovitch, and Sharon Orshalimy. "Mechanisms for Racial Separation and Inequitable Maternal Care in Hospital Maternity Wards." *Social Science and Medicine* 292 no. 114551 (2022).
Daoud, Nihaya, Ketan Shankardass, Patricia O'Campo, Kim Anderson, and Ayman K. Agbaria. "Internal Displacement and Health Among the Palestinian Minority in Israel." *Social Science and Medicine* 74, no. 8 (2012): 1163–71.
Dardona, Zuhair, Mounia Amane, Ayman Dardona, and Samia Boussaa. "Health and Environmental Impacts of Gaza Conflict (2023–2024): A Review." *One Health Bulletin* 5, no. 1 (2024): 1–12.

Davenport, Beverly Ann. "Witnessing and the Medical Gaze: How Medical Students Learn to See at a Free Clinic for the Homeless." *Medical Anthropology Quarterly* 14, no. 3 (2000): 310–27.

Davies, Thom. "Slow Violence and Toxic Geographies: 'Out of Sight' to Whom?" *Environment and Planning C: Politics and Space* 40, no. 2 (2022): 409–27.

Davin, Anna. "Imperialism and Motherhood." *History Workshop* 5 (1978): 9–65.

Davis, Angela. *Freedom Is a Constant Struggle: Ferguson, Palestine, and the Foundations of a Movement.* Haymarket Books, 2016.

Davis, Angela *Women, Race, & Class.* Random House, 1981.

Davis, Dána-Ain. "Obstetric Racism: The Racial Politics of Pregnancy, Labor, and Birthing." *Medical Anthropology* 38, no. 7 (2019): 560–73.

Davis, Dána-Ain. "Reproducing While Black: The Crisis of Black Maternal Health, Obstetric Racism and Assisted Reproductive Technology." *Reproductive BioMedicine and Society Online* 11 (2020): 56– 64.

Davis, Dána-Ain. *Reproductive Injustice: Racism, Pregnancy, and Premature Birth.* New York University Press, 2019.

Dawber, Alistair. "Babies Behind Bars: A Palestinian Fertility Doctor Has Become an Unlikely Hero by Helping Women Conceive—Even Though Their Husbands Are in Jail." *The Independent*, June 19, 2013.

Deutscher, Penelope. "Foucault's History of Sexuality, Volume I. Re-Reading Its Reproduction." *Theory, Culture and Society* 29, no. 1 (2012): 119–37.

Donath, Orna. "Regretting Motherhood: A Sociopolitical Analysis." *Signs: Journal of Women in Culture and Society* 40, no. 2 (2015): 343–67.

Dow, Katie, and Janelle Lamoreaux. "Situated Kinmaking and the Population 'Problem.'" *Environmental Humanities* 12, no. 2 (2020): 475–91.

Du Bois, W. E. B. *The Souls of Black Folk.* A. C. McClurg and Co, 1903.

Easterling, Keller. *Extrastatecraft: The Power of Infrastructure Space.* Verso, 2014.

Echchaibi, Nabil. "A Scream for Gaza." *Critical Sociology* 50, no. 6 (2024): 1021–24.

Efrati, Ido. "Arab-Israeli Doctor Leaves Job After Being Wrongly Accused of Supporting Terrorism." *Haaretz*, December 20, 2023.

Eghbariah, Rabea. "The Two-State Solution Is a Delusion." *The Guardian*, June 12, 2025.

El-Kurd, Mohammed. "Jewish Settlers Stole My House. It's Not My Fault They're Jewish." *Mondoweiss*, September 26, 2023.

El-Kurd, Mohammed. *Perfect Victims: And the Politics of Appeal.* Haymarket Books, 2025.

Elia, Nada. *Greater Than the Sum of Our Parts. Feminism, Inter/Nationalism, and Palestine.* Pluto, 2023.

Elnakib, Shatha, Mollie Fair, Elke Mayrhofer, Mohamed Afifi, and Zeina Jamaluddine. "Pregnant Women in Gaza Require Urgent Protection." *The Lancet*, 403, no. 10423 (2024).

Erakat, Noura. "Geographies of Intimacy: Contemporary Renewals of Black–Palestinian Solidarity." *American Quarterly* 72, no. 2 (2020): 471–96.

Erakat, Noura. "Grieving Palestinian Life." *Jadaliyya*, 2023.
Erakat, Noura. *Justice for Some: Law and the Question of Palestine*. Stanford: Stanford University Press, 2019.
Erakat, Noura. "Whiteness as Property in Israel: Revival, Rehabilitation, and Removal." *Harvard Journal on Racial and Ethnic Justice* (2015).
Erakat, Noura, and Marc Lamont Hill. "Black-Palestinian Transnational Solidarity: Renewals, Returns, and Practice." *Journal of Palestine Studies* 48, no. 4 (2019).
Fanon, Frantz. *A Dying Colonialism*. Monthly Review Press, 1965.
Feldman, Keith P. *A Shadow Over Palestine: The Imperial Life of Race in America*. University of Minnesota Press, 2015.
Ferrero, Laura. "Palestinian Sperm-Smuggling: Fatherhood, Political Struggle, and Israeli Prisons." In *Arab Masculinities. Anthropological Reconceptions in Precarious Times*, edited by Konstantina Isidoros and Marcia C. Inhorn. Indiana University Press, 2022.
Fezehai, Malin. "The Disappeared Children of Israel." *New York Times*, February 20, 2019.
Flaschenberg, Nimrod, and Alma Itzhaky. "How October 7 Transformed Israeli Society." *Jacobin Magazine*, October 7, 2024.
Fortier, Corinne. "Blood, Sperm and the Embryo in Sunni Islam and in Mauritania: Milk Kinship, Descent and Medically Assisted Procreation." *Body and Society* 13, no. 3 (2007): 15–36.
Fortier, Corinne. "Religious and Non-Religious Issues of Medically Assisted Reproduction in France: Sexuality, Incest and Descent." *Reproductive Biomedicine and Society Online* 11 (2020): 73–81.
Foucault, Michel. *Society Must Be Defended: Lectures at the College De France, 1975–76*. Picador, 2003 [1976].
Franklin, Sarah. *Biological Relatives: IVF, Stem Cells, and the Future of Kinship*. Duke University Press, 2013.
Franklin, Sarah. *Embodied Progress: A Cultural Account of Assisted Conception*. Routledge, 1997.
Franklin, Sarah. *Reproducing Reproduction: Kinship, Power, and Technological Innovation*. University of Pennsylvania Press, 1998.
Franklin, Sarah, and Marcia C. Inhorn. "Introduction. Symposium: IVF—Global Histories." *Reproductive Biomedicine and Society Online* 2 (2016): 1–7.
Ftouni, Layal. "'They Make Death, and I'm the Labor of Life': Palestinian Prisoners' Sperm Smuggling as an Affirmation of Life." *Critical Times* 7, no. 1 (2024): 94–109.
Ghoddousi, Pooya, and Sam Page. "Using Ethnography and Assemblage Theory in Political Geography." *Geography Compass* 14, no. e12533 (2020).
Giacaman, Rita. "Reflections on the Meaning of 'Resilience' in the Palestinian Context." *Journal of Public Health* 42, no. 3 (2019): e369–e73.
Giacaman, Rita, Hannah F. Abdul-Rahim, and Laura Wick. "Health Sector Reform in the Occupied Palestinian Territories (OPT): Targeting the Forest or the Trees?" *Health Policy Plan* 18, no. 1 (2003): 59–67.

Giacaman, Rita, and Penny Johnson. "'Our Life Is Prison': The Triple Captivity of Wives and Mothers of Palestinian Political Prisoners." *Journal of Middle East Women's Studies* 9, no. 3 (2013): 54–80.

Gilmore, Ruth Wilson. *Abolition Geography: Essays Towards Liberation.* Verso, 2022.

Gilmore, Ruth Wilson. *Golden Gulag: Prisons, Surplus, Crisis, and Opposition in Globalizing California.* University of California Press, 2007.

Gilroy, Paul. *The Black Atlantic: Modernity and Double Consciousness.* Harvard University Press, 1993.

Glissant, Édouard. *Poetics of Relation.* University of Michigan Press, 2010.

Goldberg, David Theo. "Racial Palestinianization." In *Thinking Palestine*, edited by Ronit Lentin. Zed 2008.

Goldberg, David Theo. *The Threat of Race: Reflections on Racial Neoliberalism.* Blackwell Publishing, 2009.

Goodfriend, Sophia. "Algorithmic State Violence: Automated Surveillance and Palestinian Dispossession in Hebron's Old City." *International Journal of Middle East Studies* 55, no. 3 (2023): 461–78.

Goodfriend, Sophia. "Israel's Security Theater." *Dissent Magazine*, October 8, 2024.

Gooldin, Sigal. "'Emotional Rights,' Moral Reasoning, and Jewish-Arab Alliances in the Regulation of In-Vitro-Fertilization in Israel: Theorizing the Unexpected Consequences of Assisted Reproductive Technologies." *Social Science and Medicine* 83, no. 1 (2013): 90–98.

Gordon, Avery. *Ghostly Matters: Haunting and the Sociological Imagination.* University of Minnesota Press, 2008.

Gowayed, Heba. "On Parenthood and Genocide." *In These Times*, January 15, 2024.

Gowayed, Heba. *Refuge: How the State Shapes Human Potential.* Princeton University Press, 2022.

Griffiths, Mark, and Jemima Repo. "Women and Checkpoints in Palestine." *Security Dialogue* 52, no. 3 (2021): 249–65.

The Guardian. "Any Palestinian Is Exposed to Monitoring by the Israeli Big Brother." September 12, 2014.

Gunaratnam, Yasmin. "Explosive Legacies: Gaza and Colonial Aphasia." *Sociological Review* 73, no. 2 (2025): 249–60.

Gunaratnam, Yasmin. "Infrastructures of Racial Violence, Health and Debility." *Sociology of Health and Illness* 43 (2021): 1845–50.

Hajjar, Lisa, and Basil Farraj. "Israel Is Waging War on Palestinian Prisoners." *Middle East Research and Information Project*, October 16, 2024.

Hall, Stuart. "Race, Articulation, and Societies Structured in Dominance." In *Sociological Theories: Race and Colonialism*, edited by UNESCO. UNESCO, 1980.

Hamamra, Bilal, Fayez Mahamid, and Dana Bdier. "Surviving Trauma: Gazan Women's Mental Health During Genocide." *Discover Public Health* 22, no. 229 (2025).

Hamayel, Layaly, Doaa Hammoudeh, and Lynn Welchman. "Reproductive Health and Rights in East Jerusalem: The Effects of Militarisation and Biopolitics on the

Experiences of Pregnancy and Birth of Palestinians Living in the Kufr ʿAqab Neighbourhood." *Reproductive Health Matters* 25, no. 1 (2017): 87–95.
Hamdan, Mohammed. "'Every Sperm Is Sacred': Palestinian Prisoners, Smuggled Semen, and Derrida's Prophecy." *International Journal of Middle East Studies* 51 (2019): 525–45.
Hammami, Rema. "Destabilizing Mastery and the Machine: Palestinian Agency and Gendered Embodiment at Israeli Military Checkpoints." *Current Anthropology* 60, no. 19 (2019): 87–97.
Hammoudeh, Doaa, Layaly Hamayel, and Lynn Welchman. "Beyond the Physicality of Space: East Jerusalem, Kufr ʿAqab, and the Politics of Everyday Suffering." *Jerusalem Quarterly*, no. 65 (2016).
Harcourt, Wendy, Silke Heumann, and Aniseh Asya. "Introduction." In *Bodies in Resistance: Gender and Sexual Politics in the Age of Neoliberalism*, edited by Wendy Harcourt. Palgrave Macmillan, 2016.
Hartman, Saidiya. "The Belly of the World: A Note on Black Women's Labors." *Souls* 18, no. 1 (2016): 166–73.
Hartman, Saidiya. *Scenes of Subjection: Terror, Slavery, and Self-Making in Nineteenth-Century America*. Oxford University Press, 1997.
Hartman, Saidiya. *Wayward Lives, Beautiful Experiments—Intimate Histories of Social Upheaval*. W. W. Norton and Company, 2019.
Hashiloni-Dolev, Yael. "The Effect of Jewish-Israeli Family Ideology on Policy Regarding Reproductive Technologies." In Boas, *Bioethics and Biopolitics in Israel*.
Hasso, Frances S. *Buried in the Red Dirt: Race, Reproduction, and Death in Modern Palestine*. Cambridge University Press, 2021.
Hawari, Yara. "The Political Marginalization of Palestinian Women in the West Bank." *Al-Shabaka*, July 28, 2019.
Hayes, Endia Louise, Ashley Hollingshead, Jomaira Salas, and Brooklynn K. Hitchens. "Nothing About Us, Without Us: Reinscribing Black Feminism in Sociology." In *Black Feminist Sociology: Perspectives and Praxis*, edited by Zakiya Luna and Whitney N. Laster Pirtle. Routledge, 2021.
Hazkani, Shay, and Tamir Sorek. "Yes to Transfer: 82% of Jewish Israelis Back Expelling Gazans." *Haaretz*, May 28, 2025.
Hill, Marc Lamont. "From Ferguson to Palestine." *Biography* 41 (2018): 942–57.
Hirsch, Dafna. "'We Are Here to Bring the West, Not Only to Ourselves': Zionist Occidentalism and the Discourse of Hygiene in Mandate Palestine." *International Journal of Middle East Studies* 41, no. 4 (2009): 577–94.
Holzberg, Billy. *Affective Bordering: Race, Deservingness and the Emotional Politics of Migration Control*. Manchester University Press, 2024.
hooks, bell. *Feminist Theory from Margin to Center*. South End Press, 1983.
Hovel, Revital. "Israeli Hospitals Admit to Segregating Jewish and Arab Women at Maternity Wards." *Haaretz*, April 24, 2019.
Hovel, Revital, and Ido Efrati. "In Israeli Maternity Wards, Jewish and Arab Segregation Is the Default." *Haaretz*, May 18, 2018.

Human Rights Watch. *Israel: Palestinian Healthcare Workers Tortured*. August 26, 2024.
Ihmoud, Sarah. "Born Palestinian, Born Black: Anti-Blackness and the Womb of Zionist Settler Colonialism." In *Antiblackness*, edited by Joao Costa Vargas and Moon-Kie Jung. Duke University Press, 2021.
Ihmoud, Sarah. "Countering Reproductive Genocide in Gaza: Palestinian Women's Testimonies." *Native American and Indigenous Studies* 12, no. 1 (2025): 33–53.
Ihmoud, Sarah. "Mohammed Abu-Khdeir and the Politics of Racial Terror in Occupied Jerusalem." *borderlands* 14, no. 1 (2014).
Ihmoud, Sarah. "Murabata: The Politics of Staying in Place." *Feminist Studies* 45, no. 2/3 (2019): 512–40.
Ihmoud, Sarah. "On Love, the Palestinian Way: Kinship, Care and Abolition in Palestinian Feminist Praxis." *State Crime Journal* 12, no. 2 (2024): 206–24.
Ihmoud, Sarah. "Palestinian Feminism: Analytics, Praxes and Decolonial Futures." *Feminist Anthropology* 3 (2022): 284–98.
Ihmoud, Sarah. "Policing the Intimate: Israel's Anti-Miscegenation Movement." *Jerusalem Quarterly* 75 (2018): 91–104.
Inhorn, Marcia C., and Soraya Tremayne, eds. *Islam and Assisted Reproductive Technologies: Sunni and Shia Perspectives*. Berghahn, 2012.
Irfan, Bilal, Abdallah Abu Shammala, and Khaled Saleh. "Will There Be a Future for Newborns in Gaza?" *The Lancet* 404 (2024): 1725–26.
Ivry, Tsipy. *Embodying Culture: Pregnancy in Japan and Israel*. Rutgers University Press, 2010.
Jefferis, Danielle C. "The 'Center of Life' Policy: Institutionalizing Statelessness in East Jerusalem." *Jerusalem Quarterly* 50 (2012): 94–103.
Jefferis, Danielle C. "Institutionalizing Statelessness: The Revocation of Residency Rights of Palestinians in East Jerusalem." *International Journal of Refugee Law* 24, no. 2 (2012): 202–30.
Johnson, Penny. "Living Together in a Nation of Fragments: Dynamics of Kin, Place, and Nation." In *Living Palestine: Family Survival, Resistance, and Mobility Under Occupation*, edited by Lisa Taraki. Syracuse University Press, 2006.
Johnson, Penny, and Eileen Kuttab. "Where Have All the Women (and Men) Gone? Reflections on Gender and the Second Palestinian Intifada." *Feminist Review* 69 (2001): 21–43.
Kahn, Susan Martha. *Reproducing Jews: A Cultural Account of Assisted Conception in Israel*. Duke University Press, 2000.
Kanaaneh, Rhoda Ann. *Birthing the Nation: Strategies of Palestinian Women in Israel*. University of California Press, 2002.
Kayali, Liyana. *Palestinian Women and Popular Resistance: Perceptions, Attitudes, and Strategies*. Routledge, 2021.
Keane, Fergal. "Gaza Subjected to Forced Starvation, Top UN Official Tells BBC." *BBC*, May 29, 2025.
Kedar, Alexandre, Ahmad Amara, and Oren Yiftachel. *Emptied Lands: A Legal Geography of Bedouin Rights in the Negev*. Stanford University Press, 2018.

Kelley, Robin D. G. "From the River to the Sea to Every Mountain Top: Solidarity as Worldmaking." *Journal of Palestine Studies* 48, no. 4 (2019): 69–91.
Kelly, Jennifer Lynn. *Invited to Witness: Solidarity Tourism Across Occupied Palestine*. Duke University Press, 2023.
Kelly, Jennifer Lynn. "Subjection and Performance: Tourism, Witnessing, and Acts of Refusal in Palestine." *Feminist Formations* 32, no. 2 (2020): 79–110.
Kemp, Adriana. "'Dangerous Populations': State Territoriality and the Constitution of National Minorities." In *Boundaries and Belonging: States and Societies in the Struggle to Shape Identities and Local Practices*, edited by Joel S. Migdal. Cambridge University Press, 2009.
Keshet, Yael, and Ariela Popper-Giveon. "Neutrality in Medicine and Health Professionals from Ethnic Minority Groups: The Case of Arab Health Professionals in Israel." *Social Science and Medicine* 174 (2017): 35–42.
Khalidi, Rashid. *The Hundred Years' War on Palestine: A History of Settler Colonialism and Resistance, 1917–2017*. Profile Books, 2020.
Khalidi, Rashid. "Israel: A Carceral State." *Journal of Palestine Studies* 43, no. 4 (2014).
Khamaisi, Rassem. "Jerusalem Demography: History, Transitions, and Forecasts." *Jerusalem Quarterly* 82 (2020): 110–29.
Khatib, Rasha, Martin McKee, and Salim Yusuf. "Counting the Dead in Gaza: Difficult but Essential." *The Lancet* 404, no. 10449 (2024): 237–38.
Khouri, Lama Z. "Gaza's Broken Lullaby: Genocidal Unchilding and the Impossibility of Mothering." *Studies in Gender and Sexuality* 25, no. 3 (2024): 178–87.
Kinani, Haneen, Dana Moss, and Ghada Majadli. "Challenges in Accessing Care for Palestinian Cancer Patients in Gaza During the Covid-19 Crisis." *BMJ Global Health*, July 4, 2021.
Klein, Naomi. "How Israel Has Made Trauma a Weapon of War." *The Guardian*, October 5, 2024.
Korteweg, Anna, and Gökçe Yurdakul. "Liberal Feminism and Postcolonial Difference: Debating Headscarves in France, the Netherlands, and Germany." *Social Compass* 68, no. 3 (2020): 410–29.
Kotef, Hagar. *The Colonizing Self: Or, Home and Homelessness in Israel/Palestine*. Duke University Press, 2020.
LaDuke, Winona, and Deborah Cowen. "Beyond Wiindigo Infrastructure." *South Atlantic Quarterly* 119, no. 2 (2020).
Larkin, Brian. "The Politics and Poetics of Infrastructure." *Annual Review of Anthropology* 42 (2013): 327–43.
Lemke, Thomas. *Biopolitics: An Advanced Introduction*. New York University Press, 2011.
Lentin, Ronit. *Traces of Racial Exception: Racializing Israeli Settler Colonialism*. Bloomsbury, 2018.
Lewis, Sophie. *Enemy Feminisms: Terfs, Policewomen, and Girlbosses Against Liberation*. Haymarket Books, 2025.
Lewis, Sophie. *Full Surrogacy Now: Feminism Against Family*. Verso, 2019.

Lira, Natalie. *Laboratory of Deficiency: Sterilization and Confinement in California, 1900–1950s*. University of California Press, 2021.
Lober, Brooke. "Adrienne Rich's 'Politics of Location,' US Jewish Feminism, and the Question of Palestine." *Women's Studies* 46, no. 7 (2017): 663–83.
Lowe, Lisa. *The Intimacies of Four Continents*. Duke University Press, 2015.
Lubin, Alex. *Geographies of Liberation: The Making of an Afro-Arab Political Imaginary*. University of North Carolina Press, 2014.
Lugones, Maria. "Toward a Decolonial Feminism." *Hypatia* 25, no. 4 (2010): 742–59.
Luna, Zakiya. "Black Celebrities, Reproductive Justice and Queering Family: An Exploration." *Reproductive BioMedicine and Society Online* 7 (2018): 91–100.
Madhok, Sumi. "A Critical Reflexive Politics of Location, 'Feminist Debt' and Thinking from the Global South." *European Journal of Women's Studies* 27, no. 4 (2020): 394–412.
Madmoni-Gerber, Shoshana. "From Mainstream to Social Media: The Kidnapped Yemeni Babies Affair in Israel and the Fight for Memory and Justice." *Journal of Holy Land and Palestine Studies* 21, no. 1 (2022): 1–20.
Magloire, Marina. "Moving Towards Life." *Los Angeles Review of Books*, August 7, 2024.
Maguire, Mark, and Ursula Rao. "Introduction: Bodies as Evidence." In *Bodies as Evidence: Security, Knowledge, and Power*, edited by Mark Maguire, Ursula Rao, and and Nils Zurawski. Duke University Press, 2018.
Mahdawi, Arwa. "An Israeli Bomb Destroyed 4,000 Embryos at a Gaza IVF Centre. Where Is the Outrage?" *The Guardian*, April 20, 2024.
Majadli, Ghada. "Healthcare in the Occupied Territory During Covid-19." In *Covid-19 Report: A Policy of Neglect: The First 100 Days of Covid-19 in Israel's Healthcare System*, edited by Yotam Rosner, Hadaz Ziv, Anat Litvin, Zoe Gutzeit, and Ghada Majadli. Physicians for Human Rights Israel, 2020.
Majadli, Ghada. "Silenced Voices and Militarized Spaces: The Aftermath of October 7th & the Persecution of Palestinian Physicians in Israeli Hospitals." In *Palestine Papers*. Mada al-Carmel: Arab Center for Applied Social Research, February 2025.
Majadli, Ghada, James Smith, Ghassan Abu-Sittah, and Rasha Khoury. "Why Is the New England Journal of Medicine Promoting 'Health Bridges' While Gaza's Hospitals Burn?" *Middle East Eye*, April 10, 2025.
Majadli, Ghada, and Yotam Rosner. *Responsibility Shirked: Israel and the Right to Health in the Occupied West Bank During Covid-19*. Physicians for Human Rights Israel, 2021.
Marey-Sarwan, Ibtisam, Dorit Roer-Strier, and Roni Strier. "Blurring the Borders with Anzaldua in Context-Informed, Anti-Oppressive Research: The Case of Bedouin Women." *British Journal of Social Work* (2020): 1–18.
Martin, Emily. "The Egg and the Sperm: How Science Has Constructed a Romance Based on Stereotypical Male-Female Roles." *Signs* 16, no. 3 (1991): 485–501.
Masalha, Nur. *The Bible and Zionism: Invented Traditions, Archaeology and Post-Colonialism in Palestine-Israel*. Zed Books, 2007.

Masalha, Nur. *The Palestine Nakba: Decolonising History, Narrating the Subaltern, Reclaiming Memory*. Zed Books, 2012.

Masarwa, Lubna. "Israeli Doctor Compared Killing Palestinians in Gaza to 'Eliminating Cockroaches.'" *Middle East Eye*, May 19, 2025.

Massey, Doreen. "Places and Their Pasts." *History Workshop Journal* 39 (1995): 182–92.

Mbembe, Achille. "Bodies as Borders." *From the European South* 4 (2019): 5–18.

Mbembe, Achille. "Necropolitics." *Public Culture* 15, no. 1 (2003): 11–40.

McClintock, Anne. *Imperial Leather: Race, Gender, and Sexuality in the Colonial Contest*. Routledge, 1995.

McKittrick, Katherine. *Dear Science and Other Stories*. Duke University Press, 2021.

Meari, Lena. "Re-Signifying 'Sexual' Colonial Power Techniques: The Experiences of Palestinian Women Political Prisoners." In *Rethinking Gender in Revolutions and Resistance: Lessons from the Arab World*, edited by Maha El Said, Lena Meari, and Nicola Pratt. Bloomsbury, 2015.

Medien, Kathryn. "Israeli Settler Colonialism, 'Humanitarian Warfare,' and Sexual Violence in Palestine." *International Feminist Journal of Politics* 13, no. 5 (2021): 698–719.

Meghji, Ali. "From Public Sociology to Sociological Publics: The Importance of Reverse Tutelage to Social Theory." *Sociological Theory* 42, no. 2 (2024): 114–36.

Middle East Monitor. "Israeli President Herzog Says the War on Gaza Is Not Only Between Israel and Hamas, but It Is a War 'Intended to Save Western Civilisation.'" December 6, 2023.

Mikdashi, Maya. "Can Palestinian Men Be Victims? Gendering Israel's War on Gaza." *Jadaliyya*, July 23, 2014.

Mikdashi, Maya. *Sextarianism: Sovereignty, Secularism, and the State in Lebanon*. Stanford University Press, 2022.

Mikdashi, Maya, and Jasbir K. Puar. "Queer Theory and Permanent War." *GLQ: A Journal of Lesbian and Gay Studies* 22, no. 2 (2016): 215–22.

Mitra, Sayani, Silke Schicktanz, and Tulsi Patel. *Cross-Cultural Comparisons on Surrogacy and Egg Donation: Interdisciplinary Perspectives from India, Germany and Israel*. Palgrave Macmillan, 2018.

Morgan, Jennifer L. *Laboring Women: Reproduction and Gender in New World Slavery*. University of Pennsylvania Press, 2004.

Morgensen, Scott Lauria. "The Biopolitics of Settler Colonialism: Right Here, Right Now." *Settler Colonial Studies* 1, no. 1 (2011): 52–76.

Morgensen, Scott Lauria. "Theorising Gender, Sexuality and Settler Colonialism: An Introduction." *Settler Colonial Studies* 2, no. 2 (2012): 2–22.

Moses, Dirk. *Genocide and Settler Society: Frontier Violence and Stolen Indigenous Children in Australian History*. Berghahn Books, 2004.

Mousa, Aseel, and Emma Graham-Harrison. "War Halts IVF Treatment in Gaza as Parents Mourn 'Miracle' Children." *The Guardian*, August 13, 2024.

Murphy, Michelle. *The Economization of Life*. Duke University Press, 2017.

Murphy, Michelle. *Seizing the Means of Reproduction: Entanglements of Feminism, Health, and Technoscience*. Duke University Press, 2012.
Naber, Nadine. "Arab and Black Feminisms: Joint Struggle and Transnational Anti-Imperialist Activism." In *Unequal Sisters: A Revolutionary Reader in US Women's History*, edited by Stephanie Narrow, Kim Cary Warren, Judy Tzu-Chun Wu, and Vicki L Ruiz. Routledge, 2024.
Naber, Nadine. "Reproductive Justice from Turtle Island to Palestine." *Feminist Studies* 49, no. 2 (2023): 545–46.
Naber, Nadine. "'The US and Israel Make the Connections for Us': Anti-Imperialism and Black-Palestinian Solidarity." *Critical Ethnic Studies* 3, no. 2 (2017): 15–30.
Nabulsi, Jamal. "Reclaiming Palestinian Indigenous Sovereignty." *Journal of Palestine Studies* 52, no. 2 (2023): 24–42.
Nahman, Michal Rachel. "Reverse Traffic: Intersecting Inequalities in Human Egg Donation." *Reproductive BioMedicine Online* 23 (2011): 626–33.
Nahman, Michal Rachel. *Extractions: An Ethnography of Reproductive Tourism*. Palgrave Macmillan, 2013.
Nahman, Michal Rachel. "Repro-Migration: Lessons from the Early Days of Cross-Border Migration Between Israel and Romania." In *Cross-Cultural Comparisons on Surrogacy and Egg Donation*, edited by Sayani Mitra, Silke Schicktanz, and Tulsi Patel. Palgrave Macmillan, 2018.
Nasasra, Mansour. "The Ongoing Judaisation of the Naqab and the Struggle for Recognising the Indigenous Rights of the Arab Bedouin People." *Settler Colonial Studies* 2, no. 1 (2021): 81–107.
Naser-Najjab, Nadia. *Covid-19 in Palestine: The Settler Colonial Context*. Bloomsbury Academic, 2024.
Nashif, Esmail al-. "Attempts at Liberation: Materializing the Body and Building Community Among Palestinian Political Captives." *Arab Studies Journal* 12/13, no. 1/2 (2004/5): 46–79.
Nassar, Maha. "Palestinian Engagement with the Black Freedom Movement Prior to 1967." *Journal of Palestine Studies* 48 (2019): 6–32.
Newman, Susan, and Michal Nahman. "Nurture Commodified? An Investigation into Commercial Human Milk Supply Chains." *Review of International Political Economy* (2020).
Nguyen, Mimi Thi. *The Gift of Freedom: War, Debt, and Other Refugee Passages*. Duke University Press, 2012.
Nguyen, Vinh. *Lived Refuge: Gratitude, Resentment, Resilience*. University of California Press, 2023.
Nguyen-Gillham, Viet, Rita Giacaman, Ghada Naser, and Will Boyce. "Normalising the Abnormal: Palestinian Youth and the Contradictions of Resilience in Protracted Conflict." *Health and Social Care in the Community* 16, no. 3 (2008): 291–98.
Nixon, Rob. *Slow Violence and the Environmentalism of the Poor*. Harvard University Press, 2011.

Ohayon, Leeor. "'Ragged Rats': London Exhibit Captures the Racism That Tore Apart Mizrahi Families." *+972 Magazine*, December 1, 2022.
Ong, Aihwa. "Scales of Exception: Experiments with Knowledge and Sheer Life in Tropical Southeast Asia." *Singapore Journal of Tropical Geography* 29, no. 2 (2008): 117–29.
Orr, Zvika, and Mark D. Fleming. "Medical Neutrality and Structural Competency in Conflict Zones: Israeli Healthcare Professionals' Reaction to Political Violence." *Global Public Health* 18, no. 1 (2023): 2171087.
Owens, Deirdre Cooper. *Medical Bondage: Race, Gender, and the Origins of American Gynecology*. University of Georgia Press, 2017.
Pasquetti, Silvia. "Experiences of Urban Militarism: Spatial Stigma, Ruins and Everyday Life." *International Journal of Urban and Regional Research* 43, no. 5 (2019): 848–69.
Patchin, Paige Marie. "Thresholds of Empire: Women, Biosecurity, and the Zika Chemical Vector Program in Puerto Rico." *Annals of the American Association of Geographers* 110, no. 4 (2020): 967–82.
Pateman, Carole. *The Sexual Contract*. Polity Press, 1988.
Pell, Stephanie. "Reproductive Decisions in the Lives of West Bank Palestinian Women: Dimensions and Contradictions." *Global Public Health* 12, no. 2 (2016): 135–55.
Perugini, Nicola, and Neve Gordon. "Medical Lawfare: The Nakba and Israel's Attacks on Palestinian Healthcare." *Journal of Palestine Studies* 53, no. 1 (2024): 68–91.
Peteet, Julie. "Closure's Temporality: The Cultural Politics of Time and Waiting." *South Atlantic Quarterly* 117 no. 1 (2018): 43–64.
Peteet, Julie. "Language Matters: Talking About Palestine." *Journal of Palestine Studies* 45, no. 2 (2016): 24–40.
Peteet, Julie. "Words as Interventions: Naming in the Palestine–Israel Conflict." *Third World Quarterly* 26, no. 1 (2005): 153–72.
Pitts-Taylor, Victoria *Mattering: Feminism, Science, and Corporeal Politics*. New York University Press, 2016.
Plonski, Sharri. "The Mobile and Carceral Logics of Haifa Port." *Politics* 44, no. 4 (2022).
Plonski, Sharri. *Palestinian Citizens of Israel: Power, Resistance and the Struggle for Space*. SOAS Palestine Studies Book Series, 2018.
Popper-Giveon, Ariela. "Preferring Patient–Physician Concordance: The Ambiguity of Implicit Ethnic Bias." *Ethnicity and Health* 26, no. 7 (2019): 1065–81.
Portugese, Jacqueline. *Fertility Policy in Israel: The Politics of Religion, Gender, and Nation*. Praeger, 1998.
Pratt, Mary Louise. *Imperial Eyes: Travel Writing and Transculturation*. Routledge, 1992.
Puar, Jasbir K. "'I Would Rather Be a Cyborg Than a Goddess': Becoming-Intersectional in Assemblage Theory." *philoSOPHIA* 2, no. 1 (2012): 49–66.
Puar, Jasbir K. *The Right to Maim: Debility, Capacity, Disability*. Duke University Press, 2017.

Puar, Jasbir K. "Spatial Debilities: Slow Life and Carceral Capitalism in Palestine." *South Atlantic Quarterly* 120, no. 2 (2021): 393–414.

Puar, Jasbir K., and Kathryn Medien. "Thinking Life, Death, and Solidarity Through Colonized Palestine." *Journal of Middle East Women's Studies* 14, no. 1 (2018): 94–103.

Puwar, Nirmal. *Space Invaders: Race, Gender and Bodies Out of Place*. Berg, 2004.

Qato, Danya M. "Introduction: Public Health and the Promise of Palestine." *Journal of Palestine Studies* 49, no. 4 (2020): 8–26.

Qutami, Loubna. "Why Feminism? Why Now? Reflections on the 'Palestine Is a Feminist Issue' Pledge." *Spectre Journal* (2021).

Qutami, Loubna, Inderpal Grewal, Caren Kaplan, et al. "The Genocidal Assault on Palestine: A Transnational Feminist Call to End Colonialism and War." *Feminist Studies* 49, no. 2/3 (2023).

Rabie, Kareem. *Palestine Is Throwing a Party and the Whole World Is Invited: Capital and State Building in the West Bank*. Duke University Press, 2021.

Rajvanshi, Astha. "What Pregnant Women Face in Gaza." *Time*, November 9, 2023.

Rapoport, Meron. "The 'Second Nakba' Government Seizes Its Moment." *+972 Magazine*, January 2, 2024.

Razack, Sherene H. "Race and Palestine." *Feminist Studies* 49, no. 2/3 (2024): 529–46.

Regev, Dana. "Israeli MK Calls for Hospital Segregation." *Deutsche Welle*, April 10, 2016.

Repo, Jemima. "Genocide and the Destruction of the Means of Social Reproduction in Gaza." *European Journal of Politics and Gender* 8, no. 2 (2024): 492–99.

Rexer, Gala. "Borderlands of Reproduction: Bodies, Borders, and Assisted Reproductive Technologies in Israel/Palestine." *Ethnic and Racial Studies* 44, no. 9 (2021): 1549–68.

Rexer, Gala. "How Race, Nationality, and Gender Shape Fieldwork and Data Collection." *ASA Political Sociology Section Newsletter*, Spring/Summer 2022.

Rexer, Gala. "The Materiality of Power and Bodily Matter(Ing): Embodied Resistance in Palestine." *Body and Society* 29, no. 4 (2023): 3–28.

Rexer, Gala. "Social Theory After* Gaza? Witnessing the Transnational Circuits of Race Making." *Social Text*, October 18, 2024.

Rexer, Gala. "Words Failed Us: Repairing Sociology's Haunted Past Means Finding New Language to Write About the Social World." *Sociological Review Magazine* (September 2022).

Rich, Adrienne "Notes Towards a Politics of Location." In *Blood, Bread and Poetry: Selected Prose 1979–1985*, edited by Adrienne Rich. Little Brown and Co., 1984.

Rifkin, Mark. *Beyond Settler Time: Temporal Sovereignty and Indigenous Self-Determination*. Duke University Press, 2017.

Rifkin, Mark. *When Did Indians Become Straight?: Kinship, the History of Sexuality, and Native Sovereignty*. Oxford University Press, 2011.

Rispler-Chaim, Vardit. "Ethical Aspects Concerning Sperm Smuggled by Muslim Palestinian 'Security Prisoners' out of Israeli Prisons." *Ethics, Medicine and Public Health* 14 (2020).
Roberts, Dorothy. *Killing the Black Body: Race, Reproduction, and the Meaning of Liberty*. Pantheon Books, 1997.
Roberts, Dorothy. "Reproductive Justice, Not Just Rights." *Dissent Magazine* (Fall 2015).
Roberts, Dorothy. "Race, Gender, and Genetic Technologies: A New Reproductive Dystopia?" *Signs: Journal of Women in Culture and Society* 34, no. 4 (2009): 783–804.
Robinson, Shira. *Citizen Strangers: Palestinians and the Birth of Israel's Liberal Settler State*. Stanford University Press, 2013.
Rooney, Kristin L., and Alice D. Domar. "The Relationship Between Stress and Infertility." *Dialogues Clinical Neuroscience* 20, no. 1 (2018): 41–47.
Rose, Nikolas. *The Politics of Life Itself: Biomedicine, Power, and Subjectivity in the Twenty-First Century*. Princeton University Press, 2007.
Rosner, Tal. *Heroes of Health: Israel's Healthcare System as a Model of Jewish-Arab Coexistence*. Israel Religious Action Center, 2016.
Ross, Loretta J., Lynn Roberts, Erika Derkas, Whitney Peoples, and Pamela Bridgewater Toure. *Radical Reproductive Justice: Foundation, Theory, Practice, Critique*. Feminist Press, 2017.
Ross, Loretta J., and Rickie Solinger. *Reproductive Justice: An Introduction*. University of California Press, 2017.
Rotem, Stephanie Shosh. "'A Never Ending Source of Wonder': The Women of Hadassah Create a Modern Medical Center in Jerusalem." *Nashim: A Journal of Jewish Women's Studies and Gender Issues* 38 (2021): 124–48.
Rothberg, Michael. *Multidirectional Memory: Remembering the Holocaust in the Age of Decolonization*. Stanford University Press, 2009.
Rouhana, Nadim N. , and Areej Sabbagh-Khoury. "Settler-Colonial Citizenship: Conceptualizing the Relationship Between Israel and Its Palestinian Citizens." *Settler Colonial Studies* 5, no. 3 (2014): 205–25.
Rouhana, Nadim N., and Nimer Sultany. "The Making of an Underclass: The Palestinian Citizens of Israel." *Israel Studies Review* 27, no. 2 (2012).
Rouhana, Nadim N., and Nimer Sultany. "Redrawing the Boundaries of Citizenship: Israel's New Hegemony." *Journal of Palestine Studies* 33, no. 1 (2003): 5–22.
Rudrappa, Sharmila. "No Reproductive Justice with No Ceasefire in Palestine." *Critical Sociology* 50, no. 6 (2024): 1025–32.
Sa'di, Ahmad. *Thorough Surveillance: The Genesis of Israeli Policies of Population Management, Surveillance and Political Control Towards the Palestinian Minority*. Manchester University Press, 2013.
Saabneh, Ameed. "Health Inequalities Between Palestinians and Jews in Israel: The Role of Extreme Spatial Segregation." *Population, Space and Place* 28, no. 5 (2021).

Sabbagh-Khoury, Areej. "Citizenship as Accumulation by Dispossession: The Paradox of Settler Colonial Citizenship." *Sociological Theory* 40, no. 2 (2022): 151–78.
Sabbagh-Khoury, Areej. *Colonizing Palestine: The Zionist Left and the Making of the Palestinian Nakba.* Stanford University Press, 2023.
Sabbagh-Khoury, Areej. "Memory for Forgetfulness: Conceptualizing a Memory Practice of Settler Colonial Disavowal." *Theory and Society* 52 (2023): 263–92.
Sabbagh-Khoury, Areej. "On the Monopoly of Violence: Ideal Types of Settler Colonial Violence and the Habitus of Sumud." *Current Sociology* 73, no. 3 (2025): 1–26.
Sabbagh-Khoury, Areej. "Settler Colonialism and the Archives of Apprehension." *Current Sociology* 72, no. 1 (2024): 25–47.
Sabbagh-Khoury, Areej. "Tracing Settler Colonialism: A Genealogy of a Paradigm in the Sociology of Knowledge Production in Israel." *Politics and Society* 50, no. 1 (2022): 44–83.
Sabbagh-Khoury, Areej. "Turning Theory to Practice: Palestine as a Sociological Question: ASA Resolution for Justice in Palestine." *Critical Sociology* 50, no. 6 (2024): 1033–37.
Said, Edward. *Orientalism*. Pantheon Books, 1987.
Said, Edward. "Zionism from the Standpoint of Its Victims." *Social Text* 1 (1979): 7–58.
Salamanca, Omar Jabary. "Assembling the Fabric of Life: When Settler Colonialism Becomes Development." *Journal of Palestine Studies* 45, no. 4 (2016): 64–80.
Salamanca, Omar Jabary, Punam Khosla, and Natasha Aruri. "It's Been 164 Days and a Long Century: Notes on Genocide, Solidarity, and Liberation." *Antipode Online*, April 11, 2024.
Salamanca, Omar Jabary, Mezna Qato, Kareem Rabie, and Sobhi Samour. "Past Is Present: Settler Colonialism in Palestine." *Settler Colonial Studies* 2, no. 1 (2012): 1–8.
Salih, Ruba, and Olaf Corry. "Displacing the Anthropocene: Colonisation, Extinction and the Unruliness of Nature in Palestine." *EPE: Nature and Space* 5, no. 1 (2022): 381–400.
Salih, Ruba, Elena Zambelli, and Lynn Welchman. "'From Standing Rock to Palestine We Are United': Diaspora Politics, Decolonization and the Intersectionality of Struggles." *Ethnic and Racial Studies* 44, no. 7 (2020).
Sánchez-Rivera, R. *Slippery Eugenics: An Introduction to the Critical Studies of Race, Gender and Coloniality*. SAGE, 2025.
Sánchez-Rivera, R. "From Preventive Eugenics to Slippery Eugenics: Population Control and Contemporary Sterilisations Targeted to Indigenous Peoples in Mexico." *Sociology of Health and Illness* 45, no. 1 (2023): 128–44.
Sayegh, Fayez. "Zionist Colonialism in Palestine (1965)." *Settler Colonial Studies* 2, no. 1 (2012): 206–25.
Schoen, Johanna. *Choice and Coercion: Birth Control, Sterilization, and Abortion in Public Health and Welfare*. University of North Carolina Press, 2005.

Schulman, Sarah. *Israel/Palestine and the Queer International.* Duke University Press, 2012.
Schultz, Susanne. "Reproducing the Nation: The New German Population Policy and the Concept of Demographization." *Distinktion: Journal of Social Theory* 16, no. 3 (2015): 337–61.
Seikaly, Sherene. "Nakba in the Age of Catastrophe." *Jadaliyya*, May 15, 2023.
Shafie, Ghadir. "Pinkwashing: Israel's International Strategy and Internal Agenda." *Kohl: A Journal for Body and Gender Research* 1, no. 1 (2015).
Shahawy, Sarrah. "The Unique Landscape of Abortion Law and Access in the Occupied Palestinian Territories." *Health and Human Rights* 21, no. 2 (2019): 47–56.
Shahawy, Sarrah, and Megan B. Diamond. "Perspectives on Induced Abortion Among Palestinian Women: Religion, Culture and Access in the Occupied Palestinian Territories." *Culture, Health and Sexuality* 20, no. 3 (2018): 289–305.
Shalev, Guy. "A Doctor's Testimony: Medical Neutrality and the Visibility of Palestinian Grievances in Jewish-Israeli Publics." *Cult Med Psychiatry* 40, no. 2 (2016): 242–62.
Shalev, Guy. "Helsinki in Zion: Hospital Ethics Committees and Political Gatekeeping in Israel/Palestine." *American Anthropologist* 124, no. 4 (2022): 688–702.
Shalhoub-Kevorkian, Nadera. "At the Limits of the Human: Reading Postraciality from Palestine." *Ethnic and Racial Studies* 39, no. 13 (2016).
Shalhoub-Kevorkian, Nadera. "Birthing in Occupied East Jerusalem: Palestinian Women's Experiences of Pregnancy and Delivery." *YWCA* (2012): 1–17.
Shalhoub-Kevorkian, Nadera. *Incarcerated Childhood and the Politics of Unchilding.* Cambridge University Press, 2019.
Shalhoub-Kevorkian, Nadera. *Militarization and Violence Against Women in Conflict Zones in the Middle East: A Palestinian Case-Study.* Cambridge University Press, 2009.
Shalhoub-Kevorkian, Nadera. "Palestinian Women and the Politics of Invisibility: Towards a Feminist Methodology." *Peace Prints: South Asian Journal of Peacebuilding* 3, no. 1 (2010).
Shalhoub-Kevorkian, Nadera. "The Politics of Birth and the Intimacies of Violence Against Palestinian Women in Occupied East Jerusalem." *British Journal of Criminology* 55, no. 6 (2015): 1187–1206.
Shalhoub-Kevorkian, Nadera. "Sacralized Politics: The Case of Occupied East Jerusalem." In *When Politics Are Sacralized: Comparative Perspectives on Religious Claims and Nationalism*, edited by Nadim N. Rouhana and Nadera Shalhoub-Kevorkian. Cambridge University Press, 2021.
Shalhoub-Kevorkian, Nadera. *Security Theology, Surveillance and the Politics of Fear.* Cambridge University Press, 2015.
Shalhoub-Kevorkian, Nadera. "Terrorism and the Birthing Body in Jerusalem." In *At the Limits of Justice: Women of Colour on Terror*, edited by Suvendrini Perera and Sherene H. Razack. University of Toronto Press, 2014.

Shalhoub-Kevorkian, Nadera, and Sarah Ihmoud. "Exiled at Home: Writing Return and the Palestinian Home." *Biography* 37, no. 2 (2014): 377–97.

Shalhoub-Kevorkian, Nadera, and Sarah Ihmoud. "Two Letters from Jerusalem: Haunted by Our Breathing." *Jerusalem Quarterly* 59 (2014): 7–11.

Shalhoub-Kevorkian, Nadera, Abeer Otman, and Rasmieyh R. Abdelnabi. "Secret Penetrabilities: Embodied Coloniality, Gendered Violence, and the Racialized Policing of Affects." *Studies in Gender and Sexuality* 22, no. 4 (2021): 266–77.

Sharif, Rana. "Bodies, Buses, and Permits: Palestinians Navigating Care." *feminists@law*, 4, no. 1 (2014).

Shehadeh, Lana, and Samira Alayan. "Between Colonialism and Patriarchy: The Role of Agency Among Palestinian Women in the West Bank and East Jerusalem." *Digest of Middle East Studies* 34, no. 1 (2025).

Shehadeh, Mtanes, and Raja Khalidi. "Impeded Development: The Political Economy of the Palestinian Arabs inside Israel." In *Decolonizing Palestinian Political Economy: De-Development and Beyond*, edited by Mandy Turner and Omar Shweiki. Palgrave Macmillan, 2014.

Shibli, Haneen, Limor Aharonson-Daniel, and Paula Feder-Bubis. "Perceptions About the Accessibility of Healthcare Services Among Ethnic Minority Women: A Qualitative Study Among Arab Bedouins in Israel." *International Journal for Equity in Health* 20 (2021).

Shibli, Haneen, Daiana Palkin, Limor Aharonson-Daniel, Nadav Davidovitch, and Nihaya Daoud. "Inequalities in Trust Levels and Compliance with Physical Distancing During Covid-19 Outbreaks: Comparing the Arab Minority and Jewish Populations in Israel." *International Journal of Public Health* 67 (2022).

Shohat, Ella. "Rupture and Return: Zionist Discourse and the Study of Arab-Jews." *Social Text* 21, no. 2 (2003): 49–74.

Shoman, Hala, Ashjan Ajour, Sara Ababneh, Afaf Jabiri, Nicola Pratt, Jemima Repo, and Maryam Aldossari. "Feminist Silences in the Face of Israel's Genocide Against the Palestinian People: A Call for Decolonial Praxis Against Complicity." *Gender, Work and Organization* 27, no. 1 (2025).

Shwaikh, Malaka. "Engendering Hunger Strikes: Palestinian Women in Israeli Prisons." *British Journal of Middle Eastern Studies* 49, no. 4 (2020): 507–25.

Shwaikh, Malaka M. "Prison Periods: Bodily Resistance to Gendered Control." *Journal of Feminist Scholarship* 20, no. 20 (2022): 33–48.

Shwartz, Nitza, Ilana Shoahm-Vardi, and Nihaya Daoud. "Postpartum Depression Among Arab and Jewish Women in Israel: Ethnic Inequalities and Risk Factors." *Midwifery* 70 (2019): 54–63.

Sigle, Wendy, Débora M. Nunes, Laura Sochas, Jenny Chanfreau, Siri Suh, and Kalpana Wilson. "What Reproductive Justice Brings to and Requires of the Feminist Economics Project." *Feminist Economics* 31, no. 1 (2025): 143–91.

Silva, Denise Ferreira da. *Toward a Global Idea of Race*. University of Minnesota Press, 2007.

Simpson, Audra. *Mohawk Interruptus: Political Life Across the Borders of Settler States*. Duke University Press, 2014.

Simpson, Audra. "The Ruse of Consent and the Anatomy of 'Refusal': Cases from Indigenous North America and Australia." *Postcolonial Studies* 20, no. 1 (2017): 18–33.

Slaughter-Acey, Jaime C., Devon Sneed, Lauren Parker, Verna M. Keith, Nora L. Lee, and Dawn P. Misra. "Skin Tone Matters: Racial Microaggressions and Delayed Prenatal Care." *American Journal of Preventive Medicine* 57, no. 3 (2019): 321–29.

Smith, Linda Tuhiwai. *Decolonizing Methodologies: Research and Indigenous Peoples.* Zed Books 1999.

Snorton, C. Riley. *Black on Both Sides: A Racial History of Trans Identity.* University of Minnesota Press, 2017.

Sokol, Sam. "Ben Gvir: War an Opportunity to Encourage Migration from Gaza." *Times of Israel*, January 1, 2024.

Solaimane, Mohamed. "Palestinians in Gaza Desperate to Travel Abroad for Life-Saving Treatment." Al Jazeera, January 19, 2025.

Sperling, Daniel. "Commanding the 'Be Fruitful and Multiply' Directive: Reproductive Ethics, Law, and Policy in Israel." *Cambridge Quarterly of Healthcare Ethics* 19, no. 3 (2010): 363.

Spillers, Hortense. "Mama's Baby, Papa's Maybe: An American Grammar Book." *Diacritics* 12, no. 2 (1987): 65–81.

Spivak, Gayatri Chakravorty. "The Politics of Translation." In *Destabilizing Theory: Contemporary Feminist Debates*, edited by Michèle Barrett and Anne Phillips. Polity, 1992.

Stamatopoulou-Robbins, Sophia. *Waste Siege: The Life of Infrastructure in Palestine.* Stanford University Press, 2019.

Star, Susan Leigh. "The Ethnography of Infrastructure." *American Behavioral Scientist* 43, no. 3 (1999): 377–91.

Stein, Rebecca L. "Impossible Witness: Israeli Visuality, Palestinian Testimony and the Gaza War." *Journal for Cultural Research* 16, no. 2/3 (2012): 135–53.

Steinfeld, Rebecca. "Wars of the Wombs: Struggles over Abortion Policies in Israel." *Israel Studies* 20, no. 2 (2015): 1–26.

Stevenson, Allyson. *Intimate Integration: A History of the Sixties Scoop and the Colonization of Indigenous Kinship.* University of Toronto Press, 2020.

Stoler, Ann Laura. *Carnal Knowledge and Imperial Power: Race and the Intimate in Colonial Rule.* University of California Press, 2010.

Stoler, Ann Laura. *Duress: Imperial Durabilities in Our Times.* Duke University Press, 2016.

Stoler, Ann Laura. *Haunted by Empire: Geographies of Intimacy in North American History.* Duke University Press, 2006.

Stoler, Ann Laura. "Interior Frontiers." In *Thinking with Balibar: A Lexicon of Conceptual Practice*, edited by Ann Laura Stoler, Stathis Gourgouris, and Jacques Lezra. Fordham University Press, 2020.

Stoler, Ann Laura. "Intimidations of Empire: Predicaments of the Tactile and Unseen." In Stoler, *Haunted by Empire.*

Stoler, Ann Laura. *Race and the Education of Desire: Foucault's History of Sexuality and the Colonial Order of Things*. Duke University Press, 1995.
Stoler, Ann Laura. "Tense and Tender Ties: The Politics of Comparison in North American History and (Post) Colonial Studies." In Stoler, *Haunted by Empire*.
Stoler, Ann Laura, and Karen Strassler. "Castings for the Colonial: Memory Work in 'New Order' Java." *Comparative Studies in Society and History* 42, no. 1 (2000): 4–48.
Sufian, Sandra. *Healing the Land and the Nation: Malaria and the Zionist Project in Palestine, 1920–1947*. University of Chicago Press, 2007.
Taher, Hanna al-, and Anna-Esther Younes. "Lebensraum, Geopolitics and Race—Palestine as a Feminist Issue in German-Speaking Academia." *Ethnography* 25, no. 2 (2024): 142–68.
Tanous, Osama. "Covid-19 Fault Lines: Palestinian Physicians in Israel." *Journal of Palestine Studies* 49, no. 4 (2020): 36–46.
Tanous, Osama. "The Hospital as a Place of Labor in a Settler Colonial Setting." *The Funambulist*, no. 33 (2021).
Tanous, Osama. "Israel and the Palestinian 'Womb': Racism by Numbers Rears Its Ugly Head." *Middle East Eye*, October 25, 2022.
Tanous, Osama. "'You, as of Now, Are Someone Else!': Minoritization, Settler Colonialism, and Indigenous Health." *Journal of Palestine Studies* 52, no. 1 (2023): 68–86.
Tanous, Osama, Yara Asi, Weeam Hammoudeh, David Mills, and Bram Wispelwey. "Structural Racism and the Health of Palestinian Citizens of Israel." *Global Public Health* 18, no. 1 (2023).
Tanous, Osama, and Rabea Eghbariah. "Organized Violence and Organized Abandonment Beyond the Human: The Case of Brucellosis Among Palestinians in Israel." *MSystems* 7, no. 3 (2022): e01499–21.
Tanous, Osama, and Amy Hagopian. "The Locations of Palestine and the US in the Global Map of Homelessness: Part 2." *International Journal of Social Determinants of Health and Health Services* 55, no. 1 (2024).
Tanous, Osama, and Ghada Majadli. "A Medical School in the Service of Colonialism." *+972 Magazine*, March 3, 2022.
Tanous, Osama, Bram Wispelwey, and Rania Muhareb. "Beyond Statelessness: 'Unchilding' and the Health of Palestinian Children in Jerusalem." *Statelessness and Citizenship Review* 4, no. 1 (2022).
Tatour, Lana. "Citizenship as Domination: Settler Colonialism and the Making of Palestinian Citizenship in Israel." *Arab Studies Journal* 27, no. 2 (2019): 8–39.
Tatour, Lana. "The Culturalisation of Indigeneity: The Palestinian-Bedouin of the Naqab and Indigenous Rights." *International Journal of Human Rights* 23, no. 10 (2019): 1569–93.
Tawil-Souri, Helga. "Checkpoint Time." *Qui Parle* 26, no. 2 (2017): 383–422.
Tawil-Souri, Helga. "Uneven Borders, Coloured (Im)Mobilities: ID Cards in Palestine/Israel." *Geopolitics* 17, no. 1 (2012): 153–76.

Tayara, Hania. "Health and Humanitarianism: Colonial Manifestations of Violence in the Palestinian Body." *Journal of Intersectional Social Justice* (April 2024).
Taylor, Janelle. "Confronting 'Culture' in Medicine's 'Culture of No Culture.'" *Academic Medicine* 78, no. 6 (2003): 555–59.
Temple, Bogusia, Rosalind Edwards, and Claire Alexander. "Grasping at Context: Cross Language Qualitative Research as Secondary Qualitative Data Analysis." *Forum: Qualitative Social Research* 7, no. 4 (2006).
Temple, Bogusia, and Alys Young. "Qualitative Research and Translation Dilemmas." *Qualitative Research* 4, no. 2 (2004): 161–78.
Theobald, Brianna. *Reproduction on the Reservation: Pregnancy, Childbirth, and Colonialism in the Long Twentieth Century*. University of North Carolina Press, 2019.
Todorova, Teodora. *Decolonial Solidarity in Palestine-Israel: Settler Colonialism and Resistance from Within*. Zed Books, 2021.
Trouillot, Michel-Rolph. *Silencing the Past: Power and the Production of History*. Beacon Press, 1995.
Tuck, Eve, and K. Wayne Yang. "Decolonization Is Not a Metaphor." *Decolonization: Indigeneity, Education and Society* 1, no. 1 (2012): 1–40.
Turfah, Mary. "Israel Has Created a Medical Apocalypse in Gaza." *The Nation*, February 20, 2024.
Turfah, Mary. "The World's Top Medical Journal Is Giving Cover to Genocide." *The Nation*, March 26, 2025.
Underman, Kelly. *Feeling Medicine: How the Pelvic Exam Shapes Medical Training*. New York University Press, 2020.
United Nations Human Rights Council. "'More Than a Human Can Bear': Israel's Systematic Use of Sexual, Reproductive and Other Forms of Gender-Based Violence Since 7 October 2023." A/HRC/58/CRP.6. 2025.
United Nations Office of the High Commissioner. *Thematic Report: Attacks on Hospitals During the Escalation of Hostilities in Gaza (7 October 2023–30 June 2024)*. December 31, 2024.
United Nations Population Fund. "Women of Gaza: A Year in Crisis." October 4, 2024. https://www.unfpa.org/stories/women-gaza-year-crisis.
UNRWA. "UNRWA Situation Report #172 on the Humanitarian Crisis in the Gaza Strip and the West Bank, Including East Jerusalem." May 23, 2025.
UNRWA. "UNRWA Situation Report #191 on the Humanitarian Crisis in the Gaza Strip and the West Bank, Including East Jerusalem." October 8, 2025.
UNRWA. "UNRWA Situation Report #203 on the Humanitarian Crisis in the Gaza Strip and the West Bank, Including East Jerusalem." January 6, 2026.
Valdez, Natali. *Weighing the Future: Race, Science, and Pregnancy Trials in the Postgenomic Era*. University of California Press, 2021.
Veracini, Lorenzo. "Israel-Palestine Through a Settler-Colonial Studies Lens." *Interventions* 21, no. 4 (2019): 568–81.
Veracini, Lorenzo. *Settler Colonialism: A Theoretical Overview*. Palgrave Macmillan, 2010.
Vergès, Françoise. *A Decolonial Feminism*. Pluto Press, 2021.

Vergès, Françoise. *The Wombs of Women: Race, Capital, Feminism*. Duke University Press, 2020.

Vertommen, Sigrid. "Babies from Behind the Bars: Stratified Assisted Reproduction in Palestine/Israel." In *Assisted Reproduction Across Borders: Feminist Perspectives on Normalizations, Disruptions and Transmissions*, edited by Nina Lykke and Merete Lie. Routledge, 2017.

Vertommen, Sigrid. "From the Pergonal Project to Kadimastem: A Genealogy of Israel's Reproductive-Industrial Complex." *BioSocieties* 12, no. 2 (2017): 282–306.

Vertommen, Sigrid. "Surrogacy at the Fertility Frontier: Rethinking Surrogacy in Israel/Palestine as an (Anti)Colonial Episteme." *History of the Present* 14, no. 1 (2024): 108–37.

Vertommen, Sigrid. "Towards a Political Economy of Egg Cell Donations: 'Doing It the Israeli Way.'" In *Critical Kinship Studies: Kinship (Trans)Formed*, edited by Charlotte Kroløkke, Stine Willum Adrian, Tine Tjørnhøj-Thomsen, and Lene Myong. Rowman and Littlefield, 2016.

Wailoo, Keith. *How Cancer Crossed the Color Line*. Oxford University Press, 2011.

Wang, Jackie. *Carceral Capitalism*. Semiotext(e), 2018.

Washington, Harriet A. *Medical Apartheid: The Dark History of Medical Experimentation on Black Americans from Colonial Times to the Present*. Broadway Books, 2006.

Weinbaum, Alys Eve. *The Afterlife of Reproductive Slavery: Biocapitalism and Black Feminism's Philosophy of History*. Duke University Press, 2019.

Weiss, Meira. *The Chosen Body: The Politics of the Body in Israeli Society*. Stanford University Press, 2002.

Wekker, Gloria. *White Innocence: Paradoxes of Colonialism and Race*. Duke University Press, 2016.

Wexler, Laura. *Tender Violence: Domestic Visions in an Age of US Imperialism*. University of North Carolina Press, 2000.

Whittaker, Andrea. "Reproduction Opportunists in the New Global Sex Trade: PGD and Non-Medical Sex Selection." *Reproductive BioMedicine Online* 23 (2011): 609–17.

WHO. "Hostilities in the Occupied Palestinian Territory (Opt): Public Health Situation Analysis (PHSA)." (2025).

Wick, Livia. "The Practice of Waiting Under Closure in Palestine." *City and Society* 23, no. 1 (2011): 24–44.

Wick, Livia. *Sumud: Birth, Oral History, and Persisting in Palestine*. Syracuse University Press, 2023.

Wilcox, Lauren. *Bodies of Violence: Theorizing Embodied Subjects in International Relations*. Oxford University Press, 2015.

Williams, Raymond. *Marxism and Literature*. Oxford University Press, 1977.

Wilson, Kalpana. "In the Name of Reproductive Rights: Race, Neoliberalism and the Embodied Violence of Population Policies." *New Formations* 91 (2017): 50–68.

Wind, Maya. *Towers of Ivory and Steel: How Israeli Universities Deny Palestinian Freedom.* Verso, 2024.

Wispelwey, Bram, Osama Tanous, Yara Asi, Weeam Hammoudeh, and David Mills. "Because Its Power Remains Naturalized: Introducing the Settler Colonial Determinants of Health." *Frontiers in Public Health* 11 (2023).

Wolfe, Patrick. "Settler Colonialism and the Elimination of the Native." *Journal of Genocide Research* 8, no. 4 (2006): 387–409.

UN Women. "Gender Alert: Gaza: A War on Women's Health." September 2024. https://arabstates.unwomen.org/sites/default/files/2024-09/en-gender-alerthealthsep_24.pdf.

Yacobi, Haim. *The Jewish–Arab City: Spatio-Politics in a Mixed Community.* Routledge, 2009.

Yacobi, Haim, and Elya Lucy Milner. "Beyond 'Causes of Causes': Health, Stigma and the Settler Colonial Urban Territory in the Negev/Naqab." *Urban Studies* 59, no. 3 (2022): 572–90.

Yacobi, Haim, and Wendy Pullan. "The Geopolitics of Neighbourhood: Jerusalem's Colonial Space Revisited." *Geopolitics* 19, no. 3 (2014): 514–39.

Yanko, Adir. "'She Asked No Arab Come Near Her Daughter,' Arab Medical Staff Face Racism Amid War." *Ynet*, October 31, 2023.

Yao, Xine. *Disaffected: The Cultural Politics of Unfeeling in Nineteenth-Century America.* Duke University Press, 2021.

Yiftachel, Oren. "Deepening Apartheid: The Political Geography of Colonizing Israel/Palestine." *Frontiers in Political Science* 4, no. 981867 (2023).

Yiftachel, Oren, and Haim Yacobi. "Urban Ethnocracy: Ethnicization and the Production of Space in an Israeli 'Mixed City.'" *Environment and Planning D: Society and Space* 21, no. 6 (2003): 673–93.

Yurdakul, Gökce, Gala Rexer, Shvat Eilat, and Nil Mutluer. "Contested Authorities over Life Politics: Religious-Secular Tensions in Abortion Debates in Germany, Turkey, and Israel." *Comparative Sociology* 18, no. 5/6 (2019): 706–34.

Yuval-Davis, Nira. *Gender & Nation.* SAGE, 1997.

Yuval-Davis, Nira "National Reproduction and 'the Demographic Race' in Israel." In *Woman-Nation-State*, edited by Nira Yuval-Davis and Floya Anthias. Macmillan, 1989.

Zengin, Aslı. "Violent Intimacies." *Journal of Middle East Women's Studies* 12, no. 2 (2016): 225–45.

Zengin, Aslı. *Violent Intimacies: The Trans Everyday and the Making of an Urban World.* Duke University Press, 2024.

Zikri, Almog Ben. "Bedouin Birthrate in Israel Is 'Bomb' That Needs Defusing, Far-Right Lawmaker Says." *Haaretz*, June 11, 2020.

Ziv, Hadas. "A Cognitive Dissonant Health System: Can We Combat Racism Without Admitting It Exists." In Boas, *Bioethics and Biopolitics in Israel.*

Ziv, Hadas. *The Medicalization of Armament: Gun Proliferation in the Public Sphere, Violence, and the Role of Medical Professionals.* Physicians for Human Rights Israel, December 2023.

Ziv, Hadas. *Racism in Medicine: The Politics of Segregation in Health*. Physicians for Human Rights Israel, April 2016.

Zu'bi, Bakr. "Since the War: Unprecedented Persecution of Arab Medical Workers [in Hebrew]." *Mekomit*, November 20, 2023.

Zu'bi, Himmat. "Palestinian Fertility in the Israeli Sphere: Palestinian Women in Israel Undergoing IVF Treatments." In Boas, *Bioethics and Biopolitics in Israel*.

Zureik, Elia. "Colonialism, Surveillance, and Population Control: Israel/Palestine." In *Surveillance and Control in Israel/Palestine: Population, Territory and Power*, edited by Elia Zureik, David Lyon, and Yasmeen Abu-Laban. Routledge, 2011.

Zureik, Elia. "Demography and Transfer: Israel's Road to Nowhere." *Third World Quarterly* 24, no. 4 (2003): 619–30.

Zureik, Elia. "Strategies of Surveillance: The Israeli Gaze." *Jerusalem Quarterly*, no. 66 (2016): 12–38.

INDEX

Founded in 1893,
UNIVERSITY OF CALIFORNIA PRESS
publishes bold, progressive books and journals on topics in the arts, humanities, social sciences, and natural sciences—with a focus on social justice issues—that inspire thought and action among readers worldwide.

The UC PRESS FOUNDATION
raises funds to uphold the press's vital role as an independent, nonprofit publisher, and receives philanthropic support from a wide range of individuals and institutions—and from committed readers like you. To learn more, visit ucpress.edu/supportus.

www.ingramcontent.com/pod-product-compliance
Ingram Content Group UK Ltd.
Pitfield, Milton Keynes, MK11 3LW, UK
UKHW011656180826
474168UK00002B/24

9 780520 412521